DR. HYDE AND MR. STEVENSON

To J. Garner Anthony
long a thoughtful and helpful
friend — with the highest esteem
of the author.

Harold W. Kent

July 1973

Rev. Charles McEwen Hyde, D. D.
Photograph taken by H. B. Hall & Sons, New York,
about the time of his departure for Hawaii, age 45.

DR. HYDE
AND
MR. STEVENSON

The Life of the Rev. Dr. Charles McEwen Hyde
including a discussion of the Open Letter of
Robert Louis Stevenson

by HAROLD WINFIELD KENT

CHARLES E. TUTTLE COMPANY
Rutland, Vermont, U.S.A. & Tokyo, Japan

Published by the Charles E. Tuttle Company, Inc.
of Rutland, Vermont & Tokyo, Japan
with editorial offices at
2–6, Suido 1–chome, Bunkyo-ku, Tokyo, Japan (112)

The trade edition of this book has been published with the assistance of the Juliette
M. Atherton Trust and the Samuel N. and Mary Castle Foundation of Honolulu,
Hawaii.

Library of Congress Catalog Card No. 72–83673
International Standard Book No. 0–8048–1062–1

PRINTED IN JAPAN

To
T. R. K.

CONTENTS

APPENDICES

ILLUSTRATIONS

11

ACKNOWLEDGMENTS

IN THE RESEARCH for this book, I am deeply indebted for assistance to many people. In Honolulu I enjoyed the warm and skillful support of Elizabeth Larsen and Lela Goodell of the Hawaiian Mission Children's Society, Ann Takemoto and Jean Sharpless of the Hawaiian Historical Society, Margaret Titcomb of the Bernice Pauahi Bishop Museum, and Agnes Conrad of the Archives of Hawaii.

In Massachusetts the list includes Harriet T. Brown of the Brimfield Public Library, Urita P. Bentley of the Haverhill Public Library, the staff of the Houghton Library of Harvard University. Others were Elizabeth Daly of the Lenox Library Association; Betty Dennis, Lee Library Association; Juanita Terry, Williams College Library; Ethel M. McCormick, Great Barrington Library; Janet E. Edwards, Berkshire Athenaeum; and Hildegard E. Borden, Boston Athenaeum.

Muriel H. Fellows of Philadelphia and Dr. Gerald W. Gillette of the Presbyterian Historical Society of that city supplied much needed assistance as did Carol Parke of the library of Yale University. The Rev. John A. Culver of Chicago Theological Seminary, Charles F. Stewart, Jr., of San Francisco Theological Seminary, and Arthur M. Byers, Jr., of Princeton Theological Seminary opened cordial doors to my quest. Dorothy F. Smith, Riverside, California, Library, was very helpful.

In London I had signal help from Wallace Lord and from the staff of the main British Museum and its newspaper division. Norma E. Hart of the Presbyterian Church of Australia in Sydney, Pat Lance and Faith Fogarty also of that city provided much material. Robert E. Van Dyke of

Honolulu has generously made available a number of valuable papers. J. Garner Anthony and Edward R. Bendet have advised in legal matters.

I am obligated to Hyde descendant, George Hyde Hanford of Demarest, New Jersey for advice and general assistance and for permission to quote from his grandfather's voluminous correspondence with the American Board of Commissioners for Foreign Missions.

Above all I gratefully acknowledge the readily extended expert assistance given by Gwenfread Allen, newspaper woman and author, for the long hours of critical reading and editing on the flow and content and organization of this ms. Other persons eminent in Hawaiian history have given very welcome and careful study to this ms.: Albertine Loomis, author of *To All People,* and the Rev. Dr. Kenneth O. Rewick, pastor of Central Union Church.

Much is owed Luryier Diamond, Kamehameha Schools photographer for his generous and skillful assistance with the illustrations. Cecil Keesling, Kamehameha Schools printing chief, has been ever ready and obliging in pre-publication problems. Eloise Bruns of Honolulu was extraordinarily gracious and careful in typing and proofreading this ms. Carroll E. Whittemore of Wexford, Mass., has been imaginative and tireless in his general efforts on behalf of this book. I thank him.

Finally I am grateful to my wife, Ethel, for her alertness in reading and re-reading, proofreading and advising.

To all these I extend my warmest *mahalo* (thank you) and *aloha* (affection).

Harold Winfield Kent

INTRODUCTION

WHENCE CAME HYDE? This is a most usual query, but what is more usually asked is "Why a book on Hyde?" Charles McEwen Hyde was Mrs. Charles Reed Bishop's choice, after her husband, as one of the five trustees named in her will. This Hawaiian princess of beautiful character, who died in 1884, provided for an educational foundation, the B. P. Bishop Estate, to establish and operate the Kamehameha Schools of Honolulu, Hawaii.

It was my privilege to serve as president of the Princess' institution for more than 16 years following World War II. I came to recognize Hyde as the one responsible for the creation of the program of studies and activities and policies which were to stand as the principal landmarks and guidelines of this school throughout the years.

I prize membership in the Social Science Association of Honolulu and have, each time my turn has come up, presented an essay. I had written an essay on Charles Reed Bishop, husband of the Princess, and a distinguished figure in Honolulu and San Francisco, 1846 to 1915. My next effort at an essay seemed self-pointed at Charles McEwen Hyde. His name had come to me frequently as the real force behind the founding of the Hawaiian Historical Society and the moving spirit in the development of the Library of Hawaii. Any doubt about an essay on Hyde was dispelled with the discovery that he was the founder of the Social Science Association in 1882 and was its secretary for 17 years to 1899.

As I started upon my research on the Hyde essay I chanced across Miss Ethel M. Damon's *Siloama—Church of the Healing Spring,* the story of the

15

Protestant Church in Kalawao, the leper village on Molokai island. Miss Damon had stumbled on an accumulation of forgotten church record books buried outside, at the rear of the church, in an old storage bin. She had the badly frayed and worn documents carefully exhumed and then forthwith translated into English from the Hawaiian. The mute story of the Hawaiian Church (Congregational) from the 1830's began to emerge and she was enabled to write *Siloama* from which the externally imposed confrontation between Hyde and Robert Louis Stevenson was revealed to me almost as a piece of startling news. I had never heard of Stevenson's "Open Letter" in which Hyde was pilloried following publication of his personal reply to the Rev. H. B. Gage who had inquired as to his opinion of Father Damien.

My original purpose in this essay was to describe this man Hyde for the membership of the Social Science Association and now, with the Stevenson matter, a new element became an essential aspect of the paper. It is certain that Father Damien does not need the swarm of apologists, the writers, who credit him as the first Christian leader of the leper settlement, and who aver with uniform clamor that he brought the first order, both in government and morality, out of a human chaos.

Further he did not need the broken reed of a Stevenson to mount his case. The kindly Father could and did speak for himself through his works. His voice should be the one to speak through these very works and not be dependent upon the unfounded and misguided utterances of a patterned emotional sympathy.

In the telling of the general Hyde story I confess a strong dependence upon the well preserved file of letters that flowed copiously from his pen in Honolulu to the secretaries of the American Board of Commissioners for Foreign Missions in Boston. Every letter of his 22 Honolulu years is now housed in the Houghton Library, Harvard University and this book could scarcely have been attempted were it not for privileged access to them. It would not have been possible to fill out the story in "good measure, pressed down, and shaken together, and running over" and give it a faithful Hyde "ring" otherwise.

The Rev. Dr. Hyde possessed the key elements of scholarship to high degree. He had patience and zest for research, a rare ability to analyze linguistic secrets, an orderly mind, a museumist urge. He was a classifier, an arranger, an organizer. He could have been ranked among the great researchists of Christian history, and he could have achieved this status more easily than most of the greats; he could have walked among the ruins, the idols, and the old tomes with no rip or tear in his own ecclesiastical clothing.

He was sure in his theology and so he was a free man, free to act out his life. It might have been better had he kept out of the teeming marketplace with its thrusting purpose and straying demand and instead remained within the scholarly walls of antiquity and philosophy and theology, there to stand forth in his niche in the stature of an intellectual. But he chose the marketplace and there, because of the hustling calls into every cell of human complaint and need, his intellectuality, while never feeble, was diluted to a pragmatic cause.

Hyde tended to make a career out of each of the major enterprises with which he became associated in Hawaii. Reading of this biography would be tedious if progress in the several areas were recorded chronologically. Consequently this story is based upon taking each "career" to its conclusion before picking up another.

I disassociate myself from Hyde comments on the Hawaiian monarchs of the day and likewise from the remarks about the personal characteristics of the Hawaiians. But passages on these subjects are worthy of inclusion since they constitute a largely unrepresented viewpoint in Hawaii.

Can the biography of Hyde be written to achieve for him the honorable position in Hawaiian history to which he is entitled? It is so believed and in that spirit this book is undertaken—not as an apologia. The Damien-Stevenson episode may seem such, but it is not so. Hyde has a place in that episode—in being honest in the light of his own convictions although unintentionally being cast into the role of a character assailant by the careless publication of a personal letter.

This ms. should be construed as an attempt on Dr. Hyde's life. An attempt it is, not in the vernacular sense—that has already been accomplished by the man with the scalpel, abetted *sequent* for three quarters of a century by the Stevenson writer followers—but in a special sense to turn around the unworthy image of him as bigot, traducer, slanderer; petty, despicable, obscure. The weight of the endless nouns and adjectives ill-humoredly applied piled up a staggering burden for Hyde but fortunately his life and especially the Stevenson episode do not today compel a blind stagger to the truth. And it is this truth which destroys the well of oblivion of the Rev. Dr. Charles McEwen Hyde.

Chapter 1

A PURITAN HERITAGE

The names Joseph Damien de Veuster, Robert Louis Stevenson, and Charles McEwen Hyde, taken together, do not sound as emblazoned or happy a note as might be the case with anyone of them individually.

Each of the three had certain ascriptions in common; all labored at some period in their lives in Hawaii, all were missionaries to a degree, all possessed great strengths of character, all had human weaknesses. Father Damien toiled among the leprous patients at Kalawao-Kalaupapa, Molokai; Stevenson, twice a visitor in Waikiki, looked in on the community and addressed himself dutifully to writing; Dr. Hyde toiled in his special vineyard among the native Hawaiians.

Father Damien has been exalted almost to sainthood in the Roman Catholic Church. Stevenson's niche in literary history is secure. Dr. Hyde's place in the development of Hawaii has been obscured through a chain of events involving the first two: a violation of the "warm and mutual tolerations of men."

In response to a query, Dr. Hyde wrote a personal letter highly critical of Father Damien; the letter, published, came to the attention of Stevenson who rose to the defense of the priest in an excoriation of Dr. Hyde which echoed around the world.

What manner of man was this Dr. Hyde? What role did he play in the history of Hawaii?

IN THE YEARS 1630–1640 New England was favored with a concentration of the larger share of the in-migration of the Puritans, a people at once possessed of rare intellectual vigor, deep moral instincts, and calm religious faith.

Foretoken was this decade, for these Puritan qualities were to sculpture the keystones of a new edifice of government for the future American commonwealth. As far as Charles McEwen Hyde was concerned, the impact of these qualities started in New England and spread to Hawaii.

Charles Hyde was a direct descendant of these colonial pioneers. The first forebear to migrate to New England was William Hyde who arrived in Boston in 1633 in the company of the distinguished Puritan minister, Thomas Hooker. The families settled down in Newtown (now Cambridge). But there was not enough freedom in the air nor in their efforts to establish a government compatible with their philosophy of rule. So off they went to the area where Hartford, Connecticut, now stands. Adding a third Puritan citizen of Newtown to their party, they became the founders of the town and named it Hartford.

Here these three established a version of the town system as the cornerstone of the civil order. The freedom of action inherent in this town autonomy was the insistent factor, the *sine qua non,* of the American Revolution.

Before too many years the Hyde family, in a spirit of Puritan wanderlust, moved out and this time wound up in Norwich, Connecticut, where they were again among the first settlers. Here, February 2, 1768, Alvan Hyde, grandfather of Charles Hyde, was born. He attended a spindly institution, Dartmouth College, where he graduated in 1788.

After graduation, instead of returning to his family home in Norwich, Alvan chose Lee, Massachusetts, in the southern Berkshires as a place to settle. He was "called" by the Congregational Church of Lee, June 6, 1792 where he ably and faithfully ministered to a grateful community for 41 years.

In his diary he warmly acknowledged the character and worth of his father, Joseph, ". . . a farmer of reputable character in that town (Norwich), a friend to religious orders and institutions, a constant attendant at public and family worship; but not a professor of religion. From him I received much good advice in my early years . . ." Thus the continuity of Puritan mentality and culture reached down through the Hyde generations, finally to emerge in the personality, character, and attainments of Charles Hyde.

The Rev. Alvan Hyde left an imprint of love and fidelity upon his church community. He was one of the most eminent divines of a time when the clergy were dominant in civil and religious affairs. Dignity, propriety and consistency pervaded all his actions. In his 41-year pastorate he built his church into Lee's most outstanding institution. Its widening circle of religious influence extended far into the countryside.

Because Alvan Hyde's reputation as a preacher was spreading, he was invited by the first president of Williams College, the Rev. Ebenezer Fitch, D. D., to be a trustee. He accepted in 1802 and continued as such through 1833. In 1812 he was elected vice-president and held that largely honorary title throughout the remainder of his trusteeship. The presidency itself was pressed upon him several times but he declined as frequently, in his sense of obligation to his pastorate at Lee.

Williams was chartered in 1793 and named after Colonel Ephraim Williams who had no idea he was founding a college. He had long preceded the chartering. He was killed in the battle of Lake George, September 9, 1755, but in his will had provided for the founding of a free school in its present location in the northern Berkshires. It was his trustees who opened the free school, October 26, 1791. These men ambitiously arranged the organization of the free school under the name of Williams College and applied for a state charter.[1]

Congregationalism permeated the halls of Williams College. The first four presidents, Ebenezer Fitch 1793–1815, Zephaniah Swift 1815–1821, Edward Dorr Griffin 1821–1836, and Mark Hopkins[2] 1836–1872, had degrees of Doctor of Divinity. Mark Hopkins also had an LL. D. and a medical degree. The D. D. after the names of all four is clear indication of the religious auspices under which the students were educated.

It was arranged that Alvan's four sons should go to Williams and all four completed the requirements for graduation. The fourth son, Joseph, graduated with the class of 1822 and stayed on an extra year as a tutor. Thinking of becoming a lawyer he took the stage to New York where he was accepted "to read law books" by Burr and Benedict, partners in a law firm and themselves members of old line Puritan stock. He was admitted to the New York bar and began the practice of law. In New York, he found his bride, Catherine Maria McEwen, daughter of a New York jurist, Charles McEwen. She was a lineal descendant of one of the Scottish Covenanters, the first McEwen having been engaged in some of the bloody battles of that stormy period of Scottish history. Towards the end of the seventeenth century a later McEwen sought refuge in hospitable colonial New England.

The couple tried living in Palmyra but soon returned to New York, where, shortly thereafter, a boy was born, the first of seven children. He was named Charles McEwen Hyde; the date of birth was June 8, 1832. Father Joseph Hyde and family joined the Broome Street Presbyterian Church and here became a hardworking lay family. Joseph's interest in the church encouraged him to give up the profession of law to become treasurer and general agent of the American Bible Society.

Charles entered the Collegiate School of Forrest and McElligott, of which the former, William Forrest, was principal. This preparatory school gave him a thorough start in Latin and Greek and a quick mastery of his other subjects. At the age of fourteen he was ready to enter Williams College. His father wisely delayed matriculation for two years and in the interim sent him to Ware, Massachusetts, for a taste of business life in an uncle's bank.

Experience behind a bank counter, involving contacts with farmer, storekeeper, and manufacturer and laborer, was as important to his education as formal schooling. An indelible experience this was and would forever be a resource of great value to him in his ministerial career.

At sixteen he packed his few possessions in a portmanteau and took the stage to Williamstown and enrolled in Williams College.

For a picture of his life at Williams, reference is made to an early abbreviated biography of Charles M. Hyde by his son Henry Knight Hyde, in which two classmates are quoted, affirming the continuity of Puritan background and upbringing characteristic of the Hyde line. These college years were a profound influence in shaping his character and directing his hopes towards the ministry. One of the classmates was Professor A. L. Terry who later established an enviable record as professor of political economy. He commented in part:

It was the middle of September, 1848, when the young fellows who were afterwards to constitute the core and bulk of the college class of 1852, came together.

The first term had not passed before it was well settled in the councils of the class that Charles Hyde would be their valedictorian, and that opinion was never really shaken till the end. . .His personal acquaintance was easily made and retained; he drew the confidence of everybody as a man and a Christian; and I think it may be truly said in the best sense of that much abused word, that Charley Hyde was throughout the most popular man in this college class.[3]

The other classmate, the Rev. Lewellyn Pratt, D.D., of Norwich, Connecticut, adds his bit:

It is a great pleasure to recall a student life so nearly ideal as that of Charles M. Hyde. . .one of the youngest of its members, took first place in scholarship at once, and held it steadily through the whole course, and at his graduation was the valedictorian. He never appeared to be driven or in haste but was always prepared; was about equally successful in all parts of the curriculum, and had leisure enough to do a large amount of general reading.

In manner he was always a gentleman, careful in dress and in speech, considerate of others, unwilling to give or take offense, affable and companionable, so unhurried that he could give time and help to others; and commanded the respect and confidence of the whole college. He had inherited virtue, had been well trained, he had made duty his guiding star. Reverent, faithful, true and pure, he had a charmed life in the midst of the whirls and tempests and temptations of college life, merited and obtained a good report. . .his memory will be cherished in the hearts of all his surviving classmates.[4]

His college years were marked by development in one intellectual talent which would signally mark his subsequent professional life: a facility in literary expression. Many of his numerous college essays have been preserved in the records of his literary society, Philologian, the oldest such group at Williams.

There was a halcyon touch to the tenth reunion of the class of 1852. The members met in Williamstown, at the home of Mrs. Bridges, August 5, 1862,[5] and according to the Williams College Bulletin had a merry time.

It was just as well for Charles Hyde that he would depart with happy memories, for in all his future travel he would never be able to schedule a single visit to coincide with another reunion. However, he did visit Williams College to receive a Doctor of Divinity degree, June 1872.

He also returned in 1883 to speak at the Williams College commencement. This would be his first trip back to the United States from the Kingdom of Hawaii where he was to go in 1877 on a permanent assignment.

When commencement with its honors, its ringing speeches and its chapel bells was concluded, young Hyde faced financial problems were he to enroll immediately in Union Theological Seminary for graduate work. He was offered rather lucrative terms to tutor. This he undertook at New Haven and then Savannah, Georgia. He not only received all lodging and transportation at the latter town; he had a sail on a coastal schooner from New York, through the stormy offshore waters bordering Cape Hatteras, to the seaport town of Savannah. He had never been so far away from home and alone. He tutored a boy in the family of the Hon. John Stoddard.

Upon returning to New York in the fall of 1853, he was mentally and financially ready to apply at Union Seminary. There is little information at Union of his year of study. He was, however, back in his home town among worthy companions, doing graduate work in religion and generally getting into the specifics of his training for the ministry.

There was another hiatus ahead for the prospective seminarian. His father's brother, Alexander, operated a private school in Lee, Massachusetts, and brought Charles there to teach the school year 1854–1855. There was some reluctance on Charles' part, but he felt the obligation to aid his family and not benefit at the expense of the younger children. So he taught school for his uncle.

But that year was not the end of the break with seminary plans. It was during this year that his father, Joseph Hyde, sought a better environment for the children's upbringing and moved to a farm in the southern Berkshires close to the village of Sheffield and only a few miles from Lee where he opened a school as his brother Alexander had done. He called it the Sheffield Private Boarding School. One of the principal factors in this decision was the availability of Charles, by now a teacher of some experience. It was again with some misgiving that Charles entered into the life of the school his father had set. It was not a large school and was conducted in the farmhouse where lived his parents, his two brothers and four sisters.

Large or not, the work was demanding, for not only did he manage the school and teach, he worked at the farm chores. The eldest in the family, he had little choice but to stay with this routine and this he did without complaint for four years.

He was busy with the school and farm work but not too busy to obtain a license to preach from the Berkshire South Association in Lenox on April 15, 1856. He appeared as "supply" preacher many Sundays in Sheffield, Lenox, and Lee. After five years of teaching, with what savings he had in his purse and with his father's blessing, he entered Princeton Theological Seminary in Princeton, New Jersey, in the fall of 1859. His plan was to earn a degree in theology and enter the ministry. He completed the two-year course in one.

Princeton was a seminary of stern orthodoxy. It was not only a discipline for him but it gave him an understanding and sympathy for Presbyterian theology which he came to realize differed very little from his Congregational faith; there was a difference in polity but little in theology. It was likely the early connection with a Presbyterian seminary that confused writers who were dealing with some phase or other of his life in later years. He was frequently labeled a Presbyterian.

The autonomy and democratic humanitarianism of the Congregational church were his guidelines; these from his Hyde inheritance. He was reared in that atmosphere. Congregationalism became almost a synonym for Puritanism through its freedom of worship in a self-governing church body. This was the essence of the Congregationalism of his youth.

The Rev. Gardiner Spring at Princeton was one of young Hyde's favorite professors, a Calvinist and a great teacher. Through the scholarly leadership of this man and the earlier earthy teaching of schoolmaster Mark Hopkins, Hyde was taken unquestioningly to a full acceptance of the theology of Calvin and the freedom of worship and autonomy of the Congregational Church.

Seminarian Hyde, upon graduation from Princeton in June 1860, was ready for his first church. Surprisingly, the first call came easily and without much ceremony. He was asked to supply in the pulpit of a church in a tiny Connecticut hamlet by the Biblical name of Goshen, a rural church serving a little band of Christians who made church history. By broad coincidence this may well have possessed the unconscious suggestion leading to a career in Hawaii for the Rev. Mr. Hyde who could not have missed sensing the tradition established in the 1819 ordination of two missionaries.

On September 28, 1819 Hiram Bingham and Asa Thurston who were to be members of the historic first missionary company to the Sandwich Islands in 1820, had been ordained at this Goshen Congregational Church. They were to return to that same church in September 1869 for the 50th anniversary of their ordination. The sesquicentennial of the 1819 ordination was commemorated at the same church under its new name, United Church Congregational on September 27, 1969. It was so strong a sense of tradition in Goshen that this church became known as the "birthplace of the Hawaiian Mission."

He started preaching in Goshen in the late summer of 1860 and continued there with fair regularity until the early part of 1862. Since he was a supply pastor he was not regularly "called" to the Goshen pastorate; hence, his name does not appear in the official roster of the church.

The small rural quality of this church did not constitute much of a challenge administratively or in pastoral relations but it gave nearby churches a chance to look him over.

The deacons of the Brimfield Congregational Church came, liked what they saw, and gave the young minister his first opportunity at a regular "called" town congregation. He was still single and 30 years of age. Any consideration, thus, was his own responsibility and he decided to go to Brimfield.

NOTES

1. Williams College, *Catalog*, intro.
2. President Garfield, one of Mark Hopkins' pupils, said, "A log in the woods would be a university if President Hopkins sat on one end of it and a student on the other."
3. Henry Knight Hyde, *Charles M. Hyde, A Memorial* (Ware, Mass., Eddy Press, 1901), pp. 5–11.
4. Ibid.
5. Williams College, *Bulletin*, Report First Decennial Meeting Class of 1852, Williamstown 1862.

Chapter 2

THE BRIMFIELD "CALL"

THE BULKY, rather stilted, autonomous ordination processes of a Congregational church were first officially applied in the career of Charles McEwen Hyde upon his receiving the call to his first full pastorate at Brimfield, Massachusetts. This call in the words of his son, ". . .came to him largely through the influence of his uncle William at Ware, who was well and favorably known by the Brookfield conference of churches.

"The church in Brimfield [the Brimfield Church and Society] had a long history back of it, having been organized in 1724 when the township included parts of what are now Palmer, Monson, Warren, Holland and Wales.

"Beginning at a time of close union between church and state when none but church members could vote at town elections, when the bounds of parish and town were co-terminal, and when the population was equally taxed for the support of both, it had exercised a most important influence in the town's history."[1]

This beautiful New England town, founded in 1731, is somewhat off the mainstream of traffic and is therefore preserved esthetically and culturally today, in the same appearance and with the same town manners as in 1862.

Henry Hyde goes on about the town and its people:

The town itself was one of the oldest in Western Massachusetts and though not large, possessed a number of families of good New England stock, in many cases the descendants of the first settlers. Nestling peacefully among the hills, the lack of water-power had fortunately prevented the desecration of its natural beauty by the erection of mills and factories. The railroads too had passed it by and so, larger than many New England rural communities, it had retained the characteristics of the best stage of development of such towns.

Almost entirely agricultural in its interests the town has ever maintained an active interest in church and educational work, thus living up to its best inherited traditions. The men enjoyed discussions of knotty religious problems and the women planned for the aid of religious enterprises far removed from their own borders: a people hard to move, not given to outward manifestations of enthusiasm, yet possessed of the saving characteristics of honesty and common-sense, not treating the deep things of life lightly but according them the reverence they deserved. . .A rural community like this, somewhat removed from direct contact with the larger movements of the world, naturally becomes more or less self-centered and the harmless gossip of the neighborhood relieves the pressure of isolation. As when the New England farmer makes a new clearing and starts to cultivate the land before given to forest growth, he finds the soil strong; so, when the New Englander's reserve is cleared away and the man himself is subjected to the mellowing influences of high and Christian ideals, we find him ready and responsive to them—a strong man—strong in his individuality and determination.[2]

The origins and political processes of a New England town are quaintly and tidily illustrated in the *Brimfield Town Meeting Records:*

RECORD OF THE FIRST TOWN-MEETING
Att an annull meeting holden att the meeting hous in Brimfield, to Elect town officers for the town by order of the General Court, march 16: 1731 First Robert Moulton Choos moderator the meeting and work of the day.[3]

Another item gives homely evidence of the interlaced routine of town and church:

PETITION FOR PRIVILEGE TO ERECT A PEW.
Brimfield March 12th 1759
We the Petitioners Do Send Greeting &c to the Honourable town for Several Reasons, Do humbly Beg leave of your honours that you would

give us the place over y⁰ woemens Stairs to build a pew upon our own Cost, one reason we give is that we are soe Crouded at Sundry times that we cant hardly get a seat to sit in, & the other Reasons is, that whereas there is a pew on the other Side, we Reasonably think that it will beautifie the house.[4]

Towns in New England were strong elements in colonial government. Examples of this close participation abound in Brimfield's town records:

REVOLUTIONARY WAR.

At a meeting of the town of Brimfield, January 14, 1773. To act on the following, viz.:

"To see if the Town will take into consideration the matter of Grievance that are supposed to be brought upon by certain acts of Parliment, and if they think proper to choose a committee or committees to confer with other Towns on Matters of Grievance, and in every respect to act upon it as they may think proper."[5]

Town meetings were conducted "in his Majestie's Name," the last of which (under that name) was held March 12, 1776. The following year meetings were called in the name of the "Government and People of Massachusetts Bay" and in 1783 in the name of the "Commonwealth of Massachusetts."

The Rev. Mr. Hyde details the wars and connected events supported by Brimfield town: Revolutionary War, Provincial Congress, Massachusetts Convention on the Constitution, Shay's Rebellion, War of 1812 and the Civil War. It was this last which was engaging the thoughts and energies of Brimfield citizens when he arrived. They were in the midst of enrolling another military company and loading wagons with beef. He was ordained amidst this excitement of war preparations.

The Brimfield Congregational Ecclesiastical Council was called and organized August 19, 1862. Seventeen ministers and deacons from Brimfield and surrounding villages found that Hyde had received a unanimous call, that he had his certificate of church membership, and his license to preach. The group, which included the Rev. Dr. Mark Hopkins (he had horsebacked all the way from Williamstown), examined him respecting his views of theology, his religious experience and his motives for entering the ministry. Satisfied, the council voted unanimously to proceed to ordination. The Rev. Dr. Hopkins preached in the ordination exercises.

Thus does a Congregational preacher advance into acceptance by the congregation that calls him. The church records start the 30-year-old Rev. Hyde on his ministerial path at the first business meeting September 4, 1862, in a fast roundup of assignments prophetic of the pace he would be setting for himself for the rest of his life. These are the items approved that day: "Hyde was received as a member of the Church upon the recommendation from the Congregational Church in Sheffield. . .chosen Moderator and Clerk of the Church. . .chosen member of the Standing Committee. . .received on behalf of the Ladies Benevolent Association a new communion service."[6]

The Rev. Mr. Hyde signed the minutes which he had written of this, his first meeting. He was to write in his beautiful longhand all the minutes throughout his pastorate. Actually, this was presageful, for his usual role in many of the churches, community agencies and business enterprises with which he would later be connected would be that of secretary or recorder. His handwriting for public review was carefully and meticulously done. His handwriting in personal correspondence was something else again.

The Rev. Mr. Hyde had been preaching at the Brimfield church since the first of April; he was called May 22 and ordained August 19, all in 1862. He was therefore prepared to comment on most of 1862 in his first annual report. Aside from the usual listing of church events, the report covers fully the church participation in the Civil War:

Our Church has supported the government in its defense work. The Ladies have labored with commendable diligence in furnishing the M.S. [Massachusetts State] Sanitary Commission such articles as might be of comfort to the suffering soldiers. The Young Men have volunteered at the call of our constituted authorities and left home and friends and peaceful occupations for the hardships of the Camp and the exposures of a soldier's life. This church has parted with some of its members thus for a reason and some have been brought back to find a resting place by the side of their departed kindred.[7]

His second year was reported largely in terms of the spiritual fervency of his church members and the moral support accorded the government in the war. A kind of stylized dissatisfaction marked the reference to the one while an obvious vein of righteousness in official government warfare characterized the other. Both comments are reproduced for their value as clues to Hyde thinking:

In the view of our religious history for the past year while we have occasion for devout Thanksgiving to God for the mercies we have received, we cannot but lament that we have made no better improvement of Divine favors. While we may not have been guilty of positive worldliness, preferring earthly things to spiritual, there has been too little appreciation of the supreme importance of eternal realities. Undoubtedly engaged as we have been so much of this past year on the outward business of the house of God, the attention of the people has been necessarily, in a measure, diverted from higher objects.

While mercifully spared the sight and experience of the horrors of civil war, we have not been uninterested in the contest, or, regardless of the principles of moral right and political justice, involved in it. Many prayers have been put up to the God of battles that He would prosper our righteous cause. The fourth Sabbath of the month has usually been observed as a concert of prayer for this object, and the appointments by the National and State authorities of Public Thanksgiving and Praise or Humiliation and Prayer, have been publicly observed.[8]

The Rev. Mr. Hyde was elected a trustee of the Hitchcock School December 13, 1862. This was a private school endowed by a benefactor who himself possessed no schooling, Samuel Austin Hitchcock.[9]

This man supplies a remarkable parallel to Charles Reed Bishop, banker and philanthropist, who was to be a close Hyde associate in charitable and cultural interests some years later in Hawaii. The parallel is significant in that both were self-made merchandisers and generous donors to churches, schools, and other community enterprises. His father was a hatter and a tailor; but he and two partners opened the first dry goods commission house in New England. Then he became the prime mover in the Hamilton Woollen Co., retiring in poor health to Brimfield.

His charities and grants were enormous for his day; $175,000 to Amherst College, $120,000 to Andover Theological Seminary, $5000 to Hyde's church in Brimfield as a "fund to aid in support of an Evangelical Calvinistic Orthodox Trinitarian Congregational Minister," $90,000 to found the Hitchcock Free High School, and many others.

Hyde was chosen for the school's Prudential Committee which regulated the employment of teachers and handled the building program. He was re-elected each year until his resignation from the Brimfield church in 1870. But the need of his counsel followed him to his next parish at Haverhill, as in 1875 the legislature added four nonresident trustees to the board, and among them was named "the Rev. C. M. Hyde of Haverhill."[10]

There is a record of brief war service in the Hyde file. In 1864 the students learned he was going into the army as chaplain and asked him to defer his going to give them some of his time for religious exercises. A modest postponement seemingly caused no problem with army authorities—his work could be undertaken at will—so he conducted the exercises requested. As a result, fifteen students united with the church.

He then left for the service which took him away from Brimfield for seven weeks. His duty was in a field hospital at City Point, Virginia. No description of this service has been found.

But the greatest event in 1864 was the marriage of Mary Thirza Knight and Charles McEwen Hyde. She was a graduate of the first class of Hitchcock Free School and a native of Brimfield, born there August 6, 1840. She was further educated at Mrs. Willard's Seminary, Troy, N. Y., and at Oberlin College. "Disregarding the old advice," wrote Henry Hyde, "never to marry in one's own congregation he wooed and won Mary, the youngest daughter of Dr. Ebenezer Knight, the village physician. Unlike in many ways, each seemed to possess in part what the other lacked and no better argument was ever made for the marriage of opposites than their long and happy married life, in which a common ideal of consecration and service dominated the minor differences of thought and temperament."[11]

They were married October 10, 1864 in their Brimfield church. Mary Hyde entered immediately with zest into the role of minister's wife. She achieved great praise as a religious leader among women.

The Rev. Mr. Hyde reviewed 1865 much as he wrote of 1863:

Never before has the general health of the community been better, never before has there been much greater deadness in spiritual things. The outward business of the house of God was never in better condition, but the spiritual condition of the church has been far below the apostolic standard of holy living.

The year has been one of great public excitement. The closing scenes of the Slaveholders' Rebellion, the assassination of Pres. Lincoln, the entrance of a new President and Congress upon the conduct of national affairs in a most critical juncture in the nation's history, have demanded appropriate notice in the exercises of public meetings.

This generation can never forget the Sabbath which followed the murder of the President, the deep feelings of sorrow and horror it occasioned, and yet also the calm trust which the people evinced in the God who delights to exercise loving kindness, righteousness, and judgement in the earth.

With the return of peace, with a government now free from complicity with the iniquitous system of negro slavery, with indications on every hand of unprecedented prosperity, we need now to feel more than ever our dependency on the blessing of God for any real permanent good. In the privileges and opportunities with which we are in these days favored, we have high incitements to duty. God is calling his church in this nation to earnest endeavor. Let us consecrate ourselves anew and certainly to the will of God, the service of Christ, to the spread of holiness, with fidelity, love and zeal.[12]

In the next year's report he noted with no great joy the completion of a chapel by the Adventists at nearby East Corner. This kind of "invasion" usually bothered him as a disturbing factor in his church territory and it was to happen again and again. Opposing Protestant denominations had little sensitivity for territorial jurisdiction. This feeling was deep in the Rev. Mr. Hyde's mind because his church was the town church, well established in its historic beginnings and, as far as he was concerned, effectively filling the Brimfield needs.

Young and restless he organized the Pastor's Bible Class. This he taught on Monday evenings and attendance quickly soared to the point where it became a major item in his Brimfield program.[13]

In analyzing the Scriptures he had to prepare his own curriculum and regularly outlined the material on a blackboard. He was developing a formal instructional approach which would reach its most effective employment in Hawaii. His role was to be chiefly that of teacher.

In 1869 he translated into action his earnest annual complaint, of spiritual matters being secondary in growth and purpose to material affairs. This was a great revival undertaken in January, February and

March. It was most satisfactory to him. With the enlistment of the greater number of the business leaders, the revival was well planned and almost the entire town came into the fold.

In the summer of 1869, the Rev. Mr. Hyde and his church played host to the fiftieth anniversary party of the Sunday Schools of the Brookfield Association (23 churches). He gave the historical address. He had an innate sense of history which was hand-to-hand with his sense of mission to teach.[14]

But Brimfield, although a major parish, was not an important religious goal. The time to consider a larger church had come. In undergoing the resignation process he found it as complicated as the summons to the position, only in reverse:

At the close of the afternoon service, the Pastor announced his resignation of the pastoral office, and asked the Church and Society to unite with him in calling an Ecclesiastical Council that the pastoral relation might be duly dissolved, according to the forms and usages of our denomination.

A meeting of the church was called and the resignation accepted. This was communicated to the Parish and invitations to be represented at an Ecclesiastical Council were announced.

The Ecclesiastical Council was convened May 21, 1870: Minutes of the Ecclesiastical Council called in accordance with the tenor of the letter of invitation, copied above to consider the expediency of dismissing Rev. C. M. Hyde.

We cordially commend Bro. Hyde to the churches as a sound and effective preacher of the Gospel. He is regarded by his brethren in the ministry as a scholar of rare attainments, able in his presentation of truth, wise in counsel, devoted and faithful in his work as a pastor.

Reasons for his resignation have to be advanced *and* accepted. The reason stated in this Ecclesiastical Council Minutes, ". . .the want of generous support, which since the Society has such ability, we regard as sufficient. . . "[15]

Either a friendly naivete was being employed by the Council members to ease Charles Hyde's determination to move to a larger church or if he placed great stress on this point himself he was the one being naive for the "want of a generous support" was to haunt him all the days of his life. The real motivation was simple. He was seeking new vistas, new fields to apply his restless energy—and climb another step up the ecclesiastical stairs. He was "dismissed" to Centre Church in Haverhill, Massachusetts, November 1870, with "recommendations."

NOTES

1. Henry K. Hyde, *Charles McEwen Hyde, a Memorial*, pp. 15–17.
2. Ibid.
3. Charles M. Hyde, *History of Brimfield*, (Springfield, Mass., Bryan Printers, 1879), Appendix, p. 287.
4. Ibid., Appendix, p. 307.
5. Ibid.
6. Brimfield Congregational Church, Records of the Clerk, Sept. 4, 1862.
7. Ibid., Annual Report, 1862, Jan. 1, 1863.
8. Ibid., 1863, Jan. 1, 1864.
9. Charles M. Hyde, *Samuel Austin Hitchcock* (Boston, Alfred Mudge & Son, 1874), pamphlet.
10. Ibid.
11. Henry Knight Hyde, op. cit., pp. 19–20.
12. Brimfield Congregational Church, op. cit., 1864, Jan. 1, 1865.
13. Ibid., 1865, Jan. 4, 1866.
14. Ibid., 1869, Jan. 1, 1870.
15. Ibid., May 21.

Chapter 3

THE HAVERHILL PASTORATE

CHARLES HYDE officially ended his work at Brimfield May 31, 1870. Even before his resignation the Mount Vernon Congregational Church of Boston had a committee in Brimfield checking his fitness to undertake an associate ministry with the famous Rev. Edward Morris Kirk, D.D. Hyde had actually preached from the Mount Vernon pulpit on at least two occasions and had made a favorable enough impression to warrant the committee's trip to Brimfield.

The committee could find nobody in Brimfield who would be critical of his ability, work habits and leadership. One man thought his walk was peculiar, as it was, in a sense; Hyde bounced each step as if on a miniature spring board.

But the committee **upon** reporting back found that Dr. Kirk had already blocked the **possible call.** He did not want an associate—any associate. So the search died there and then.

Shortly after the door closed at Mount Vernon, the congregation of the Centre Congregational Church at Haverhill, Mass., opened its door. Either Boston's Mount Vernon or Haverhill's Centre would have been an excellent church for him.

Haverhill, some 60 miles north of Boston, was a bustling town on important land and water highways. Son Henry describes this town:

Fairly homogeneous in population, its inhabitants principally engaged in the manufacture of shoes, it had not then passed into a position of such commanding importance in that line of industry as it now occupies, nor had it then been made the battleground for the fierce conflicts between capital and organized labor of later years. Many of the operatives at this period were still of native stock, the influx of French Canadians then having hardly begun. The congregation of the Centre Church was in part made up of the better class of these operatives, cutters for example, whose work demanded sufficient intelligence to gain for them good wages.[1]

The record book of Centre Church contains the minutes of the Ecclesiastical Council called for the examination and installation of the Rev. Mr. Hyde:

Pursuant to letters missive from the Centre Congregational Church, Haverhill, an Ecclesiastical Council was convened at the vestry of that church, November 15, 1870 to assist in the examination, and if thought advisable, the installation of Rev. Charles M. Hyde as Pastor of said church. . . . .

After prayer by the moderator, the Council listened to the reading of the documents relative to the dismissal of the Pastor elect from his former charge, the call of the Centre Congregational Church to become their Pastor, and his acceptance of the same. The Council then proceeded to the examination of the candidate, first as to his Doctrinal belief and then as to his religious experience; at the close of which it was voted that the Council "be by themselves." The Council being by themselves, it was voted that the examination "be deemed satisfactory and that we proceed to the Installation of the candidate in the P.M."[2]

After installation he plunged not only into the problems of the church but also lined up with educational forces in the community. "Dr. Hyde, for so he was familiarly known in the later years of his life, possessed the happy faculty of original suggestion. . . to comparatively few is it given to see passing events in their true perspective and seize on those worthy of distinction."[3]

The Haverhill pastorate, in and of itself, was an effective crusade for Christ, deeply appreciated by a grateful following, but for purposes of narrative, relatively unexciting. Attention is therefore given in this Haverhill period to other services he rendered.

He was Haverhill's most community spirited leader in efforts involving

education and charity. He engaged in a broad sweep of town interests—
the rehearsal for an incomparable drama of acts and scenes that he would
later stage in Hawaii.

Temperance does not classify strictly as either a church or community
activity. It is a combination of both, and unlike either is an activity where
the zeal of the crusader is the indispensable ingredient for success. The
Rev. Mr. Hyde had not mixed in temperance causes until he reached
Haverhill. Likely enough he had never witnessed drinking or its effects
comparable to what he was now seeing. The problem was acute in this
manufacturing area; but with the intuitive touch of the crusader he became highly successful in fashioning approaches and solutions in the best
temperance tradition.

The Monday Evening Club of Haverhill had been formed about the
time Hyde was at Princeton Seminary. Shortly after his arrival in Haverhill he was tapped for membership.[4] Usually composed of 20 men, intellectual lights, it met monthly with programs composed of impromptu
comments on the current social science scene climaxed with a major paper
or essay. This latter item was usually a carefully prepared literary effort
of the membership, each one taking his monthly turn.

A club of this nature could be found in many towns throughout New
England, but was certainly a traditional adjunct of Massachusetts towns.
Hyde had formed a club akin to this in Brimfield—a Book Club where
the men met and discussed literature of all ages. To accept membership
in the Haverhill Monday Evening Club was like transferring from one
club to another. The whole exposure to this idea would later find him
restless in Honolulu until he could round up a small group of reasonably
compatible individuals and start another Monday Evening Club under
the name of the Social Science Association.

His participation with these twenty "social scientists" in the pursuit of
literary and cultural objects illustrates his widening intellectual curiosity.
A list of his impromptu *Five Minute Talks* excerpted from the minutes
clearly pictures his mind at work:

The French cession of Alsace and Lorraine to Germany
A recent will provides for the ringing of a bell periodically for all time
Dr. Bacon's article on Railway Legislation
Affairs in Japan
New discoveries in the Polar Sea by Captains Olaf and Johnson

Bulgarian visitor's description of wine culture
Philosophy of Herbert Spencer
Fascination of the scenery of the St. Lawrence and its rapids
Pulmonary subjects find relief in Colorado parks
Accuracy of engineering in the Hoosic Tunnel
Life of Powers the sculptor
Dr. Schleimann at the site of ancient Troy
Attachment of Fitz Greene Halleck for a Quaker lady
"Et tu Brute" not historical but original with Shakespeare

Wide differentiation and variety mark this list which is far from complete. Even this sample shows a remarkable range of human interests.

In the essays (called Exhibits in the minutes) Hyde donned a cloak of hard dry fabric. He prepared two essays in his six years at Haverhill and in these treated controversial subjects head on. In the *Darwinian Theory of the Origin of Species,* he contended that the hypothesis quite failed to establish its own obligations or to explain conflicting phenomena and was on the whole quite unable to withstand a careful criticism. This essay roused animated discussion!

The other essay dealt with the "Nature of Suffrage, its rightful qualifications and practice and the Safeguard of Popular Government." Here was Hyde the teacher using the blackboard to develop his theme graphically. His unsurprising conclusion was that "hope for good government lay in selecting upright nominees."

Aside from any other benefits, this Monday Evening Club was a totally different pulpit than the one at Centre Church. Here he could maintain a layman's dialogue with his fellow townsmen on nonreligious subjects.

Public education was another interest. He was a member of the Haverhill School Committee for 1872 and 1873 representing Ward 4. "During his term of office, the Committee decided to vacate the Old Haverhill Academy Building that had been used as a high school since 1837 and to build. The new building, 'the long-looked for Canaan,' was occupied in 1874."[5] Generally the Committee was concerned about the qualifications of teachers and examinations of pupils. The Rev. Mr. Hyde was a "visiting" committee member, stopping in at schools and classes with some regularity.

A private school, Bradford Academy, appointed him to its Board of Visitors, a group formed in 1863 to take over from the trustees the annual check on student progress. This school stood on the other side of Haverhill's Merrimack River, away from the town proper. His first appointment was at the bottom of the roster in 1872. He moved rapidly to the top of the list. In his last year in this assignment, 1876–1877, his residence was listed from Boston.

"The Board of Trustees were overly conservative . . . apathetic . . . elected for life . . ."[6] The School, founded in 1803 was, despite its trustees, a strong academic force in the Haverhill area. On one occasion, he reported he "had never seen more thorough work in Latin at any school or college."

The public library drew his attention also. He rejoiced in successful overtures to obtain a $30,000 grant for a new free public library from the Hon. E. J. M. Hale. He reported on this gift to the Monday Evening Club and covered it in his announcements from the pulpit. He urged his parishioners to support the project.

On one occasion, in company with Dr. Seeley, a local fellow preacher, he started a movement to establish a "Women's Union for Good Works."

He had ever had a dedication to the field of foreign missions, a feeling nurtured by exposure to discussions in early family years, the seminary and the pastorate. Suddenly, through an incident connected with his School Committee role, the light of the mission field was turned on for him.

The school authorities wanted the site on which the old Atwood house was standing for a new high school building and the City of Haverhill purchased it for that purpose. Harriet Atwood, the third of nine children born there, had died at the age of 19, just as she arrived in India as a missionary. She was one of the many young people who thronged to the mission fields under the authority and guidance of the American Board of Commissioners for Foreign Missions.[7]

The Rev. Dr. Hyde, filled with the message as he related it at the memorial service and subsequently wrote it out for publication, found the poignant trail beckoning to him. Dr. Rufus Anderson of the Prudential Committee of the American Board heard of Hyde's recital of this touching tragedy and of course had followed his highly successful work in the Haverhill pastorate and the earlier Brimfield charge. A ministry school in Hawaii for natives was in need of resuscitation and Anderson began to feel that Hyde might be the one for the job. It was not in response to the "beckoning" however, that termination of his services was, shortly after that memorial service, recorded in the Haverhill church minutes. He had no immediate mission plans:

. . . The five years of pastoral labor which I shall have completed tomorrow in connection with this Centre Congregational Church and Society have been to me a busy and blessed period of service . . .

In the Providence of God, however, consideration of personal duty in reference to the present conditions of affairs in this Church and Society, have convinced me that I ought to ask your consent, as I do herewith, to the termination of my pastoral relations to you, in order that I may be free to enter into other engagements, in another field of labor.[8]

When this letter was read, a committee was appointed to wait on the Rev. Dr. Hyde to express regret and ask that he withdraw his resignation. He thought this over and two weeks later the clerk read his reply:

The request of the church that I would, if consistent with my views of duty, withdraw my resignation, I cannot but regard as a gratifying testimonial of persistent confidence and affection . . .

But to those who would thus interpose what they may consider a needless and unaccountable termination of a five year pastorate of harmony and prosperity, I must say that I have not acted unadvisedly. I cannot see it to be my duty to withdraw my letter of resignation and I reiterate the request I have made.[9]

Following essential Congregational landmarks an Ecclesiastical Council was convened December 15, 1875 at the vestry to listen to Dr. Hyde. After hearing his explanation the Council deliberated in secret for half an hour:

. . . After listening to the presentation of all the facts in the case it was unanimously resolved that it is expedient that the Pastoral Relations now existing between Rev. Charles M. Hyde D. D. and the Centre Church and Society be dissolved at the close of the year 1875 . . . We are surprised and pained to learn of the Existence of a state of things in this Church and Society which makes it seem to Rev. Dr. Hyde to be his duty to withdraw from a position which he has so ably and successfully filled. We are happy to make special note of the Ministry of Rev. Dr. Hyde in this place, as having been attended with the blessing of God in the Conversion of Souls; in the quickening and enlargement of the Church; and in the compacting of this Religious Society and we do most heartily commend our Brother to the Confidence of our Churches as an able Preacher, a tender and faithful Pastor, and a Christian man, whose character is a recommendation of the Doctrines he has taught and a pillar of strength to any cause . . .[10]

All in all this was a strange termination. No record shows or will ever show the convincing testimony he must have presented. Thus, irrevocably, the pastorate at Haverhill was ended. In retrospect, a famous theologian, the Rev. Dr. Charles M. Clark, commented on how the Hyde-Haverhill record was of such quality that it seemed providence had shaped his path to Hawaii:

Mr. Hyde was a man of fine presence, urbane manners, genial spirit, "a loving pastor, devoted to his flock, and greatly beloved in the houses of those whose hearts were pressed by want, or anguished in grief." Like his two predecessors, he was a man of unusually scholarly tastes and abilities. Even while here he was greatly interested in education. He was also greatly interested in missions. To his scholarly tastes and ability he added a quite uncommon executive capacity, the ability to conceive large plans and to move strongly and wisely and successfully for their accomplishment. It was not strange, therefore, that he was chosen to lead in a new educational institution, under the American Board in Honolulu, for the training of a native ministry, and that he became a foremost factor in all educational work in the Hawaiian Islands from his arrival there in 1877, till his death in 1899. In Dr. Hyde there was embodied in peculiar degree the instinct of New England Congregationalism for education, and the capacity of the Congregational ministry to lead in educational work. Dr. Hosford was pre-eminently a pastor; Dr. Munger, a preacher; but Dr. Hyde . . . a teacher and educator.[11]

Eighteen seventy-six turned out to be a year of the unexpected. Charles Hyde's sudden conclusion of the Haverhill pastorate temporarily made him a free lance. His visits to the old home towns of Brimfield and Lee stimulated invitations to write their town histories. By coincidence, but for different reasons, each town was ready for a celebration and a publication.

The town of Lee was observing the centennial of its founding in 1877 and because the Hyde families had been long and favorably associated there, and one member of a Hyde family had achieved renown throughout New England as a scholar and a preacher, it was decided to ask this man to deliver the Centennial Address and prepare a history for publication—the Rev. Dr. Charles McEwen Hyde.

The history of Lee, as prepared by Hyde, is a massive compendium of war, rebellion, and peace. It takes in town meetings, industries, institutions, crises, biographies, roads and trails, rivers and mountains. The research led Hyde across the breadth of Massachusetts.[12]

The Brimfield history was not based on its own centennial but was rather a spontaneous response to a joint resolution of Congress. The United States was due for its centennial shortly. For an account of the project and Hyde's involvement in it we turn to the book of Brimfield history as he organized it:

Be it resolved by the Senate and House of Representatives of the United States of America, in Congress assembled, That it be, and is hereby recommended . . . to the people of the several states, that they assemble in their several counties or towns on the approaching Centennial anniversary of our National Independence, and that they cause to have delivered on such day an historical sketch of said county or town from its formation . . . and [a] . . . copy in print or manuscript, be filed in the office of the Librarian of Congress.

By vote of the Legislature of Massachusetts, a copy of this resolution was transmitted June 13, to the clerks of each of the cities and towns of the Commonwealth.

On receipt of this communication Mr. Henry F. Brown, the town clerk of Brimfield, presented the matter to a few of the citizens, who, while approving of the object, thought it desirable to postpone the matter to a later date than the one named in the Resolution of Congress, and on Sunday, August 27, a notice was read in church inviting all persons interested in securing as many of the facts of the settlement and early history of the town as might be done by a Historical Address and other means, to meet at the Selectmen's room the following evening. At this meeting . . . Rev. Dr. C. M. Hyde was selected to prepare and deliver the Address.

Wednesday, October 11, dawned one of Autumn's brightest, and at an early hour the roads from every direction were thronged with teams and foot passengers, all eager to be on hand for Brimfield's grandest and proudest occasion . . .

[a] procession marched to the church, where it arrived about 11 o'clock, and which was filled to overflowing before but a small part of the people had been admitted. Prayer was offered by Rev. M. L. Richardson of Sturbridge, after which the president delivered the address of welcome, introducing the orator of the day, Rev. C. M. Hyde, D. D.

. . . it was voted "that the Rev. C. M. Hyde, D. D., be requested to write out for publication, with such additional facts as he may wish to incorporate, his historical address on the early history of Brimfield, delivered October 11, 1876."[13]

Carefully and thoroughly he assembled thick files of notes, and was preparing the manuscripts when the interrupting hand of providence was laid on his head; now, his destiny was in Hawaii. He could not deliver the Lee Centennial Address, nor could he finish the town's history. He turned over the completion of the task to his uncle Alexander; with the work so far advanced, he was credited with the authorship. The Brimfield book was also given over to other hands, but again, because the notes, statistics, and genealogies had been largely completed, Hyde was designated author. This history was published in 1879, the Lee history in 1878.

He was hard at work on the research and text of the histories when an inquiry from the American Board of his possible interest in the mission position in Hawaii reached him. This was in November 1876.

His life was confusion in the agonizing weeks of consideration until January 16, 1877 when the clouds lifted and he could see his way clear to a new horizon, the Hawaiian Islands.

NOTES

1 Henry Knight Hyde, op. cit., pp. 23–24.
2 Centre Congregational Church Records, 1856–1886.
3 Henry Knight Hyde, op. cit., pp. 21–22.

4 Monday Evening Club of Haverhill, Minutes. "December 12, 1870. Rev. C. M. Hyde nominated for membership . . . January 61, 1871. Rev. C. M. Hyde ballotted on and the result was unanimous."

5 Letter Donald C. Freeman to author, Jan. 6, 1970.

6 Jean S. Pond and Dale Mitchell, *Bradford, A New England School* (Haverhill, 1954).

7 The American Board of Commissioners for Foreign Missions of Boston was largely a non-denominational effort. In this book it is referred to as the American Board, ABCFM, or simply, Boston.

8 Centre Congregational Church Records, 1856–1886, Nov. 18, 1875.

9 Ibid., Dec. 1.

10 Ibid., Dec. 15.

11 The Rev. Charles M. Clark, *Historical Sermon* given at the 75th Anniversary exercises of Centre Church Oct. 11–12, 1908. Clark was The Waldo Professor of Ecclesiastical History, Bangor Theological Seminary.

12 Charles M. Hyde, *Lee, A Centennial and a History* (Springfield, Mass., Clark W. Bryan & Co., 1878), pp. 352.

13 Charles M. Hyde, *History of Brimfield*, Historical Celebration of the Town of Brimfield (Springfield, Mass., Clark W. Bryan & Co., 1879).

Chapter 4

"BEHOLD . . . AN OPEN DOOR"

CAPTAIN JAMES COOK, discoverer of the Hawaiian Islands, seldom was wrong even in prediction. The Rev. Dr. Hyde, however, was later to allude to one error in Cook's judgment in a sermon to the newly organized Central Union Congregational Church in Honolulu:

In Captain Cook's account of his Voyages to the South Seas, when he has given his description of the people whom he had seen, he says in regard to the probability of their even hearing the Gospel: "It is very unlikely that any measure of this kind should be seriously thought of, as it can neither serve the purpose of public ambition, nor private avarice, and will without such inducements, I may pronounce that it will never be undertaken." What a mistake Captain Cook made in his calculations! How little did he imagine that his published narrative of what he had seen, was one of the divine providences for accomplishing the very thing which he predicted would never be undertaken! It was Carey's reading Cook's Voyages that stirred his heart with the desire to go to the heathen, and so the *whole vast scheme of Modern Christian Missions originated*.[1]

It was the fortuitous placement of a native Hawaiian boy, Henry Obookiah,[2] in friendly Congregational hands in Connecticut that led to his becoming the first native Hawaiian to be baptized as a Congregational church member, April 9, 1815. He had shipped aboard the *Triumph*, a trading vessel, in Kealakekua Bay, Hawaii, in 1808. He was sixteen. Befriended by the Captain of the ship, then by students at New

45

Haven's Yale College and by members of New England churches, the young Hawaiian went from total illiteracy to eloquence in English in less than a decade. His short ten years in Connecticut inspired the American Board to an action that would irrevocably involve the Sandwich Islands, as Hawaii was then familiarly known.

In two contrasting coincidences, young Henry arrived in New Haven about the time of the founding of the American Board and died in Cornwall, Connecticut February 17, 1818, close to the date of the death of Kamehameha I of Hawaii. The first company of missionaries was formed in 1819 and sailed to establish the American Board's first mission in Hawaii.

The mission, supported by sailing after sailing of successive "companies" of missionaries, extended to 1863. In those 43 years[3] more than 50,000 natives were received into the church, solid coral stone meeting houses were erected, the Hawaiian language was reduced to writing with an alphabet of its own, the Bible was translated from the Greek. A constitutional monarchy and a public school system were established. Private boarding schools for the native boys and girls were opened on all the islands. The churches flourished with large congregations. The gospel message had reached a large majority of the Hawaiians.

Then "came the time where the islands were to be recognized as nominally a Christian nation and the responsibility of their Christian institutions was to be rolled on themselves."[4] The Civil War was placing a strain on American Board finances and this, coupled with strong demands for service from all quarters of the globe, hastened a visit to Hawaii by Dr. Rufus Anderson, senior secretary of the American Board.

In June 1863 he met with the Hawaiian Evangelical Association for twenty-one days of debate. The Association agreed to assume the responsibility for self-support and autonomy and no longer look to the American churches for management and control. The mission, as such, was disbanded.

John Erdman, seventy five years later, commented on that "annual Meeting of the Missionaries in 1863 [at which] several momentous questions were decided":

First, should the large parishes handled by the missionary fathers be divided into a number of separate churches and Hawaiian ministers be placed in charge of them? The answer was yes, and this was adopted as a policy so that gradually the original 22 churches, during the next 10-year period, became 58 with only six of them under *haole*[5] pastors.

Another great question was, should new missionaries be sent from America to fill vacancies caused by death and withdrawal of the early missionary fathers? The meeting decided that although there was still work to be done by the missionaries, probably the children of the missionaries who knew the Hawaiian language could meet the situation. Previous to 1863 the Hawaiian Evangelical Association had been composed of missionaries only, but now the constitution was amended so as to include Hawaiian ministers and a certain number of deacons, and the language of the meetings became Hawaiian.

This momentous gathering also set up an Executive Board called the Board of the Hawaiian Evangelical Association composed of 18 elected members, six of whom were Hawaiians. This Board was authorized to help needy churches, to send missionaries to other lands, to train ministers for the churches, to train suitable wives for them, and to publish books.

Thus was the whole missionary movement radically altered. Rev. S. C. Damon in the *Friend* of July 1863 states, "This marks an important crisis in our ecclesiastical affairs. Hereafter we shall refer to 1863 as the period when the Christian Evangelical Community on the Islands attained its majority and assumed the attributes of manhood."

The church work had been set up and geared to minister to a homogeneous people speaking one language, living a simple life. But that people in the next four decades rapidly diminished in number from 67,000 in 1860 to less than 38,000 in 1900. Rulers and chiefs who had been influential sustainers of the Christian movement were replaced by others . . . Great economic development with its concomitant influx of masses of aliens changed the whole tenor of life. The total population more than doubled, from 70,000 in 1860 to 154,000 in 1900. Instead of being practically the single element in the population, the Hawaiian people became a small minority group. Inevitably this seriously affected the Christian movement.

These ministers, devoted men as they were, had not the background nor the training to adjust themselves, nor lead their people to cope with the rapidly changing conditions. These pastors of the numerous Hawaiian churches found that the formerly substantial churches were rapidly decreasing in size through death and dissension and could no longer provided adequate salaries. Some of them were compelled to take time out of pastoral work for raising their own food and catching their own fish. Others entered the field of politics and were elected to the legislature. In either case, economic necessity proved a handicap to vigorous church work.[6]

Biographer Henry Hyde summed up the serious question of the American Board's decision to cut the Hawaiian mission loose upon itself:

After events have seemed to call in question the wisdom of this action; though at the time circumstances seemed to render such a course imperatively necessary. While the success of the Gospel had been marvelous in its transforming power, it was almost too much to expect that a nation, but one generation removed from barbarism, should acquire in that length of time the stability and persistence of ideals to be found in older Christian Communities.[7]

Dr. Hyde gave his views of the unhinging impact of the withdrawal after he had been on the scene for some time:

It seems to me that the radical mistake made in 1863 was the giving over of everything into the hands of the Hawaiians so completely, without checks and balances. It might have been all right in theory; but its application of self support to mere children has proved a fatal error in practice. How now to redeem the past, and retrace and retake the lost ground is the question of the hour. . .[8]

This sense of misjudgment would never leave him. Two years later he again expressed himself:

I hope the Board will not abandon any other Mission as summarily as they did the Sandwich Islands. Words do not mean the same things in the Board Rooms at Boston as the realities out in this mid-Pacific. A national life cannot be manufactured to order and the prophesy about a nation being born in a day cannot be construed into constituting a nation Christian by vote of a Mission Board.[9]

Long before these pronouncements, however, the Prudential Committee of the American Board had convinced itself that a limited reentry in the Hawaii field was necessary. It decided to amend the 1863 agreement which basically had established an autonomous church in Hawaii, largely staffed and operated by native Hawaiians.

In Hawaii also, the local people had already attempted helpful adjustments and measures of their own. Classes of hopeful theological prospects had been recruited from among the natives and instructed in the details of parish work and in principles of exposition and homiletics. It was specifically in this area where, in the wisdom of the Prudential Committee, the remedy should be applied.

The American Board's decision to re-enter the mission field in Hawaii was recorded in the proceedings of its annual meeting at Hartford in October, 1876 with a decision to send a man who could give leadership to the native pastors.[10] In attendance were two Hydes: Uncle William Hyde of Ware, a corporate member of the American Board and highly regarded among the commissioners and Dr. Hyde, who had suspended his history writing at Lee, for the week of missionary talk and action at Hartford. The latter was registered as an Honorary Member since he had no pastorate at the time, but he was a delegate.

The proceedings placed him on the Mission Committee for Madura and Ceylon. His name was not linked to the stated proposal to reactivate the mission work in Hawaii. There was no doubt of his acquaintance and popularity as a coming Congregational minister for he was already known and respected for his labors in the pastorates at Brimfield and Haverhill. He had some inquiries about possible pastorates but was too engrossed in the immediate pressures of the history work to think of taking on a new assignment. He returned to Lee.

New England ministers largely with the New England Congregational stamp upon them had dominated the evangelization of the Hawaiian Islands since 1820. It was natural that the Prudential Committee would look for its Hawaii man from among such as these. Needed was an able pastor, a parish specialist, an educator, and one whose bearing and being would lend themselves to counseling weak and struggling churches.

In the remaining weeks of 1876 the Prudential Committee weighed the possible prospects and as the search progressed the finger pointed more and more to Dr. Hyde. Finally, on the first day of the new year, 1877,

Hyde had a caller: the Rev. E. K. Alden, one of the secretaries and, in this instance, an emissary of the American Board.

He bore the invitation to go to Hawaii as a paid employee of the American Board to reorganize the Theological Seminary,[11] and set up and conduct a program of theological education for natives as pastors in Hawaiian churches and outpost stations of Micronesia.

Although he was aware that he was being considered, he was surprised, even stunned, that New Year's Day. Now the decision was in his hands and the American Board was in a hurry! His strong inclination to accept was restrained by the state of unfinished business (the histories) and his family circle. The one he could pass over to other hands; the family situation was the one which almost wrestled him down.

His letter of acceptance gives the details of the ordeal of decision:

When Dr. Alden, two weeks ago today, asked me if I would go to Honolulu, I had just begun to think out a sermon I was preparing to preach the next Sunday, from the text: "Behold, I have set before thee an open door."

The work to be done, as Dr. Alden represented it to me, seemed a grand opportunity to do important service for Christ around the world. It was in the line of my own cherished plans and preferences. "Yet," I said to myself, "it is not an open door to me." For my family relations and circumstances are such that work in a foreign land seemed impracticable. I had had two pleasant pastorates in New England and hoped to do such pastoral work for several years more either here or in some other part of the home field. Several times since I resigned the pastorate of the Haverhill Church, I have declined opportunities offered to me to engage again in pastoral work, or in some more general service for the Master. "Now again," I thought, to myself, "God is strangely presenting to me in his providence an opportunity for Christian service which I shall have to decline." But, most unexpectedly, I found encouragement where I had thought there would be only insuperable obstacles. Friends whom I consulted approved of the project. My wife's aged mother, who long ago gave herself and her children to Christ, gave her hearty consent to any sacrifice that the service of Christ might seem to demand. My wife expressed not merely a willingness, but an earnest desire to engage in such work as she would find to do at one of the outposts of Christian civilization.

So that now in regard to this Special Service, it seems as if the Master were saying to me, "Behold I have set before thee an open door." Step by step, the way has been opened for me to signify to you now my readiness to engage in the work that needs to be done at Honolulu for the islands of the Pacific if the Board sees fit to appoint me to take charge of it. From the earliest years of responsible life it was a conviction often impressed upon my mind by providential indications, rather than by direct utterance, of my parents, that my work in life was to be the work of a New England Congregational pastor, such as my grandfather of venerated memory had been long years ago. "When," (as Paul says of the time of his conversion), "it pleased God to reveal His Son in me," this desire was clarified and intensified. Before I left Theological Seminary I had to consider and settle the question whether I should not. . .(work) in some Seminary in the foreign mission field. For family reasons I could not then go abroad. During my first pastorate my parents and my sister had a home with me. I still am under obligations, in connection with my youngest brother, for my sister's support. But my wife's mother and sister propose to go with us and to help make home, and New England home-life, a power for good in Honolulu.

Both my wife and myself are in full vigor of health. We have always been and are now in fullest sympathy with the spirit and regulations of the Board.

In the experiences of life hitherto I have found myself strangely guided and controlled in all the evidently crisis hours of decision as to plans and preferences. And in view of all these circumstances and considerations, in regard to the work of training Hawaiian pastors and Pacific Islands missionaries I am ready to give myself to it heartily and unreservedly, hoping that in this work I shall find fulfilled in the Master's special promise, "Lo, I am with you always."

Yours in the fellowship of the Gospel
Chas. M. Hyde[12]

This was a typical Hyde letter, tender in restraining concern for his family and resolute in answering a spiritual summons. He remained at Lee for almost two months after the Alden call, working not only on preparations for the journey to Hawaii but on the two histories which he wanted to be able to deliver in such shape as could readily be completed by successor hands.

He was told by Alden that there would be a "Missionary Convention" in Chelsea, Mass., March 21, 1877. He closed up at Lee, March 12, took a horse and carriage on the two-day trip to Brimfield, where he continued final preparations. He wanted to sell his Brimfield home but was finding no market. "It is a poor time to sell," he said, "and property off the line of the railroads is very unsaleable." He was writing to Alden from Brimfield and went on to say, ". . .If you do not find an opportunity for me to preach next Sunday, I shall stay here till Monday. Is there anything expected of me at the meeting in Chelsea? Has the order of service been arranged? Do you wish Mrs. Hyde to be with me there? . . .We already talk of Honolulu as 'home' and are planning and eager for the life work we anticipate there."[13]

He also wrote to his seminary confidante of Princeton days requesting a copy of the course of theological study for possible application in Hawaii. "I have many pleasant memories of my year at Princeton and hope that I may succeed in impressing upon others, as deeply as was impressed upon my own mind, the necessity of thorough Bible study, and the supreme authority of the Bible as every preacher's standard of truth and righteousness."[14]

Finally, after the many weeks of negotiation, Rev. Hyde was commissioned to the Hawaii mission as "head of this school of the Prophets." The official commissioning service was held at the First Congregational Church of Chelsea, March 21. The farewell exercises were those customarily held prior to departure for the field. This day there were ten missionaries of the American Board who would immediately leave for their respective fields. Dr. Hyde was one of the ten—his destination, Hawaii.

It was decided that the Hyde family, which now included two growing boys, Henry K., and Charles K., as well as Mrs. Hyde's sister and mother, Eunice B. Knight and Mrs. Thirza W. Knight, would all go to Hawaii.

The party of six did not need to suffer the long perilous voyage around Cape Horn. The travelers could get across to San Francisco in six days following the newly completed composite route by rail. Ten additional days, more or less, would land them in Honolulu.

Dr. Hyde in his usual painstaking way wrote back to the Rev. N. G. Clark, one of his correspondents on the American Board, as the party traveled westward. At Oberlin he preached at a fund raising service. He preached at Brimfield, Indiana, a town undoubtedly named for his former residence in Massachusetts. By May 14 the party was in Salt Lake City and in a few days had arrived in San Francisco where the departure of the S. S. *Zealandia* for Honolulu was awaited.[15]

The ocean leg of the journey forced a letup in literary activity, but Dr. Hyde conducted church services aboard ship. Finally, the Hawaiian islands came into view. He wrote his impressions of the physical beauty of the islands while still aboard. He finished with a description of the reception at dockside and the immediate details of settling in, the first free moment allowed him on land. This would constitute his first Hawaii letter to the American Board correspondents. The arrival portion of the letter can speak for anyone who has come to the islands by ship:

On the morning of the Eighth day out, Thursday, May 30, we came in sight of the islands, whose romantic history has interested many hearts most deeply, and in whose future destiny, spiritually, we had come to take a strong personal interest. As we neared the island of Oahu and the dim cloudy outline of the distant view unfolded, more and more clearly, the scene before us was one of enchanting beauty. Above the jagged outlines of the sharply serrated volcanic peaks, lay a mass of clouds repeating in soft vaporous folds the forms of solid majesty below. The morning sunlight brought out in bold relief the brown slopes of the mountainsides in sharp contrast with the intensely black shadows that marked the valleys which furrowed the ridges. Turning Cocoa [sic] Head, still lovelier scenes met our gaze. The bright soft brown of the steep slopes, was varied with patches of a bright, soft mossy green. The white fringe of breaking waves, dashing on the coral reef, was topped by a line of tall cocoa palms, whose graceful outlines served as a heading to the fringe. Diamond Head stood boldly out, its broad, serrated, hollowing top making it look like a solitaire, set with clasping circulets of gold. Passing this we had our first view of Honolulu.[16]

The ship's approach had been "announced" from a Diamond Head lookout so that unbeknownst to the passengers the welcomers with great anticipation were hastening to the dock from all parts of town to greet the newcomers. Their arrival had actually been looked forward to for several months. His letter continues:

At the head of the recess of a broad mouthed roadstead lay a low lying mass of greenery over which towered here and there, steeples and flags. Beyond, stretched up the steep mountainside a shady cleft, looking dark and cool, which we knew must be the famed Nuuanu Valley, —"valley of the cool ascent." A rounded summit of barren brownness on the right was evidently Punchbowl Hill. To the left, westward, the irregular outline of the Waianae's shadowy peaks closed in the view. The long roll of the open ocean was changed to short dancing waves. The deep blue of the outer water changed to green and then to brown the nearer we approached the shores. The pilot was in the offing, ready to guide us through the narrow channel, where the coral reef is divided by the fresh water of the stream flowing down Nuuanu Valley and finding its way oceanward, making it impossible for the coral insects to build up their barrier-home, where its water flows.

The sailors in the pilot's boat were the first Hawaiians whom I had ever seen. They had the swarthy faces of dwellers in tropic climes, but they were bright with intelligence, their features pleasing from an air of intellectual discrimination, apparent in their countenances, as well as the look of generous hearted good nature. We soon neared the lighthouse on the reef, outside of which lay fishermen's canoes, long, narrow, deep, hollowed out of a tree and with curious projecting outriggers. On one of the canoes was piled a mass of nets and the little flotilla was patiently waiting the appearance of some school of fishes, when they would surround and capture them.

The anchorage for vessels between the reef and shore was much smaller in extent than I had fancied. Three Russian men-of-war, and another flying English colors, intimated, how easily the quietness and calm of these Pacific seas, might be broken in upon by the booming of cannon and the crash of the ponderous balls. The islanders had even surmised that the appearance of these war vessels indicated that hostilities had already begun between the Czar of all the Russias, advancing his armies too far Southward to suit English ideas, and the Queen of England, lately proclaimed Empress of the Indies. Strange that a quarrel on the banks of the Danube should inaugurate bloody strife in these far off seas!

A motley assemblage soon gathered on the wharfs at which we were to land. It took more time to turn our steamship in the narrow precincts of the anchorage. Some of our passengers in haste to greet waiting friends, put off in small boats that flitted about. Some, tired of the monotony of the steamer's narrow quarters, went ashore to indulge in a horseback ride about the town before breakfasting on shore at the Hawaiian Hotel. It was just time for the usual breakfast on board the steamer. . .soon we were surrounded by a multitude of friendly visitants, ready to welcome us to our new home and proffer the hospitalities of generous hearted friendliness. Dr. Damon's smiling face and cheery greetings were the only familiar features of the scene.

Introductions to new friends were soon followed by a distribution of our parcels. And then we were escorted ashore and to the carriages in waiting to take us to our temporary homes. We had paid the purser the head money, $2 for everyone over 12 years of age who lands on these islands to spend more than thirty days. These fees form a fund for the support of any sick stranger at the Queen's Hospital.[17]

The remainder of this very long letter reviews the maelstrom into which he had been drawn within days, not to say, hours, following disembarkation. The local church workers had saved their concerns!

Charles Hyde had been reared in the narrow cultural pattern of Puritan New England, educated in a small Christian college, trained in strongly orthodox seminaries, and had now arrived in a mixed social confusion utterly foreign to anything he had ever known. The people in the top echelon of the American Board, even though they had visited the islands, and had visits and letters from their missionaries in the islands, could not prepare him for Honolulu.

But here he was! It was June 1, 1877 and he was facing at the age of forty-five, his second career; twenty-two years in Hawaii.

NOTES

1 Charles M. Hyde, sermon, "The Prime Motive in our Missionary Enterprises," Central Union Church, June 10, 1888 (The *Friend*, July 1888).

2 Obookiah is the phonetic English version of the way he pronounced his name as understood upon his arrival in Hartford. Years later, when Hawaiian speech was reduced to writing, his name was corrected to Opukahaia.

3 The first company arrived in Kailua, Hawaii, April 4, 1820.

4 Henry Knight Hyde, op. cit., p. 30.

5 *haole*, foreigner, largely applied to Caucasians.

6 John Erdman essay, *After the Early Mission, What?* Social Science Association, Honolulu, Oct. 4, 1937.

7 Henry Knight Hyde, op. cit., pp. 29.

8 Letter Hyde to the Rev. E. K. Alden, ABCFM, July 31, 1888.

9 Letter Hyde to the Rev. Judson Smith, ABCFM, Apr. 5, 1890.

10 ABCFM, *Annual Report,* Hartford 1876, Oct. 3–6, 1876.
11 The Theological Institute was renamed the North Pacific Missionary Institute after Hyde's arrival.
12 Letter Hyde to the Rev. N. G. Clark, ABCFM, Jan. 16, 1877.
13 Letter Hyde to Alden, Mar. 13.
14 Letter Hyde to Prof. W. H. Green, Princeton Theol. Sem., Mar. 15.
15 Letters Hyde to Clark, May 1, 14, 23.
16 Ibid., June 19.
17 Ibid.

Chapter 5

LODGING AND LANGUAGE
THE NEW WORLD

THE GENERAL religious, economic, and social fabric of the Kingdom of Hawaii at the time of the arrival of the Hyde family was summarized by son Henry Hyde:

Landing in Honolulu in June 1877, the hospitable home of Mr. and Mrs. S. N. Castle was thrown open to them and here their first impressions of Hawaiian life were received. The reciprocity treaty with the United States had but lately gone into effect. Under its provisions Hawaiian sugar was to be allowed free entry into American ports and an enormous and profitable market was thus opened for what was already the largest product of the islands. The stimulus thus afforded to the leading industry of the community gave a bright promise for its commercial future.

As yet it had not begun to effect the changes in the city which in the two succeeding decades practically transformed it. The social life of the community was delightfully simple, although the seeming unconventionality was often strictly limited by the rules of local etiquette.

The predominant element in business and social affairs being composed largely of the descendants of the missionary fathers and mothers there was a strict regard for the observance of religion's requirements . . . This created a distinctly religious atmosphere as well as a power to be reckoned with in connection with important undertakings. The majority of the foreign element was thus by birth and training disposed to entertain kindly feelings for the Hawaiians, not attempting to exploit them for their own advantage. . . . The natives themselves for the most part cherished no ill-will against their white brethren . . . due in part to the wisdom displayed by Dr. Judd and his associates, who, when called upon to assist in the establishment of a civilized form of government, had been keen enough and loyal enough to their adopted land to maintain the native rulers and officials in their positions. No carpetbagging schemes could be alleged against them; and the Hawaiians, thus upheld as the nominal rulers of the land at least, were not subjected to the indignities so often concomitant with the advance of Anglo-Saxon civilization.

They had been fearfully reduced in numbers since Capt. Cook's visit, when he estimated the population to be some four hundred thousand. The ravages of disease had practically decimated their numbers and they seemed unable to hold their ground in the midst of their new conditions. Superstition was alarmingly rife amongst them and to counteract this, together with its attendant train of fears, a fresh infusion of moral and intellectual courage was needed. Their simple wants were easily satisfied, for a day's wages would ordinarily suffice to provide for the family needs for a week. To arouse them from apathy, the sure fore-runner of decay, they must gain a new appreciation of the value of labor and education.[1]

The number of engagements that were crowded into Dr. Hyde's calendar was incredible. On his first Sunday he preached at Kawaiahao, the great Hawaiian church, with his sermon translated into Hawaiian. In the afternoon he attended a prayer meeting aboard the missionary sailing vessel, *Morning Star,* shortly under way for Micronesia. That evening he preached at the Bethel, the original church for foreigners in Hawaii. The congregation was made up in part of visiting seamen.

Beginning June 5 the Hawaiian Evangelical Association held its annual meeting, its fourteenth since the changeover in 1863. Hyde had several "instant" memberships—election to the board of directors and appointment to four standing committees: foreign missions, publication, education and appropriations from the American Board. He also headed the list of preachers for home evangelization.

The Theological Seminary, the school he was to direct, stood in a compound in the general vicinity of Kawaiahao Church, Kawaiahao Female Seminary, the residences of the Cookes and Pogues and the

Depository of the ABCFM. He drew a rough sketch of the area as one page in a June 19 letter to Clark in Boston.[2]

One other instant affiliation was effected; on June 23 Punahou School elected him as trustee. "The following trustees were elected by ballot. In place of E. H. Allen, resigned, Hon. A. F. Judd. In place of Revs. Mr. Frear and Pogue, whose terms expired this month, were elected Rev. W. Frear and Dr. C. M. Hyde."[3] The minutes also speak of his assignment to the Education Committee of Punahou School a few days *before* election as a trustee.[4]

He did not have much time to enjoy the beauties of the Honolulu countryside. He was there to do church work and he plunged into it. The Theological Seminary, his basic mission in the islands, was renamed the North Pacific Missionary Institute.

Pastoral service in the Brimfield and Haverhill churches, preceded by experience as tutor, school teacher and school board member, had shown him the practical power of closely linking education and religion in evangelistic endeavors. Because of this, and the fact that it permeated his thinking all the rest of his life, excerpts are introduced here of some observations he made at the Hilo Boys Boarding School's jubilee:

. . . The Apostles . . . give this Gospel of God's grace its world-wide and lasting triumph by systematic teaching. An evident fact in the progress of Christian missions is that the teacher's platform occupies a position of coordinate importance with the pulpit of the preacher. In this Sandwich Islands Mission the School preceded the Church. As soon as a few of the natives had learned the art and mystery of written language they began at once to teach others the little knowledge they had acquired. In a short time the whole nation was at school.

But it was soon found that the meager attainments of these first teachers must be supplanted by wider knowledge and better skill, if education was to make any further progress. The old mustang methods of mental nurture must give place to the careful and orderly arrangements characteristic of organized and settled Christian communities. So it came to pass that the years from 1830 to 1840 were years of marked intellectual development as well as of wonderful spiritual change in the mission. No such numbers were ever before or since converted to Christ as during that decade. Never has there been such another period of book-making, especially for schools, as in those ten years. The eagerness of the Hawaiians to learn was met by the readiness of the missionaries to provide books for their instruction in the rudiments of knowledge, and also the elementary principles of the higher departments of learning; geometry and trigonometry in mathematics, universal history, grammar, political economy, moral science, systematic theology . . .

It is not sufficient to give a people or an individual the bare knowledge of important truth. If these truths are to influence the character, they can reach their highest effectiveness only as they become permanent principles of action. To do this, some length of time, and some varied experiences, are absolutely essential. In no other way can these essentials be so well secured as in the Christian "Home School," as in the records of the Mission these Boarding Schools are very frequently called. From the very beginning of the Mission, the Christian home has been held up before the Hawaiian people as the great object to be desired and sought in reorganizing society on these islands. For in the origin and development of Christianity the family rather than the individual has been presented as the unit in all methods of aggressive movement or of permanent growth . . .[5]

As Dr. Hyde wrote, so he acted. The program of studies, enriched with lectures, chores, socials, excursions, church meetings, and intellectual games, was but a reflection of his early experiences.

Insistent as the demands of the Institute came to be, he found it a necessity to pursue two rather unrelated goals immediately. The first of these had to do with family housing and the second with mastery of the native language.

Transactions by which a lot became available for the Hyde home moved along rapidly as soon as word reached Honolulu that the Hydes were coming. The Benjamin F. Dillinghams deeded a rather large piece of land on Beretania Street near Alapai Street to the Harvey Rexford Hitchcocks February 1. These people in turn deeded the property to Samuel N. Castle and the Rev. Elias Bond as trustees for the American Board June 27. The Hawaiian Board received $2000 from the American Board for construction of the house with $1500 to be raised locally. Dr. Hyde hurried the plans which were ready in mid-July, 1877. " . . . the house is plain, neat, commodious . . . I can assure you that we feel grateful enough for our home. The lot is a very large one, I have smoothed over the surface, kept out the weeds, let the grass cover it, and the lawn and trees make it most restful and attractive to every eye. The house is excessively plain, but the large, light rooms, and their whole arrangement give everyone the impression of a pleasant home . . . "[6]

In September 1878 construction and furnishing were well enough along that the Hydes could entertain the Rev. Elias Bond of Kohala, Hawaii island, a substantial contributor to the American Board for salary and other expenses for the new arrivals. Hyde derived much comfort from the new house. " . . . I had the pleasure of entertaining Bro. Bond at dinner at my house. He was delighted with the arrangement and gratified at the economical yet tasteful finish . . . Every visitor is pleased with the plan of the house, and there is no house in Honolulu that surpasses it in economy of expenditure and convenience of arrangement . . . I do the chores myself."

There was a slight defensive tone in the letters. Someone from Honolulu had written that the Hyde home was a bit on the showy side. "So when you hear of the fine Establishment we keep up . . . please remember there is another side to the story. Yankee wit and thrift can 'Keep up appearances' and make a little go a great way. I have written you fully as you requested in regard to this matter . . . "[7] He went on to say that Mrs. Hyde managed to do without any help in the kitchen except that paid student help did most of the washing and ironing.

Robert Louis Stevenson also was to arraign the home as a pretentious manse in his *Open Letter to the Rev. Dr. Hyde of Honolulu.*[8]

But Hyde needed no defense. The home became almost a public meeting and housing facility. The Social Science Association met there frequently as did the students of the Institute, and countless other individuals and groups came to enjoy the warm hospitality. The Hydes took in the missionaries stopping over from Micronesia, some of them sick, needing weeks and even months of rest and recuperation. The place was home, hospital, and hotel.

The Hydes renovated the buildings in 1892 and comment was made that "Mrs. Hyde's taste has put the rooms into such shape though at a very moderate cost, that a second Robert Louis Stevenson may grow green eyed with envy again at what money cannot do, but a little Yankee ingenuity can, taking material that other people would despise and by attention to the fitness of things, making a *toute ensemble* that is very charming to every eye . . ."[9]

One incident of Honolulu living illustrates the intimate annoyances to which people were subjected. "I did not mean to convey the impression that the mosquitoes, which troubled me at the time I wrote you, were a new pest. Far from it. They are the one continued drawback to comfort in rest or in labor every evening, seven times a week. But some evenings they are worse than usual. I found very soon after my arrival here that I must protect myself against them or my evenings and mornings too would all be lost. So I manufactured a canopy for my study table, and under cover of this I can generally defy the innumerable host of hungry and noisy insects. When I moved into the new house I enlarged the canopy and every evg if we wish to have any comfort reading or writing, or talking or listening, the whole family takes shelter within this mosquito-proof . . . ''[10]

Dr. Hyde had not, until his arrival, heard a word spoken in the Hawaiian language. While he had given some thought to acquainting himself with the language, he encountered an urgency not to mere acquaintance but to mastery. That first Sunday morning, as he faced the great audience of natives in Kawaiahao, where he was preaching to the people he had come to serve and where his every phrase had to be translated, he made up his mind he would learn the language.

Said he after a few weeks had passed: "The spoken language is different from the English, making so much of the vowel sounds and paying so little attention to consonants, that it will require much practice to be perfect in it. Its grammatical construction is very simple, but there are a great many particles, expletives like That man *there* and The fire burned *up* everything where appropriate use seems more a matter of instinctive propriety than of regulated usage."[11]

As the summer months passed he gained enough proficiency to attempt teaching oral English to the native students. Few methods can so quickly prepare a person in speaking a foreign language as this and it is quite likely he grew faster in Hawaiian than the new fall term students did in English. He elicited a pat on the back from a fellow minister: "You would have been gratified could you have heard with us Dr. Hyde's address of twelve minutes in Hawaiian without notes to a large audience in Kaumakapili Church last sabbath evening. . . . ''[12] He was in his eighth month in Hawaii and the Hawaiian language!

He could say in another month that he could "find no difficulty in conducting a recitation in Hawaiian."[13] At the end of the school term he proudly described his first annual report; "I wrote out a full report of the Institute (in Hawaiian) for the Ass'n and a similar report (in English) for the Board which I have just read this evening."[14]

Dr. Hyde spoke of one practice which certainly contributed to his orderly intimate understanding of the language. " . . . I am committing to writing every hint and suggestion I can get in regard to the language, hoping to make easier for others the work of acquiring the tongue."[15]

Nothing gives a better insight into Hyde's patience and persistence than a shoe-box sized container I recently stumbled upon at the Bishop Museum. It held these minutely pencilled notes of his on the Hawaiian language. Here even a cursory look speaks of a bonanza. Here is an incredible quantity of Hawaiian phrases and words—thousands— organized under numerous headings; name lists of Hawaiian ducks, bananas, fishes, and others; word lists for work, play, hulas, places; colloquial expressions, proverbs. The accumulation represents remarkable source material for the grammarian, the dictionary compiler, and the translator.

"The language," he said, "as spoken sounds to me like the broken speech of one without a palate. There are nice distinctions in the vowel sounds, hard for one to catch, whose tongue has been trained to the use of consonants. There is a guttural hitch or catch, which is cognizable rather by the throat in utterance than the ear in hearing."

On his first trip to any of the other islands he visited Maui and Hawaii. It was in August 1878 and was a hurried trip which could have almost been termed a "dictionary" trip. The venerable "Father" Lorenzo Lyons of Waimea, Hawaii, had, with the assistance of an old native over a three-year period, entered correct accents which had been entirely omitted by the Rev. Lorrin Andrews in his enlarged 1865 dictionary of the Hawaiian language.[16] Dr. Hyde had his own copy of the Andrews dictionary rebound with blank pages inserted among the printed pages and at Waimea spent seven ten-hour days copying the accents. His biographer son comments that "these blank pages are now well filled with the finest of writing, containing words not incorporated in the Andrews edition, together with derivatives and shades of meaning. Every word of which he had made a study is marked and there are few words without these pencil notations. Some of the results of this language study he embodied in a Hawaiian Grammar published in 1896."[17]

His scholarly insight into the origins, the meanings of roots, the values of accent and elision, is nowhere more clearly evidenced than in his two-part paper in the short-lived *Hawaiian Monthly,* "Random Notes on the Hawaiian Language." Here he presents useful comparisons of root meanings, points out errors in accepted versions of definitions, and discusses double meanings. He characterizes the language as "not mono-syllabic like the Chinese, nor inflectional like the English. It belongs to the second great division of languages, the agglutinative, called Turanian by some philologists."[18]

The efforts seem prodigous when it is realized they were expended in the interstices of activity-filled days. " . . . I have completed a full catalog of all publications in the Hawaiian language. My intention is to assign some of these books to each student for private reading in additon to the regular studies of the Institute. I wish them to be especially well informed in Biblical knowledge. I intend now to prepare some elemen-tary treatises on subjects not yet put into shape in the Hawaiian language, publish them in a series of newspaper articles and then preserve some copies in scrapbooks for the students."[19]

He reviewed the program of studies at the end of December 1878 and described a new use for the Hawaiian language. " . . . On Tuesdays, a translation from English into Hawaiian. I am pressing into this service in the way of translating Moody's Gospel Hymns two of the students who have some knowledge of music and metre. The translations are of such pieces as are suitable for publication in the native newspaper . . . Thursdays we translate Hawaiian into English, using for this purpose the Hawaiian textbook on Moral Science."[20]

The translation of hymns did not much involve him until the death of Father Lyons in 1886. Lyons, known as *Laiana,* and Miss Ella H. Paris, known as *Hualalai,* in the credits at the tops of their respective hymn pages, were the most prolific translators in the Hawaiian hymn field.[21] In a comment in an ABCFM letter Dr. Hyde said, "The students sang finely melodies adapted to and arranged for male voices only. The words were translations that I made myself. Now that Father Lyons has gone his work of translation has thus developed upon me in addition to my other work."[22]

As he gained facility in the language he applied use of it in new direc-tions. He prepared an essay on Hawaiian literature for a YMCA Quarter-ly Meeting February 21, 1879 on which the *Friend* commented:

. . . The main feature of the evening was the reading of an essay by Dr. Hyde on the subject of Hawaiian literature, which consisted mainly of the Doctor's notes and comments in making up a catalogue of all the works published in the Hawaiian language. Of these there are 107, but only one collection comprises them all, and some copies of early editions of the Bible, primers, maps and engravings, which attracted much attention.[23]

By the end of August 1880 he was on another path:

. . . I hope now to be able to write for newspapers in Hawaiian, having Mr. Forbes revise my work. I want very much to prepare a Sunday School Paper, that shall be wholly religious in its subject, language, illustrations, and without advertisements. My idea is to publish one paper for children on the first of each month—I want to furnish the papers at 25¢ each year if it is possible to do so— I want to take this year to prepare materials, and begin publication Jan. 1, 1882. . .[24]

1882 letters to the American Board referred to other beginnings in language employment. "I am beginning," said he, "also a collection of Hawaiian meles [songs], traditions and legends."[25] Again, "I have also annotated, amended, and enlarged Andrews' Hawaiian Dictionary which has 30,000 words alphabetically arranged . . ."[26] He was off a bit on his word count. The figure was closer to 15,000.

"I am making up now," he went on, "a set of laws and government reports. These would be of no special value in your library but they help me in mastering the language. I am gathering also old Hawaiian newspapers but this work goes on very slowly. I doubt whether a complete set can be picked up. I have just written to the Rev. S. J. Whitman of Samoa, inquiring about his projected Cooperative Polynesian Dictionary and offering to help on furnishing lists of Hawaiian words. I early began keeping a classified list and find it a great help . . ."[27]

Practical results of classroom motivation were reported; "And that reminds me of one of the exercises I have given to the students to rouse their intellectual abilities . . . to write out some of the sayings that are popular among the Hawaiians and suitable for use in sermons or addresses. I have now a collection of over 250. From these, I have prepared an article which is to appear in Thrum's Hawaiian Annual for 1883 . . . It classifies some of them in order to give in this way some idea of Hawaiian modes of thought and speech . . . "[28]

He was definitely taken with the importance of preserving the pure Hawaiian tongue. It is therefore understandable that he would firmly stress the study of it in the public schools. In a long letter to the *Gazette* he said:

The greater number of new and commodious schoolhouses, the increasing number of able and faithful and acceptable teachers, are evident facts that redound greatly to the credit of the present Board. But some, who are interested especially in the welfare of the Hawaiians, have been led to query, whether the present policy is as advantageous in some respects, as it certainly is intended to be, to the best interests of the Hawaiian children.

Mr. Knudsen has had most favorable opportunities for personal knowledge in regard to the Hawaiians on Kauai . . . In the letter from him recently printed in your paper, he deprecates the exclusion of the Hawaiian language from the schools for Hawaiians. In this particular, I wish to express my concurrence with his opinion and view of the situation, rather than with the stand taken by Principal Scott in his reply . . . It is not so much the study of English exclusively, which marks the divergence of views in regard to the policy of the Board, as the exclusion of the Hawaiian language from the schools, in which according to the last census Hawaiians and halfcastes constitute 81 per cent of the school population. The question is not merely in regard to the superiority of one language over another as a medium of instruction, nor to the superior economical view of the English in a business point of view. No one can deny the immeasurable advantage of the English language . . . no sane person would think of insisting on making Hawaiian the language of the schoolrooms, and require the teachers that came from the States to acquire the Hawaiian language . . .

But the fact is as stated by Mr. Knudsen, a condition of things to be deplored and remedied that the present generation of Hawaiian youth is growing up in ignorance of their own language, unable to read or write it properly. And they are also growing up without that knowledge of the rudiments, the fundamental principles and facts in mathematics, geography, grammar, history and physical science, such as would better fit them to be intelligent and capable members of civilized society . . . the policy of the Government should be to encourage and strengthen, not throttle, the Hawaiian element in our heterogeneous population.

The charge has often been made, unjustly, so any well informed observer would say, that those who came from the States to Christianize the Hawaiians, tried to make them over in a cast from a mould of New England pietism. It seems to me that our modern scientific humanitarians in the policy they are adopting, are trying to make over the Hawaiians after the prevailing standards of nineteenth century mercantilism. The cry is, "Away with this people, not fit to be capitalists and managers of trusts, nor trades-union leaders, seeking for the horny hand of toil the scepter of rank and power." If it be true that Hawaiians cannot be boss mechanics, or merchant princes, or leading lawyers—and who, that knows them, has any idea they ever will achieve such social distinction?—have they no right to life, independence, and social activity in such fashion as may best suit their national peculiarities, even if this should lie in style not in accordance with our ideas of culture? The Westminister Catechism does not give the consummate ideal of deity; it leaves out beauty altogether in its enumeration of the divine characteristics. Modern materialism does not uphold the highest type of humanity in making economic values the sole test of human worth and dignity. Help the Hawaiians to be good Hawaiian men and women, is the true policy, in my opinion, even if they should not be Christians of such high-toned spirituality, as Edward Payson or David Brainerd; or such mechanics, and inventors, and corporators as Pullman, or Edison, or Jay Gould.[29]

A few years later a final reference to his language activity occurs in a letter as he was "coasting" in health but working resolutely at everything regardless. "I have just had sent to me the final revision of a little manual, I have prepared, of the Hawaiian Grammar in the Hawaiian language, and if life and health are spared, I want to prepare other such helps after the style of the Chautauqua textbooks."[30]

This recital of native language efforts reveals an intellectual vigor which was of great effect in his unending labors among the people constituting his mission.

NOTES

1 Henry K. Hyde, op. cit., pp. 34–35.
2 Letter Hyde to the Rev. N. G. Clark, ABCFM, June 19, 1877.
3 Punahou School, *Secretary's Records*, June 23.
4 Ibid., June 20.
5 The *Friend*, Supplement, Hilo Boarding School Jubilee Notes, December 1886. C. M. Hyde, "Relation of the School to the Mission," pp.2–3. This is the monthly publication of the Hawaiian Board, founded in 1842.
6 Letter Hyde to Clark, Dec. 7, 1881.
7 Ibid., Sept. 28, 1878.
8 Robert Louis Stevenson, *Open Letter to the Rev. Dr. Hyde of Honolulu* (Sydney, Australia, Ben Franklin Printers, 1890).
9 Letter Hyde to the Rev. Judson Smith, ABCFM, Feb. 2, 1892.
10 Ibid., Mar. 18, 1878.
11 Ibid., July 17, 1877.
12 Letter the Rev. Hiram Bingham to Clark, Feb. 19, 1878.
13 Letter Hyde to Clark, Mar. 18.
14 Ibid., June 18.
15 Ibid., June 19, 1887.
16 Lorrin Andrews, *Dictionary of the Hawaiian Language* (Honolulu, H. M. Whitney, 1865).
17 Henry K. Hyde, op. cit., p. 72; Charles M. Hyde, *Piliolelo Hawaii, Hawaiian Grammar* (Honolulu, Hawaiian Gazette Co., 1896).
18 *Hawaiian Monthly*, Honolulu, Vol. I, Nos. 9, 10, Sept. Oct. 1884.
19 Letter Hyde to Clark, Sept. 28, 1878.
20 Ibid., Dec. 23.
21 Hymns translated by Rev. Hyde are listed below. All were first printed with music in *Leo Hoonani* by Theodore Richards in 1902.
    O Day of Rest and Gladness *(Ka La Hoomaikai Keia)*
        English Poem by Christopher Wordsworth
    I Know Whom I Have Believed *(Na Iesu No I Haawi Mai)*
        El. Nathan
    Sweet Peace, The Gift of God's Love *(Mai Kai E Launa Me Oe)*
        P. B. Bilhorn
    The Eye of Faith *(Aole Au E Imi Mau)*
        Rev. J. M. Maxfield
    Sound the Battle Cry *(Ala! Oho E!)*
        Wm. F. Sherwin
    Throw Out The Life Line *(Ho Mai Ke Kaula O Ke Ala Mau)*
        Rev. E. S. Ufford
    Only Remembered *(Eia Ke Ala)*
        Horatius Bonar
    To Live in Christ *(No Iesu No Owau A Pau)*
    Jesus, My All *(Iesu Ke Alii Mau)*
    Song of the Soldier *(E Na Koa O Ke Ola)*
22 Letter Hyde to Smith, June 29, 1887.
23 The *Friend*, March 1879.
24 Letter Hyde to Clark, Aug. 30, 1880.
25 Letter Hyde to the Rev. H. M. Hagen, ABCFM, Jan. 14, 1882.
26 Ibid., Jan. 28.

27 Ibid.
28 Letter Hyde to Clark, Dec. 16.
29 Letter Hyde to editor *Hawaiian Gazette,* Jan. 1, 1889, p. 4.
30 Letter Hyde to Smith, Oct. 28, 1896.

Chapter 6

THE MINISTERS' SCHOOL

EVEN BEFORE the American Board withdrawal in 1863, the local Congregationalists had clearly perceived the most striking key need of the Hawaiian mission and had so reported to the church association:

In view of the present and prospective wants of Hawaiian churches, in view also of the pressing call for Hawaiian preachers among the benighted islanders of Micronesia and the Marquesas groups, the time appears now to have fully arrived in which it becomes us to make higher efforts than heretofore for the education of a pious and efficient ministry, for the purposes above mentioned.

It is therefore recommended

1. That the pastors and other members of this association, select such pious and educated members of the churches, and who appear to possess the proper talents for the ministry, to be taken under the care of the clerical associations, on trial, as candidates for the ministry, and to be put under a course of instruction for that object.

2. That we elect one of our number as teacher of a Theological school, for the thorough training of these candidates.

3. That we correspond with the secretaries of the Board [ABCFM] soliciting their approval of the above object, and asking for aid in support of the Teacher of the Theological School.[1]

A missionary training center at Wailuku, Maui island, in 1863 was the first local effort. The Rev. W. P. Alexander was placed in charge. When he departed for a visit to the Marquesas Islands in 1870 the school was closed. In 1872 the buildings of the U. S. Marine Hospital, 56 Punchbowl Street, between Beretania and Hotel Streets in Honolulu, were purchased at the suggestion of Dr. G. P. Judd and refitted as the Theological Seminary. The Revs. J. D. Paris, Benjamin W. Parker, and A. O. Forbes served successively for short periods through June 1877.

The problems of staffing the school were largely caused by the not unusual subordination of the work to the pressing duties of whatever regular assignment may have prevailed at the time. A full time worker was the only solution and the Rev. Charles McEwen Hyde, D.D. of Haverhill, Massachusetts was appointed.

By strange coincidence the Rev. Mr. Parker, who had acted as one chairman of the Theological School, passed away almost at the hour of the commissioning exercises of Dr. Hyde to the new leadership at Chelsea, Massachusetts, March 23, 1877.

The Rev. Hiram Bingham, Secretary of the Hawaiian Board, treated the arrival of Hyde with an unusual fervency in a letter:

To the Missionaries of the Hawaiian Board cooperating with the American Board,

You will truly rejoice with me that God has sent us an able man to take charge of the North Pacific Institute, in the person of Rev. Charles M. Hyde, D.D. We trust, his efforts among us will result in raising up well qualified reenforcements for the Gilbert and Marshall Islands Missions. Dr. Clarke writes of him, "as a very accomplished scholar, one of the best and most highly esteemed in this state (Mass.) and with ripe experience in the ministry, carrying with him the esteem and confidence of our churches; XXX a first class man, earnestly devoted to the missionary work. We doubt not you will earnestly and frequently remember him and his work in your prayers."[2]

At the first chance, Dr. Hyde took a quick interested look at his future school home. In the June 19 letter to Boston he stated a few details and included a rough sketch of what must have seemed a disappointing layout. Said he, "The main building is 22 x 56, giving two large rooms, each 22 x 28. The front room is the Recitation room; the rear, is the

Library . . . It is whitewashed and on the walls are hung missionary maps and a map of the Holy Land."[3]

The North Pacific Missionary Institute opened under his leadership October 2, 1877 with a roster of 15 students, 14 Hawaiian and one Chinese, most of whom were married. From letters to the American Board, from the *Friend* and other sources comes the story of his aptitude for teaching. His simple direct teaching resourcefulness was noted by observers and as faithfully reported. "Dr. Hyde," said the Rev. Mr. Bingham, "has as many students as the premises of the Institute will accommodate. He has entered into his work with all his heart and strength, and we will cease not to hope and pray that his labors may be largely blessed. The efforts of Mrs. Hyde in behalf of the wives of the married students are praiseworthy."[4]

In the same ship mail a Hyde letter was also on its way to that American Board correspondent. In this Dr. Hyde wrote first impressions of the native. " . . . The Hawaiians seem to be a people whom it is very easy to interest. But interesting as they are, there are lacking in their national characteristics some elements, which are indispensable to true and permanent national prosperity. They have more of the French grace *vive* and dash *elan* than the English grit and pluck. I cannot but be pleased with the apparent quickness and readiness with which they take any suggestion from me."[5]

Later that year he added further analysis:

The people have no mental training from the past like the Oriental. They have never learned the art of thinking logically, or of thinking properly so-called at all. Yet they are not dull or stupid: on the contrary, they are quick and bright. I have not heard anything striking from them in the addresses or conversation. The student talks the first evening seemed to me like our little children's "Sunday School Meetings!"

They look with reverence to a *makua*,[6] and are ready to obey, much more than to command. They allow "friends" to eat them out of house and home because they don't know how to get rid of the intruders.[7]

"I have been troubled," he wrote to Clark later, "as other teachers have in former times, by an influx of *makamakas*,[8] friends of the students. No Hawaiian, as a general thing is master of his own house. He is liable at any time to be eaten out of house and home by friends who quarter themselves on him till his food and property are well spent. I have interfered to protect the students, and summarily dismissed some of such unwelcome guests, that in Hawaiian style had camped down in the rooms."[9]

Towards the end of his first school year he detailed some of his adventures in teaching and referred to the role that Mrs. Hyde was taking in backing up his work:

. . . I am greatly disappointed at being unable to give them some English text books to study. My attempt to get a simple Biblical Geography has not succeeded . . . I have Binney's *Theological Compend.* Improved. It is about the size I should like, but it is not written in as terse and simple English as is needful for immature and uncultivated minds— and it is a Methodist book . . . I have given them orally and on the blackboard what is technically called "Isogogics"—"Introduction" to the Pastoral Epistles, and required them to recite back in Hawaiian and English. When they had finished the study of the two Epistles to Timothy, I invited some of the clergymen in the city to visit the Institute, and without any previous drilling for the performance examined the students in what they had been studying. I was gratified with the manner in which they acquitted themselves, with the blunders they made as well as with the measure of fluency and accuracy they had attained in a few weeks of imperfect instruction.

We have just finished the study of Gallender's *Child's Book of Natural Theology* (in Hawaiian). I am now leading them on in Biblical Archeology—the chronology of the Scriptures, the Social and Domestic Life of the Jews etc etc giving topics from the Tract Society's Biblical Dictionary (in Hawaiian) and requesting one person each day to give a review (in English) of the previous lesson. I give them a half dozen Hawaiian sentences each day to translate into English and as many English sentences to write from dictation, hoping to prepare them thus to write an Outline Study of Systematic Theology.

. . . I have forgotten that on the evening of the same day (Tuesday Mar 12) in which the students were examined, Mrs. Hyde invited them all to come to the house for a social gathering, the married ones with their wives. There were 22 present and they enjoyed the occasion very much. They had been afraid of awkwardness in the use of knives and forks but sandwiches prevented any need of such timidity. After an hour spent in looking at pictures, conversation and singing after the collation had been disposed of, they left the house with many *"alohas"* and *"mahalos."*[10]

A Hyde letter telling of his first session with Sunday School teachers is graphic. He had volunteered to head the Sunday School at Kaumakapili Church:

At a Sunday School teachers meeting one evening . . .I told them of the books in use in Christ's time. The fact was mentioned that a physician in Honolulu who had visited the Holy Land, had in his possession the book of Esther in Hebrew manuscript . . .I read some of it in the Hebrew, and the corresponding passage in the Hawaiian Bible. Children and grown people gathered around the pulpit at the close of the exercises with eager curiosity to see the words in which the Bible, so familiar to them in their own tongue, was originally written, and the parchment roll, described to them actually seen, and its folds still smoky brown, with the slow consuming touch of time, were reverently handled as a memorial of centuries of bye gone years.[11]

The first annual report of the Institute was a good report of the initial Hyde year. It was handwritten in English and Hawaiian and read to the annual meeting, the Aha Paeaina, of the Hawaiian Evangelical Association and printed in the proceedings. The report referred to the school as the Ministers' School and Hyde signed as *teacher*. Excerpts follow:

. . . Hyde taught mostly in English. The students read and translated the English reader, together with the grammar. Hyde taught the Sunday School lesson every week. He explained the Epistles to Timothy, Titus, Philemon, Jude and II and III John. The students memorized some divisions of the Bible dictionary.

All the students worked outside every Friday only one hour, cleaning the premises. They worked every afternoon to get their food. They get almost enough by means of their work without outside help. "If anyone desires to be a minister, he desires a good work." Laziness is unsuited.

The gifts of the Hawaiian Board were insufficient to accomplish everything, but four rooms have been renovated and prepared with funds given by the four churches. C. M. Cooke gave window curtains for the dining room. Rev. E. Bond gave $100 for the new building. Mrs. Dickson and Miss Judd gave material for the rooms—a bed, a bureau and mats.

The Rev. S. B. Dole gave Latin books for the teacher and Mrs. Pogue gave all the books of her late husband, Secretary of the Hawaiian Board, recently deceased. There are almost 300 of these valuable books. Some old books in Hawaiian and English were sent from Lahainaluna, but this school needs books in Hawaiian.

This year we have seen merely the new beginning. Like trees after a storm, this school has begun to bud forth again. We have many reasons for being hopeful. It is not well to forget the words of the Lord, "Pray the Lord of the harvest that he will send forth laborers into his harvest."

It will be well for this Association to appoint a committee every year to test the qualifications of the students. You all are requested to attend the examinations of the School on Monday at 8:30 a.m.[12]

Immediately following is the brief but heartwarming comment of the examining committee. "The school was examined on June 6 and the committee was wide-awake for the job. We thank God for this school. The work is progressing. Great has been Dr. Hyde's speed in learning Hawaiian, also his power to impress his ideas on his students."[13]

There was no acceptance on his part of the pagan theology of the native but he had an uncanny ability to analyze it in terms of what he wanted to teach. He cited a teaching incident of this kind in a letter to the American Board:

One item I may mention as some encouragement to me in my work that the students now in the Institute seem to be so thoroughly and staunchly devout believers, earnest defenders of the faith of the Gospel. I have commenced talking on Systematic Theology. When considering the fundamental truth of God's existence, wishing them to regard theological study as practical common sense, not merely speculation or dogmatic opinions, I asked them why the Hawaiians worshipped the shark, the owl, big stones etc etc. They told me, "because of the divine power these things had. If any were shipwrecked and called on the shark god for help, they would be brought safely to land; otherwise not. If any fisherman wanted a good haul, and would put his votive offering on a certain stone, he would be successful, otherwise he would labor in vain. If a person was sick and drank *awa*[14] to the owl he would be cured. And this has been tried so often, people could not help believing in the divine power of these things." They said that many church members, *and ministers too,* believed this, but all declared it was not believed at all by them. They told me of one minister who had just died of consumption who made the circuit of Hawaii in the effort to regain his health by this *pilgrimage* in honor of the old divinities! They could not show the absurdity of such a belief. All they could do was to assert their own deep conviction of the truth of Christianity. So I tried to give them a short method of dealing logically with such superstitions and establishing by sound argument their own position as witnesses for God . . .[15]

A second year came to a conclusion bringing a second report. This is quoted in some detail for the valuable allusions to the solid progress of the Institute:

In the good providence of God the work of the Institute, has gone on without interruption and without much change from last year. Ten students have been in attendance the whole of the past year. These were all connected with the Institute last year. One other was pronounced a leper and did not return. No new students have entered this year. These students have not by any means devoted themselves to study, in such a way as is expected of young men in the U. S. in their position. But as a general thing they have labored with fidelity and diligence in the work assigned them.

The studies pursued have been after the same general programme as last year. Beginning at 8:30 a.m. the whole morning of each day except Saturday had been devoted to study and recreation. Rev. M. Kuaea and Rev. S. E. Bishop have given their services, this year as last, instructing respectively in Church History and in O. T. Interpretation.

A Catalogue of all the books in the Hawaiian language has been prepared giving titles, pages, editions, and it is hoped to secure copies of all the books. Among these are several valuable manuscripts, one a Commentary on Acts, begun by Mr. Pogue, which has been filled out partially completed in connection with studies and recitations on that Book.

Judge McCully has given a Chandelier for the Recitation Room, and

Her Highness Ruth Keelikolani has given a piano, formerly owned by His late Majesty Kamehameha V.

During the coming vacation, arrangements have been made for the students to supply vacant churches. It is hoped that their labors will be blessed both to themselves and to the Churches. Where are the young men to take the places of the class that will graduate next year? The government needs intelligent and ambitious young men for its service. Various industrial interests call loudly for active and enterprising young men. Teachers are needed in the schools. Never was there a time when a young man had so many attractive opportunities offered him as here in *Hawaii nei* today.

But higher than all other claims is the call of Christ on his disciples to enter into His service. A register has been prepared of all Hawaiians who have been preachers and pastors. The record is a most honorable one. May God in His mercy call many young men, like Saul of Tarsus or Timothy of Derbe, to be the spiritual leaders of this nation turning many to righteousness and in heavenly glory shining like the stars in the firmament for ever & ever.[16]

He wrote of writing and teaching, illustrating the motivating force of competitive effort:

. . . I am writing this year Commentaries on Hebrews, Ephesians, and Romans. The students write from dictation and when I have finished the Exegesis of one character, give some suitable "practical remarks and suggestions." I hope in that way to train them to think, and to apply Bible truth for themselves. To the student who shall in the judgment of the Committee have done best in this study, shows the best mss. etc I offer to give *"The Portable Commentary"* in two vols. (by Jamieson, Fawcett & Brown) in English. The students are reading in English and translating Binney's *Theological Compend,* and reciting in Hawaiian from questions in Hawaiian . . .[17]

A practical teaching device was briefly referred to in another letter. "I propose," he wrote, "to build a model parsonage at the Institute. It will serve the double purpose of adding housing for more students here and give them all a concept of acceptable and essential standards in such housing when they get to their church."[18] He forgot about this for a while; " . . . the chapel, the main building of the School was burned down one night . . . the Government will rebuild at once . . ."[19]

By the winter of 1882–1883 the Hydes were ready to plan a "refresher" return to the United States. He worried about the fitness of his students to take summer pastorates in the churches on their home islands while he would be away. "I wish we had a better set but if we are to have Hawaiian ministers we must take them with the characteristics of the Hawaiian people. *God's infinite patience bears with our manifold defects and infirmities—why should we—be discouraged . . . with the human weaknesses and follies of our fellow laborers?* With all their faults there is something pleasant and lovable in Hawaiians and I shall hope on hope, ever labor, study, & pray for their improvement and progress . . . "[20]

Leprosy as a subject for correspondence appears for the first time in 1884. " . . . Hitherto I have dealt with it (Leprosy) on my own responsibility, quickly dropping out the individuals I have found from year to year who were tainted with the terrible malady. But now I have found three out of fifteen students are certainly lepers; that another student and two of the wives have suspicious symptoms . . . "[21]

He wrote off in all directions for advice with questions about symptoms, remedies, hospitalization. He assembled the opinions of the experts in a major article in a local paper.[22] These writers represented a cross section of the best thinking about leprosy. The disease, its causes and effects, would surface in his mind almost as a nightmare as he was later to become involved in it in a way he could not possibly have foreseen.

By the end of 1884 he could write pragmatically of school conditions and effects. "I am more than ever convinced," he wrote, "of the importance of this work. The churches are the centers of good influence and ought to be supplied with capable and efficient pastors. One third of the parishes have no pastors, one third ought not to have such as they now have. I cannot take more than 15 students at any one time, and as the course of study ought to take generally at least four years, I cannot very soon overtake the needs of these twenty vacant churches. But out of a church membership of over 1250 to get four theological students every year is enough to keep good the supply, were all other conditions favorable."[23]

He further analyzed native abilities and shortcomings:

. . . This is the great difficulty in trying to elevate the Hawaiians—in their total lack of our feeling of push and energetic endeavor. I have to put this into these students, and it is gratifying to see how marked a change two years residence at the Institute works in these young men, and in their wives too. You know, perhaps, that this is a Manual Labor Training School. The students take care of the grounds, paint, chop wood, do carpenter work, and thus get enough money to pay their support, about $3.00 per week . . . Last class had some bright ones who worked in printing offices, and as commission buyers . . . Industrious effort to support themselves . . . help to develop such traits of character as fit them for managing their household and church affairs in a business way. Then I have to train them to think and talk correctly, give them lessons in English and logic, so that they get some notion of the elementary principles and laws of language and mind . . .[24]

Throughout the following spring (1885) he advanced plans for a summer school of practical theology for the benefit of Hawaiian ministers. He blew this idea up into an almost impossible dream:

. . . There is much enthusiasm about my proposed People's University, a sort of Church Correspondence School, a Chautauqua Literary & Scientific Circle with our Pastor as Head . . . I propose to publish 4 books with 12 lessons each to be recited to the pastor, and at the end of every lesson to have examination papers provided and circulated, the answers to be written and sent to Honolulu for correction: at the end of six months print a list of members and names of those who pass over 75% correct replies . . . This is a project I have had in mind for three years . . . I propose mingling general information with Biblical study and for the first four books have planned a Hawaiian Grammar, a Biblical Geography, a General History, and Biblical Introduction to the Old Testament.[25]

While the People's University never left the planning boards for the post office, preparation of the suggested materials continued as he created new study helps and texts and refined old ones. He was perennially at this. "I have also prepared a Manual of Parliamentary Proceedings, the Common Rules of Order, for deliberative bodies, and after careful study of the church Manual, the Students have conducted in due form on assigned topics, a church meeting, a committee meeting, association meetings."[26]

Excerpts from later annual reports bespeak the never ending kaleidoscope of Institute affairs; "In 1886 there were 14 students, all married, some with 3-4 children. The medical examination, now required, cleared all adults and children . . . All gather together for a sunrise prayer meeting, Sundays. A Bible School has been maintained for the children."[27]

"The Rhetorical Society has held a weekly meeting for training in the management of public assemblies, an effective style of extemporaneous speaking, logical discussion of mooted points, and tersely written homiletical discourses . . ."[28]

Among visitors registered in the guest book at the Institute for 1888-1889 was the English portrait painter Edward Clifford. He gave $10 for the use of the school, which spent the money framing photographs of the different classes. A visit to the leper settlement and Father Damien was Clifford's primary purpose in visiting the islands. He was there two weeks and stopped over afterward in Honolulu.[29]

There was steady growth in the school program. There was little change in enrollment but the preparation of text materials, improvement in instructional methods and the selection of students, summer pastorates in town and country, ordinations for local island parishes and for work in Micronesia, went on apace. A new set of facilities was needed: dormitory space for married students, more and better equipped classrooms, and an improved chapel.

A campaign for funds was launched in 1888. Soon sufficient money was in hand and the contract for the new facility was let for $8327. The same site on Punchbowl Street was used. J. Outerkirk was the contractor, H. W. McIntosh, the supervising architect. There were 16 suites of rooms included among the other facilities.[30]

Dr. Hyde liked the new building. "Other forms of faith may advocate and exemplify asceticism and squalor based in sordid notions of human life. But the gospel of the grace of God, as it comes to us, is a gospel of beauty and delight as well as sympathy with affliction and suffering."[31]

He covered other activities in his annual report in 1891. "One pleasing development of practical Christianity is the readiness and success with which some of the students have taken up the work of street preaching.

This meeting, face to face, a crowd of men indifferent to religion, or opposed to its claims, has reacted intensely and favorably on the piety of the students themselves. Students visit from house to house for conversation and prayer, Bible reading and distribution of religious reading in connection with the Hawaiian Evangelical Association."[32] Dr. Hyde in his Institute had reached an optimum level of performance.

"I enclose a program," he wrote to the American Board, "of the closing exercises of the NPMI. Ten out of the 19 students will graduate this year, and for all of them vacant parishes are ready."[33] There was even greater drama in a parallel excerpt a year later. "But what is better, every one of the present class of students has signified his readiness to go to Micronesia into the foreign missionary work. What theological seminary on the mainland can show a record like that? Eight out of the ten are married, and the wives are equally ready with the husbands . . . It will not be an easy matter for the Hawaiian churches to support them, and so I write to urge again the propriety of the American Board's assuming the support of the Gilbert Islands Catechists, sent out from the G.I. Training School."[34]

He had foreseen more clearly than anyone the need of an understudy who would be trained in his way of operation and would then be ready to assume the leadership role. His first mention of this was long before, in 1883. He kept up a running barrage of reminders to the point of its being a matter of self-torment. ". . . I hope," he wrote Judson Smith in 1888, "you will see the importance of having someone on the ground in training to take up my work when it may be necessary for me to retire. I never was stronger or better physically than I am now, but no one can tell when the debilitating climate may tell on my strength so severely that I may break down. There is no indication now of anything of that kind, though I feel that brain-work here is so exhausting as to use up one's brain power entirely. I am not wearied merely, but all such power is gone, as utterly, as if the brain were a log of wood. The will is as vigorous as ever, but the tool is blunted past all *possible* use. I have to stop because I cannot go on: I cannot *think*. It is a curious sensation to have this full physical vigor, but the brain power all spent . . . "[35]

He may have been sounding such a note of despair just to provoke action in Boston. His greatest intellectual accomplishments illumined the final and golden decade of his life. Still nothing happened. March 7 he wrote another letter to Boston. He was planning his next mainland trip scheduled for the summer of 1890. " . . . One reason I am asked to go on is to secure some one as a helper in the Institute who can be in training to take my place. I cannot calculate on more than ten years of active work in the future, and some one ought to be in readiness."

Even the pressure of a personal survey that summer produced no results. So absorbed was he in this continuing failure to enlist a helper, that in the comparative seclusion and relaxation of the ship returning him to Hawaii in September, he composed an article for the reputable *Congregationalist* under the title, "New Times, New Men, New Methods." It was built around the need for strong leaders and constituted a review of the times generally; education, religion, and social and economic life. If it were dated 1970, it would still be applicable.[36]

Institutions fashioned by the personality and energy of one man are in jeopardy if adequate succession is not assured. And it was likely more of a problem in the Institute since Dr. Hyde did not have a board of directors specifically and solely charged with direction of the work. But he recognized this potential hazard and it became an obsession: " . . . I do wish," he wrote, "That you would secure someone such as I have specified, for an assistant in the NPMI. Some one ought to be here and in training to take my place. No one that might come after me could possibly receive such help as I did from the old missionaries then living, and as I stand ready to give to anyone that comes while I can give help."[37]

For the next three years a letter seldom went to the American Board without mention of the NPMI succession. He employed any favorable opening to press the matter. Once he capitalized on a personal injury. " . . . I went inside my toolroom last Friday to get some curtain fixtures to repair a broken window shade at the Institute. I was standing on a box and fell . . . "[38] He bruised his muscles, dented a pail, etc. Another time he reported availability of $5500 in cash to subsidize an assistant.[39] Still with all this, except for one false start, nothing happened.

The Hydes had taken a long respite from Hawaii in the summer and fall of 1893. He was invited to attend the eighty-third annual meeting of the American Board in Worcester, Massachusetts, October 10–13; he accepted, and delayed his Hawaii return accordingly. It was his first visit to such an annual meeting in 17 years. He was 61.

Seemingly his campaign for an associate might be advanced by a personal appearance. It is likely the following portion of the ABCFM Annual Report was prepared by Dr. Hyde:

And we recommend also the early appointment of an associate for Dr. Hyde, in order that the new and increasing work at the islands may be carried on with the energy commensurate with its importance.

The island work illustrates the important influences exerted upon our missions by foreign powers; for example, that German interference should so distract and threaten the work in the Marshall Islands; that Spanish interference should still exclude our missionaries from Ponape; that English protection should so encourage and facilitate work in the Gilbert Islands. All these facts put stress upon the critical political situation in the Hawaiian Islands. It is not too much to say that the results of the works of the American Board of Commissioners for Foreign Missions in these islands, social, educational, religious, are imperiled by the present political complications. In view of these complications your Committee will submit the following resolution:

Resolved, that without any sense of political interference, the Prudential Committee consider the wisdom of a representation to our government at Washington setting forth the great work accomplished by the Board, at such cost, in the Hawaiian Islands, in part represented by the large American colony, and the claim which these results make for some immediate and vigorous action of the government which shall tend, in the interest of Christian civilization to secure these results from injury or destruction by any intestine confusion in the government of that land.[40]

The report was adopted and he could start the long journey home in the high hope of early realization of his quest. The reference to a communication to the government at Washington was a thinly veiled suggestion for action either in support of the Provisional Government in Hawaii or outright annexation. It had been anticipated that were Queen Liliuokalani to be deposed, annexation would come immediately. This did not occur and some emergency makeshift governmental control was in order; hence, the Provisional Government. Crisis in Hawaiian affairs was coming to a head at the very moment he was sitting in his chair at this annual meeting.

He was forbearant for awhile after his return but the winter of 1893–1894 passed and still nothing happened. A most unusual idea came to the Hydes. In a carefully worded, well organized letter in his finest penmanship, signed by both, an offer was made to the American Board:

When we gave ourselves to the service of Christ in the public ministry of the Gospel, as our life-work, we had no hesitation in doing so, because of any possible lack of means of support. We have felt it a privilege to be able to do Christian work as the Lord has opened the way, and He has provided abundantly for all our needs. We have tried to do the best work possible in the wisest way. We are interested deeply in the special work we have been doing these seventeen years for Hawaiians, and for the general welfare of this Community in various departments of Christian activity. We feel that the present is a period of special importance in prosecuting Christian work among the Hawaiians. We have for several years looked in vain for an associate in this work.

The work has grown under our care, and so broadened out, that one man alone cannot attend to all the details personally, as ought to be done, if the work is attempted at all. We feel the urgent necessity of speedily securing some one, who can bring special qualifications and experience to the training of young Hawaiian Christians for aggressive work. We regret that the falling off this year in the resources of the Board, seems to discourage the hope or endeavor to secure at this time such a worker as is now imperatively needed here.

For some time, we have been planning, that upon meeting the necessary expenditures for the education of our children, we might relieve the Treasury of the Board from any expense for our support. We have not thought that we were quite ready to do this, but circumstances are such at present, that we have concluded not to wait for any better ability. Our oldest son is occupying such a position of trust and emolument, as not to need any assistance from us. We had hoped that our younger son would fit himself for some public profession: but as he has shown no fondness for books, we hope to have him make his home with us, while earning his livelihood in some active business in this city. Since the death of Mrs. Hyde's mother, there has been received quite an addition to her private means, which with such economies as we have always practiced, will suffice for our present needs. We have never called upon the Board for any additional aid, beyond our salary, whether for repairs, or for our travelling expenses, or our children, or the expenses of their education.

We have therefore decided now to make to you a proposal, which we hope will put your work in these Islands on a more effective basis. We will relinquish our salary entirely, and will devote ourselves wholly to the special Christian work we came to do, under the direction of the Board as heretofore, on condition

(1) That we shall be granted the free use of the home, that has been provided for us, which we have furnished, and occupied all these years, and where we hope to spend the remainder of our life.

(2) That as long as we continue in this work, we shall receive an annual grant of five hundred dollars, from which we will pay the cost of insurance, water rates, taxes, repairs, and care of the premises: that is, all we ask of the Board is a home, and an allowance sufficient to keep it in good repair.

(3) That the fifteen hundred dollars, thus relinquished and made available for other use, shall be applied to the salary of the new worker, whom we hope the Secretaries will try to secure at once. We are confident that with the money, given for the purpose, now held by the Hawaiian Board, a suitable home can be purchased for the associate whom you may send.

If this proposal is accepted by you, it shall take effect on the first of October of the current year, so that the Institute may be opened at that date on this new basis.[41]

The commissions of the Bishop trusts allowed the Hydes to make the volunteer surrender of salary.

He had not reached the finish line yet, however. In August, 1894 as another school term was about to open, and another annual meeting of the American Board would follow, his patience was thin. " . . . I see that you are aware that I would like a person of some experience, a vigorous worker, tireless, resourceful, persistent, yet pleasant."[42] He sounded as if he were enumerating his own personal qualities. "Pray do not send me anyone for the sake of sending somebody," he wrote later. "That will only make the situation worse . . . You will understand how I rejoice with trembling . . . we need now an aggressive piety, evangelistic in spirit and method."[43] He finally burst forth in a lament that pleaded for action. "I would like to have some definite expectation," he wrote, "so that I can make the needful preparations. There are students to be secured, if I am to have an associate, a house to be bought, a course of study to be mapped out, hours of work determined, and a new basis of organization adopted. I do not dare go away from Honolulu, for if the mail should bring any definite tidings, I should have all I could do, to make these absolutely necessary preparations. The time is slipping by and nothing has been done. I am like a pent-up stream; but in face of such obstacles can only draw a longer and longer breath, ready for some explosive utterance, bye and bye."[44]

Even as he was placing his letter in the boat mail, the wheels of compliance were turning in Boston. The Rev. John Leadingham was the appointee and arrived in Honolulu November 3, 1894 on the S.S. *Australia.* He fitted in well under the worrying eye of a critical hopeful leader. "Mr. Leadingham is taking hold of work," he wrote, "in sensible manly fashion, and will work into larger activities as opportunities open. I have been suffering from nervous prostration ever since his arrival till a week ago Sunday when I felt conscious of returning vigor and can now do a full day's work with all the vim and comfort of yore."[45]

Assimilation of the new associate was fully realized with the opening of the next term of the Institute. Hyde could write in settled mood about his relief. He could now reshape his own schedule of work. "Mr. Leadingham will relieve me from much of the personal care of the students, distributing the personal rations of oil, bread, rice, salmon, tea, sugar. For two years I have been obliged to deal in these commodities, as the students could not earn enough to support themselves without this aid. He will relieve me also of all classwork Mondays and Fridays. I want one day for correspondence and literary work, and another day each week for the various duties that have been devolved upon me in connection with Oahu College, the Hawaiian Board, the Kamehameha Schools, the Bishop Museum, and the Bishop Trust."[46]

By the end of 1898 Hyde's health was failing rapidly but Leadingham was sufficiently adjusted to the Institute to allow a drastic curtailment of duties. Doctors advised a change of climate and on May 13, 1899 a very sick Dr. Hyde sailed for the United States mainland. Sick or not he maintained his concerns for the Institute. Upon arrival in San Francisco he got off a letter to W. W. Hall in Honolulu, requesting he submit a resolution to the Hawaiian Board applying income from a recent Charles M. Cooke gift of $50,000 to the operational budget of the Institute.[47] Dr. Hyde and his travel party then took the train to Ware, Massachusetts.

Unhappily, the Institute story did not run far beyond his decease, five months after this letter was written. The Rev. Mr. Leadingham was an able man but he was no Dr. Hyde. He was unable to mount a campaign for the $150,000 endowment planned by Hyde before the last mainland trip. He did not have the understanding knack of recruiting new students. The Institute came to a quick halt in 1902. Too little, too late!

Dr. Hyde had in his singlehandedness created a religious seminary; he gave it an orderly and intellectually stable program of studies. The products of his teaching skill were scattered in effective mission work throughout the Hawaiian Islands and the mission stations of Micronesia.

NOTES

1 Report, Committee on Theological Education, Minutes Hawaiian Evangelical Association, June 1861.
2 Letter Hiram Bingham to Missionaries of the Hawaiian Board Cooperating with the American Board, April 1877.
3 Letter Hyde to Rev. N. G. Clark, ABCFM, June 19.
4 Letter Bingham to Clark, Feb. 19, 1878.
5 Letter Hyde to Clark, Feb. 17.
6 *Makua*, a relative in the role of parent, benefactor, provider.
7 Letter Hyde to Rev. E. K. Alden, ABCFM, Oct. 28.
8 *Makamaka*, intimate friend with whom one is on terms of giving and receiving freely.
9 Letter Hyde to Clark, Nov. 14.
10 Ibid., April 16. *Aloha*, greeting. *Mahalo*, thanks.
11 Ibid., Jan. 20, 1879.
12 Hyde, North Pacific Missionary Institute, *Annual Report*, June 11, 1878.
13 Ibid.
14 *Awa*, a shrub, its root a source of a narcotic drink.
15 Letter Hyde to Clark, Jan., 20, 1879.
16 Hyde, North Pacific Missionary Institute, *Annual Report*, June 5, 1879.
17 Letter Hyde to Clark, Oct. 27.
18 Letter Hyde to Clark, Jan. 19, 1880.
19 Ibid., Apr. 8.
20 Ibid., Feb. 12, 1883.
21 Ibid., Jan. 10, 1884.
22 *Hawaiian Gazette*, May 14.
23 Letter Hyde to Rev. Judson Smith, ABCFM, Oct. 15.
24 Ibid., Nov. 1.
25 Ibid., June, 1885.
26 Ibid.
27 Hyde, NPMI, *Ninth Annual Report*, June 2, 1886.
28 Hyde, NPMI, *Tenth Annual Report*, June 9, 1887.
29 Hyde, NPMI, *Twelfth Annual Report*, June 4, 1889,
30 The *Friend*, Oct. 1889.
31 Hyde NPMI, *Twelfth Annual Report*, June 4.
32 Hyde, NPMI, *Thirteenth Annual Report*, June 11, 1891.
33 Letter Hyde to Smith, June 16.
34 Ibid., Apr. 26, 1892.

35 Ibid., May 3, 1888.
36 Hyde, "New Times, New Men, New Methods," *Congregationalist* Boston, Oct. 23, 1890. pp. 364–365.
37 Letter Hyde to Smith, Feb. 9, 1891.
38 Ibid., Feb. 2, 1892.
39 Ibid., Oct. 17, 1891.
40 ABCFM, Annual Report, Oct. 10–13, 1893.
41 Ibid., April 28, 1894.
42 Ibid., Aug. 3, 1894.
43 Letter Hyde to Dr. C. H. Daniels, ABCFM, Aug. 18.
44 Ibid., Sept. 15.
45 Letter Hyde to Smith, Dec. 8.
46 Ibid., Oct. 26, 1895.
47 Letter Hyde to W. W. Hall, Honolulu, May 22, 1899.

Chapter 7

THE HAWAIIAN BOARD

THE NORTH PACIFIC Missionary Institute was the compelling care of Dr. Hyde's multi-phased religious beat in Hawaii. He never slackened his efforts on its behalf. He never failed it as he stalked the whole field of religious objects moving across his horizon. He was omnipresent, he was available, and as much as anything he was willing to serve. He could endure long hours of work. These qualities, permeated with an unusual intellectual and judicious grasp, drew him into almost every religious activity in the American Board program in Hawaii. The Institute was his primary mission but the church community work in which he deeply involved himself constituted a second career.

A starting point was membership in the Fort Street Church and its successor, Central Union Church. This was his "parish" church, not a base for operations but a home church. He became a member of Fort Street Church at Communion in December, 1877. In writing of this step he also mentioned attending "worship at one of the native churches. I also have a class of young (native) men in the Sunday School. Mrs. Hyde has one of young (native) girls at Kawaiahao. In the afternoon I visit some out district and take part in the Sunday School teaching and the conference talk of these afternoon meetings. I have also accepted appointment as one of the Trustees of Kawaiahao Female Seminary. I was chosen President."[1]

None of his scheduled religious activity was part of the Fort Street Church-Central Union Church program. He served his parish church only on special occasions. He was elected Moderator of a Council to ordain Mr. E. N. Dyer as minister for Kohala Foreign Church on Hawaii island.[2] Another time he gave the pastoral charge to the Rev. E. G. Beckwith who was called as pastor.[3] He preached by invitation occasionally; once on *Foreign Missions,* in which he sketched the missionary work of the Hawaiian and American Boards, another time on *Idolatry Among the Hawaiians.*[4] One of the most touching of his Central Union messages was given on December 12, 1898 when he extended "William Morris Kincaid the right hand of fellowship as pastor of Central Union Church."[5] He himself was a sick man and scarcely able to weather a pulpit experience. This enumeration is selective and merely suggestive of his Central Union role. He was speaking elsewhere two or three times every Sunday of his life but it was usually a special purpose that lured him back to his own church.

When Bethel Union Church was destroyed in the disastrous downtown fire, April 16, 1886, the Hydes were everywhere about, working with the victims of the fire, housing, feeding and clothing them. Later when Bethel Union and Fort Street Churches merged into the new Central Union Church, they became charter members.

This merger and the see-sawing preceding it was not a simple transaction. Bethel Union members were invited to use Fort Street facilities. Initially, each congregation had its own worship and Sunday School, but burned-out Bethel people also immediately entered into plans of fund raising and rebuilding and this had the full support of Dr. Hyde. A year passed and the Fort Street hosts liked their Bethel guests. Almost a year to the day, he wrote some of the circumstances of a proposed merger and his regret in the matter:

. . . Another complication has arisen. The Bethel people undertook to rebuild after the fire. Their pastor, Mr. Oggel, has made strenuous efforts and has raised $16,000. Before engaging in the work they discussed the advisability of uniting with the Fort St. Church and decided against it. Negotiations with the Government and the Seaman's Friend Society enabled them to dispose of their right and title to the site of the old Bethel in such a way as to receive in exchange a new and very eligible site. They had perfected their plans and were to meet and vote on the propositions of the contractors. Just then Mr. Cruzan (pastor of Fort St. Church) resigned. It was proposed in a prayer meeting at Fort St. Church to unite with the Bethel and join in building a new church for the united congregation. It was so voted and a committee was appointed to carry out the project . . . I have no responsibility in the matter but I deeply regret it. The mere proposal voted by the Fort Street prayer meeting was sufficient to kill the Bethel people's enterprise.[6]

Dr. Hyde doubted the merger would be approved, but it was. There was some discord arising in and from the fusion proceedings and he was relieved that the Rev. E. G. Beckwith was called as the first pastor. This man was one of Punahou's most gifted leaders. Although he had left the school and the islands 28 years before, he was remembered for his level-headedness and tact. The imprint of his schoolmastering on his Punahou students aided in his return. Beckwith did a great job and laid the groundwork for a noble and enduring Congregational effort. Dr. Hyde could recognize this and wrote to the American Board, " . . . Dr. Beckwith's influence was telling on the people . . . The prayer meetings are taking on a more spiritual type . . . Dr. B's sermons are of a high type, and such truths must finally tell on character and conduct. The change is very great from what it was under the former pastorate. Dr. B is orthodox to the back-bone."[7]

Hyde was just as orthodox in his views, " . . . this talk of *liberality*," he continued, "reminds me very much of some small patterned men that are all the while talking about their *dignity*, and ready to pick a quarrel with any who disregards their ideas of their own dignity. When in organizing the Central Union Church this article of faith in regard to eternal punishment came up, it is my impression that the majority were ready to vote it down. But the few of us who did believe it were so evidently and so fully decided in our convictions of the truth of the doctrine (not the plausibility of some hypothesis) that the matter was not pressed."

The American Board in Boston had been experiencing a liberality revolution of its own and elicited this comment from Dr. Hyde: "I am very sorry to hear of the revival of theological differences, but it seems to be 'in the air' everywhere. I doubt whether Central Union Church here has another 'orthodox' evangelical pastor, whenever Dr. Beckwith shall retire."[8]

But there were also varieties of orthodoxy that displeased him. " . . . Elder Starr of the Central Bible Institute, Chicago, has been giving 'bible readings' insinuating the principles of interpretation of the Seventh Day Adventists. It seems too bad to admit such schismatics to the Central Union Church and the YMCA, but our good Christian people are so afraid of being denounced as 'Sectarian' that they give place to the messenger of a perverted Gospel and see no difference."[9]

While doctrine was being debated, the masons and other artisans were following the plans on the trestleboard. The magnificent new church building with walls of dressed lava from Yoachim quarry and Kapena Falls was completed and readied for dedication. At the service, Dr. Hyde gave an address, "The House for a Church." A congregation numbering 1037 "seated" was in attendance that December 4th, 1892.

Dr. Beckwith handled Central Union's first years with marked success but retirement was inevitable. Prospect of this worried Dr. Hyde. "The special item of interest is Dr. Beckwith's resignation. While it appears to be his own voluntary action, yet he could have wished to have spent three years more in the pastorate here, retiring when he reached the age of 70. But the coming of Mr. Rader (Dr. McLean's assistant at Oakland) to occupy the pulpit during Dr. Beckwith's vacation, has precipitated matters. Some of our younger and more flighty people want such a minister, rather than one of Dr. B's mature piety, intellectual superiority, and judicious conservatism. It comes to me as a personal loss."[10]

Grumble as he did, Dr. Hyde needed the heartiness and understanding inherent in the circle of agreeable friends at the church. The understanding of his intimates and trusted acquaintances, re-enforced by his religious faith, equipped him to strike out with ever fresh zest.

It was the native Hawaiian who called him and as was his nature, his approach was rarely that of circumambulation. It was "attack, attack, attack!" His North Pacific Missionary Institute was his attack route but the flanks bristled with unfilled needs and opportunities not altogether free of booby traps and mine fields.

Kaumakapili Church was, in a sense, the second-ranked Hawaiian church. Kawaiahao Church was the largest, but aside from occasional sermons and incidental meetings Hyde did not include it in his tour of duty. At Kaumakapili he found work. "I have been chosen S.S. Super-intendent at Kaumakapili and after consultation with friends have accepted the position and begun the work."[11] In 1879 the congregation raised $14,000 of a needed $15,000 for a new church. His first year in the Sunday School was then coming to a close. He agreed to stay on but intense dissension developed over the political inclinations of the Kaum-akapili pastor, over the questionable handling of the building fund, and even over Dr. Hyde's participation in the work of the church. " . . . I thought it best to decline peremptorially to serve any longer as S.S. Supt. I was chosen unanimously, however, and it was gratifying to know the reason. They wanted someone who could teach them Bible truths. I consented to take charge of the Teachers' Meetings as before. I think I shall also take charge of the Women's Bible Class."[12]

But things would not smooth out. The Congregational tenet of local autonomy was sorely tried in a situation such as this at Kaumakapili. It was so serious, it was carrying the practice of autonomy into a gro-tesque weakening of the very mission itself. This happened in many Hawaiian native churches, "We are nonplussed as to what to do about Kaumakapili," he wrote. "Nominally the church has the charge and responsibility of its own affairs but if any Hawaiian Church is left to run itself without any supervision from time to time, records are lost, funds are made away with, parsonages sold, churches mortgaged, discipline neglected, unworthy and disreputable persons get control of church work and church affairs."[13]

A growing racism was edging between the natives and the foreigners. Hyde was in mental turmoil, and King Kalakaua was definitely pro-moting this cleavage. The King had gone so far as to attempt to persuade the Hawaiian churches to place a religious stamp of approval on his political actions. This, of course, outraged Hyde's sensibilities and tended to estrange him from this native church.

The Board of the Hawaiian Evangelical Association, more commonly called the Hawaiian Board of Missions or just simply the Hawaiian Board, was the broad working base, the real vehicle, for Dr. Hyde in his work with the native churches. His effort with Kaumakapili was an independent, personal gesture.

The Hawaiian Board coordinated the work of the Congregational Church in Hawaii, except those projects directed by the American Board such as the North Pacific Missionary Institute. Work of the Board was carried on largely at the level of the individual churches in island associations, a division of which was the island ministers' association. Here the ministers could get together on their own in semiannual meetings. The first of the ministers' meetings that Hyde could attend was in March, 1878. He wrote his impressions to the American Board:

I was very much pleased with my first attendance at a meeting of the Oahu Association of Ministers. It was the semiannual meeting held this year at Waikane, 16 miles N.W. of Honolulu. Accompanied by one of the students as guide, I left home [horseback] last Tuesday at 6 AM. The morning was lovely and we had frequent dashes of rain. But we were only too thankful for the rain so long withheld and would not have been disappointed if it had poured down in torrents. I presume you have taken the same ride through Nuuanu Valley, down the Pali, across the plains of Kaneohe below, and along the seaside to the charmingly sweet and peaceful nook, with the long stretches of green rice fields from beyond which stands out conspicuous from the whole distance of the plain the white spire of the pretty little church . . . the evident freshness of the paint on the church building and the newness of the fence around the church grounds of the Evangelical Society betokened enterprise and thrift . . . There was no great depth of thought in anything said at the gathering but there was genuine Christian humility, kindness, and interest.[14]

He was asked to preach the Home Missionary sermon at the annual meeting of the Hawaiian Board in June 1878. He was also chosen Recording Secretary at that meeting. In 1879 and 1880 he was elected Moderator of the Association Churches.

The idea of a Biblical Museum occurred to him and he presented, not only an expanded outline of the project to the American Board, but described some preliminary steps he had taken to get it underway:

. . . Another project has occurred to me in taking up the study of the Life of Christ. I want very much a Biblical Museum to illustrate the manners and customs to which allusion is made in the Bible. Cannot your Secretaries secure from our missionaries in Turkey a collection of coins, utensils, clothing, manufactures, jewelry etc. which would be of service to me. Why not have such a collection available at the Rooms of the Board in Boston as a Loan Museum for Sunday Schools, Institutes, Conventions etc? I have written to our Hawaiian Missionaries to send a collection of such things from their various islands. When the *Morning Star* (steamer) comes back from her trip, she will probably bring me such a collection that I may be able to make out a duplicate set and forward to Boston.

Then if any special information is desired about the Micronesian Mission, little books could be prepared to accompany the collection for exhibition in various missionary gatherings. I have already many items gathered up which might easily be arranged into such a pamphlet illustrating life in these Pacific Islands before the Advent of the Gospel and its civilizing influences. Do you think favorably of this project?[15]

While nothing came of the proposed Biblical Museum, as such, it served to stimulate his conception of organizing the Bernice Pauahi Bishop Museum. Artifacts from the mission stations in the Pacific accumulated in the storage spaces of the Charles R. Bishop homes in Honolulu, while simultaneously a collection of materials from missions around the world piled up in the rooms of the American Board in Boston.

The two unclassified sets of Polynesian treasures were eventually absorbed in the Bishop Museum. Hyde, whether the museum would be Biblical or Bishop, was in the vanguard of museum thinking for his day.

About this time the American Board inquired if the Hawaiian churches could assume more of the Micronesian mission work. His reply was largely discouraging. He first listed the obstacles; among them: the native women were unwilling to go to Micronesia, the support of Micronesia would slow up the work in Hawaii, the pecuniary ability of the Hawaiian churches was diminishing, the population (of natives) was decreasing, the price of sugar in the world markets was down, salaries and budgets of the "foreign" churches were at too low a level, and there was added work with the newly arrived immigrants of several races. He followed this enumeration with a broad sweep across the Hawaii horizon of community income and outgo:

. . . In Honolulu, we have the various national charitable societies with expenses of $2000 a year, Free Masons and Odd Fellows with their halls and monthly dues, the Hospital, the Ladies Benevolent Society, the Stranger's Friend Society, the Sailor's Home, the Public Library, Kawaiahao Seminary, Oahu College etc etc besides daily calls to help individual cases of special need. The Bethel Church is making a heroic effort for that small handful of people to raise $2400 salary for their pastor, the Fort Street Church pays Mr. Cruzan $3200 besides a large sum for music, sexton etc. Under Mr. Cruzan's leadership that church is spending on itself and its city missionary work as much as $1500 or $1800 a year. Their sympathies are not with Foreign Missionary work, as was true of Mr. Frear. We have also to pay $1500 to the General Secretary of the YMCA and $500 to the Janitor, $200 to the Reading Room. Besides the contributions from churches and individuals to the Hawaiian Board, the Woman's Board raises annually $700 mostly for Micronesia. The Gleaners get $400 most of which goes to Rand on Ponape. Mrs. Hyde's little Hawaiian girls' sewing society supported last year 3 girls in Kawaiahao Seminary at $50 each, and gave $40 to Mrs. Lono, the wife of the returning Hawaiian missionary stationed at the Gilbert Islands mission. The Cousins Society raises annually $2000 mostly given to the Micronesian Mission, and every time the *Morning Star* goes, she takes individual remembrances of more or less value to every one of the Micronesian missionaries. Do you think we are now doing our part for the Micronesian Mission, generously and not neglecting either the pressing necessities of the work in our own community? What one church in the States will you find that begins to do what Fort Street Church has done for years and years, without a single member that can be called wealthy?

It ought to be considered that the total population of Honolulu [1885] is only 20,487, of this 10,853 are natives, 1164 only are Americans, 5265 are Chinese, 791 are British, 580 Portuguese. The whole white population is less than 3200. The American residents would represent a population about the same size as Brimfield, Massachusetts, where I was formerly pastor. You know the town. Think of that community doing anything like what I have shown above this community has been doing for years.[16]

The American Board had been reading his optimistic reports on NPMI activity, in preparing successfully its graduates for ministries in native churches in Hawaii and Micronesia. On its own side it was attempting to satisfy ever-increasing pleas from its far flung missions. It had built up the sanguinary hope that the Hawaiian Board might have by now accumulated sufficient funds to shoulder the burden of direct aid to the Micronesian cause.

This hoped-for takeover was not possible, but the Hawaiian work among the Micronesians, buffeted by the occupation forces of the French, Spanish and Germans, and also subjected to political changes under American leadership, would never cease. The propinquity trail to Micronesia would dim, but the dollars, clothes barrels and men and women of Hawaiian churches would find their way there over the years, even to this year, 1972, when this book is being written.

Dr. Hyde, ever so often in his letters to the American Board, would burst into a religious lyricism graphically depictive of his idealistic nature. One such reflection appeared in a letter to Judson Smith:

. . . Fifteen years have passed since the public celebration here of fifty years of missionary work in the North Pacific. We are making no such missionary history now as the fathers did. Our monumental stones are more likely to be like those that the disciples saw in Herod's temple, and of which the Master said, "Not one shall be left upon another." If it is true that God buries the workman but carries on the work, it is also true that our ideals are often lost in the fullness of a larger hope. This Hawaiian people may fade away, but as in growth of vegetation, the primitive gives place to the higher. The black coals of primeval forests are turning the wheels of varied industry and developed arts, that are transforming the face of the earth, and making it neglect the thought of man as well as the glory of Man. Oh for the coming of the day when every thought of man shall be holiness unto the Lord![17]

He also stood on solid ground in explanation of the transfer of two church workers from plantation towns. "Rev. H. S. Jordan has given up the foreign church at Kohala, and goes to the coast on the next steamer, Feb. 20. Rev. Isaac Goodell also gives up at Honokaa, Hamakua, Hawaii. The fact is there is no possibility of building up a church on our sugar plantations. They have but few white men, and these very often are 'hard characters.' A minister's work is like a chaplain of a state prison, except that the chaplain is sure of an audience, and a minister on a plantation is not."[18]

Church land holdings were another problem of the Hawaiian Board. "My interest," he wrote, "in the Hawaiian Churches (Land titles) led me to prepare at the last annual meeting the appointment of a committee of investigation, and the Ass'n appointed me immediately."[19] He asked the Hawaiian Board to authorize him to secure a complete record of all the land titles of the ABCFM in Hawaii.[20]

This was a matter plaguing the Board then. It still does. Properties were held under different kinds of grants, titles, trust deeds, provisions and much could and did happen to dissipate the ownership and controls. Hyde grasped the serious lack of orderly inventory and spent much time in gathering title data.

One result of this title search was a decision of the Hawaiian Board to create a Finance Committee, the first in its history, which "shall decide what investments shall be made of the special and permanent funds of the Board . . . have charge of the real estate held by the Board in fee simple or in trust. . . . " It was provided for on November 5, 1889 but was slow in getting under way. It had its first meeting in 1893 and Hyde picked up another secretaryship. He maintained his usual standards here: never missed a meeting, wrote the minutes longhand and signed each set. The precedent established in this modest plan of management of church properties has been followed continuously. In 1969 a companion foundation was chartered devoted solely to this purpose.[21]

Seldom was a Board meeting held at which he failed to suggest a new enterprise. He usually came away as the appointed chairman of whatever project he espoused. One looked to the reorganization of Christian work in the islands. Still another came out of the Committee on Evangelization. His comment on this was a bit ingenuous: "The Committee on Hawaiian Evangelization have met and organized as you will be duly informed. That I should be chosen chairman of the Committee was an idea that had never occurred to me. I did not like to oppose the suggestion lest I should seem churlish and ungracious in relation to this new work, which you well know has never been my attitude. The additional burden of responsibility involved makes me shrink from accepting the position; but for the present it seems best."[22] At this time he was a member of several standing committees of the Hawaiian Board, including foreign missions, home missions, education, appropriations from ABCFM, and he was chairman of the publications committee. He could have enjoyed a full life just being a committee man!

Had he not made a career of the ministry he would have gone down in history as an educator. He was an astute organizer, programmer and teacher. Despite the channels of ocean separating the islands, despite the lava coasts and the tangled vegetation and rough mountains, he worked up an educational landscape which encompassed the island chain. His interests extended from boys' and girls' boarding schools on Hawaii island through schools on Maui and Oahu to a seminary on Kauai. Most of these enrolled and housed native children. His mission to the natives was perhaps more effectual through the medium of the schools than the churches.

Hyde was really but an instrument of the Hawaiian Board in his contacts with the boarding schools. His interest in these institutions stemmed from the NPMI. Through correspondence and personal visits he assisted in the recruitment of teachers, improvement of the program of studies, installation of facilities and buildings and development of finances. In only one of these schools, Kawaiahao Female Seminary, did he actually participate in administration and instruction. This school had started, as had most boarding schools in Hawaii, as a family or home school. The Rev. and Mrs. Luther Gulick occupied the former residence of the Rev. E. W. Clark, in close proximity to the mission printshop and only about a block from Dr. Hyde's Institute. The Gulicks took in some Hawaiian girls, added a teacher, and the Hawaiian Mission Children's Society assumed most of the expenses. Hyde's arrival in Hawaii coincided with a Hawaiian Board decision to place the school under the special charge of a board of five trustees. He was named both trustee and president. A quick look at the buildings designated for school and dormitory use revealed the need of immediate construction of a modern facility. This constituted his first fund raising and building work. Miss Sarah R. Sage, sister-in-law of his Uncle William Hyde of Ware, supplied the major portions of the funds.

Another boarding school, Waialua Seminary, closed in 1882 and he asked the American Board to apply the proceeds of that closing to the Kawaiahao Seminary account. Mrs. Bernice Pauahi Bishop gave $5000 as a bequest in her will. The Board of Education made several annual contributions and finally a whole new set of buildings was in use. He was also his own maintenance man. His 1884 summer in Honolulu was in part devoted to cleanup. "There is no one looking after Kawaiahao School," he wrote, "so I am superintending cleaning and repairs, hoping

to have the place in order by the time the new Principal comes."[23]
Repair and maintenance generally were as natural to his hand and endless energy as matters of greater purpose.

Tragedy struck the native people in October, 1884, in the passing of
Bernice Pauahi Bishop. The high-ranking wife of one of Honolulu's
most respected leaders was the daughter of Hawaiian royalty. Her great
grandfather was Kamehameha I, the Conqueror. Her husband was
Charles Reed Bishop, a visitor from Glens Falls, N. Y. in 1846. He
remained in Hawaii and rose through clerk, accountant, storekeeper
and banker to become one of Hawaii's most trusted and community
minded leaders.

Dr. Hyde became well acquainted with the Bishops. He had come to
be their confidante in their major community interests. It therefore was
not unexpected that when Mrs. Bishop's will[24] was probated, December
2, 1884 he would be named one of five trustees, along with her husband,
of her vast royal family land holdings in the islands.

This trusteeship set Hyde to dreaming. He wrote to Clark in Boston,
a few days after the will was probated:

I am in hopes to get $5000 immediately from Mrs. Bishop's estate; and
this with the money from the sale of the Waialua property, with the
addition of money from the Government will give enough to put up the
new building for Kawaiahao Seminary. But someone has put in an
appeal to set aside the will on the ground that Mrs. Bishop ought to
have given the property to her relatives! This is an interruption to the
progress of the legal proceedings, though nothing more probably. The
Trustees named to take charge of the Kamehameha Schools have therefore not accepted the trust as yet. It may be that I can so arrange matters
as to have the Kawaiahao School take girls under 12 while the Kamehameha School will at first take only older girls . . . I want next week to
begin to plan the new buildings for Kawaiahao Seminary.[25]

The drive of impatience, an overriding quality, brought quick results:

I have at last succeeded in securing a lease of land, 75 x 150 feet, in
rear of Kawaiahao School for ten years $80 per annum, and am au-
thorized to put a building 68 x 38, two stories, as an extension to the
Westward of Sage Hall. This will provide a dining hall, office, sewing

room, on the first floor, chambers for teachers, and a new dormitory for pupils 26 x 38. The outbuildings; bathroom, laundry, ironing room, carriage house, will be put on the leased land, with the hope that it will ultimately be purchased for the use of the school. As the title to premises now occupied by the schools is in the name of the ABCFM it is desirable that the whole property should be so held.[26]

A crisis occurred in the relationship of Dr. Hyde with Kawaiahao Seminary toward the end of 1886, growing out of the acceptance of an invitation to the boarding students to attend a palace pageant celebrating King Kalakaua's birthday. The dispute found the trustees arrayed against the teachers. The children sat it out in the dormitory the night of the pageant. The next day, unsettled by this turn of affairs, he wrote with some feeling to the American Board, "The lines must be drawn, and they all divide not on the color line, not on church lines, but on the lines of social purity and fundamental righteousness. White folk and good folks will be on the side in favor of heathenism and indecency, because forsooth! it is the King's side and we must *honor* the *King* . . . The crisis has not yet come, but the times are nearing such a point. It is the white people and their conduct that have given Kalakaua his opportunity. Weak goodishness goes down in this community like our rice crop before our heavy rains and the whole season's work is a loss. I do not know what the outcome of this affair may be. I expect to be blamed and misrepresented for the stand I have taken; but no duty ever seemed to me clearer or more unpleasant."[27]

This was perhaps Dr. Hyde's most frustrating experience. Here he was standing against the sophistication of a Honolulu society. "If there is any man in all the missionary fields of the Board that needs special sympathy from you at home, and earnest prayer for guidance and support and comfort from above, I believe that I am such a man," he wrote, "I have little sympathy from the Christian community here though I believe the tide of public sentiment will turn before long and disgust and abhorrence take the place of the present toleration and approval."[28]

In that same boat mail he repeated his "cry in the wilderness" to another American Board secretary. He had a feeling of being cast adrift. About the only men who staunchly upheld his decision in holding the boarding girls away from the King's birthday party were fellow trustees, the Rev. S. E. Bishop and the Hon. A. F. Judd, and his banker friend, Charles R. Bishop. Hyde could have stayed clear of the commotion for it was reasonable that the school principal make the decision. But he was not about to give any sign of approval or favor to a Kalakaua production:

I have learned facts about the King's measures and objects, which convince me that with the cunning of the savage and the tirelessness of revengeful animosity, he is seeking the overthrow of Christian institutions and the utter demoralization of society. His aim is to restore heathenism with its absolute power of the chief and licentious orgies of wasteful indulgence. Yet good people here are afraid to make any open opposition, but we should have a revolution. Many too so misinterpret the Scripture as to think it is their duty to show outward reverence and give tacit approval to a man whom they know to be thoroughly vile and unworthy, but he is King. I am surprised and pained to see how many good people have no spark of indignant abhorrence of gross wickedness, so long as it does not interfere with their own ease and comfort. They deprecate anything and everything that will make trouble, and so disturb their quiet enjoyment. You see in what a predicament I am placed, and how difficult it is for me to take a stand, and maintain uncompromising fealty to right, without giving occasion for recrimination and even denunciation of such obstinacy and hardness of heart . . . [29]

He was walking his heart out as he trod a deteriorating untenable path strewn with the artifices of the King and the affronted opinion of the Seminary teachers. Each boat mail took another chapter, sometimes two, to Boston. On December 21 he wrote separate letters to two secretaries of the American Board. To Judson Smith he said, "The imbroglio with the Kawaiahao teachers has taken on a new phase. Having found that I have been sustained in every position I have taken, the teachers have dropped every other issue, have no complaint to make against anyone else, but insist upon it that I give up the Presidency of the Board of Trustees, or they will resign." To E. K. Alden, "It's the old story of the snake in the grass biting the heels of the horse and throwing the rider. Only I don't think I shall be thrown. I have had to reconstruct for the third time my theory of the case, and believe now that what I supposed to be at first a *regular volcanic* eruption, is only a very ordinary piece of *contemptible incendiarism.*"[30]

No matter how overly puritanical his decision to overrule the principal may have been or may seem to have been he could not compromise the principle involved. He mulled the matter over during the holidays and finally, despite his lingering obstinance, wrote his resignation to the Hawaiian Board on January 11, 1887. The Rev. S. E. Bishop and A. F. Judd resigned at the same time. While his informed reasonings went into letters to the American Board, any action regarding Kawaiahao Seminary would go to the Hawaiian Board:

. . . In endeavoring to maintain an open, firm, and consistent opposition to such practices that have been foisted upon an enduring community, I do not expect nor wish to force upon others my individual opinions in regard to rights and duties. Nor do I intend knowingly to compromise myself by any action that may seem to indicate approval of the position of those who are foremost in their attempts to override Christian sentiment. Nor can I acquiesce in the policy that deprecates and blames open, firm, consistent opposition to the un-Christian and anti-Christian policy now rife . . . However painful it has been to differ from those I love and esteem who take divergent views of duty and lines of action, it has been still more painful to me to find that in carrying out the expressed sentiments of all the Trustees of Kawaiahao Seminary there has been unwittingly aroused a degree of animosity, which makes any further responsibility for the management of the school only an occasion for manifold vexation and anxieties . . . In view of these considerations, I herewith resign my position as one of the Trustees of Kawaiahao Seminary . . .[31]

The resignations were referred to a special committee which recommended the following minute for adoption by the Board:

. . . We desire to put on record our regret that they have thought it best to withdraw from that over-sight and care of this school, which this Board has so long entrusted to them.
And we also desire to express our appreciation of the able manner in which that trust has been administered. The continuous increase in the number of pupils; the growing influence of the school for good, to the Hawaiian race; and the great material changes in the way of new buildings and appliances speak more loudly than words possibly could, of the

ability, sagicity [sic] and self-denying labors of these brethren during the past nine years.

And we feel that very much of this success has been due to the indefatigable labors of the Rev. C. M. Hyde, D.D. who as the Executive Officer of the Board of Trustees has carried this school in his heart and given it freely, his time, his thought, and his unwearied endeavors.

And we also desire to express our approval of the care with which the moral interests of the school have been conserved and with which the powerful influence brought to bear upon the Hawaiians to drag the race back to the old idolatrous and pagan superstitions have ever been resisted by our brethren in their oversight of the school . . .[32]

There is more but this is enough; a fairly obscure action but one of deep implication for the character of his work with the natives. The Seminary continued under its new board of trustees until 1894 when circumstances seemed to warrant its closing. This surrender of the trust brought Hyde back into action. "Nobody wants to see the school abandoned, but nobody has done anything to keep it open. So far the last two weeks I have been busy working out a scheme for its continued operation."[33] He came back into the picture on two counts; the American Board held title to the land and the Hawaiian Board wanted the school continued.

He prevailed upon Charles R. Bishop for a grant and tried then and later to persuade his fellow Bishop Estate trustees to take over the Seminary as the care of the newly discussed Kamehameha School for Girls. These efforts were not successful, but the Seminary did continue until its merger with Mills School as the Mid-Pacific Institute a decade later.

Two other girls' boarding schools felt the imprint of the Hyde influence. East Maui Female Seminary was founded as the "Home" school by the Rev. C. B. Andrews, a missionary of the American Board. It was a very successful undertaking under the able and devout leadership of great teachers like the Misses Carpenter, Malone, and Alexander who successively headed the work. This was a favorite object of charity of Charles R. Bishop.

Here Dr. Hyde played the role of visiting missionary advising on curriculum matters, employment of staff and building problems. The school was first named East Maui Female Seminary, then Makawao Female

Seminary, later Maunaolu Seminary. Today the school is named U.S. International University—Mauna Olu Campus, a coeducational school.

Kohala Girls' School in the Kohala district of Hawaii island had been opened in 1874 with 21 girls, all of native families. Miss Elizabeth ("Lizzie") W. Lyons was the teacher and the school flourished under her charge. But by 1887 she had to resign and for lack of a teacher the school was closed. The Rev. Elias Bond, resident missionary in Kohala, a great friend of Dr. Hyde, decided to reopen in the next year. The property was deeded to the Hawaiian Board which voted to send Hyde to oversee the reopening which was delayed to the fall of 1889 for unavailability of a suitable teacher. October 2, 1889, Miss M. F. Whittier arrived as head teacher. Hyde described his part in this during the summer preceding her arrival. Everything seemed to fall into place: teachers, repairs and alterations, cooperation of the nearby Hawaiian churches, student recruitment. It was like opening an entirely new school:

I reached Kohala at 11 am and after dinner got the key to the school buildings and gave them a thorough inspection. The next morning I went throught them again with Cornelius Bond, and agreed as to the repairs and alterations. In the afternoon went to the Rev. A. Ostrem's and consulted with him about securing the necessary funds. Had a meeting of the local Trustees in the ev'g and presented plans and suggestions which were adopted. The next day went through the district and secured $200 contribution toward expenses of repairs etc. The next day visited one half of the Hawaiian homes of well to do people with children and interested them in the school. Sunday held 3 meetings, the preaching service, the Sunday School, and the Deacons' meeting. The church voted to raise $200 for the School. Came home & wrote to every Hawaiian pastor, urging them to secure funds & scholars and also sent a circular . . . to all foreigners in Hawaii likely to take any interest . . .[34]

He was happy with the solid growth of the school. He took Mrs. Hyde back on periodic visits and both delighted in observing the classes at work. A maximum enrollment of 60 girls was reached in four years after the 1889 reopening class of fourteen. The school facilities still exist but no longer serve as a girls' boarding school. They house short-term retreats, conferences and camping enterprises.

As for the boys' boarding schools, Mills and Hilo, he had little to do. In the case of Mills School he was an interested observer as Francis Williams Damon attended to the alterations on his home to accommodate the first 15 resident boys. This was 1892. The Chinese work had grown to become one of Hyde's interests and this little Mills School was for Chinese boys. "Thus simply has begun what may grow into an important institution."

Hilo Boys' Boarding School also did not require his attention as to buildings, student recruitment and the like. He was interested in channeling Charles R. Bishop money into endowment and student scholarships. Mr. Bishop was generous in his gifts to the Hilo school and his total giving was close to $70,000. It was its principal, the Rev. William Brewster Oleson, who was engaged in 1887 to head the new Kamehameha School for Boys. Hyde had a hand in this transaction as one of Mrs. Bishop's first trustees of the school established in her will.

Thus we reach the end of a review of his contact and association with the churches and schools standing in Congregational relationship with the Hawaiian Board. His was a large effort of unceasing endeavor in both church and school, and while his output cannot be closely measured objectively, it is gross understatement to qualify it as only significant.

NOTES

1 Letter Hyde to the Rev. N. G. Clark, ABCFM, Jan. 8, 1878.
2 The *Friend*, March 1886, p. 1.
3 Ibid., Jan. 1888, p. 5.
4 Ibid., July, p. 1.
5 Ibid., Jan.
6 Letter Hyde to the Rev. Judson Smith, ABCFM, Apr. 8, 1887.
7 Ibid., Dec. 22, 1888.
8 Ibid., Jan. 17, 1890.
9 Ibid., Nov. 10, 1891.
10 Ibid., Nov. 16, 1893. Dr. Beckwith's letter of resignation to the congregation was dated Nov. 29, 1893.
11 Ibid., Jan. 20, 1879.
12 Ibid., Jan. 17, 1881.
13 Ibid., Sept. 25, 1882.
14 Letter Hyde to Clark, Apr. 16, 1878.
15 Letter Hyde to Rev. E. E. Strong, ABCFM, Nov. 15, 1884.
16 Letter Hyde to Smith, May 15, 1885.

17 Ibid., Aug. 31.
18 Ibid., Feb. 15, 1886.
19 Ibid.
20 Ibid., Jan. 13, 1887.
21 Records of the Financial Committee of the Hawaiian Board, 1893–1910.
22 Letter Hyde to Smith, July 26, 1888.
23 Letter Hyde to Clark, Aug. 1.
24 "Last Will and Testament of the Late Hon. Mrs. Bernice P. Bishop," Oct. 31, 1883.
25 Letter Hyde to Clark, Dec. 15, 1884.
26 Letter Hyde to Smith, Apr. 1, 1885.
27 Ibid., Nov. 17, 1886.
28 Letter Hyde to the Rev. E. K. Alden, Nov. 20.
29 Letter Hyde to Smith, Nov. 20.
30 Letters Hyde to Smith and Alden, Dec. 21.
31 Letter Hyde to the Hawaiian Board, Jan. 11, 1887.
32 Hawaiian Board, Minutes, Jan.
33 Letter Hyde to Smith, June 28, 1894.
34 Ibid., Aug. 23, 1889.

Chapter 8

RECIPROCITY BEGETS THE IMMIGRANT

DR. HYDE never swerved from his primary assignment to the cause of the native Hawaiian. He was always willing to broaden his horizon among all peoples, but even in his ventures among the Chinese, the Japanese, and the Portuguese, he related, in the larger context of the kingdom of Hawaii, to the Hawaiian race, its welfare, its progress, its promise. His capacity for work was a never-failing resource and he employed it to reach out from his center core of the natives to the multitudinous problems of all races and peoples in Hawaii.

Three major ethnic groups, Chinese, Japanese, and Portuguese, were brought to the islands in the order named, to work as laborers on the sugar plantations. There were both Chinese and plantations before 1876, the year the Reciprocity Act was passed (September 9). The Royal Hawaiian Agricultural Society was behind the first shipment of 200 Chinese in 1852 and other small groups dribbled in over the years. After the 1876 Act the plantations which numbered 35 in 1874 almost doubled (63) by 1879. The immigration stream took on the proportions of a flood, with many problems.

One immigrant group, a single family of six, was by coincidence making its way to Hawaii's shores to work not on a plantation but in a vineyard—this family headed by the Rev. Charles M. Hyde—Caucasian from New England. The immigrant Chinese and the immigrant Hydes were not long in meeting.

Excerpts from Dr. Hyde's correspondence with the American Board clearly picture the developing story of his work with the Chinese. "I have been busy the last week drafting a set of Rules, a Creed, and a Covenant for a Chinese Church here in Honolulu. It seems as if the time has come to have such a church organized. We are trying to make arrangements to have Sat Fan go to Haiku, Maui and do evangelistic work among the Chinese. Tit Moon [Sit Moon] has ret'd to Honolulu and could be the pastor of the Chinese church if one should be organized."[1]

"I am much interested," he wrote later, "in the Chinaman I am training for Christian work among his countrymen. I cannot tell how much or how little he knows but he seems very studious in his habits. I have been to hear him preach and was impressed with his earnestness. He has a congregation of 50 to 80 every Sunday evening. I have taken him to the hospital where he is to visit every Thursday & to the prison where he will hold service every Sunday morning. I am trying through him to get a register of all the Christian Chinese in Honolulu, variously estimated from 80 to 120."[2]

The problem of the sudden release of thousands of Chinese upon the islands was so demanding that the resources for Christian work were taxed beyond their strength. It was aggravated at this point because whole families began to come instead of just single men. "The Chinese colporteur," he noted, "who has been studying with me since January is expecting his wife and children to come. So God is introducing Chinese *families* here, and we have a work on hand to care for these which is greater than we can attend to with our resources only. With 6000 Chinese men, women and children to care for we need an educated American missionary skilled in the Chinese as well as his mother tongue to labor among them. But where is he to be found?"[3]

The YMCA, which had come to the islands in 1869, only a few years earlier, became a strong evangelical force through its street meetings, house calls, and prayer meetings. Its leaders took on the Chinese work as a "part of program." Probably the person most interested was the Rev. Samuel Chenery Damon who had come to Honolulu in 1842 to serve the Bethel Church. Dr. Hyde worked closely with him in preparing summation of Chinese work for a quarterly meeting of the YMCA, February 21, 1879. Services were being held regularly each Sunday morning at the Lyceum, at the Bethel vestry in the evening, a prayer meeting Wednesday evenings and a Sunday School class at 3 p.m. on Sundays. Measures were being taken to organize a church among the Chinese. Articles of faith had been drawn up and two Chinese men were qualified to take on the work.

An Ecclesiastical Council was called June 8, 1879 to consider the "expediency of organizing a Chinese Church."[4] The Rev. Mr. Damon presided as Moderator and Dr. Hyde was appointed Scribe. The Council's findings were affirmative and the Council adjourned for Communion at Kaumakapili Church. Hyde reported this action to the annual meeting of the Hawaiian Board later in June and wrote informally about it to the American Board. ". . . One of the pleasant incidents . . . was the organization of the Chinese Church. 34 names of church members with letters were presented . . . Trustees have been chosen, and are to be duly incorporated . . ."[5]

The Chinese Church received its charter, purchased a lot at Fort and Beretania Streets and launched a campaign for funds for a building. By January, 1880, $7000 had been raised and the building was started with some indebtedness, but confidence was strong in the congregation. Hyde, with great satisfaction, wrote to the American Board, ". . . I am doing what I can to help on a Fair some ladies propose to hold in the new Chinese Church for the benefit of the building fund. We hope to have the building ready for the formal opening exercises on the first Sunday in January . . . This enterprise is one in which I have taken interest from the beginning. It is the *first Church building,* so far as I know, built by the Chinese themselves. It is *not* a mission chapel, originated by other Christian people here, but an enterprise of the *Chinese* Christians. *Goo Kim* is the brains, the purser, and the soul of it all, as far as the Chinese are concerned . . . The Colporteur, Sit Moon, who has been in the employ of the YMCA for seven years, is acting pastor. After Jany [sic] first his salary will be paid by the Chinese Chruch."[6]

With even greater pride he pointed to his own contribution by way of assistance. "I send to the *Conglst.* this mail an account of the dedication of the Chinese Church. It has fallen to my lot to engineer the whole movement that has now resulted happily. I saw to the constitution, organization and recognition of the Chinese Church in 1878 and so too I have engineered the project of building them a church."[7]

He also had to place the church records in order, as he wrote to a friend: "I send you by this mail the *Gazette* with a/c I wrote of the dedication of the new Chinese Church. I went to their prayer meeting the Wednesday evening following and straightened out their church records for them. I propose to keep them in English myself for the present. They are utterly unused to our methods of proceeding in deliberative assembly."[8] It is also likely he was unused to the Chinese writing in vertical lines and from right to left on the page.

At this very time a smallpox epidemic, probably introduced by some of the Chinese immigrants, laid low the town. During its seven-month span, the labor force was swollen with incoming shiploads of fresh immigrants. "Another steamer," he wrote, "yesterday brought 600 more. Five more steamers are on the way. This looks like an invasion, even if it be a peaceful invasion. At this rate the Chinese men will soon outnumber the Hawaiian men so completely that it might be considered a Chinese colony."[9]

One bright shaft of light broke through the lowering gloom. Young Francis Williams Damon returned from a world tour full of zeal for the Chinese work. He joined the YMCA, superintended a Sunday School and taught a Friday evening singing class. All of these services were related to Chinese needs. He was "destined to be the great leader of the Chinese work,"[10] said Hyde.

There was a surge in the immigration statistics for 1883. "6100 Chinese laborers dumped on Honolulu . . . another steamer from China, the *Coptic* of the O. & O. Line has come bringing 1000 Chinese. The *City of Sydney* our regular steamer from San Francisco of the P.M.S.S. Line brought 345 . . . our present officials are incompetent to deal wisely with the situation."[11] Thus he worried. By October 1884 there were 20,000 Chinese in the islands.

He summarized his part in the launching of the Chinese work to Judson Smith of the American Board: "I have planned and pushed the work for the Chinese that has been done since I came,—the organization . . . incorporation of the trustees, building of the church, appointment of the Colporteurs, etc etc. I have served as Clerk . . . and administered every Communion but one, keep the register of Chinese Christians, give certificates of membership, letters of dismission etc etc."[12]

He had been busy learning and using the Hawaiian language in his work with the natives but wisely undertook no such self-instructional program in Chinese. He had to make out with interpreters, and when it came to church documents, charter, statement of faith and the like, he had to send to competent translators in San Francisco for correct Chinese expression.

His work with the Chinese did not continue at this full pace beyond 1884 but to the year of his death he administered Communion every Sunday evening that it was scheduled.

The other major racial groups that thronged to these islands were the Portuguese and the Japanese which were not far apart in their arrival.

The plantations had an urgent need of field labor. The Hawaiian Immigration Society in cooperation with the government tried all over the world to locate immigrants. 338 Gilbert Islanders—men, women, and children—were brought in by charter. Hyde remarked that he was "not pleased with their fitness as a people to be integrated in Hawaii and the plantations were not either." Other Micronesians and Polynesians were tried as well as Chinese, but the latter provided the largest sources, and possessed the best assimilative qualities.

In the 1870's Dr. William Hillebrand from careful observation as a temporary resident in Portugal recommended natives of Madeira and the Azores for the consideration of the plantation managers in Hawaii. He was granted special status, and, with instructions and a suggested contract form, proceeded in the face of many obstacles to arrange a first contingent of Portuguese men, wives and children. A German ship, the *Priscilla,* finally anchored in Honolulu September 29, 1878 with 120 Portuguese immigrants from Funchal, Madeira. Other ships swiftly discharged larger and larger groups; the plantations liked them for their thrifty, industrious, and law-abiding habits.

Authorities in Portugal, however, became restive with the mass departure of its families. The Hawaiian government sent Hon. H. A. P. Carter to Portugal to negotiate an immigration treaty. Through his tactful representations an immigration convention was signed.

Carter's mission did not result in a "provisional convention" until May 2, 1882, but that negotiations would succeed, there seemed to be little doubt in Honolulu. Long before May 2, Dr. Hyde wrote about this and of his need for help. " . . . We are to have a treaty with Portugal so that more Portuguese can be brought in. It is an interesting fact that a dozen or more have asked for a meeting of themselves. We have one converted Portuguese, and he held a meeting with them in Kawaia-hao Church, two weeks ago. If we only could find some one to take up this work here in an opening in that line of Christian work. You see in how many different directions our Christian zeal and labor can be drawn out in this polyglot of nationalities . . . "[13]

Portugal was largely a Catholic nation with a few pockets of Protestants centered in Madeira and the Azores. Some of these, fleeing the social oppressions of the majority church, filed for the contract work in Hawaii. Others united in a colonization venture in Central Illinois. The two groups had their faith as a common tie. Propinquity and homesickness sent a few of the Illinois Portuguese to Hawaii. One group of families came from Kankakee, another from Jacksonville and still another from Springfield, the center of the Illinois colony.

Still, most of the Portuguese in Hawaii were Roman Catholics and only a few converts took to the Congregational faith despite the evangelical work by the Protestants. The work involved very few people and moved slowly albeit solidly.

Dr. Hyde's capacity for work was to be tested as never before. He could not neglect his Hawaiians. The Chinese were swarming in, the Portuguese were coming and the Japanese were just over the horizon. He was beginning to operate on several parallel racial tracks and while there were no collisions, there were also no blendings. The racial groups tended to follow a self-segregation pattern. His activity within and on behalf of the Hawaiian Board was, of necessity, multiroad.

The attention of Mrs. Hyde's sister, Eunice B. Knight, was drawn to the many Portuguese children who seemed to be loose on the streets. Many families moved into town upon the completion of the father's contract. Miss Knight raised the question of their religious training in

an 1887 meeting of the newly organized Central Union Church. A
Sunday School was started the next Sunday afternoon in an old native
Church at Beretania and Miller Streets.

Progress was slow—too slow—for Dr. Hyde. He suggested in 1889
that Joseph Emerson, who was making a trip to the United States,
make a side trip to the Illinois Portuguese colony to ascertain the possibilities of assistance for work in Hawaii. He spent a Sunday at Springfield, interviewed the pastor, the Rev. Robert Lennington, and found a
young Portuguese, J. J. Almeida, who expressed interest in the work in
Hawaii.[14]

The baton, however, was passed to other parties in Springfield.
"Rachel Fernandez, daughter of John Ignatius and Mary Augusta
Fernandez, was born in Springfield, Illinois, Feb. 7, 1862. Her parents
belonged to a little colony of converts who left Madeira in search of a
home where they should be free from grievances they could no longer
endure. She united with the First Presbyterian Church of Springfield
in 1872. On Oct., 11, 1883 she was married to Antone V. Soares."[15]

When the Hydes were planning their 1890 trip to the United States
they were asked to bend their return journey through Jacksonville,
Illinois to interview the Soares family for possible missionary work among
the Portuguese in Hawaii. The contact was made successfully and the
Messrs. A. V. Soares (accompanied by Mrs. Soares), J. K. Baptiste and
E. N. Pires arrived in Honolulu in mid-September 1890.

It was deeply satisfying to Dr. Hyde to act as moderator of the Council
that examined and ordained Messrs. Soares and Baptiste as evangelists
in June 1891. Honolulu was the field of work for Soares; Hilo for Baptiste.
These were the leaders who stimulated the Christian work among the
Portuguese. With the ardent push of Dr. Hyde they organized the Portuguese Mission as a department of the Hawaiian Board.

Prior to the arrival of the Soares party the few devout Portuguese
Protestant laymen had held school and church services in temporary
quarters in both Hilo and Honolulu. Full-fledged compounds were now
to be constructed for church, Sunday School, day school and free kindergarten. Hyde, as a delegate from Central Union Church, went to Hilo
in January 1892 to attend a Council to organize a Portuguese Church
and dedicate a new chapel.

In Honolulu, on February 15, 1895, a land and building project was
launched. In the fund drive, which realized over $16,000 in 18 months,

these names appear as subscribers; Charles R. Bishop ($500), Bank of Bishop & Co. ($250) and Charles M. Hyde ($25). The church, school and parsonage—beautiful and spacious—were erected on the site at the corner of Miller and Punchbowl Streets adjacent to the *ewa* side of Queen's Hospital.

In the midst of the fund drive tragedy struck. The gracious and talented Rachel Soares (33) passed away. The funeral services held November 20, 1895 listed Hyde as delivering the eulogy.

A Portuguese Benevolent Association was formed with Mrs. Hyde as one of the leading organizers. She worked amidst great odds but achieved signal success in giving guidance to this association over a period of many years.

Dr. Hyde maintained continued interest in the Portuguese Mission; it had been a long drawn-out development but he had remained with it. He made frequent appearances at Portuguese church happenings but with the growing self-sufficiency of these devout immigrants he was able to give more time to the third major plantation group, the Japanese. The stream of Portuguese laborers and families continued unabated until 1888 when it was largely cut off due to the acceptability of the Japanese who were closer, and who came as single men at much less cost than the families of Portugal. But by that year over 6000 Portuguese workers had entered Hawaii.

The first Japanese immigrants arrived shortly after the Portuguese had made their entry. The two migrations were almost simultaneous and continued on a parallel disembarkation from vessels from the east and west for about a decade.

The difference in the Christian work of the two peoples, as far as Dr. Hyde and the Hawaiian Board were concerned, was chiefly in religious and cultural backgrounds.

Henry Hyde offers a clear picture of the waves of oncoming immigrants from the Land of the Rising Sun:

By special treaty arrangements, laborers for the plantations were allowed to emigrate from Japan, at the time when the government was jealously guarding its citizens from foreign enticement.

When the tide of immigration began, it flowed at a rapid rate for some time. The influx of such numbers of Japanese induced their government to station a diplomatic representative at Honolulu to look after their interests . . .

The Japanese are a fascinating people. Their courtesy and alertness produce a favorable impression on those who are brought into contact with them for the first time. Their wonderful power of adaptability and imitation makes them unique among the nations of the world . . . The march of events is steadily carrying them forward to a position of greater prominence.

As in Japan, so in Hawaii, there was the same speedy disposition to look with favor on things foreign. This created a state of mind favorable to the reception of Christian truth, an opportunity which the seed-sowers in Honolulu were not slow to improve. Dr. Hyde ever regarded his work among them as the romance of his missionary career . . . He established a regular service at Queen Emma Hall, speaking through an interpreter.

All the members of the legation, including the Consul General, Mr. Taro Ando, were regular attendants and soon Mr. Ando acted as interpreter . . . Mr. Ando himself, then all members of his family, then the attaches of the legation, and finally the servants of his household, publicly confessed their faith in Christ. This came about directly as a result of Dr. Hyde's preaching, which later was supplemented by the efforts of Rev. Mr. Miyama who came from San Francisco that he might preach to the Japanese in their own tongue . . .[16]

Hyde's first mention of the Japanese in a letter to the American Board was April 8, 1882. He spoke of the Japanese Commissioners coming to study the routine of the courts in handling criminal cases. He mentioned that the American missionary influence was instrumental in securing for these people their national rights.[17] He could also have mentioned the services rendered by his friend, Charles R. Bishop, to the Japanese government upon the occasion of this visit of the commissioners. So gratified were these men at their reception they recommended the awarding by the Emperor of the Order of the Rising Sun, First Class to him.

Except for a small contingent of 148 Japanese workers obtained by Consul General Eugene Van Reed in 1868, no Japanese immigrants came to Hawaii until February 9, 1885 when 956 filed ashore in the wake of Consul General R. W. Irwin, their sponsor.

When Irwin left for Japan to arrange the immigration of Japanese laborers he agreed to send with the first contingent a man who would be qualified to do Christian work among them. In further anticipation of this arrival, Hyde was appointed by the Hawaiian Board to solicit special donations for a building to be used as evening school and reading room in Honolulu for Japanese. Needed also would be a house for the Christian worker.

He described the arrival of the first immigration vessel. Somehow, he did not suspect that this particular ship was carrying laborers:

. . . Last Sunday the *Tokio* was reported off the harbor. I went to the wharf to send a message and proffer hospitalities to any Missionaries from China or Japan who might be on board. I met Mr. Irwin, the Hawaiian Consul for Japan, and learned that there were none; but that he had brought the first batch of Japanese immigrants, 949. I have had some talks with Mr. Irwin nearly every day since. I have visited the Japanese in the Immigrant Depot. I must say I am perplexed. I think Mr. Irwin must have made some very rose colored statements, about the Islands, to induce so many of the farmer class to leave their country for the poor chances offered here. He calls them "Puritan Fathers," only to me they are not Puritans, nor Fathers of a new country . . .[18]

Also aboard the ship was Shinichi Aoki, a Christian worker, nephew of a pastor in Japan who cooperated with Dr. Hyde in starting work among the Japanese and assisted him as an interpreter. As with the Chinese language, Dr. Hyde, probably wisely, did not attempt to learn Japanese. When Aoki left after about two years in Honolulu, he donated his entire library of 200 Japanese books for the start of a Japanese library.

The Rev. Takie Okumura, later one of the outstanding Congregational workers among the Japanese, wrote of Dr. Hyde's initial efforts, "Dr. C. M. Hyde, who was then secretary of the Hawaiian Board, seeing the importance and necessity of reaching the steadily increasing mass of Japanese immigrants with the Christian gospel, rented a room in Queen Emma Hall on the corner of Queen Emma and Beretania Streets and commenced religious meetings. Mrs. H. C. Coleman and Mr. Bidwell led the Sunday School and English night school."[19]

By the following April the evening school numbered 24, the building fund was progressing favorably, but Hyde had reservations. "If the experiment is a success, I hope it will ultimately be a Japanese chapel. If not it will be available for our Hawaiian work."[20] He wrote a month later, "We have 12 regular attendants at our evening school for the Japanese. It is opened regularly with reading of the Scriptures and prayer by the young Japanese preacher. I have attended regularly Sunday morning service for the Japanese in the YMCA Hall. Next Sunday evening I mean to begin an evening service for them in the school room at the NPMI."[21]

Within 30 months the organization of a Japanese church began to take shape. He could report rather optimistically now:

The Rev. K. Miyama, a Japanese convert and local preacher in connection with the M.E. Mission [Methodist Episcopal] in San Francisco came by stmr two weeks ago to look after his countrymen here. He was sent out and his passage paid by the Japanese in S. F. I don't think he intends to start a M.E. Mission here. Mr. Damon and myself have welcomed and helped him in every way.

Taking advantage of his being here, we have worked up the organization of the Japanese on a Christian basis, forming a Japanese Benevolent Union for aid to their sick, poor, etc. and also a Japanese YMCA[22] for religious, social and educational work among them. Such work has been going on all the time. I have met with the Japanese every Sunday morning for a religious service ever since they came. This organization of the work among them looks towards receiving some into church membership and forming the nucleus of a Japanese church . . . We are to change the hour of the Japanese service, next Sunday so as to close at 11:30 with the hope of getting out those at household service. They are a very interesting people to work for, as amiable as the Hawaiians, and the upper classes as intelligent, refined, and courteous, as our own people. They have not the Chinese self-sufficiency and are more cleanly . . . Another interesting incident has been a visit to the Quarantine Grounds where 1400 Japanese are quartered previous to assignment to the various plantations. I arranged to have a meeting this afternoon. The scene was most impressive. Imagine a clear space of 15 feet in diameter and around this 1400 people seated on their haunches, all listening intently, amusedly, responsively as well as reverently to the Rev. Miyama's fervent presentation of salvation by Christ as the one hope for man. What an opportunity is this for such a Christian worker![23]

The reference to the formation of a Japanese Benevolent Union foreshadowed a significant community institution. Mrs. Ando, wife of the Japanese Consul General, was the Union's first president. Its early days were slow moving. Mrs. Sunamoto, wife of Pastor Teikichi Sunamoto of the Honolulu Japanese Church, revived the movement among the church women and became its second president. The members held weekly meetings and their purpose was to look after sick and distressed people.

Again it languished but was revived in 1892. Men were admitted, the name was changed to the Japanese Benevolent Society, and the inaugural meeting, February 27, 1892 was "addressed by Dr. C. M. Hyde of the Hawaiian Board." It was this society which led to the establishment of the Kuakini Hospital in Honolulu.

Mrs. Hyde had a singing school Friday evenings and her choir was made up of people who had never sung before. A Sunday School was started on Sunday afternoon. A Rising Sun Temperance Society was formed. Central Union Church took on a project of supplying funds for the services of Mr. T. Shimizu, a licensed Methodist preacher brought out from San Francisco to work under the direction of a committee of the Hawaiian Board.

Dr. Hyde, however, was about to send up distress signals. The Rev. K. Miyama made a quick round trip to San Francisco to assist in setting up certain arrangements for entry of the Methodist Church into the Hawaiian Islands as a mission field. Methodist Bishop Fowler revealed this in commissioning "The Rev. Miyama to open a mission of the M.E. ch. in the Sandwich Islands for the Japanese." This was most upsetting to the Rev. Hyde. In fact he was indignant. "He (Miyama) was not invited to return by the Hawaiian Board, nor by Mr. Damon, or myself . . . It was presumptuous in Bishop Fowler to begin a M.E. Mission here . . . It might answer in the United States where all are on an equality. But here we are to help in any such work and it cannot be done without our help . . ."[24]

He lost no time rushing to the defense of what he considered the integrity of his Congregational duty. He utilized his "instant pursuit" tactic. Off went a letter to Bishop Fowler signed by himself and the Rev. S. E. Bishop as the Committee of the Board of the Hawaiian Evangelical Association and adopted in a hastily called meeting of the entire Board. The letter in the handwriting of Hyde protests the new

mission and hopes that "some working plan of effective Christian cooperation be devised and adopted. If you feel disposed to cooperate with us,
as we most earnestly desire, in the common Salvation, would it not be
well that Mr. Harris, or yourself, should visit us, with authority to
consider and agree upon some suitable methods of cooperation?"[25] The
letter continues with a succinct passage delineating the historic position
of the American Board in Hawaii.

Meanwhile progress was reported in the Japanese work:". . .We
had the semi-annual meeting of the Japanese YMCA last Saturday ev'g.
This time the numbers present wanted to *vote by ballot.* Mr. Damon and
myself were unanimously re-elected. (I have been Pres. & he V.P. for the
last 1/2 year). . . It is astonishing to note how easily the Japanese adopt
our usages. The Sunday morning congregation which I address at Queen
Emma Hall, is over 40 in number, exceedingly decorous, and as well
dressed in European style, as any equal number of the congregation in
Fort St. Ch. . . . "[26] An answer to the query of the Hawaiian Board
was not long in coming. The Rev. M. C. Harris disembarked from a San
Francisco steamer a few weeks later. He found the Methodist work had
fanned out among all the islands, chapels erected, workers on duty and
the mission generally in good health.

Despite Dr. Hyde's fears a warm friendly feeling prevailed. Fort
Street services including baptisms, sermons and Communions were
conducted jointly by Congregational and Methodist leaders. An informal
conference was called with Harris, Beckwith, Judd, Bishop, and Hyde
in attendance. No decisions were made but a united approach without
any sense of union or merger was the way it was left. Harris returned to
San Francisco, church matters involving the Japanese settled down, and
Dr. Hyde was not unhappy.

By the end of July, 1888, things were well enough in (Congregational)
hand to suggest letters to the Methodist Mission in San Francisco and the
American Board in Boston. The Hyde letter to Harris was a *modus vivendi*
in which the Committee of the Hawaiian Board offered cooperation outside of merger or union.[27] The same boat mail carried a letter to Judson
Smith. "It seems," he wrote, "no organic union were possible, but the
loose cooperation scheme on which we are to work need not occasion any
friction. . .Whatever sharpness I may be inclined to employ as occasions
may arise will be modified by the genial wisdom of Dr. Beckwith and the
loving spirit of the Rev. S. E. Bishop. . ."[28]

DR. HYDE AND MR. STEVENSON

A week later he illustrated the distinctions in polity between the two denominations: "As I look at it, the M.E. Church is a big machine with wheels and cogs. For myself I prefer Cong'l forms where I feel that I have my individual choice as a man about my actions, neither a cog nor a wheel."[29]

Consul General Taro Ando in the customary rotation of assignments returned to Japan. An affectionate community farewell was extended to the Ando family. He was a highly regarded consular agent and added to that was a leader in the evangelical work among the Japanese. Dr. Hyde conducted the reception proceedings at Queen Emma Hall.

A Christmas entertainment arranged by the Japanese Church people pleased him. "The Japanese surprised us all," he warmly commented, "by the simple elegance with which they got up a Christmas entertainment with speeches, singing, tree, refreshments etc. The 'Lyceum' was beautifully decorated. The exercises were simple, brief, pleasing. At their request a quartette from the NPMI sang a Christmas hymn in Hawaiian . . . There was a heartiness, a good humor, a good taste about all this, that was very charming. The Japanese will evidently not make such angular Christians as our New England Calvinism stiffens people . . . Here come these Japanese with a bonhomie and an abandon, that show how much pleasure they can bring into the dull round of ordinary life when they bring Christian joy with it . . ."[30]

Shortly after the Christmas festival, the SS *Yamashiro Maru* from Japan docked with a long passenger list of immigrants. At the usual religious service at the Immigration Depot, addresses were made by Japanese church workers, a Rev. A. N. Fisher of Buffalo, N. Y., and Dr. Hyde. Fisher had come from San Francisco as a representative of the Methodist Mission there. His job was to study and to recommend future policy regarding Methodist work in Hawaii. Now too long after his return to San Francisco a letter arrived from the Rev. Mr. Harris. The blue skies of Hawaii never seemed more beautiful to Hyde than that day in September, 1891 when he read Mr. Harris' words! "This mail will bring to the Hawaiian Board new responsibilities. I never doubted for a moment, that God called us to the Islands to help save the Japanese. Mr. Fisher has reached the conclusion after careful study of the problem, that the Methodists should withdraw from the field and leave this work to your Board. I have joined with him in a letter making a tender of the Mission and all that we have under our supervision to your care. I trust you may see your way to release us of all further responsibility so that we may devote all our time to the increasing number of Japanese on the Pacific Coast . . ."[31]

In the Harris letter reference is made to a "tender of the Mission." The accompanying official document signed by both Harris and Fisher covers this point:

We are instructed by the authorities of the Conference to proffer retirement from that field upon condition that said Board (Haw'n) assume care and conduct of the Mission . . . It will be expected that the Japanese membership on the Islands will take such name and relationship as the Board may determine, and any items of property acquired shall come under control of the Board.

The salaries of the brethren have been paid to Aug. 31 and there is no indebtedness against the Mission as far as is known to us. We have in hand six hundred dollars . . . will pay the salaries for the month of Sept . . . and will pass the balance to the credit of the Board should this proffer be accepted.[32]

It is a rare thing to find one Protestant conference surrendering its mission, including workers, money and buildings to another denomination. The increase of Japanese in the west coast states may have been too demanding, at least for the moment, to care for an island missionary project 2400 miles out in the Pacific Ocean. It may have been the Rev. Mr. Fisher's impression when he checked over the Mission on his visit to Hawaii that Hyde and company were doing an adequate job and the Methodist hand was not needed.

But the assimilation that ensued was an uneasy procedure. Some of the workers were "too Methodist" to accept a new denominational command. There were troubles outside the Congregational fence that soon brought the Methodists back in a renewal of their own work. A political upheaval of the Hawaiian kingdom resulted in a series of *pro tem* governments, ending in annexation by the United States. This was a revolution which had Dr. Hyde's warm support but in the process further protest about Methodist activity in Hawaii was to no effect.

Imagine his feelings when with no advance warning he read in the *Gospel in All the Lands* that the California M.E. Conference had voted to resume work in Hawaii and had appropriated $1000 for a M.E. Mission to the Japanese here.[33] The Congregationalists, who had been the only major Protestant force in Hawaii for three quarters of a century, now had a new partner.

Hyde should have welcomed the fresh impetus and new strength. The Congregational Conference was finding deep inroads in its work from the Catholics, Mormons and Buddhists. Furthermore, the native population was dwindling to a dramatic low; and it was the Hawaiians who were the main reason the American and Hawaiian Boards were in Hawaii. He did, however, accept the situation with reluctance but with a good grace. At the time he read the announcement he was worrying up a program for the local Japanese churches to adopt the "Ruk Lagoon (Micronesia)" as their missionary field. The Japanese were colonizing in this area of the Pacific and "Japanese traders . . . peddled among their wares a questionable grade of whiskey." He was also carrying on a stepped-up correspondence regarding American Board efforts with church people in Japan, particularly in regard to training Christian field workers.

But now as the Methodists were settling in and the political skies were clearing, his health was declining. His doctors advised an ocean voyage and visit to Japan's spas, mountain resorts, and hot springs. Careful arrangements were made and with the Rev. Mr. Leadingham in charge at the Institute, the Hydes took passage on the SS *Doric*, August 1, 1897; first stop, Minoshita Springs, four hours from Yokohama by train. In this trip of almost four months, Hyde did not allow himself much time for rest and recuperation. He was entranced with Japan. He followed his usual habit of letter writing and reporting. Chiefly, he prepared long colorful descriptions of town and countryside for the *Pacific Commercial Advertiser* and the *Hawaiian Gazette*. The articles started as a series of different releases to each paper but about halfway through the trip he submitted the same story to each. He also prepared articles on impressions of religion for the *Friend*. He was like a child with a new toy in this fascinating country. So he revelled in being pushed up the mountain trail to the Fujiya Hotel by three "jinricksha men." He loved Nikko and its mountain lake above with the "edge-of-the-precipice road" connecting the two. He enjoyed his old friends, Japanese repatriates from Honolulu, among them Consul General Ando, the Rev. K. Miyama, Dr. Iwai, dentist. He thought the trains were good but "not noted for their speed."

The palaces, processions, schools, military training, worship customs, currency intrigued him. He was astonished by the number of imitations of foreign goods made in Japan. He quickly sensed strong devotion, in all levels of Japanese life, to a continuous program of personal training. He could see the development of a discipline both inwardly in the individual and outwardly in the community. The mountain resorts, the rains and the winds delighted him. Visits were made to leper colonies, kindergartens, schools, expositions, missionary retreats and churches.

In articles to the *Friend,* official monthly publication of the Hawaiian Board, Hyde reported on Doshisha University and Osaka Seminary. Doshisha University in Kyoto originally was a Theological School of the American Board. Here in his visit he was troubled by its emphasis upon ethical rather than evangelical principles. He found it deteriorating in respect to physical condition, and the enrollment and faculty diminishing. This was due, he wrote, to the spirit of nationalism which flushed the minds and hearts of the Japanese after their recent naval and military successes. "Foreign influences were minimized; foreign ways discarded; foreign teachers sent adrift. So Doshisha suffered . . ."[34]

The work in Osaka Seminary, on the other hand, was different. Here were four evangelical churches, a hospital and a girls' boarding school. There was also a residence erected with contributions of the Woman's Board of Missions of the Hawaiian Board.

Generally, in the articles to Hawaii, he analyzed Christianity in Japan and its influence on Japanese life and character. "There are missionaries from twenty-seven different organizations, besides some independent missionaries, at work in Japan."[35] He thought they were all needed, that the major groups worked well together:

As to the influence that Christianity is now exerting in the Japanese national 'ife and character, it is acknowledged that the radical change which is needed in Japanese civilization can come only from the spread of gospel truth. But . . . the change of controling ideas and habits in individuals and social life is the work of time and of providential discipline . . . The Japanese are still wrestling with problems they never confronted before and are floundering along with many mistakes in policy and method . . . They want to project themselves and their own ideas into God's work, and to claim the glory for themselves, just as they employ architects and engineers from abroad. And when the work is nearly done dismiss them, put some Japanese in charge and claim the finished product as a proof of Japanese skill. That is what is really meant by this claim for a Japanese Christianity, of which we hear so often, but of which we can never get a clear statement as to its character and validity. It must be Japanese however. Just here is the chief weakness of Japan, an intense self conceit; and that patriotism, of which we are told there is an utter absence in Christian teaching, is, much of it, only an exaggerated vanity. It is self conceit magnified and reduplicated, as one's individual face is in those mirrors that have a multitude of faces . . . It is this exaggerated "selfhood" that largely interferes just now with the rapid spread of Gospel principles and of the Gospel spirit that was characteristic of the work a little while ago.

The desire for change, a restless search for novelty, as if the new were surely the good, seems to have taken possession of the leading minds in this Japanese nation. Under the old social system, every individual's place and work were strictly defined. What the father did the son was expected to do. What dress a mother wore, the daughter was expected to wear . . . I am astonished to see how far the national dress is being supplanted by European toggery . . . but some little want of fitness betrays the wearer as not to the manner born . . . The Japanese, like the Hawaiians, lack an inbred sense of moral obligation . . . There is the same desire to make things smooth and easy, underlying all Japanese courtesy, that makes the Hawaiian confound the *pono* with the *oluolu,* the right with the agreeable . . . When the responsibility for control of means, and leadership of men, is put upon the newly Christianized Japanese, it comes upon them as unprepared for such positions of trust and influence as the Hawaiians . . ."[36]

This fall trip in 1897 was a revelation of ornamental landscape and human philosophy representing new experiences to the Hydes. In his orderly reporting of the scenic beauties in travelogue style and in his analyzing Japanese personality and its relation to Christianity, he has provided a valuable record.

The Hydes returned on November 19 and a month later he gave the Central Union congregation a scholarly summary of his views of the Japanese Christian work.

Through such a recital of Chinese, Portuguese, and Japanese work, it must be remembered that the Hyde program only *included* the work with the superimposed races. The native program was uppermost in his mind and in this he continued his orderly research, his correspondence, his community purposes. There is more to the religious aspect of his biography before we consider his community involvements; these remaining topics treat of the YMCA and the American Board itself.

NOTES

1 Letter Hyde to the Rev. N. G. Clark, ABCFM, Feb. 17, 1878.
2 Letter Hyde to the Rev. E. K. Alden, ABCFM, May 11.
3 Letter Hyde to Clark, Sept. 3.
4 The *Friend,* YMCA, Supplement, July, 1879.
5 Letter Hyde to Clark, Sept. 1.
6 Ibid., Dec. 18, 1880.
7 Ibid., Jan. 17, 1881.
8 Letter Hyde to Mrs. C. E. Armstrong, Jan. 18.
9 Letter Hyde to Clark, Feb. 14.
10 Ibid., Nov. 19.
11 Letter Hyde to the Rev. J. O. Means, ABCFM, Apr. 19, 1883.
12 Letter Hyde to Smith, June 15.
13 Letter Hyde to Clark, Jan. 14, 1882.
14 Letter Hyde to Clark, Dec. 14, 1889.
15 The *Friend,* obituary of Rachel F. Soares, Dec. 1895.
16 Henry K. Hyde, *op. cit.,* pp. 60–63.
17 Letter Hyde to Clark, Apr. 8, 1882.
18 Letter Hyde to Smith, Feb. 14, 1885.
19 Rev. Takie Okumura, *Seventy Years of Divine Blessings* (Honolulu, June 1939, Printed in Japan).
20 Letter Hyde to Smith, Apr. 1, 1885.
21 Ibid., May 1.
22 Hyde was elected president, F. W. Damon vice president.
23 Letter Hyde to Smith, Oct. 20, 1887.
24 Ibid., Mar. 26. 1888.
25 Letter Hyde and Bishop to the Rev. C. H. Fowler, D. D., Mar. 27.
26 Letter Hyde to Smith, Apr. 9.
27 Letter Hyde to the Rev. M. C. Harris, July 25.
28 Letter Hyde to Smith, July 26.
29 Letter Hyde to Alden, July 31.
30 Letter Hyde to Smith, Dec. 12, 1889.
31 Letter Harris to Hyde, Sept. 17, 1891.
32 Agreement, the Rev. M. C. Fisher and the Rev. M. C. Harris to Hyde, Sept. 1891.
33 Letter Hyde to Smith, Jan. 1, 1894.
34 The *Friend,* Nov. 1897, pp. 85–87.
35 Ibid., pp 84–85.
36 Ibid.

Chapter 9

"DOERS OF THE WORD"

IT WAS THE AMERICAN BOARD of Commissioners for Foreign Missions which had dispatched Dr. Hyde to Hawaii. No matter how far afield he might roam within the religious fences or the more complicated world of politics, business, and publication he never lost sight of that primary assignment. He could be gently critical of the Board, thoughtful of its anniversaries, and a stout defender against its enemies. "You will be celebrating the seventy fifth anniversary of the ABCFM when this letter of mine reaches you," he wrote in 1885. "I hope for a revival of missionary zeal as the review of three quarters of a century brings to mind what great things God has wrought . . ."[1]

He boiled over when authoress Kate Field made careless reference to missionary wealth after her visit to Hawaii in 1886:

I have been very much gratified, casually meeting a J. W. Scovill of Chicago, to find him one of the corporate members of the Board, and interested in our work. In fact, one of his motives in coming was to learn for himself the truth in regard to the stories of missionary wealth he had heard from a Miss Kate Field, who had been at the Islands, picked up various slanders, never came near any of us to find the truth, and went back to California to spread the scandalous gossip wherever she went. I think Mr. Scovill has learned the facts in the case, and will go back to the States, knowing more and thinking better of our work than ever before . . .[2]

Consultative visits by American Board members were exceedingly infrequent. The real bond linking the Board and Honolulu was a correspondence channel via ship and rail with an accompanying time lag. Missionaries stopping over in Honolulu on their return from the mission field were full of recommendations: areas for new work, statistics, *Morning Star* (missionary schooner) problems, reassignments; book, supply, and food needs and the like. These kinds of information were assimilated and reduced to advice to the American Board by Hyde and others.

Missionaries, during a routine stopover or an emergency visit to Honolulu, were very frequently housed with Dr. and Mrs. Hyde who came to appreciate the considerable part played by temperament and health in the work in Micronesia. When Mrs. Albert Sturges, missionary wife, arrived in Honolulu from the mission station in Ponape, she was desperately in need of care; weight 77 pounds, she was a sick woman. She went directly to the Hyde residence for weeks of recuperation.

Some years later the *Morning Star* made an emergency trip to Honolulu carrying Dr. Sturges who had suffered a stroke and needed a Honolulu rest period before seeking medical assistance in California. The Hydes housed him in a rough whitewashed dwelling. The sheer starkness of the accommodation was at the insistence of Sturges. Another time missionary Doane was taken in feeble health from the ship to the Hyde home for several weeks. These samples of Hyde "nursing home" hospitality taken with many others caused him to observe that he "was sorry, sorry that the Micronesian work . . . needs people who are not nervous or delicate. None such should be sent. Persons of equable temperament and rugged health are the only ones who should think of going."[3]

In 1880–1881 the chief issue concerning the Micronesia Mission in the Hyde letters was the location of the Kusaie School directed by missionary Pease. The American Board supported one site and the Hawaiian Board to a man wanted it placed elsewhere.

In 1882 a local committee was formed with Hyde as recorder to investigate a massacre on Tapiteuea island, the result of a fight between natives and Hawaiian missionaries over land ownership.[4] Problems in Micronesia ranged from the routine to the unexpected and were endless.

He strongly urged the Ponape School be moved to Auk, not Mortlock. Mr. Rand's training school should supply Ponape, Pingalap and Mokil.[5] He spoke of the trade of the *Morning Star*, of the German island group acquisitions, the metes and boundaries of the Ponape Mission lands and he wanted Paaluhi sent to Ruk, Lutera to the Gilberts and so on.[6]

Another element which gave impetus to the involuntary expanding of concentration of Micronesian affairs in Honolulu hands was the sending forth to the field the native missionaries by the Hawaiian Board; after 1877 all new workers would come from Dr. Hyde's Institute.

In addition to the welfare of the missionaries his attention was also drawn to the provisioning, outfitting, scheduling, and repair of the *Morning Star* in Honolulu. This seaport was in effect becoming its terminus. His introduction to the schooner had been only a few days after his arrival in 1877. He was appointed by the Hawaiian Board as "chairman of a committee . . . to determine the compensation of the Captain of the *Morning Star* . . ."7

Morning Star III was wrecked on a reef at the entrance of Kusaie harbor in 1884. Earlier the American Board, knowing the vessel was old and would soon need replacing, had ordered construction of a new ship to be called *Morning Star IV*. After launching and commissioning at Bath, Maine, it sailed, with steam added, for Hawaii and entered Honolulu harbor in April 1885. It was already being built when the wreck of *Morning Star III* occurred.

Dr. Hyde was delighted with this beautiful new ship but was disappointed that so little fuss was made over it:

. . . I felt as if we were not making enough of the coming of the *Morning Star No. 4*. No one seemed disposed to "enthuse" on the subject. So I suggested and carried out successfully three gatherings on board the *Star*.

Last Thursday evening the Entertainment Committee of the Cousins' Society arranged for some literary and musical exercises with ice cream and cake . . . Mrs. Dillingham, daughter of Mrs. Lowell Smith, our poetess, favored us with an original poem.

Saturday evening we held our regular Cousins' Society monthly meeting on board the *Star* . . . We used the main hatch for a platform; had the piano and the secretary's table on that. The hatchway was garlanded with maile . . . We had photographs of the various missionaries and copies of publications of the five different languages spoken in the different missions. Then we had brief addresses from Judge Judd, President of the Hawaiian Board, Capt. Bray, Rev. Messrs. Bingham, Bishop, Foster and myself . . .

Sunday afternoon we had a meeting of the Hawaiians and there was a very good attendance. I took Leleo, the returned blind missionary from Apaiang, and Lono, in my carriage down to the *Star*. We had addresses from them and two other returned Hawaiian missionaries, Pali [sic] and Kamakahiki. We had plenty of singing . . .[8]

He referred to that Honolulu harbor celebration a few weeks later. "I propose to print a Chronological Record of the Micronesian Mission in connection with the address before the Cousins' Society which I delivered Monday night. I prepared it for the meeting of reminiscences we held on board the *Star*."[9]

He was usually clear and firm in his suggestions to a seemingly slow-moving American Board. He could be roused to vehemence:

Mr. Forbes tells me that you have written to him to have the *Star* go directly to Ruk . . . The Hawaiian missionaries in the Gilbert Islands depend on the *Star*'s coming regularly about such a time every year. They may be left to suffer for want of expected provisions while the *Star* is going West. You will see that this is an objection to the plan of an annual gathering of the Missionaries. Nor do you seem to comprehend that a voyage to Ruk is equivalent to 1/3 of the circumference of the globe: nor that the necessities of sailing a ship compel a long sail to the North West in order to get winds that will carry the vessel Eastward and Southward to Kusaie or to Honolulu: and that the *Star* is not a *steamer,* its sole superiority over the former vessels being its ability to steam, instead of lying idle, in calms. It is a poor sailor, cannot beat to windward.[10]

This was plain talk. Obviously such crises as these arose from running the ship and the program under two masters 5000 miles apart. He entered deeper into Micronesian affairs with each layover of the *Morning Star:* coppering the ship's hull, setting Honolulu departures, charting of sailing times and distances among the atolls, detailing itineraries based upon favorable winds, accessible harbors, and the specific areas of missionary work.[11]

An examination of a hitherto forgotten box of notes on Micronesia in the Bishop Museum gives Hyde a fantastic mark for his throughness in preparing himself and keeping up on the Micronesia Mission. There are hundreds of sheets of his sketches and tables showing distances in miles and days among the island groups, logs of the *Morning Stars* on inter-island travel and to Boston and Honolulu, lists of missionaries and families at every station, school and church building details, and statistics. He must have known more about the geography of communication, the people best adapted to doing mission work and the most strategic places for carrying it on than any other person in Boston, or Honolulu, or Micronesia—and he had never set foot in the field.

There was criticism of this Honolulu direction in *Morning Star* matters. Hyde was considerably nettled with missionary Pease's denunciation of the American Board for letting the Hawaiian Board schedule the vessel. Pease was specifically referring to Hyde's attention to route making.[12]

A strongly worded explanation was mailed by Hyde to the American Board:

You speak of the *Morning Star* Committee [Honolulu] as planning the voyages. It is the Foreign Missions Committee of the Hawaiian Board that has always studied up and laid out the program. The *Morning Star* Committee is of recent origin and was organized especially to look after the *financial* management in consultation with the Captain, an advisory board to *share* the responsibility and guard against possible extravagances of expenditures. We take it that you intended to have the *same* committee as before attend to the working of the *Star* on her missionary service.[13]

The American Board was unable to mount any measure of Boston control so Hyde, in Honolulu, continued as a member of both of the above described committees to coordinate and mediate *Morning Star* activity.

International politics began to affect Micronesia. The far-off power plays of the Germans and Spaniards, and the recent sharp interest of the Japanese, inserted an ominous overlordship as an entirely new element of missionary concern. The area was becoming an ocean of troubles with the United States not participating except through minor commercial traffic and the peaceful work of the missionaries. Hawaii, as an independent country, would be an excellent outpost of information and any consideration of American strategy in the Pacific would have to include that almost perfect defense bastion, Pearl Lagoon. Hyde kept in touch with the political actions of the European and Oriental nationals and did not like what he heard and said so. He wrote feelingly of the massacre of the Ponapese by the Spanish governor and soldiers in 1887. He was incensed the next year when a German sea captain assessed a fine on a church at Ebon because the "natives refused to buy of trading vessels, whose captains sold liquor. A copy in German of an agreement signed by Rev. Bingham and twelve others, Oct. 31, 1885 was shown me and I was asked if these were missionaries, if Ebon was not a dependency of Jaluit, if the people of Ebon were not included in a 'so-called treaty of friendship' made with some German captain in 1878 which put them under the jurisdiction of the German Consul away off in Samoa, and if the Ebon people did not understand what things their chiefs had signed."[14] Hyde explained to Glade, the German Consul in Honolulu, the misconceptions held and wrote a memorandum of fact for him on the subject.

Then the Spaniards:

News rec'd by the last stm'r, Sept. 27 [1890] brought us the news of the fresh disturbance on Ponape, the killing of the Spanish officers and soldiers and the saving of the lives of 2 priests and 4 soldiers. I was appointed a committee in connection with Mr. Emerson to lay this matter before the U. S. Minister.[15]

I tried to impress upon Stephens [John L. Stephens] in my talk with him this point—that if the U.S. Government does not deign to protect its citizens at the outset of this Spanish and German arbitrary rule, then as the American commerce is extended in the Pacific, our citizens will be liable to still greater indignities and injustice under the idea that their government does not care and will not protect their interests. The people at Washington should be reminded that the Pacific States are growing rapidly, that this commerce of the Pacific is one of the developments of the near future, and the Pacific States will be in a position soon if not now regarded, when they will demand a policy of protection vigorously carried out.[16]

Throughout the 1890's he witnessed and reported the steady erosion of the mission work caused by the race of the national giants to obtain footholds in one island group or another in Micronesia.

In December 1886 an about-face was suggested by the American Board. It would consider sending missionaries to Hawaii again and defer part of the costs. Normally a voluntary gesture like this would set the missionary bells ringing, but Dr. Hyde had been sensing an imminent change in the government of Hawaii—a change for the better he would have regarded it—and wanted to wait for a more propitious moment. In his reply he spoke of the impending change of government and declared that the American Board should stay clear of Hawaii. "The King has the vantage," he wrote, "and until he loses his vantage he rules the day." Hyde simply would not approve of introducing new laborers at this time.[17]

This strong request for delay was based upon his acute awareness of a wide town movement to curtail King Kalakaua and his powers sharply. He felt that this action against the king could happen in a few weeks. Actually it did not take place for six months. But no matter, even if he wanted a delay, planning for new people in new positions had to precede any moment of decision. He was named head of a committee of the Hawaiian Board to report on personnel needs in Hawaii. He checked off several in a letter to the American Board. One man was needed for the work with the 1100 Portuguese, another to help Damon with the Chinese, a revivalist, a man to reopen and head Kohala Girls' School and others. But he still urged delay.[18]

By the middle of June the focus centered politically in a reorganization of the government. Kalakaua would not be deposed but the direction and impact of his rule would be changed for the better.

Immediately the Hyde plea for delay dissolved into an excited pressure to move the new people to the Hawaiian field. "Now is the time when we want new men to come. The old fraudulent, pretentious display of Hawaiian ability is out of the way. We shall have a sensible, dignified, orderly good government. Now is the time for the friends of the Hawaiians to rally and help reorganize Christian work among them, simultaneously with the reorganization of the Government."[19] His enthusiasm could scarcely be contained. "Now is the time to push things . . . Don't wait for things to turn up, but put in and turn things . . . We need devoted, humble, zealous, intelligent men to send out here and send them at once, simple, earnest, sympathetic men."[20]

The business of recruiting new and able men had reached a serious stage in Christian leadership. The stalwarts of the Mission in Hawaii were either growing too old to be effective or had passed away. The letdown in the work was noticeable back in Boston, occasioning some second thoughts as to the wisdom of the American Board's withdrawal in 1863. "One sentiment often expressed," wrote Dr. Hyde, "is that the

ABCFM naturally feels reluctant to go before the American public with an appeal for funds for the resumption of missionary work, as such actions would be a virtual confession that the giving up of the Islands as a *mission* field was a mistake. Naturally, people here, informed with the necessities of this work, feel that it is very important that something should be done and done immediately."[21]

He pursued this thought in another letter listing suggestions for handling the new proposal that the American Board re-enter the field in Hawaii and through a Committee of Five start the Mission again. He felt the North Pacific Missionary Institute could be enlarged to handle it.[22]

The Hawaiian Board's Committee on Evangelism, with Hyde as chairman, made a quick review of the picture in a memorandum written by the Rev. W. B. Oleson, principal of the newly formed Kamehameha School for Boys, as scribe. The committee was specific. It listed discouraging as well as hopeful aspects, and in summation said, "We believe the signs are favorable for an onward movement of Protestant Christianity among the Hawaiians. The times are propitious and the needs are urgent."[23]

He wrote about American Board re-entry in 1891. "I hope that if the Board did make a mistake in withdrawing too soon from the mission field, they will not now make another mistake by refusing to enter into the fullest possible cooperation with friends of the Hawaiian work at the islands, who would be glad to have the Board resume the work and push it under the new and changed conditions."[24]

His concern was that "Boston" might want to run the Mission from Boston. It was not only the spirit of autonomy which was deeply imbedded in the minds of Hawaiian workers; there was the almost certain promise of anything but effective administration from so far away.

One final comment on this relationship went to the Board:

I can only wonder, what change, if any, the new condition of affairs will have on the relations of the Board to the Islands. Shall we be considered any longer, as belonging to the foreign fields? As to need of work and help there is no question about that. It was a mistake on the part of the Board not to keep up active work on the islands. Hawaiians only two generations removed from barbarianism, are not fitted for self-government. They have no conception of the fitness of things. They cannot reason logically. They know things only superficially *as* they *seem*, not as they *are* in their relations, and *must* be in accordance with the eternal principles of truth . . .[25]

During the years of missionary work in the islands, the American Board and later the Hawaiian Board acquired title to many properties by purchase, grant, or gift. These lands included many tracts closely related to Hyde's life: the three Kawaiahao Seminary lots, the two on which the Hyde home was built, the Bingham premises at Punahou and many many more. Management of these properties was but infrequently well maintained. Records were not too carefully kept. Often some urgency would call for a search of title, or an inventory of properties on one island or on all the islands. One instance arose in 1892. Hyde was given power-of-attorney along with Messrs. Hall and Emerson to bring the entire portfolio of holdings up to date. This meant a review of all abstracts of title, examination of all mortgages, surveys and royal patents. After much work Hyde speaks of it. "I have been trying to straighten out the land titles of the ABCFM of which an abstract has been made, but some *lacunae* required a great deal of personal investigation and correspondence with people on other islands, which occasions some vexatious delays . . . I have been put on the Finance Committee of the Board, so that what I have been doing unofficially, as opportunity offered, I am doing now officially as a matter of obligation."[26]

Among other trips taken by the Hydes to other islands in the Hawaiian chain, to Japan, Europe, and the United States, one stands out. Annual meetings of the American Board were held in the late fall but it was not until 1893 that Dr. Hyde was able to cover things sufficiently at his North Pacific Missionary Institute to allow his being away. Politics in Hawaii were stablizing with the Queen dethroned. The Columbian Exposition in Chicago was beckoning. The climax of the trip would be his participation in the annual meeting of the American Board at Worcester, Massachusetts. In one report printed in the proceedings there comes to light a striking pen portrait of this man, now 61 years of age and a veteran of 16 years in Hawaiian work:

Dr. Hyde is one of the venerable missionaries whose years of experience in the field have given a knowledge of the Hawaiian Islands that but few possess. He is a man of fine presence, of good height, erect, hair almost snow-white, pleasant, attractive, dark face, with, however, the "chin of determination" which bespeaks for him, underneath the quiet manner, the strong commanding character which has served him so long in his work. He speaks with a directness that does not need the tricks of oratory to gain for itself an audience. A glance around the well-filled hall while he was speaking showed by the attitude of the faces the exact direction in which they had to look to see the speaker.[27]

This was a rather unusual entry for the factual business-type reporting that was characteristic of the ABCFM proceedings. But there was more. A liberal element was unseating the conservatives at this annual meeting that Hyde was attending and he was certainly not a liberal. Yet his comments, which were recorded also, were temperate and thoughtful and warmly applauded:

I wish simply to say, as one of the missionaries of the American Board, that I voice the sentiments of many with whom I have spoken, if not all, that this large assembly interested in the work of the Board should adopt the report of this committee. Both a condition and a theory confront us now. You have heard much in relation to both of these aspects of this question. In relation to the theory let me say that in my opinion, in the stress of God's providence, we have been called upon as Christian believers, not to change our position, but to change our front. We, who go as missionaries to the heathen, speak to them not so much of salvation from death as a new life in Christ. Then again, as to the condition confronting us, do not, I beseech you, make the practical blunder of seeking to save your consistency instead of saving souls. I plead with you not to thrust your fist into your brother's face, but lock hand with him and walk together to save souls.[28]

Correspondence with the American Board continued without abatement to the last week of his life. Here was his listening post, here his platform to espouse causes, here his confessional. The American Board may have seemed impersonal in its far-flung bigness but it had a deep consistent personal concern that gave intimate encouragement and support to its helpers out in the field. The Board was an enormous source of strength to Dr. Hyde.

An unofficial arm of the American and Hawaiian Boards was the Hawaiian Mission Children's Society, commonly referred to as the "Cousins' Society." This nickname originated from the familiar use of "sister" and "brother" in salutation among the missionaries. Their children were the "Cousins." Organized for the missionaries to Hawaii and their descendants, it provided selected participation in the work of the mission.

The Society was holding its 25th annual meeting simultaneously with the Hawaiian Evangelical Association in 1877 and Hyde, scarcely disembarked in the islands, was invited to "address miscellaneous remarks to the Society." He was elected director, 1878–1879; president, 1879–1880; and president again for 1884–1885. In his address, as retiring president June 5, 1880, he summed up the transition from paganism to Christianity in Hawaii:

Great has been the change in these islands since that voyage of the Brig *Thaddeus* from Boston around Cape Horn. Only a brief time before the arrival of the missionaries, the King had been the foremost actor in throwing off the oppressive restriction of a religion of cruelty and terror. It is because of the religion then introduced and accepted that today the Hawaiian Kingdom, the solitary instance of such beneficent and radical change of national as well as ecclesiastical polity, stands among the nationalities of Christendom, an independent and co-ordinate sovereignty. It was not because of its commercial importance, or its political greatness, but because it was recognized as a Christian nation, that this little archipelago secured its acknowledgement by the great powers of Christendom as an independent sovereignty. In 1820 the need and the demand of the hour was foundation work for Christianization and for civilization . . . The same diligence of endeavor, the same fixedness of purpose is needed now as then . . . Those who doubt or deny such truths as the existence of a personal God, the spiritual nature of man, the authoritative utterances of revealed truth are lauded by many as the advanced thinkers of the day . . . It is only as we believe that men have souls to be saved or lost, as well as bodies to be clothed and fed we can even begin rightly to estimate the worth of one single human being . . . What if there are many keen enough to see the weaknesses of our well-meant but often ill-advised labors for the salvation of souls, and quick to ridicule such weaknesses? Is ridicule the test of truth? The criterion of excellence? Is the power of sarcasm so beneficent in its influence that we should exalt it to the highest place of honor in our esteem?[29]

In 1885 he reported again as retiring president. This time he outlined the brief history of the "Cousins" and stressed the need for reinforcements for the changed condition of Christian work in the Kingdom. Mission children had held a well-organized farewell to Dr. L. H. Gulick on June 5, 1852 as he was about to leave to begin work in the Micronesian Mission. This farewell led to the formation of the Hawaiian Mission Children's Society. He went on with statistics of the Mission's 33 years and the significant part played by the several successive *Morning Stars*. He described Hawaii's society in its manifold aspects and stated a "reinforcement" need in each area: that is, in business, government, and education; and lastly said he, "there is need of reinforcement in Christian work of the courage, the hopefulness, the devotion that made the fathers and mothers of this Sandwich Islands Mission the moral heroes that they were."[30]

He was addressing himself to a group of important people in Hawaii; they were the descendants of missionary, church, school, business, and government families. Collectively they were a power for religious action; as individuals each in his own way had a contribution to make in spreading far the work so ably portrayed albeit rather sonorously by Dr. Hyde. He tended to over-ornamentalize his public utterances.

There were other tasks for him during the early years of his association with the "Cousins." He headed a committee to re-word a sensitive bylaw, the one covering eligibility for membership. He was chairman of the Historical Committee which collected biographies of the missionaries.

The *Maile Wreath* was a literary effort of the Hawaiian Mission Children's Society and an outlet for Hyde activity. Speakers on various topics, not necessarily of religious nature, were invited for intermittent gatherings at different homes, frequently at the Hyde residence. Papers presented were usually hand copied into the *Maile Wreath*, a modest journal—in effect a minute book of speeches. Speakers were sometimes listed as editors. There were also printed journals bearing the name *Maile Wreath*, but not at this time.

Dr. Hyde read no less than ten papers before the Society, one of which[31] was inspired by a recent book, James Bryce's *American Commonwealth*.[32] Here was a treatise that calmed him and offered sensible direction to his thinking regarding the workings of Hawaiian government. His paper to the *Maile Wreath* audience was devoted to the checks and balances inherent among the three divisions of American government. He quoted

Bryce: "Each [of the coordinated departments] is appointed by the people to its special work, for the purpose of harmoniously coordinating their action. Their business is to work *together,* and not at *odds* [italics Hyde's] . . ."

In another paper, "Immigration Assisted and Immigration Resisted," he worked up a thesis supporting the immigration of Asiatics to Hawaii.[33]

Another venture of the "Cousins" fitting the Hyde idea of interesting paths to follow was a project named the "Sewing Girls' Home." This was in 1890. "Some think it wrong," he wrote to the American Board, "to train girls to be genteel with no society into which they can move with such training."[34]

The islands were entering a depression, and there was thought of closing, but operation was authorized for another year under the name "Working Woman's Industrial Home." Shortly however, the Society withdrew entirely from any Hawaiian evangelization and in doing this "closed out this pleasant home for about a dozen girls . . . reformatory, uplifting Christianizing work needs to be done . . . [where] could we get for such work the $1600 we must pay [annually] for the Home?"[35] This rather belated plea had no effect. The enterprise closed.

Dr. Hyde was engaged in other directions and did not see much of the "Cousins" in his last years. The Society had taken part in evangelical work in which he was more than an interested bystander. But now its emphasis was shifting and continued to shift, finally to become an important research center of missionary effort.

While he entered into his public preaching and teaching with evangelical fervor he could also relax in the quiet hours in his almost instinctive urge to write and print. He was equally at home in religious tracts and periodicals, in English and Hawaiian, in secular papers and publications. He mentioned an early project in a letter to Boston: "I am thinking of papyrographing a little monthly paper, *The Helping Hand,* for the Hawaiian pastors. I believe such a work would be of great value to them, if I can find the time to carry it on. I want to accumulate some material before I begin the enterprise so that I shall not feel pressed for want of copy."[36]

Another time: "I have made out a list of all licensed preachers and theological students, whose names I can learn, with dates of ordination, installation, years and school of preparation, and other such facts . . . I have the names of 146. Can any other mission make such a statement as that?"[37] In another letter he wrote of a history of female education that he was working on. In this he had an impressive list of boarding schools he planned to describe: Kawaiahao, Kohala, East Maui, Waialua, and others.[38]

In August 1886 the Hyde family went out to Waikiki to a seaside cottage belonging to Mrs. S. C. Damon. "We are on the beach with fine facilities for bathing, boating etc. I have brought down my Mss. and such books as I need and am prosecuting such literary work as I have long had in mind, but not found leisure to undertake. I have copied off many of the old deeds, and perfected my form for incorporation for trustees of our Hawaiian churches. I have also finished for the printer a revised copy of our Church Manual and I have other work in hand that the two remaining weeks will hardly give me time to complete . . ."[39]

"I have translated several new hymns, as I have done now since Father Lyons' death, for the anniversary exercises of the Institute."[40] About this same time Hyde authored a brief but detailed history of the writing and publishing of hymns in the Hawaiian language.[41]

"I am just starting in to get the S. S. Handbook for 1892 ready for publication. If I only had the leisure I could add a great deal to the Hawaiian religious literature."[42]

In three letters to the American Board Dr. Hyde writes of his desire to launch a Hawaiian religious newspaper.[43] Curiously, it was not so much a lack of time on his part as the unavailability of pressmen. The newspapers, both English and Hawaiian, were deluged with additional printing of books, magazines, manifestoes, annual reports. He did succeed in starting one publication. "I have been busy getting out a S. S. magazine in Hawaiian, *Ka Hoahana,* the *Fellow Worker.* It is 16 pp. 8vo with a cover, on which is a list of the S. S. lessons for the year, a calendar, the Lord's Prayer, Apostle's Creed, Ten Commandments 8 pp. News of the churches, S. S. items, YMCA, and the Home Circle each 2 pp. If the venture is successful, at the subscription price of $1 a year, I may increase the size another year. It will cost $40 a month. I have $250 in hand from the S. S. Assn. and expect to raise the rest from subscriptions, publishing an edition of 500."[44] In another year he sensibly changed frequency of publication from monthly to quarterly.

He published the *Hoahana* faithfully right up to his last weeks in 1899. The magazine, edited by others, continued publication for many years.

He wrote of publications again. "I am at work in my spare moments preparing Doane's Grammar and Vocabulary for the press. As the Dictionary is not alphabetically arranged this involves a great deal of work. I hope to get the new Museum Trust to publish the Grammar and Vocabulary of each of the 4 Micronesian languages."[45]

There were other irons in the fire. "My *Hawaiian Grammar,* in Hawaiian, is in the hands of the printer . . . I shall begin work at once on another textbook on Elocution, Rhetoric, and the conduct of public assemblies; and keep on at such work in addition to Institute and Trustee work, and Secretary work for various organizations; and look forward to busy months ahead."[46] There is some understatement here.

His confidence in the corresponding secretaries of the American Board was such that he could unburden himself unashamedly when some crisis in his Honolulu march of events was cutting him down or some "extra" liberalism at the national level, affecting the integrity of his Congregationalism, offended his religious sensibilities. Frequently, in such comments he revealed his innermost feelings regarding his faith and his church. "From a boy," he once wrote, "I have always wanted good men to keep away from Evil and not to countenance it; to call bad things and bad men by the names that belong to them. The feeling has not grown weaker with the lapse of years. I want to see truth and righteousness triumphant. I have felt that the best way to influence the King was to build up an influence outside that would counteract his schemes for the debasement and ruin of his people."[47]

In some respects 1887 and 1888 were not of his easier years. He had run up the white flag at Kawaiahao Seminary. He did not favor the merger of the Fort Street Church and the Bethel into the new Central Union Church. At Oahu College the trustees were, in his thinking, grossly mishandling a teacher relations problem. The veto power was being returned to the King. There were Hawaiian Board incidents, there were Board of Education incidents. He wrote to the Rev. E. K. Alden for advice, and again he poured out his distress:

I used to say I was never sure of my *backers.* Now I am forced to say I am not sure of my *foundation.* I have been victimized and ostracized everytime I have attempted to stand up for truth and right. Events afterward have proved that I was right and saw the truth from the first.

But the utter indifference with which all the rest of the community treat it, makes me ask myself again and again, as I have had to do many

The Rev. Dr. Charles M. Hyde, age 58, and Mary T. Knight Hyde
(Mrs. Charles M.), 1893. Photos from the Hawaiian Mission Children's
Society Collection.

Upper left: Town House, Brimfield, Massachusetts, erected 1878. The town government moved out of the jointly used church facilities into its own town meeting house, landmark evidence of the evolving separation of religion and government. Sketch by F. Bolles. *Upper right:* Home of the Congregational Church and Society of Brimfield, Massachusetts, erected 1847. Sketch by F. Bolles. *Below:* Hitchcock Free High School, Brimfield, Massachusetts. Hyde was a trustee 1862–1875.

Upper left: William Hyde, banker of Ware, Massachusetts, and uncle of C. M. Hyde. He was a corporate member of the ABCFM which commissioned Hyde for missionary work in Hawaii. *Upper right:* Charles M. Hyde, pastor of the Centre Congregational Church, Haverhill, Massachusetts, 1870–1876. *Right:* Centre Congregational Church, Haverhill, Massachusetts, about 1865. Demolished 1948. Photo from Haverhill Public Library Collection.

Top: The C. M. Hyde residence on Beretania Street between Alakea and Ward Streets. Erected 1877. *Middle:* First Honolulu home of the Theological Seminary, formerly the Castle home, on King Street. *Bottom:* North Pacific Missionary Institute on Punchbowl Street between Beretania and Hotel Streets. Planned and constructed by C. M. Hyde, 1889.

times before, can I be mistaken? Have I lost my wits? Are these honorable Christian men who are doing these things? What am I to think and feel and say? Must I keep quiet and let all this deviltry go on unrebuked?[48]

This was about the longest letter, twelve pages, that he ever wrote. It was a cry in the wilderness, a wail, an almost childlike plea for support.

In November 1888 he commented rather sadly on the missionary image in Honolulu. ". . . These inconsistencies of professedly good men sadly interfere with the progress of Christ's Kingdom in this community. Missionary is a term of reproach in Honolulu, very likely because so many of our people have done things utterly inconsistent with their professed beliefs, and so little confidence is felt in men whose principles of character and conduct are contradictory . . ."[49]

He achieved a rationale that allowed him to evaluate religion in terms of practical activity. He revealed this in a letter to Boston. "We do not magnify the grace of God by entertaining some lower estimate of sin. Yet as I remember what changes have been wrought in the trend of public opinion during my short life, and watching the drift of sentiment now, it seems to me that Christian experience in the future will be more and more in the line of practical activities, rather than a mere 'liberal' sentiment. At the Judgement Day the test will be of *life* rather than *belief* . . ."[50]

His moods were ever-changing. In measured optimism he could write a few months later, ". . . I want to see here to help us some sense of large abilities and personal influence. This is going to be an important center in the years to come as the mighty march of travel and traffic sweeps over this Pacific Ocean, and we ought to build for *Christ* and his *Church*."[51]

He was troubled by local Honolulu liberals and his concern and impatience included the "advanced thinkers" who were beginning to influence the American Board. "I have read," he complained to the Board, "with some indignation the article in the last *New Englander* on 'Protestant Vaticanism.' There is a venom in it, which does not show up well these new advocates of 'sweetness and light' in opposition to the stern Puritanism of the old New England theology. The cool assumption of these new lights that they are the 'liberal' thinkers expressing the 'advanced thought' of the Christian century is paralleled by the organization here in Honolulu of a Chinese Society, 'The Learned Destroyers of Christianity.' "[52]

Periodically he sent off blasts against the changing philosophers of the church. Two years later he wrote this: "I grieve over the new departure in theology which seems to be not so much a departure into realms of speculation of which we know as little as we know of dying; but rather an attempt to overthrow or set aside plain Bible statements of facts. There is a feverish agitation kept up about this theory of probation after death, which is far removed from the fixedness that is one element of certainty. Agitation is not necessarily the sign or method of reform; it may be the precursor of dissolution . . ."[53]

In church polity Dr. Hyde clung tenaciously to the Massachusetts brand of church government:

I have gone through out here this scheme of making the *churches* the controlling authority in managing Christian work. It simply gives a set of men, who *don't do the work,* the power of nullifying the actions of those who are pushing the work to the best of their judgement. That judgement may sometimes be mistaken, but the sense of responsibility that comes from doing the work is of more importance than concentrating all authority in outside parties who nominally control it. There must be *authority* these folks say; else there is no *responsibility.* This making an ecclesiastical body the directing and controlling power as Connecticut folks have been trying to do, is contrary to the genius of Massachusetts Congregationalism. The old Bay State has always given fullest scope to individual enterprise, and *that* is the line on which the highest and most satisfactory developments have been made, *not* in any ecclesiastical organism.[54]

He applies this unacceptable thinking about church polity to the American Board itself:

I remember old time discussions about voluntary *Societies* and Ecclesiastical *Boards* and wonder why our young ministers are so eager to change the breadth and freedom of the old ways of managing our benevolent societies, in the name of *liberality,* for the manipulations and dominations of *Elected Boards,* by delegates of ecclesiastical organizations, not *churches* . . . This new kind of liberality which seeks to denominationalize the American Board, and make it the executive committee of committees of associations, that have in themselves no ecclesiastical authority, seems a very mongrel and inconsistent mimicry of Presbyterianism, with its authoritative judicatories . . . But I should be stigmatized as an old fogy and any opinion of mine, adverse to the "advanced thought" of some "rustlers" would be derided as only a "back number" of no value simply because it is not dated as a new issue.[55]

There was little compromise or give in the definite conviction that he applied to his total work. He would rather walk away if he believed his principles of Christian belief were being aborted or abused. This fault, if indeed it were a fault, was perhaps his greatest personal shortcoming. He allowed his sense of disenchantment with those who violated the sacred proprieties and principles of the Bible and Congregationalism to become an often permanent block to further communication.

He was a conformist's conformist. He walked his beat in the churches, homes, streets of Honolulu, a gospelist of his Puritan upbringing. He sensed divine direction and found his great strength in the singleness of purpose explicit in that guidance. There was no compromise within his own thinking as to his personal conduct, and he carried this passion for adherence to principle into expectancy of comparable adherence to principle in every human.

The story of Dr. Hyde's religious career has now largely been told and the page is turned to consideration of his community efforts.

NOTES

1 Letter Hyde to the Rev. Judson Smith, ABCFM, Oct. 1, 1885.
2 Ibid., Mar. 27, 1886.
3 Letter Hyde to the Rev. Mr. Means, ABCFM, Apr. 9, 1883.
4 Letter Hyde to the Rev. N. G .Clark, ABCFM, July 1, 1882.
5 Letter Hyde to Smith, Oct. 31, 1885.
6 Ibid., Mar. 5, 1886.
7 Letter Hiram Bingham to ABCFM, June 15, 1877.
8 Letter Hyde to Smith, May 1. 1885.
9 Ibid., June 15.
10 Ibid., May 7, 1886.
11 Ibid., July 26, 1889.
12 Ibid., Apr. 30, 1890.
13 Ibid., July 14, 1891.
14 Ibid., Jan. 8, 1888.

15 Ibid., Oct. 18, 1890.
16 Ibid., Jan. 8, 1891.
17 Ibid., Dec. 21, 1886.
18 Ibid., Feb. 11, 1887.
19 Letter Hyde to the Rev. E. K. Alden, ABCFM, July 1.
20 Letter Hyde to Smith, Aug. 27.
21 Letter Hyde to the Rev. E. E. Strong, ABCFM, May 31, 1888.
22 Letter Hyde to Smith, July 2.
23 Memo Hawaiian Board to Smith, July 28.
24 Letter Hyde to Smith, Jan. 23, 1891.
25 Ibid., Feb. 28, 1893.
26 Ibid., July 20, 1892.
27 Eighty-third Annual Meeting, ABCFM, Worcester, Mass., Oct. 10–13, 1893.
28 Ibid.
29 28th Annual Report, Hawaiian Mission Children's Society, June 5, 1880, pp. 24–28.
30 33rd Annual Report, Ibid., June 8, 1885, pp. 30–40.
31 C. M. Hyde, "Co-ordinate? or Sub-ordinate?" *Maile Wreath,* May 9, 1889.
32 James Bryce, *American Commonwealth* (New York, Macmillan, 1888).
33 Hyde, "Immigration Assisted and Immigration Resisted," *Maile Wreath,* Sept. 17, 1889.
34 Letter Hyde to Smith, June 30, 1891.
35 Ibid., July 20, 1892.
36 Letter Hyde to Clark, Mar. 17, 1879.
37 Ibid., May 12.
38 Letter Hyde to Smith, Jan. 30, 1885.
39 Ibid., Aug. 14, 1886.
40 Ibid., May 14, 1889.
41 Hyde, "Hymn Books in the Hawaiian Language," the *Friend,* June 1889.
42 Letter Hyde to Smith, Nov. 25, 1891.
43 Ibid., July 27, Aug. 8, Sept. 12, 1892.
44 Ibid., Jan. 4, 1895.
45 Ibid., Sept. 24, 1896.
46 Ibid., Dec. 3.
47 Letter Hyde to Alden, Nov. 1, 1884.
48 Ibid., Feb. 27, 1888.
49 Letter Hyde to Smith, Nov. 15.
50 Ibid., Dec. 12.
51 Ibid., Mar. 14, 1890.
52 Ibid., Oct. 1, 1885.
53 Ibid., July 29, 1887.
54 Ibid., Mar. 4, 1889.
55 Ibid., Nov. 16, 1892.

Chapter 10

AN EVANGELICAL CHANNEL

PRAYER MEETINGS, street corner services, and Bible classes were routine and typical of the early YMCA years. Organized in London in 1844, the movement spread to the United States in 1851 and reached Hawaii in 1869, only eight years before Dr. Hyde stepped ashore in Honolulu. It was evangelical in its program and purposes and Hyde was an evangelist. Nothing could be more natural than that he should fall into stride with its work.

The YMCA was in no sense taken over by Dr. Hyde but he found it a vehicular affinity well suited to his inclinations and purposes. The minute books of the YMCA carry frequent references to him. The monthly meeting of the management board was the center of action; for many years there was no paid staff worker. The various board members through committee assignments handled the program and reported their progress at the meetings.

The first mentions of Dr. Hyde in the YMCA minutes have to do with a Chinese boy, Sat Fan, whom he was preparing for missionary work. "Drs. Hyde and Damon were appointed a committee to consult with Sat Fan and Sit Moon and for a month or so, pay them what was proper, until it could be decided which one would remain as a colporteur for Honolulu for the YMCA."[1]

Two other matters appear in the minutes, on the same date. "Dr. Hyde read a very interesting paper before the members present, on the printed literature of the Hawaiian Islands and gave the History of various publications. Also brought a number of the first books printed here to show the audience." Here, although in a modest way, he was giving his

147

listeners a sample of his competence in shuffling, rearranging, cataloguing and compartmentalizing the facts in a situation in order to make an orderly presentation. This quality was a chief factor in his success as a scribe or clerk, a valuable supportive role in all his Hawaii activity. He thus was scribe and collator as well as commentator and writer.

The other reference was also typical. "Dr. C. M. Hyde suggested that at the regular meetings of the association as variety in the way of entertainment that topics be given out on religious subjects, to be looked up during the month and discussed. The matter was thought favorably of." In accordance with this idea, "Rev. Frear and others were appointed to dissect the book of Job for the next meeting."[2] The discussion group technique was another Hyde specialty and would emerge in its most refined form in the Social Science Association which he started a few years later. He subsequently gave an essay of his own before the YMCA board on the "Hawaiian Language." The essay was also an indispensable component of the future Social Science effort.

Prison visits were a part of the YMCA program. G. C. Lees reported that "in junction with Dr. Hyde he had held service at the prison, speaking of the same as the most interesting meeting he had ever attended."[3]

Another time the minutes recorded, "Dr. Hyde as one of the Prison Committee reported quite a large number of Foreigners present at the services held there on Sunday mornings. They gave good attention and he felt there are cases of genuine repentance, many desiring to live a better life. Three services are held at the prison on Sundays at different hours viz Foreign, Hawaiian and Chinese."[4]

Liquor and opium issues brought the YMCA leaders into open conflict with King Kalakaua. "Dr. Hyde and Sanford B. Dole were authorized to prepare and circulate for signatures among the managers, owners, and agents of the various Sugar and Rice plantations petitions to be presented to the King in favor of maintaining the present prohibitory laws against liquor and opium . . ."[5]

Temperance and intemperance were the same in Dr. Hyde's book. He was a teetotaler to his last day. Since the King and Legislature were not moved to climb on any temperance bandwagon he acted:

. . . We have now begun a Temperance movement in a somewhat novel way, appointing an Executive Committee of twenty-one to take charge of the work. We have no constitution but are responsible to the public for fidelity and success, holding monthly meetings to make report of our work and striving in various ways to arouse the dormant Temperance sentiment of the community. As it was a word or two from me that started this movement, I have been chosen chairman of the Committee and under the circumstances did not feel justified in declining the position . . .[6]

The movement quickly gathered momentum. Captain Bray of the missionary schooner *Morning Star* was successful, when in San Francisco, in persuading Mr. M. L. Hollenbeck to schedule himself for a series of temperance talks in Honolulu. An associate of the famous evangelist Dwight L. Moody, and a distinguished and effective speaker, he addressed capacity houses, night after night, on such subjects as How Men Become Drunkards, How to Get at the Drunkard and What is Gospel Temperance? The movement during Hollenbeck's brief speaking tour became a revival. "One of the first fruits of the revival," wrote Dr. Hyde, "is a Saturday Evening Gospel Temperance Meeting at the Bethel, the very kind of work I had in mind when I suggested the necessity of a special effort for the suppression of intemperance . . . we have voted to wear the blue ribbon badges . . ."[7]

The blue ribbon had become the official emblem of the Blue Ribbon League, a temperance body started only a few years earlier in the YMCA of London. Dr. Hyde paraded his blue ribbon proudly and faithfully.

"In our YMCA I am planning to secure for this work (helping drinkers) a 'Temporary Relief Fund' to make small loans to such men out of employment to be repaid without interest as soon as they have the means."[8] Hyde could not only preach fervently on evils of drink; he could also sympathetically lend an ear and a hand to the victim of alcohol.

Not to be outdone by the men, a ladies' temperance movement had been gathering steam. Frances E. Willard and a group of friends in Evanston, Illinois, put together a temperance society under the name, Women's Christian Temperance Union (WCTU). Miss Willard sent a letter on possible Honolulu participation to the president of the YMCA. A local chapter was quickly formed by outstanding Honolulu women and shortly thereafter received its charter from the national headquarters in Evanston.

In this movement it was not the Rev. Dr. Hyde but his wife who participated and she served well: treasurer of the chapter the first two years, then as "Superintendent of Public Meetings," as member of the committee on Chinese work and as vice-president.

The WCTU, as operated by the women of Honolulu, tended to relieve Dr. Hyde of some of his temperance efforts. It allowed him to confine himself largely to planning and leading gospel temperance meetings for the natives. He prepared a temperance pamphlet for free distribution among his listeners. He also came upon some useful visual aids. "I think Sewell's plates representing the drunkard's stomach might make an effective object lesson. Mr. Forbes found in the old Chamberlain house in a box, 8 of them of large size 2 1/2 ft × 3 ft. I mounted them on a frame, and lectured about them in Kaumakapili Church during the week of prayer."[9]

Early in 1887 another temperance speaker, R. T. Booth, a representative of the Blue Ribbon League for England and her colonies, gave a month to temperance work in Honolulu on his way from New Zealand to the United States. "As I was the one," said Dr. Hyde, "who advocated and urged the project, I was anxious to insure success of the movement. Our YMCA Hall was thronged night after night for two weeks. Over 300 signed the pledges. Only one night was given to the Hawaiians, but the interest was so great, over 100 taking the pledge, that Mr. Booth has been invited to speak to the natives Sunday, Monday and Tuesday evgs . . ."[10]

It was fortunate that Hyde was able to use the YMCA resources and program in support of the temperance work. It was not a likely aspect of the Hawaiian Board program although he had the sympathetic backing of most of its members. The first temperance meetings were held at the Bethel because of the complete lack of a YMCA hall. Not only the temperance activities but the entire program of the YMCA pressed for something more than the borrowed office space in J. T. Waterhouse's "Lyceum" on Beretania Street. In September 1881 Hyde wrote to the American Board; "I happened to suggest to the YMCA at their last meeting the need of a building for Christian work among the many young men now coming to our city. The idea took hold at once, $4000 was pledged and I was appointed chairman of the Building Committee."[11] A. F. Judd and P. C. Jones were the other members. At the same time he was named to a committee to prepare a charter to enable the YMCA to hold property.

Upper left: Fort Street Congregational Church about 1885. Corner (*makai-ewa*) of Beretania Street. *Upper right:* The original Central Union Church, a dressed lava stone structure, was dedicated December 1892. This was the Hydes' home church. *Below:* Bishop Memorial Church, erected by C. R. Bishop at his own cost. This was dedicated to Mrs. Bishop in 1898.

Above: Missionary vessel *Morning Star III* was in service on a Boston-Honolulu-Micronesia run when Hyde arrived in Hawaii in 1877. He assisted materially in its schedulings, outfittings, etc. The ship was wrecked in 1884. *Below: Morning Star IV* was launched August 6, 1884, sailed from Boston, Massachusetts, November 5, 1884 in the service of the ABCFM.

Above: Bethel Church and Temperance Fountain. The original "foreign" church in Honolulu. *Below:* The first Kaumakapili Church for Hawaiians. It might be called the second Hawaiian Church, Kawaiahao Church being the oldest and largest.

Drawn by F.A. Olmstead   G.T. SANFORD. 1841.   Lith of Endicott

Upper left: Charles K. Hyde, second son of the C. M. Hydes. *Upper right:* Henry K. Hyde, older son of the Rev. Dr. and Mrs. Hyde. Author of the *Memorial To Charles McEwen Hyde.* This picture was taken in 1887, age 21. *Lower right:* Mrs. Irene Ii Brown-Holloway. Part Hawaiian girl, ward of the C. M. Hydes and lifelong friend. All photos on this page from the Hawaiian Mission Children's Society Collection.

Building plans were drawn and about a year later a cornerstone laying ceremony was held. "Our YMCA Building has begun [makai-ewa corner of Hotel and Alakea Streets]. The cornerstone is to be laid next Thursday aftn. We are hoping to get an address from Mr. Joseph Cook then. The President, Professor Pratt of Punahou[12] is to give the Historical Address, I am to read a description of the building . . ."[13]

His account was graphic. It took in the size and irregular shape of the lot, details of the entrance and exterior with a step-by-step listing of room sizes, furnishings, and the contents of the box in the cornerstone. One of the features among the furnishings was a collection of "nine magnificent paintings of volcanic activity by Mr. [Charles] Furneaux . . . These pictures are valued by the artist at fifteen hundred dollars. They were purchased and kindly placed in our hall, as the most fitting place, by the generosity of the largest business firms in the city, and by Mr. Furneaux, the artist."[14]

The Minute Book reflects the ever changing assignments of the board members. Hyde was no exception. He served and reported variously on Chinese work, temperance, prison visits, Japanese work, Queen Emma Hall, Hawaiian YMCA branches, the reading room, YMCA cemetery lots, employments, and devotional services. The shifting of assignments also brought him into periodic editorship of the YMCA Supplement of the *Friend*.

His effectiveness was enhanced by his association with many Honolulu resources. As a need appeared he could muster men and money and even agencies. Thus in 1883 he was able to arrange the transfer of the Chinese work to the Hawaiian Board. A bit later he obtained permission from that same Board to start a 6:00 a.m. Sunday service for the Japanese.

His turn on the Reading Committee gave him great pleasure. He reviewed the magazine subscriptions and the nature of the books on the shelves and applied fairly strict puritanical standards to their appropriateness for reading room listing. He mentioned one instance; "In a lively discussion with regard to the *Signs of the Times* newspaper it was finally decided to let it remain on our tables still."[15]

He also gave a statistical report of the number of readers or visitors at the reading room. He did this compilation each month. It was heavy traffic for small Honolulu town—about 250 per week.

In February 1885 he worked with Shinichi Aoki, the divinity student, to form a Japanese YMCA and became its first president.

The summer of that year found him on Molokai representing the Honolulu Association at a convention of YMCA native branches at Pukoo. After addressing the convention in Kaluaaha Church, he left for the leper settlement at Kalaupapa, by the same interisland steamer which had brought him to Molokai. Here he and other YMCA officials joined the church people in the dedication of not one but two Hawaiian (Congregational) Churches. One was the restored Siloama Church at Kalawao and the other the new Kanaana Hou Church at Kalaupapa.

The YMCA at the latter place was the gift of G. N. Wilcox and with the approval of the Board of Health was given over to the Hawaiian Board for operational care. This was an active YMCA and the special object of assistance of Honolulu friends.

In 1887 the late Queen Emma's beautiful home on Beretania Street was rented by the YMCA from the Queen's Hospital. It was renamed Queen Emma Hall and it supplied a much needed facility for YMCA work, primarily among the Hawaiians and also the Japanese and Portuguese. A. F. Judd, P. C. Jones, Henry Waterhouse and Hyde were designated as the committee on management. Said Dr. Hyde; "I have been busy this week fitting up 'Queen Emma Hall' for the Hawaiian Branch YMCA. I have secured from the various business firms donations in their several lines, and Mrs. Hyde has got subscriptions of over $50 from some of the white married ladies. We shall organize at once singing classes, debating society, English classes, Temperance meetings, lecture courses etc."[17]

Dr. Hyde worked on this old house of the late Queen for three weeks making it ready. As secretary of the committee he assumed general management of the new facility. The days of this venture were numbered from the beginning; native work of any religious nature was reflecting the divisive influence of the politics of the times. The Japanese work was moved into the Hall. But race was being pitted against race, native against missionary. Even raising the $900 yearly leasehold rent was difficult. Hyde tried to interest the Hawaiian Board in taking it over, obtained contributions covering the rent for a period, but there was no viable solution. Queen Emma Hall was returned to Queen's Hospital for other disposition. He dropped out of active YMCA work but continued making observations. Noting the upcoming 50th anniversary of the YMCA of Albert Hall in London, he suggested a letter of congratulation. Another time he put in a word for the YMCA at Kalaupapa. "A letter was read from Dr. Hyde by D. W. Corbett in regard to needed help for the YMCA at the Leper Settlement on Molokai . . . It was voted that a committee of two be appointed by the chair to carry out, if practicable, the suggestions in Dr. Hyde's letter with respect to the Leper Settlement YMCA. The President appointed Edwin Benner and D. W. Corbett as such committee."[18]

This was one of the rare instances where Hyde the advocate did not also get the action. The aggravation of his illness and the increasing pressure of other activity did not hinder him from another personal effort. In 1897 he decided to start some Sunday afternoon Bible classes. "I have recovered my strength so far as to give the YMCA a course of 8 studies on Ephesians in March & April . . . They have no Bible classes at all now. I shall repeat the same in Hawaiian on Friday evenings for the Hawaiian YMCA."

He also reported to the YMCA board that John R. Mott, a great international figure in the YMCA work, who had just arrived from Japan, would spend two weeks in Honolulu YMCA service. "We hope to have some stirring talks from him."[19]

The strong element of evangelical purpose in the YMCA program in the years Hyde was associated with it was the magnet that attracted and held him to the work. Evangelism was of kindred purpose among the American Board, Hawaiian Board, and YMCA. Dr. Hyde never gave a thought to uniting them in any way but he could and did apply the potent power of evangelism harmoniously among them all in his Christian endeavors.

NOTES

1 Honolulu YMCA, Minute Book, Feb. 21, 1879.
2 Ibid., May 22.
3 Ibid., Oct. 16.
4 Ibid., Feb. 17, 1881.
5 Ibid., Special Meeting, June 1880.
6 Letter Hyde to the Rev. N. G. Clark, ABCFM, May 9, 1881.
7 Ibid., Dec. 7.
8 Ibid.
9 Letter Hyde to the Rev. Judson Smith, ABCFM, Jan. 30, 1885.
10 Ibid., Feb. 11, 1887.
11 Letter Hyde to Clark, Sept. 24, 1881.
12 Professor Amasa Pratt, Pres. Punahou School, 1875–1878.
13 Hyde letter to Smith, Sept. 25, 1882.
14 *The Friend*, Supplement, May 1883, p. 44.
15 Honolulu YMCA, Minute Book, Feb. 21, 1879.

16 *Hawaiian Gazette*, Sept. 16, 23, 1885.
17 Letter Hyde to Smith, Mar. 5, 1887.
18 Honolulu YMCA, Minute Book, Oct. 10, 1895.
19 Letter Hyde to Smith, Feb. 10, 1897.

Chapter 11

"AS THE TWIG IS BENT"

PUNAHOU SCHOOL

Education in the Hawaiian Islands has flourished under both private and public auspices with strong overtones of missionary influence and leadership. The need for a supervised home life while classroom pursuits were followed caused the opening of many boarding schools. Vocational courses drew great attention and were emphasized in some degree at the expense of the academic studies.

Missionary children were accorded a somewhat segregated exposure to the classicism of the New England schools. Punahou School[1] was organized in 1841 for them. Its founding, its purposes and Dr. Hyde's initial identification with it are set forth in his son's book:

Considering the character of the missionary fathers and mothers, it is not strange that in their self-imposed exile from their native land, they should be extremely anxious for the education of their children. This early led to the establishment of a school for their benefit at Punahou, some two miles out on the "plains" from Honolulu near the entrance to Manoa Valley. Here under the wise instruction of Rev. Messrs. Dole, Mills and Beckwith, and their associates and successors, the mission youth had the foundations of their education laid. The standard of the school was high, its graduates usually fitted to enter the Sophomore class of any eastern college. From its halls a constant procession of young men went forth to pursue their studies in the schools of the home land. As a general thing, they maintained a high degree of scholarship and reflected credit on their adopted land and the homes and school from which they came. For years Williams College was not without a student from the islands and it is safe to say that from no other single source has it received any better material. This college honored itself as well as the recipients, when it bestowed the degree of LL. D. on two of its sons, Gen. S. C. Armstrong and Pres. Sanford B. Dole, both graduates of Punahou.

As the commercial life of the islands increased, so did the number of foreigners engaged in business. Many of them were also desirous of educational advantages for their children. Gradually the scope of the institution widened, although it has always remained a distinctly Christian school. It was inevitable that from the outset it should occupy a position of commanding importance in the educational life of the islands and such, in truth, has been its record. It has always been able to command the services of the best men in the community on its Board of Trustees and so it was no small honor to Dr. Hyde that he should have been elected to the Board within a month of his arrival . . .[2]

His first assignment was to the education committee of which he was member or chairman for the next 22 years. On the examining committee he alternated between member and chairman. In addition to these functions he was given a minor chairmanship on the spelling committee.

Shortly before his arrival matters had come to the point, at Punahou, where admission to the higher school needed a better preparation in some lower school of primary and grammar nature and the Punahou Preparatory School was decided upon as the answer. It was organized and housed in the basement of the main school building. Hyde was troubled by the inadequacy of the facilities and close proximity to the higher school. His feeling was that the face of Punahou could not be lifted as long as the Preparatory School was under heel. He moved swiftly on this thought. "The Trustees regard favorably another measure I have proposed; viz, to cut off the Preparatory from Punahou entirely and establish a Preparatory School in the city. I have in mind some eligible lots, and my plan is to build a schoolhouse with three rooms, two grades in a room . . ."[3] But no "eligible lots" were available. For the site *and* facilities he wound up at the old Armstrong[4] house in town.

The property was purchased from the Roman Catholic Church for $10,000, a healthy price for those days. He was voted "a committee for attending to the repairs and alterations . . . at an outlay of not more than $500."[5] He was always eager to get at something where he could work hand-loose and unhampered. ". . . I am just now involved in extra labor in opening the Punahou Preparatory School. The Trustees have put the premises in my hands."[6]

The education committee was the hub of his Punahou trusteeship. He it was who largely gave direction to the program of studies, acted on employments including two presidents, and conceived and planned new facilities. An example of the all-inclusive nature of his education committee routine was his proposal for a physical science department. He described this idea to the American Board. "I have long felt that we needed on these islands a naturalist to help discover and develop their physical resources and capabilities . . . I proposed a series of Resolutions, which were unanimously adopted, to the effect that we secure for Punahou . . . the services of some *Christian* naturalist for this work, one not touched with infidel notions and tendencies . . ."[7]

The moving of the preparatory, construction of a dormitory and dining hall, and planning a Punahou anniversary sidetracked the science course for a while but the obstacles were cleared away and Dr. Hyde happily announced that Mr. Bishop had agreed to give $15,000 towards a science building provided matching funds were raised elsewhere. The requirement was met with an oversubscription of $3,000 realized well within the deadline.

This gift climaxed successful correspondence with a promising candidate for the science teaching position. Hyde presented the name of Professor Lucius L. Van Slyke of Ann Arbor, Michigan, to fill the "chair of Chemistry and Natural Sciences." To attract the professor he consulted the Planters' Association and the government about supplementary work that would reinforce his pay—a kind of sponsored "moonlighting."

Hyde pored over the plans of the building and kept a close watch on the construction much like a "clerk of works."[8] The hire of Van Slyke and the completion of the science building coincided nicely for the opening of the new department.

For Punahou's fortieth birthday in June 1881 President Jones and Dr. Hyde were given the task of compiling a history. Research and writing fell largely to the latter. The book with the oversized title, *A General Catalog of the Trustees, Teachers, and Pupils of Punahou School and Oahu College, June 16, 1881,* was printed in an edition of 1000 copies, barely in time for the festivities. It was replete with statistical and historical data.

Dr. Hyde was given the first of two president-hunting assignments in 1883. He was spending his first summer in the United States since his 1877 arrival in Hawaii. He told of the successful search in a letter to the American Board:

> You will rejoice with me that my tribulations in search of a President are satisfactorily ended. On consultation with Mr. Frear I thought Rev. W. C. Merritt of Woodland, Cal. the most suitable man.
> . . . We took two days for a full and free conference and last night I received his acceptance of the Presidency . . .[9]

A few weeks after Merritt's arrival Hyde suggested a public reception for the new president. He was named Chairman for the event.

Things did not go well for President Merritt. "We are in trouble at Punahou. Mr. Merritt has got the ill will of all the boys, which they have shown by teasing him in various ways; hiding the School Bible, taking off the tongue of the bell, removing the hands from the clock, kindling a fire in the schoolroom, and their last act was shearing his horse's mane and tail. The boys, who did this act of meanness, have been found out and expelled; but fourteen others left the school and went elsewhere. There are rumors of Mr. M's having resigned, but I hear nothing as yet from him . . ."[10]

Merritt continued in the presidency until 1890. When he did resign, Hyde was off to the United States on his second presidential successor search. He was given full power to close a contract and "offer as high as $2400 salary if necessary." This time he made a "ten strike." Mr. F. A. Hosmer of Great Barrington, Massachusetts, and Mr. J. I. Wood were employed, the latter as assistant. "Mr. Hosmer is winning his way to the favor of the scholars and the public. I hear no unfavorable criticism whatever. So I may trust I have not 'gone through the woods to pick up a crooked stick at last' . . . Mr. Hosmer and Mr. Wood, his assistant, are immensely popular with the boys and girls. I feel grateful for such a result & the favoring providence that has brought it all about.

"Mr. Hosmer found the college already in successful working order, stepped right in, took the helm, & is Master of the situation from the very first. The boy that gave Mr. Merritt most trouble is Mr. Hosmer's most vigorous ally and champion. It is wonderful how much a little tact will accomplish."[11]

His delight spilled over into a letter to General S. C. Armstrong, president of Hampton Institute and himself a graduate of Punahou. "It seems as if I was specially favored in getting such a man as Mr. Hosmer for Punahou. . ."[12] He reached a peak of enconium in speaking of his new president.

Punahou's semi-centennial was now at hand. Hyde suggested that General Armstrong be invited to address the gathering. He also felt that an endowment gift by banker Bishop would be appropriate for the commemoration. He was successful on both counts; Armstrong delivered the semi-centennial address and Bishop gave $50,000 in 6% bonds with no conditions attached.[13] Hyde spoke on the program, representing the Punahou trustees.

In 1892 he gave the Punahou commencement address in a "handsomely decorated Central Union Chruch." About this time he wrote of serving on building committees for Oahu College and the Kamehameha School for Girls "for both of which we have received unique and attractive plans from our resident architects, Ripley & Reynolds."[14] The new building at Punahou was a much needed recitation hall, donated by Mr. Bishop and named Pauahi Hall after Mrs. Bishop. A year later Dole Hall, costing $70,000, was completed.

"President trouble" haunted the Hyde trail, cropping out again in 1895. ". . .several teachers who wanted to get rid of Prof. Hosmer have resigned and have brought charges of the most frivolous character. We have sent to Boston for new teachers, and hope the trouble will blow over . . .As chairman of the Educational Committee, much of the work, as well as the opprobrium of this scandal, comes on me personally, but so far nothing has disturbed my equanimity. I feel very sorry for Mr. Hosmer, so unjustly put upon his defense. Few men could show so clear a five years' record under the severe scrutiny to which he has been subjected. . ."[15] Hosmer survived the ordeal and continued on to round out ten years of sound service to the school.

Hyde had filled in as secretary of the trustees from time to time but beginning with the meeting of January 10, 1894 he filled the secretaryship continuously with permanent election to the position June 19, 1894. By mid-1898 his health was so precarious that he asked relief from further service in that capacity. In May 1899 he gave up his cherished membership on the Education Committee.

His was a contribution to Punahou growth and well-being that has never been fully described. Someone at any institution of this character assumes the thankless task of watching over personnel: the employments, the resignations, and the dismissals. Inherent in these matters are the student dissents, the teacher positionings, the administration defects. As he worked with tremendous energy on curriculum, anniversary celebrations, fund raising, construction, and personnel matters, and his efforts here were notable, it was opprobrium, as he himself termed it, which he of all of the trustees had to endure the most. Walking into the troublous agitations of individuals seems to produce the same negativism that accompanies the stride of the zealot or crusader. Be that as it may, Punahou is deep in his debt for his faithful, energetic and intelligent service.

THE KAMEHAMEHA SCHOOLS

Unlike his quick assimilation into Punahou School affairs within days of his arrival in Hawaii, Dr. Hyde's connection with the Kamehameha Schools did not commence for seven years. In Punahou he started his trusteeship in a small but "old" school; in the Kamehameha Schools that were yet to come he would be starting from scratch.

Not long after the Hydes came they met Charles Reed Bishop and his wife, beautiful Hawaiian Princess Bernice Pauahi. A warm friendship developed which would ultimately cast Hyde in a leading role in most of the community and charitable efforts supported in part or in full by the Bishops.

Their first meeting was likely in the Fort Street Church, officially known as the Second Foreign Church and Congregation of Honolulu. Bishop had just been re-elected a trustee of the church as the Hydes were nearing Honolulu harbor in June 1877. They joined the church as regular members. As the weeks and months rolled on Bishop could observe the energy and dedication of Dr. Hyde in project after project. At the same time Hyde was subconsciously hitching his ecclesiastical wagon to Bishop's economic star.

In the long Bishop-Hyde friendship there were many varying bases of dialogue.

Among charities Bishop was not so inclined to go all out into missionary and church ventures as Hyde desired to lead him. He was more education minded, perhaps because of some lacks in his own schooling which ended with the eighth grade. He was not concerned whether the education he might support was carried on under missionary direction—he was for education. At the time of the Hyde arrival Bishop was president of the Board of Education under appointment by King Kalakaua. Industrial education was stressed while he occupied the position.

Hyde was a frequent visitor at Bishop's bank and the families exchanged visits at their respective homes and at picnics as often as busy schedules would permit. The Bishops lived in a beautiful two-story house, *Haleakala* (house of the sun), in the heart of old Honolulu, on the site of the present Bishop Trust Co., Ltd., building.

Dr. Hyde, as his visits here increased in regularity, was welcomed more and more as a counsellor. On one occasion discussion arose concerning lands which Mrs. Bishop had inherited from her cousin, Princess Ruth Keelikolani, who died May 14, 1883. These had come to Ruth from Princess Kamamalu and Governor Kekuanaoa and made up a substantial block of the royal family acres. Combined with those Mrs. Bishop already owned they gave her one ninth of the land of the Kingdom of Hawaii.

Ownership of this enormous acreage was a responsibility of grave proportions. She was now an individual possessed of great wealth, far greater in potential value than anyone could dream. Decision on a testamentary distribution was urgent because of Mrs. Bishop's physical condition. She was a sick woman.

The Bishops talked with friend Hyde about suitable charities. Mrs. Bishop wanted an institution, perhaps a hospital, but it must bear the name of her illustrious great grandfather, Kamehameha I. There was a hospital in Honolulu, Queen's, and it was a viable house of mercy.

Dr. Hyde made observations of his own in the talks. His was a concern for the welfare and education of native youth. He had studied the needs of the natives closely. His mission from the American Board was directed to them. He had organized anew the North Pacific Missionary Institute; he was a leader in the management of Kawaiahao Seminary; he was closely in touch with the operation of the Hilo Boys' Boarding School.

The idea of a school, two schools, one for boys and one for girls, situated in Honolulu, for boarding and day scholars, emerged from their talks. The details were worked out in her will and codicils by Francis March Hatch, distinguished lawyer of Honolulu.

After Mrs. Bishop's death October 11, 1884, the five trustees named in the will started the work of organizing the Kamehameha Schools. Her husband, Charles R. Bishop, was first named among the trustees followed by Dr. Hyde, a trusted first choice of Mrs. Bishop.[16] The others were William Owen Smith, Samuel Mills Damon, and Charles Montague Cooke. Hyde's role was not so much with business of the trust. He was to become the centering force in evolving the philosophy, principles of operation, and the program of studies of the new institution.

In the flow of letters to the American Board he made little mention of his work with the new schools. It was almost a life apart for him. He did write fully of his trusteeship when the provisions of the will were published:

I have sent to Dr. Clark a newspaper with full accounts of the funeral of Mrs. C. R. Bishop. He will remember having met her when he visited the Islands. She was the last of the Kamehameha blood. Her husband is one of the party that came to the Islands enroute to Oregon, but were persuaded to stay in Honolulu. Judge Lee was another of that party of young men in search of a fortune. He drew up the system of laws for the Islands, and was the first Chief Justice of the Supreme Court. His widow returned to the States and there married Pro. Yeomans, (of the *Popular Science Monthly*). Dr. Wood was another (now living on his income at Newton, Mass.). Mr. Bishop became a banker, and has a large property in his own right. Mrs. Bishop received most of her estate from Ruth Keliiokalani [sic], sister of Kamehameha IV and K V. She has now devoted it, as you will see from the paper, by the terms of her will, mainly to the Education of boys and girls. She names five Trustees, myself among the number. I had often talked with Mr. and Mrs. Bishop about such schools.

The provision she has made is an exceedingly wise and liberal one. The Trustees have very few restrictions. The fund will probably amount ultimately to $500,000, when all the life interests shall have reverted to this fund for the Kamehameha Schools.[17] Her wish was that a boys' school should begin at once. Mr. Bishop will pass over at once to this fund the property in which a life's interest was willed to him, so that it can be available immediately towards putting up a building. There have been heavy expenses in putting into proper order the real estate inherited from

Ruth, but by Dec. 2, when the will is to be probated, shortly after which probably the Trustees will begin their official duties, the annual income of the estate will be known and what part of it can become available at once for the support of the schools. This provision for Christian education, so wise and so ample, relieves my mind of one great occasion for anxiety in forecasting the future of the Hawaiian people. The work done by the missionaries is now to be carried on by this fund given by a Hawaiian chiefess for the lasting benefit of her people, as notable and honorable a gift, as was Kamehameha III's gift of lands to every occupant of the soil, at the time he gave them also a constitutional government. If the young can be trained to become useful men and women, a long step has been taken towards counteracting the many evil influences now at work, and tending to the speedy extinction of the whole Hawaiian race.[18]

A valuable proponent of Hyde's vocational education idea was the Rev. William Brewster Oleson, principal of the Hilo Boys' Boarding School. They had met when Mr. Oleson made a brief stopover in Honolulu on his way to Hilo to take charge of the school. In the fleeting encounter Oleson greatly impressed the Hydes. Deeper acquaintance caused Hyde to exclaim, "I think if there is a Christian hero in these islands it is Mr. Oleson. He has accomplished a wonderful work in keeping up and developing the Hilo Boys' School in the face of obstacles and opposition that would have cowered completely anyone with less self-sacrificing devotion to Christian work. . . I find Mr. Oleson's school, as a school, even more admirable than I had anticipated. It is a model institution for self-government as well as self-support, and the boys who go out from it must have in fine development this most essential element of a manly character. But I am pained to see how little Mr. Oleson has to do with. It calls out the constant exercise of ingenuity and patience but also drains terribly the nervous vitality."[19]

Mr. Bishop was also becoming acquainted with Oleson after Hyde had introduced them. In meetings which followed, Oleson was drawn into the Bishops' inner circle where he could freely air his views regarding this industrial or vocational education. So impressed was Bishop, he started contributions to the account of the Hilo school. Hyde was behind the promptings of these charitable gifts.

The Bishop family conferences led directly to the employment of Oleson as the first principal of the Kamehameha School for Boys under salary conditions worked out by Dr. Hyde. "We give him $3000 a year with house and pasturage free (somewhat larger salary than I have you see) and six months leave of absence, salary continuing while he visits the States to get ideas and recuperation. . .We have spent nearly $2000 already in simply fencing in the school lot, but have $21,000 cash in the bank. Mr. O. wants to make this a distinctively Industrial School not simply 'manual labor' as was the Hilo school."[20]

The impact of Hyde's pursuit of Bishop Estate matters was profound. Mrs. Bishop's land holdings were a material blessing of unknown promise and her husband's sage and unfailing judgment was as solid a contribution to her purposes as the remarkable lavas, soils, and ponds of her wealth. Hyde was favored to work in this blend of physical and human resources. He did not depart from his original mission to the Hawaiian natives. But being Hyde he would adorn the path the schools would take with solid Christian principles, thereby gaining greater practical realization of his mission than he could possibly have done otherwise.

How important he was to the new task can be determined in a brief look at his attendance record at Bishop Estate board meetings and the proportion of these meetings in which he as vice-president would fill the chair in the absence of Bishop. Frequency of meetings per month varied with the need; always one, sometimes as many as four. His record was without a blemish. He missed no meetings except when he was off the island. Bishop presided from the inception of the trust through August, 1887. Beginning then, Hyde was in the chair; three meetings in 1887, ten in 1889, all in 1891, half in 1892, and all from January, 1893 through May 5, 1899. This last was his final meeting with the trustees before his decease. Even when William Fessenden Allen was elected president in 1898 and could not preside due to absence from Honolulu, Hyde continued to serve as chairman. This recital from the record therefore is evidence of his importance to the trust.

He was aware of his responsibility. "Hon. C. R. Bishop leaves for the States today. This leaves me nominally at the head of the Kamehameha Trustees," was his laconic comment.[21]

As the time for opening the Boys' School was approaching it became apparent that the wording of Mrs. Bishop's will needed some clarification or interpretation. No one, not excepting her husband, was as well qualified to do this as Hyde. He was "appointed a Committee of One to present a Report at the next meeting in the matter of a situation [site] for the Boys' School: its object, aims, method, time and extent."[22] He brought his report, previously circulated, to the meeting of December 23, 1885. *The Prospectus of the Kamehameha Schools,* his own title, was quickly adopted. Except for minor alterations at that meeting, it has constituted a principal guideline, after the will, of Mrs. Bishop's intentions as to the purposes and direction of the schools.

It is now apparent why Mrs. Bishop named him to a trusteeship. Someone was needed from among the five trustees who understood the problems of educating the native youth and could apply himself to that aspect of the administration of the trust. It worked out that way. Generally, the responsibility for managing staff, operation, and program of the schools was his, and its successful outcome can be credited to him.

The trusteeship did something for him in turn. Here was a newfound solidity and satisfaction which added buoyancy and confidence to his step as he walked his religious and community beat in Hawaii.

If there is any one popularly misunderstood intention of Mrs. Bishop as regards her will, it likely centers in the question of admission. She had two men, her husband and Dr. Hyde, standing by to assist lawyer Hatch translate her hopes into legal language. As approved by her, the will states, in part, a broad provision for the education of youth with only a single conditional preference for native youth: "[the trustees shall] devote a portion of each year's income to the support and education of orphans, and others in indigent circumstances, giving the preference to Hawaiians of pure or part aboriginal blood. . . I also give to my Trustees full power to. . . regulate the admission of pupils. . . "[23]

These brief quotations indicate the stature and dignity of her will, a great document; one which has survived many attacks but still continues to provide clear guidelines as to her fixed purposes. The restriction to part or full blooded natives, as followed from the first class admitted in 1887, results from the power given the trustees by Mrs. Bishop in her will but it undoubtedly was in line with Mrs. Bishop's inclinations and has been perpetuated because of the availability of qualified pupils. The flow of applicants has never slowed. With intermarriage through the years, children of some Hawaiian ancestry present many other strains and the result is a student body in whose veins flows blood of races from every corner of the globe.

Dr. Hyde assumed an enormous burden in his efforts for the schools, one which the other three trustees (Bishop was in San Francisco most of the time) were not unwilling for him to take. It was he who drove out to the campus in his horse and buggy, almost daily, to check the maintenance, the well digging, the program of studies, the print shop, dining hall and kitchen, religious program—in short, everything! *He* was the education committee of the board of trustees. Bishop invariably wrote to him about construction, scholarship, supplies, salaries, food costs and the like. He also maintained the letter writing to mainland teaching aspirants, a job in itself.

But this was only half of it! The same trustees, plus two more, directed the Bishop Museum. Here Hyde helped with most museum matters except finance. The other trustees again had no quarrel with the arrangements. The wonder of it is that he could handle the schools and the museum and have any time for his NPMI or any of the other myriad agencies on his schedule.

The Rev. Mr. Oleson arrived in Honolulu from Hilo to start his Kamehameha principalship in early summer, 1886, with neither a school nor a house. He too was a planner and builder and was due to be closely associated with his old friend, Dr. Hyde, in the latter's role of educational trustee. A glimpse of some of the action is revealed in an American Board letter: ". . . I have been very busy with Mr. Oleson in plans for the buildings and organization of the Kamehameha Schools. We have tramped over the 85 acre lot hither and yon, but are not yet decided where to locate the buildings and how to group them. The lower part of the lot is a pile of lava boulders, strewn around in inextricable confusion: but the upper part has two slopes and a plateau that afford magnificent views of the City, the peaks and valleys, the ocean and the Waianae Range."[24]

The school opened about the first of October, 1887 but the opening exercises had to be delayed until November 4; two of the teachers did not find the promised passage from San Francisco available. When a program of opening could be held it was a community celebration. Dr. Hyde was in charge. King Kalakaua and members of the royal family attended. There were members of the legislature, people from the board of education and public and private schools. Hyde's keynote address praised Mrs. Bishop and her purposes in making the substantial bequest for the new school. The King spoke, expressing his pleasure that such an enterprise was now available for the education of native subjects.

Trustee commissions came as an unexpected new kind of income.

Hyde, probably pleased, was perplexed. With typical candor he submitted his reactions to the American Board:

. . . One of the rules of the Board, as I understand it, is that no outside income can be allowed the missionaries. It must all be accounted for to the Mission. Now, as there is no *Mission* here, what I asked was, that the commission I receive (unexpectedly to myself and entirely unsought) as one of the Kamehameha Trustees, I might be allowed to spend, for the present, in repairs on the house I occupy. . . In such a community as this, where there is so much idle gossip, I do not want it thrown in my face that in addition to my regular salary I take and use for my own emolument, without any authority so to do and in contravention of the rules of the Board, the money I received as a Trustee of the Kamehameha School. . . The Apostle Paul has set all ministers an example of special carefulness about responsibility of trust funds. . .[25]

The commissions hovered around an annual thousand dollars in the first years of the estate, climbed to about $1500 in 1892 and reached $2000 in 1898. Hyde adjusted a relinquishment of his salary in almost exact proportion as his commissions mounted. Since they about equalled his $2000 salary in 1898 he surrendered the whole salary at that time.

In June 1888 he wrote, "Hon. C. R. Bishop is putting up at his own expense a building for a Home School for Boys, a Preparatory Department for the Industrial School for larger boys."[26] The idea for this departure from Mrs. Bishop's will came to Hyde as he observed the numbers of homeless and orphaned six, seven, and eight-year-old boys uncared for in Honolulu. He took the problem to Mr. Bishop who moved quickly to authorize plans. He asked the trustees to approve his new project at the same meeting at which he showed the plans. This became his favorite object at the campus.[27] Bishop picked up the running expenses of the youthful school when budget money of the estate was too tight.

Scarcely had the Preparatory Department settled into its new quarters when the Boys' School was readying itself for its first graduation exercises. Ten boys had completed the course of study. Each had some part in the literary recitations of the June 1891 evening. General Armstrong who had been invited by Dr. Hyde to speak at the Punahou Commencement (semi-centennial) was one of the speakers. "This is a long step in advance above everything attempted by Hawaiian boys," he said.

A change in leadership in the Boys' School was shaping up. Oleson had in surpassing fashion completed the opening-to-graduation cycle. Hawaii's politics were involving him as an anti-royalist to the point of personal danger. Tired and worried he decided to resign to take effect July 1893. A Hyde report of this to the American Board followed. ". . . The assistant principal, Mr. Richards (son of Mr. Richards formerly printer of the *N.Y. Observer*), is engaged to a daughter of J. B. Atherton. They are to be married in June. The young couple will then spend a year in the States, and on Mr. Richards' return he will take Mr. Oleson's place. . . I consider his [Oleson's] departure a great loss to the Islands."[28]

Bishop and Hyde wrote Richards frequently with suggestions as to what and where to study and visit and of the emphases that should obtain at Kamehameha. In one letter Hyde spoke of hoping a "Christian" machinist could be found. It was about this time that he was searching for a "Christian natural science teacher" for Punahou.

In another letter he covered his attitude toward textbooks. "In regard to the purchase of schoolbooks, you will remember that the school has been managed hitherto without much use of textbooks. The effort has been to make the accurate use of *language* the main feature of instruction. To this end we do not need many textbooks to be studied by rote; nor those to be used in 'the higher branches' so called, for which we are not prepared and do not want introduced. Bearing this in mind, yet aware that textbooks may be of great value as books of reference, alike for teacher and pupil, it was voted to authorize you to purchase such books as you might wish to secure for the school, limiting the whole amount so appropriated and available to $50."[29]

A few days later he wrote of the experimental nature of the school, higher education, and a schedule of manual training schools:

The whole school is experimental. The Trustees do not fix anything without sufficient trial. The tenure of office for teachers must at first be tentative. We can't give too much and we don't want to give too little, and qualifications cannot be measured by any percentage system and graded by salaries into classes . . .

We do not want higher education at all in the Kamehameha Schools. Provisions for that will be made in other ways in exceptional cases. Mr. Bishop is giving the two boys (Charles E. King and Samuel Keliinoi) at Oswego, a fine opportunity because they had the stuff in them that seemed to warrant it. . .

I hope that you will see all you can of the Manual Training Schools. I suppose you have seen the Trade Schools, and the Pratt Institute, the Drexel in Philadelphia, the Boston School of Mechanic Arts, Purdue University, Chicago, Toledo, St. Louis, the Miller (?) School in San Francisco. You can pick up a great many hints.[30]

Hyde introduced the idea of mainland visits for stimulation and information and administrators and others continue such study trips to the present day.

The Girls' School was next. "Mr. Oleson wants the new Kamehameha Girls' School built near his Boys' School. I myself favor a location in the other direction far from the boys. I see by the newspaper that the question has come up in Boston with decided action in favor of mixed schools as against separate schools for boys and girls. I do not know how the other Trustees stand in regard to this matter. We are just beginning to talk it over."[31]

His reflections on the subject of mixed education appear somewhat unresolved. But such was not the case. He had operated in a climate of unmixed education in all his contacts with youth. His was the lead in placing the condition, "two schools, one for boys and one for girls" in Mrs. Bishop's will. Two schools were eventually established and remained apart, except for some extra curricular activities, each largely autonomous, until recent years.

Money, ever a hurdle, was not coming in rapidly enough to satisfy Mr. Bishop; and the current upheaval in kingdom politics, whereby royal rule was being altered in favor of successive forms of less autocratic government, added to his concern. In the estate minutes of May 6, 1893 he speaks "against starting the Girls' School now."

Shortly, however, income increased, politics changed for the better and to such degree that in the spring of 1894 we find Miss Ida May Pope hired away from Kawaiahao Seminary as principal of the new Kamehameha School for Girls. She followed the Hyde formula and went to the United States for the customary visiting while building plans were started for a site "as far away as possible," on the *makai* side of King Street.

Hyde was enthusiastic about the new school and as usual was engrossed in construction progress. "I hope to get out soon a woodcut from the new Kamehameha Girls' School," he wrote, "with a description of the buildings which are unique yet very tasteful though simple in style, V shaped with Assembly at the apex, and at the terminal points the Dining Hall and Gymnasium. I sketched a plan as a hollow square, but our architects have done better, for convenience and for attractive appearance."[32] The school was officially opened December 19, 1894, Mrs. Bishop's birthday.

He waxed ecstatic, "It is a pleasure to be connected with such an institution as the Kamehameha Schools where there is no lack of money; but the Trustees can do whatever the welfare of the schools demands."[33] Mr. Bishop would scarcely have subscribed to such exultation as regards money and spending. He was frugal personally and demanded frugality in any operation in which he might be involved. He could not tolerate deficit spending and this applied at Kamehameha as well as anywhere else.

Miss Ida May Pope proved an excellent choice as principal. She initiated the custom of celebrating Mrs. Bishop's birthday at a Girls' School Founder's Day dinner. Hyde said, "I wish that the Deputation could have been guests at the dinner given in the Girls' School, cooked and served by the girls, the matron taking her seat among the guests. It would have been a revelation of the possibilities there are in Hawaiian girls."[34]

He commented again 18 months later:

The Class Day Exercises were given in as good *style* as I have ever seen anywhere. Of course the essays were not much above the ordinary *level*. Last evening the Graduating Class read their essays and sang their songs. The whole affair was most creditable to Miss Pope and her assistants. In fact, we have as fine a corps of teachers as I have ever seen brought together in any Girls' School. Admiral Beardslee said to me as we came away that he was more impressed with the evidence of Missionary work in Honolulu than in any community among the many he had visited where Missionaries had labored. There was a delightful combination of a high ideal of life and careful attention to the practical duties of ordinary every day work.[35]

There were now alumni, and activity for them was in order. The matter was talked about, but with expenses growing at the Boys' School and the Preparatory Department, and with the opening of the Girls' School and the departure of Oleson, alumni activity was delayed to a better day. It was not until the formation of the Chas. R. Bishop Trust in 1895 that alumni needs could be funded.

Theodore Richards, now principal of the Boys' School, was a staunch advocate of an alumni association and he gently urged support of it upon Hyde. Shortly, Richards was pleased to learn from him of favorable action:

I wish to bring to your notice one of the provisions made by Hon. C. R. Bishop in a deed of trust, executed Aug. 1, 1895, so that any action you may take in connection with an alumni association of the Kamehameha Schools may not be taken in ignorance of this provision of the Trust, and its conditions.

"Under Subdivision 5, Article 8: For aiding in the support of an Alumni Association, or Social Club, for the benefit of those who shall have attended Kamehameha Schools not less than two years, the sum of three hundred dollars [annually], said sum to be expended under and in accordance with the rules to be approved by my said Trustees and their successors."[36]

This annual contribution from the Chas. R. Bishop Trust is discretionary with the Trustees, but through the years of payment it has been a lifeline to the continuity of alumni action.

A chapel for Kamehameha was next on the list. Mr. Bishop had departed for San Francisco in March 1894, never to return, although his ashes were brought back to the islands in June 1915. He sold his Bishop & Co. bank to Samuel Mills Damon; he was faring well financially in the Bay area. He could afford the money to build the chapel he had discussed frequently with both Hyde and Theodore Richards. An initial gift of $50,000, supplemented by half as much more, provided a beautiful church edifice on a campus site *mauka* of King Street, close to the present Farrington High School auditorium. It was constructed of the reddish brown lava stone from the quarry above the campus which was also the source of stone for the recitation building of the Boys' School and the first buildings of the Bishop Museum.

Correspondence streamed between Mr. Bishop in San Francisco and Dr. Hyde in Honolulu regarding construction details. The structure was dedicated December 19, 1897 with addresses by Damon and Hyde. The latter also read the Prayer of Dedication. The schools had a chapel; they now needed a minister. He wrote at once to the American Board. "I write to ask if you know of any young minister who has had experience enough in the pastorate to know that he is not mistaken in his calling, whom you would recommend as chaplain at our Kamehameha Schools. Our chapel was dedicated on the 19th ult. and I send you the *Gazette* with a picture and an account of the exercises. We do not want anyone who is pokey, dull or broken down."[37]

Time was running out for him. He left for the United States on the last "sick call" in 1899 and could arrange nothing more for his chapel. There was one more letter, his last one on school matters, which he addressed to Uldrick Thompson. It bravely illustrates his mental energy and drive even in the face of approaching death:

I have sent to Mr. Carter the reports of Hampton School for this year. . . I think you will find them suggestive of possibilities for development of the Kamehameha Schools. I have just had a call from Mr. and Mrs. Oleson who wished to be remembered to you. I am most decidedly stronger than when I reached here, but cannot say I am a "well" man. Mr. Oleson is suffering from kidney trouble also, I am sorry to learn. It would seem as if we were never to have a mail from the Islands. I am getting very impatient to know what is being done.

. . . I would like to see our Kamehameha Schools doing for the Hawaiians what is well expressed in the matter of this year's graduating class at Hampton, 'We lift as we rise.' There are a great many perplexing features in the problems before us and I wish I could bring to them better power of thinking than I have now in my disabled condition.

. . . The religious tone of the schools is of preeminent importance, though some of the Trustees may not give it much attention.[38]

Dr. Hyde was connected with the Kamehameha Schools for only 15 years. Within that time as a trusted associate of Mr. Bishop he supervised its early beginnings. He was favored with sterling workers who were given the complex responsibility of creating the several parts of Kamehameha: William Brewster Oleson, Uldrick Thompson, Sr., Theodore Richards, and Ida May Pope.

All moved in concert with him, thus establishing a tradition of trustee-sharing of management which rounded out an enduring relationship among trustees, administrators, instructors, students, and parents which

50 years later I could fairly describe as the "Kamehameha Family." Intimate trustee participation in school affairs could be onerous on school administration but it has assured an unbroken emphasis with the native student upon character, willingness to work, and self-discipline.

PUBLIC SCHOOLS

Dr. Hyde turned up in unexpected roles upon occasion, one of which was in public education. He could have been expected to be seen in the public schools dealing with curriculum, building, or personnel. It was none of these. "It is only since I came," he wrote to the American Board, "that the number of teachers has so increased that they could find in their numbers the necessity and the warrant for any special bond. I have talked over this matter with some of the principal teachers and called a public meeting last week in which a constitution I had prepared was adopted and printed for signatures from teachers here and on other islands wishing to join such an association. It is proposed to have a Teachers' Convention the first week in January. We shall have essays, discussions, methods of teaching etc etc."[39] This undertaking in the teaching profession was the forerunner of the Hawaii Education Association.

At successive annual meetings of the teachers he expounded on but one subject, "industrial education." This was also a fetish with Bishop, who was on the Board of Education from 1869 to 1894 with the exception of a few years when not reappointed by Kalakaua. It was among such men as Bishop, Oleson, Armstrong, and Hyde that an educational philosophy based upon good work habits, the dignity of work itself, and its importance to the social and economic welfare of the State was preached and promulgated. It affected the educational policy of every private boarding and day school and public school. Hyde was an ardent disciple of this thought and chose to utilize the public school teacher group as one means of promoting the idea. This was evident as he himself admitted: " . . . While I cannot in self respect have anything to do with the present Board of Education, I have thought it a good opportunity through the Teachers' Convention which I organized three years ago to call public attention to the alarming increase of vagabonding among young Hawaiians and urge as partial remedies the opening of Evening Schools and the development of a system of Industrial Education for boys and girls in connection with the government common schools[40]

. . . I have built up an influence outside of that Board, to which it is compelled to give attention and various useful reforms have thus been secured. . . "41

When Kalakaua was forced to make more acceptable appointments in July 1887 and Bishop was restored to the Board of Education, Hyde expected too much, too soon, in public education. His only recorded criticism of his banker friend came at this time:

. . . Nothing has made me feel so sore since I came back to the Islands as the conduct of the present Board of Education. One would have thought that Hon. C. R. Bishop, Prof. W. D. Alexander, and S. M. Damon would have had some regard for the interests and morality, not to say the poor Hawaiian children, in their appointments. But to my great grief the Kohala school is put in charge of the Anglican preacher, and an old man who never taught a day in his life, notwithstanding Father Bond's earnest remonstrances. Mr. Hitchcock has been summarily dismissed from Lahainaluna notwithstanding Father Castle's appeal in his behalf. (He himself is away, superintending the printing of an English-Hawaiian Dictionary in San Francisco). Men of open immorality and brazen infidelity are retained in schools though I begged Mr. Bishop to put decent appointees in their places. . . Unfortunately I know of no capable teachers, whom I could recommend, and so have no power to counteract all this mismanagement by urging the appointment of suitable teachers. As I look at things, it would have been very easy for the present Board to have empowered Mr. Hitchcock to look up suitable teachers in California. . .42

An incomplete sequel was described a year later:

You may remember that I protested in vain last year against the action of the Board of Education in dismissing Mr. Hitchcock, and appointing as Principal (Lahainaluna) one against whose character there were most disparaging stories. The result has been as I feared. The man has shown out his real character, and has been asked to resign. I have been asked to nominate someone for the Principalship. It is too bad to have this old missionary school run down as it has done. . . but it is a hard place to fill. I do not know anyone I could recommend. Do you know of any Christian teacher who would like such a position, salary $1500 and a house? For help, there is the pick of the boys in school to do the house-work. . .[43]

There was ample justification for Bishop's appointments. The public schools, under Walter Murray Gibson as president of the Board of Education, had been allowed to deteriorate; pupil inattendance, teacher indifference, and inept supervision had damaged their character. There was a serious drop in inquiries from potential teaching applicants. When Bishop and the others came back into direction of school affairs, they were compelled to pick up the close-at-hand school leaders available.

Public education was not a field that appealed to Hyde. He had to operate under restraints inherent in all public institutions. He could not fully apply his dreams of Christian dignity and creed as he could and did in his private school world, but he tried.

FREE KINDERGARTENS

Free kindergartens were thought of as a partial solution to family and home problems. In the development of such schools. Hyde, with his wife perhaps more in the lead, became involved. "A few of us met at Mr. Damon's [Francis W.] home to talk over starting a free kindergarten for Hawaiian children of 3-6 years of age. It seemed a very desirable under-taking and Mrs. Hyde agreed to be one of a Committee to try and raise the necessary money for 6 mos."[44]

Money was tight, but if a new door could be opened, he would never hesitate. He wrote soon again; "We are expecting to start this afr'n a Kindergarten for Hawaiian children; Mrs. Hyde is on the Executive Committee. Mr. F. W. Damon and myself constitute the Advisory Board. It was Mr. Damon's idea, a good one, if we can only get the means and the teacher to make it a successful experiment."[45]

Things moved. One month later: ". . . we are now planning to open a Kindergarten for the Portuguese. Mr. Damon has had one in operation for the Chinese for the year past, supported by a friend of Mrs. Damon in the States. She has agreed to pay the running expenses of the school for the next year also. Mrs. Hyde made an appeal for the Hawaiian Kindergarten at the last meeting of the Woman's Board, and it was so cordially received that she is emboldened to go on still further and make an appeal at the next meeting to start a Portuguese Kindergarten. . .

Mrs. Rice who has unexpectedly received $500 from some investment has offered to give it for a schoolhouse for the Portuguese Mission."[46]

One can sense his pride in his wife's engagement in this work. About a year later he was writing again on her newest effort. "Mrs. Hyde has organized the Kindergarten Department of the Woman's Board for the better supervision and sustenance of these schools now in operation among the Chinese, Japanese, Portuguese, and Hawaiian."[47]

Mrs. Hyde was housewife to her family and hostess to the continual flow of missionary families and the periodical meetings of church groups, Cousins' Society, Social Science Association, and the like. These activities could command her full time and therefore her husband did not press her to assume outside duties; but she found time for a few, among which was this work with the little children.

But Dr. Hyde did the reporting to the American Board. "The Kindergarten Schools are full to overflowing," he wrote enthusiastically, "and the ladies are taking much interest in the extension of the work. It has hitherto been managed as a Department of the Woman's Board, of which Mrs. Hyde is President. A plan is now on foot to organize a Kindergarten Association, making Mrs. Hyde, President of the new organization. The meetings of the Woman's Board are full & enthusiastic & visiting ladies are full of expressions of admiration at the amount of work done and the executive ability manifest in the work. There are few communities of the small size of Honolulu, where can be found so many ladies of such more than ordinary ability."[48]

His only other comment in a letter to the American Board came in 1897. "The Kindergarten work is making headway every year. Mrs. Hyde went to Ewa with a large company last Saturday, to open officially the *Ewa Plantation* Kindergarten, the first of many we hope to see."[49]

This forerunner of public school kindergartens still fulfills a pre-school need in Hawaii today as the Kindergarten & Children's Aid Association —a notably successful continuation of the starting days when Mrs. Hyde was one of the workers.

NOTES

1 The name Oahu College was given to the school in 1841 and was used along with the name Punahou School, somewhat confusingly, until 1934 when the school officially became Punahou School.

2 Henry Knight Hyde, op. cit., pp. 49-51.

3 Letter Hyde to the Rev. N. G. Clark, ABCFM, Apr. 8, 1882.

4 The Armstrong premises, originally the site of the Rev. W. L. Richards' home when he was advising Kamehameha III, became the founding site of St. Louis College and after use as Punahou Preparatory School, were added to the grounds of the Anglican Cathedral.

5 Punahou School, Secretary's Record, Dec. 13, 1882.

6 Letter Hyde to Clark, Dec. 16.

7 Letter Hyde to Clark, Jan. 17, 1881.

8 Clerk of (the) works, a building inspector hired by the owner to check construction.

9 Letter Hyde to the Rev. E. K. Alden, ABCFM, Sept. 21, 1883.

10 Letter Hyde to the Rev. Judson Smith, ABCFM, Jan. 14, 1887.

11 Ibid., Sept. 26, Oct. 18, 1890.

12 Letter Hyde to General S. C. Armstrong, Hampton Institute, Oct. 20.

13 Letter Hyde to Smith, June 30, 1891.

14 Ibid., Feb. 3, 1894.

15 Ibid., Aug. 1, 1895.

16 Lydia Aholo, a child at the time and a member of the first class at the Kamehameha School for Girls, a friend of the Bishops and a lifelong friend of the Hydes, told me that Dr. Hyde was Mrs. Bishop's first choice as trustee.

17 His estimate was generous for that time but far from an estimated market value of a thousand times that sum and more in 1970.

18 Letter Hyde to Smith, Nov. 15, 1884.

19 Ibid., June 26, July 15, 1885.

20 Ibid.

21 Ibid., Apr. 12, 1889.

22 B. P. Bishop Estate, Minute Books, Aug. 6, 1885, p. 3. The Prospectus is printed in the appendix.

23 Hon. Mrs. Bernice P. Bishop, *Last Will and Testament*, Oct. 4, 1884.

24 Letter Hyde to Alden, Nov. 6, 1886.

25 Letter Hyde to the Rev. E. E. Strong, ABCFM, June 13, 1888.

26 Ibid., June 27.

27 The new campus of the Preparatory Dept. on Kapalama Heights is named the "Charles Reed Bishop" campus.

28 Letter Hyde to Smith, Mar. 29, 1892.

29 Letter Hyde to Theodore Richards, Mar. 28, 1893.

30 Ibid., Apr. 8.

31 Letter Hyde to Smith, Nov. 21, 1890.

32 Ibid., June 28, 1894.

33 Ibid., Mar. 6, 1895.

34 Ibid., Dec. 26.

35 Ibid., June 30, 1897.

36 Letter Hyde to Theodore Richards, Dec. 13, 1895.

37 Letter Hyde to Smith, Jan. 7, 1898.

38 Letter Hyde to Uldrick Thompson, July 24, 1899.

39 Hyde Letter to Clark, Nov. 19, 1881.

40 Ibid., Jan. 10, 1884

41 Letter Hyde to Smith, Dec. 30.

42 Ibid., Sept. 12, 1887.

43 Ibid., Oct. 20, 1888.

44 Ibid., Jan. 11, 1893.
45 Ibid., Feb. 1.
46 Ibid., Feb. 28.
47 Ibid., Mar. 3, 1894.
48 Ibid., Mar. 6, 1895.
49 Ibid., Feb. 10, 1897.

Chapter 12

HYDE THE COLLECTOR

THE BERNICE PAUAHI BISHOP MUSEUM

"Dr. Charles McEwen Hyde, afterward secretary of the Museum Trustees, should be credited with the earliest suggestion of a museum of Hawaiian material. . . "[1] So wrote Dr. William Tufts Brigham, director of the Bernice Pauahi Bishop Museum, in his annual report for 1915.

Dr. Hyde had acquired many skills useful in any museum genesis. He had organized comprehensive exhibits for benefits, and planned a religious museum with portable educational units. He could readily size up an object for its museum value. On one occasion he had heard of an ancient printing press. " . . . Mrs. Andrews has just died here and I am told has in her cellar an old Ramage Press on which so many Hawaiian books were printed! Also some of the wooden blocks from which were printed the picture of animals etc etc in the early days of work here. I shall try to secure them against such thoughtless and irreparable loss as was the sale years ago of the copper plates for their value as old copper. . . "[2]

One project that had an unforgettable museum flavor about it was a public library benefit, a major share of which was conceived and executed by Hyde. This was several years prior to any definite museum plan. A comprehensive exhibit of Bishop-owned artifacts with other items from many Honolulu homes was assembled and catalogued all in a museum style. Hyde labored long hours in preparing the pamphlet for the printer and in receiving and arranging the generous supply of display materials. Impression of the professional touch to the exhibition and of a community well pleased with it would linger long in Bishop's memory.

Hyde did not take Bishop to a decision on a museum. Mrs. Bishop's priceless collection of Hawaiian and Polynesian antiquities was stored, unsecured, on the ground floor (high basement) of the late Princess Ruth's 21 Emma Street home. Safekeeping was a worry. He had also been exposed to the same kind of careless disposition of ancient materials as had Hyde. As he contemplated these problems a practical measure suggested itself. "Why not build a museum room to house these objects as a source of information for Kamehameha students about their progenitors in the Pacific and Hawaii?" This thought was to govern the site selection. The museum was incorporated in the heart of the Boys' School campus.

In 1864 the Bishops entertained two young scientists from Boston. Horace Mann, son of the distinguished American educator, and William Tufts Brigham were on a Harvard University field trip in the interests of botany and zoology. Bishop began to fit all of these separate elements together: Mrs. Bishop's collection, human weakness in museum security, Kamehameha student needs, library benefits—and William Tufts Brigham!

The turning point was described by Brigham many years later:

Six years after her death [Mrs. Bishop died October 16, 1884], Mr. Bishop completed (as he supposed) his monument to the memory of his wife, the Bernice Pauahi Bishop Museum. . .This was built in the midst of the grounds of the Kamehameha Schools, and was to be cared for by the teachers of the schools, a merely school cabinet of curiosities. . . I had not visited the . . . building that was very nearly complete. . . when one afternoon Mr. Bishop . . . asked me . . . to see what he had done. . . he . . . showed me some of the things to be placed in the rooms when ready, and he asked me to arrange the collection in the finished building. This I agreed to do that I might thus show my respect and affection for the memory of my friend.[3]

Brigham's employment as head of the museum was not an immediate result of that first visit, but after much discussion an arrangement was

agreed to and he went to work. Unfortunately, no good working relationship was ever to be established between the trustees and the new man.
The contentious self-sufficiency in Brigham's makeup precluded this.

Hyde presided over most of the trustees' meetings and even he could
do little better than to keep out of the curator's way. Bishop was usually
content to give Brigham his "head." Still there had to be a museum
committee from among the trustees; Hyde was named:

The Kamehameha School Trustees have asked me to take upon myself
the duty of supervision of that work [Brigham and Museum]. I do not
have any details of the work to perform. For that we have a very capable
and responsible curator, Professor W. T. Brigham from Boston. But
I have to have an individual oversight over his work and approve all
requisitions from him for running expenses. We are just about publishing
our preliminary Catalogue of the *Kahili*[4] Room and the samples of *Kapa*.[5]
We have of these two Polynesian articles the largest and most varied
collection in the world. Mr. Bishop intends to enlarge the Museum
building in which as at present arranged all available space is needed
for Hawaiian curiosities so that we shall have here the fullest collection
of all that can be exhibited to give you a true idea of the manners &
customs of all the races of Polynesia.[6]

Brigham's grasp of his work relieved Hyde of being an "operations"
trustee. But there were projects in which he entered with his usual gait
and dash. One was to buy the very complete collection of Polynesian
and Micronesian artifacts and antiquities which had come into American
Board possession over all the missionary years, and which were housed in
a special exhibit room in Boston. The Board turned down the first offer
made by C. R. Bishop, whereupon Hyde wrote to the Rev. Judson Smith
in Boston." . . . I suggested to him [Bishop] that instead of offering to
purchase the *whole* collection of Hawaiian curiosities, he should make a
specific offer for the few articles he would like to secure for the Museum.
You have no idea what a magnificent piece of architecture it is."[7] He
had changed the subject; he was referring here to the completion of the
outer walls of the first dressed lava stone building of the museum group.

"Mr. Bishop's Museum," he went on a few weeks later, "will not be
finished and ready for reception of curios for some time yet. He will
probably be in no haste to apply to the Board a second time. . . Mr.

Bishop has money enough to pay any price for what he wants, but is a cautious, as well as gentlemanly business man."[8] While the processes of this acquisition were developing, Brigham suggested his need of the scientific books on conchology donated by Bishop to the public library. He was engrossed in identifying and classifying specimens. Hyde went directly to the Department of Interior and obtained temporary transfer of "sundry books of reference." Ultimately through the effect of the loan as a first step, the books became the property of the museum library.

Bishop's generosity provided additional buildings to the museum. The second unit was significant in its implied commitment to physical expansion as growing needs would require. This building was called the Annex and later named Polynesian Hall. In reporting on this addition, Hyde had another opportunity to write about the Boston artifacts:

We shall open to the public on Founder's Day [December 19] the Annex to the Museum in which we have a fine display of ethnological and Natural History Collections from Micronesia & Polynesia. The Hawaiian collections occupy the Museum building first erected. The whole structure is admirable both in architecture and arrangements. . .

[The ABCFM curios] will be of more interest and value here. . . than in Boston. . . I should think that my own personal assurance of the desire of everyone of the missionary descendants, now resident on the Islands, would be amply sufficient [for favorable action].[9]

This letter brought a sudden and successful conclusion to the matter. The special committee appointed to consider the request of the Museum in Honolulu for a loan of certain articles now in the Board's Museum reported the following resolution:

Voted, that at the request of the Trustees of the Bernice Pauahi Bishop Museum, established at Honolulu, all the articles now in the Board's Museum, and belonging to the Board, which originated in the Hawaiian and Micronesian Islands be loaned to the Trustees of the said Museum for the purpose of being exhibited in their Museum. . .[10]

This collection, the largest and most valuable ever acquired by the Bishop Museum, was quickly packed and freighted to Hawaii. Hyde was asked to prepare the agreement covering the loan.

The excitement attending the unique exhibit was stimulating to visitor and curator alike. "There has been a great increase in the number of visitors to the Bishop Museum to see all the antiquities sent from Boston," wrote Hyde in his regular letter to the American Board. "Prof. Brigham grows more enthusiastic. . . He wants Mr. Bishop to build an addition . . . to house safely simply the Hawaiian department."[11]

Hyde alluded to a new legal instrument of Bishop's devising, a deed of trust that would exercise a profound influence upon the Hyde-Bishop partnership in the distribution of the latter's charitable gifts:

It is not to be publicly mentioned but it will soon be known here that Hon. C. R. Bishop has sold his banking business to Hon. S. M. Damon for $800,000, and has passed over to the Trustees the whole of this money, now in promissory notes @4% interest with 5 and 10 years to run. The same persons who are Trustees of the Bishop Estate are to act as Trustees of this Charles R. Bishop Fund, with specific directions to pay over certain sums annually to certain specified charitable objects and with large discretionary powers for the remainder. But at the end of 10 years the fund will still be $400,000 and continue on forever at that figure, the income only to be spent. . .[12]

Organizing details, including the role that he was to play, were listed in a follow-up letter. "We have organized under the trust of which I wrote you as 'Trustees of the Charles R. Bishop Fund.' Mr. Bishop is President, as of the Kamehameha Schools Trustees, but I am Secretary instead of Vice President."[13]

As with the conch shell books, loans have a pattern of becoming permanent even to title. This was the outcome with the American Board's collection of antiquities. Bishop wrote into his newly formed Chas. R. Bishop Trust a provision (Para. 10) for payment of $8000 to the American Board for the collection: $3000 down and $5000 upon acquiring title. The trust deed was dated August 12, 1895. Bishop, even while waiting out the return of the signed agreement of loan, deliberately placed the $8000 purchase item in the new document.

On the day the trust deed was received and reviewed by the Bishop Estate Trustees, Hyde passed the news on to Boston. "I notice that one provision of the Trust is to pay $3000 to the ABCFM whenever they are willing to give the Hawaiian Curios outright to the Museum and in case the proposition should come from the ABCFM without any conditions $5000 is to be paid down instanter."[14]

On January 14, 1896 the Prudential Committee acted. "The Finance Committee reported on the proposal of the Charles R. Bishop Trust to purchase articles loaned by the Board to the Bernice Pauahi Bishop Museum, recommending that the Board's title to all of the said articles be transferred to the said Museum. . . "[15]

Thus, the years of campaigning to get the artifacts to Hawaii in the ownership of the museum were ended. Credit for the transaction is Hyde's. He had the able assistance of Gorham Gilman[16] in Boston and the cautious dollars of Bishop to bring it about.

The Chas. R. Bishop Trust was no sooner launched, with an election of officers September 4, 1895, than Bishop prepared the third of the Bishop trusts. This was the Bernice Pauahi Bishop Museum Trust. Its deed was adopted by the trustees July 23, 1896. This marked the final separation of the museum from the schools. The rationale that led Bishop to create this new trust included also the need to separate the museum from potential entanglement with the distribution of his funds to charitable objects under the Chas. R. Bishop Trust. In its new freedom the museum moved slowly and soundly to become one of the great museums of the world, certainly the greatest dealing with the Polynesian culture.

About this time Bishop stated his pioneering principle about land leasing in a letter to Dr. Hyde. "The capital of the B. P. Bishop Estate," he said, "should not be any further reduced, and as there can be no better security than the lands owned by it they should not be *sold;* but they should be leased in large lots or tracts, or small lots and for long term or short term at just and fair rates of rent, such rate as one can with good conscience insist on prompt and full payment of."[17] This policy applied with equal force to museum lands.

Bishop was attempting to compartmentalize his correspondence with the trustees. He was finding himself repeating the same advice or information to two or three of them in each mail. "Hereafter my letters on matters of the Estate," he wrote Hyde, "will be addressed to you as vice-president; on matters of the Museum, to Mr. Holmes, as Treasurer, and on matters relating to the C. R. Bishop Trust, to Mr. Carter, as Treasurer. All intended of course for the consideration of the respective Trusts. . ."[18] However the correspondence was divided, Hyde concentrated on being

Bishop's agent in school matters, charitable objects, museum collecting, and in acting as "curator" of Professor Brigham.

Bishop wrote more cautions, more don'ts, than anything else to Hyde. He did not want any more purchases of wooden dishes, adzes, or *poi* pounders "unless they were *quite different.* . ."[19] The museum should not get into the book printing business. Printing labels was satisfactory but not books. "The Museum should get out of debt, and never go into debt again."[20]

But his recurring subject in correspondence was Brigham himself. "You know that I was very anxious to have Mr. Brigham continue, long enough at least, to finish the literary work undertaken—which had already cost a goodly sum—and the new Annex, and I shall be very glad if he will so conduct himself toward the Trustees and others, as to go on comfortably and not exhaust their patience. Appreciation of his good work is all that has saved him. You will, I know, do all that you can for harmony and success. I am sorry that Mr. Brigham's experience does not make him more careful as to giving offense. He has to be taken, as he is, for what he is worth, and not as we may wish him to be."[21]

Brigham was indeed a personality of controversy; each publication, each field trip, each employment required a deft and not always successful handling. If there was a cross to bear in his museum trusteeship, Dr. Hyde found it in the conflicts within Dr. Brigham, who, while affronting practically every new tourist, visitor, or scientist with whom he may have had but a passing introduction, kept pounding away at his museum duties with ingenious and energetic application. Bishop and Hyde could see behind the belligerent facade; they understood him as well as anyone. Brigham had other "handlers": Henry Holmes, counsel, and Sanford B. Dole, museum trustee; but Hyde was the liaison.

One of the Brigham "cases" concerned the youthful scientist R.C.L. Perkins. Here was an imaginative field collector of bird-skins, insects, and shells, among the foremost in his profession and in the employ of the University Museum of Zoology, Cambridge, England. He collected specimens on several islands of the Hawaiian chain.

Bishop became acquainted with him on stopovers in San Francisco and was impressed with him to the extent of hoping that Brigham might not only relax in his newfound antagonism toward this able young collector but also might employ him. Hyde also came to know Perkins in

Hawaii through supplying him with necessary field equipment, and he presented his name to Brigham who refused any consideration and who, as a matter of fact, threatened to resign. Had he gone through with it, Hyde was prepared to recommend Perkins as head of the museum.[22]

The translation of David Malo's *Hawaiian Antiquities* was the subject of much talk in Hyde-Bishop correspondence. " $300 seems to me a good deal to pay. . . and to that would have to be added the expense of publishing, and then it would be in a book which could not be sold to recover any considerable amount of the cost; but if the Trustees think that it would be worth the cost, and that the translation would be satisfactory, I will pay for it."[23]

Through Hyde's remaining years, Bishop leaned heavily on him in museum as well as school matters. He wrote on a number of things: volunteering payment of part salary of Perkins who was collecting for the British Societies, the museum making no loans of its artifacts, obtaining the Koebele insects, inventorying the collections and encouraging Brigham through frequent trustee visits to the museum. He urged that Brigham gather *meles*,[24] speeches, etc. (the museum had acquired a phonograph). Bishop's suggestions and queries were treated as directives and accordingly followed through carefully and promptly by Hyde.

Dr. Brigham, working and building, resigning and reconsidering, was tactfully and patiently passed along year after year. The restraint of his associates was fully justified by his peerless contribution, the creation of the Bernice Pauahi Bishop Museum. Dr. Hyde's part was to hold a protective umbrella over him and generally to play out the provocator and to ease the provoked.

NOTES

1 William T. Brigham, Bishop Museum, *Director's Report*, 1915.
2 Letter Hyde to the Rev. N. G. Clark, ABCFM, Mar. 17, 1879.
3 Brigham, *Hawaiian Annual,* 1916, p. 70.
4 *kahili*, feather standard symbolic of royalty.
5 *kapa, tapa*, paper fabric or cloth made from mulberry bark.
6 Letter Hyde to the Rev. Judson Smith, ABCFM, July 20, 1892.
7 Letter Hyde to Smith, Aug. 30, 1889.
8 Ibid., Oct. 19.
9 Ibid., Dec. 8, 1894.
10 American Board, *Minutes,* Dec. 26.
11 Letter Hyde to Smith, June 17, 1895.
12 Ibid., Aug. 12.

13 Ibid., Oct. 1.
14 Ibid., Aug. 12.
15 American Board, *Minutes,* Jan. 14, 1896.
16 Gorham Gilman, former resident of Hawaii, friend of C. R. Bishop and at the time of the "artifacts" campaign a citizen of Boston.
17 Letter C. R. Bishop to Hyde, Nov. 7, 1896.
18 Ibid., Feb. 11, 1897.
19 Ibid., Mar. 19.
20 Ibid., Feb. 20.
21 Ibid., Nov. 18, 1898.
22 Although Perkins did not get the museum job he went on to collect in Arizona and California with world renowned scientist Koebele. Arrived home in England he carried out his promise of dividing the specimens of birds and insects with the museum. He was a principal contributor to the monumental four-volume work, *Fauna Hawaiiensis,* edited by David Sharp and published in England (Cambridge University Press, 1899).
23 Letter Bishop to Hyde, Apr. 28, 1896.
24 *Mele,* song or chant of any kind, poem.

Chapter 13

SCHOLARLY PURSUITS

THE PUBLIC LIBRARY

The in-migration of Caucasian nationals to Hawaii in the 19th century was accompanied by the re-creation of the cultural agencies of the homelands of origin; among them, schools, churches, and public libraries. An attempt to open a library was made in 1853 when the Honolulu Circulating Library was organized. There followed various library attempts including the Mechanics' Library and the Honolulu Library Association. Initially, emphasis was placed on reading room needs, then circulation of books, and later book accumulation. The reading room priority served the needs of visiting seamen and locals alike. Throughout the early years of the successive libraries the statistics were almost solely related to the number of readers.

Dr. Hyde could have been an outstanding librarian. He was an avid reader, a collector of books, a classifier of facts and general information, a writer and a publisher. Honolulu was ready for a major attempt at a library in 1879, a little less than two years after his arrival in the islands. William Johnson assembled a starting committee, consisting of C. R. Bishop, W. D. Alexander, M. M. Scott, T. G. Thrum, C. M. Hyde, S. B. Dole, the Castles, and A. S. Hartwell.

On March 1 an organizing meeting was called at the Knights of Pythias Hall and a Temperance Reading Room was proposed. The name however did not meet approval. It was changed by the end of that same meeting to the Honolulu Workingmen's Library Association.[1] A week later it was changed again to the Honolulu Library and Reading Room Association.[2] Its charter was received June 24.[3]

The name of Hyde does not appear in the minutes until the meeting of September 6, when he was elected vice-president and Thomas G. Thrum, president.[4] Two weeks later "H. R. Hollister, C. M. Hyde & Dr. Rodgers were appointed to advance the work of the Society, specifically to take steps towards holding Debates, Lectures, and Essays."[5] This sounds like a Hyde suggestion, similar to one made for the YMCA program earlier in the year.[6]

In this library association he was re-elected vice-president through 1882 when his role was changed to trustee to which post he was returned each year until his death.

In 1882 a committee of five, S. B. Dole, A. J. Cartwright, C. M. Hyde, F. W. Damon, and C. T. Rodgers, was appointed to arrange a loan exhibition fair for the benefit of the Association.[7] In the midst of the preparations, Hyde snatched a moment for a letter to the American Board. " . . . I suggested the Exhibition, agreed to be responsible for Archaeology, Hawaiian Antiquities etc. I worked very hard, Thursday, Friday & Saturday. It seemed a perfect chaos Satdy but by 5 p.m. things had taken orderly shape and were secure for the night . . . we will fill two rooms each 40 x 80 ft. and 12 ft. high with pictures, bronzes, statues, articles of natural history, Chinese and Japanese wares, Haw'n antiquities & varieties from foreign lands. . . . "[8]

A complete 48-page catalog was prepared for printing. In this he listed 1337 items by number and title in the several major categories:

  I. Pictures; oil paintings, water colors, engravings, photographs
 II. Statuary; Bronzes, Carvings, Ceramics
III. Coins, Plate, Jewels, Lace, Embroidery
 IV. Natural History
  V. Chinese and Japanese Department
 VI. Antiquities. Curiosities, Costumes, Autographs[9]

Over $2000 was realized. Another such exhibition in 1884 almost reached the goal of $12,000 set for the new library building.

This kind of fund raising was novel to Honolulu and aside from the monies collected served to unite the community in a common cause. Everyone who had a valuable or interesting item or a whole collection made loans. The quality and variety of objects were impressive. In such an exhibition can be detected the early gropings toward future institutions—the historical society, museum, art academy and archival agency.

In writing about the next fair, Dr. Hyde said, "We have had a Fair for the benefit of the Library Association and the gross receipts were $3155. As one of the Directors I felt it my duty to protest against any raffling, or lotteries of any kind, and am glad the protest[10] was successful in checking at once all such schemes. We had secured all but $600 of the $12,000 needed for the new building."[11]

The Trustees decided to go ahead with the construction of the library's first permanent structure on the property now occupied by the Merchandise Mart at the corner of Alakea and Hotel Streets.

Close association of the library with the YMCA gave Hyde ample room to exercise his ideas of improving the Honolulu moral climate for young men. As a trustee he was assigned to the Literary and Hall Committee. Here he was in a delightful confusion of books and magazines. As in the YMCA reading room he scrupulously followed the selection of newspapers and periodicals and was quick to disapprove any which did not measure up to his code for young people.

The periodical list was long and all issues were nicely arranged for reading. He reported in 1886 that 14,248 readers used the library hall.[12] But not only were there in-readers; a call went out for bundles of old publications which were supplied to Queen's Hospital and the prison and placed aboard various vessels including naval ships.

A collection of books and pamphlets printed in Hawaiian was given by the Hawaiian Board of Missions through the suggestion of Dr. Hyde.

In another instance he used his Punahou trusteeship to successfully right a discriminatory regulation of the library board. "I am instructed by the Trustees of Oahu College and Punahou Preparatory School," he wrote, "to request that your honorable body will grant the same privileges in regard to the use of books to our students as are now accorded to the scholars of the Public Schools. Believing that this request will commend itself to your favorable consideration as fair and just and awaiting your consent to this request, I remain . . ."[13]

His last motion (his last meeting) was made on April 17, 1899: to accept the offer of A. J. Cartwright of his library of 800 volumes.[14]

Here was another community enterprise greatly influenced by Hyde. In his 20 years of close association with library business he was in the "Chair" for over a third of the meetings. He was by far the most regular attendant. He obtained major gifts totaling $45,000 from his banker friend, Charles R. Bishop. He was, perhaps with the exception of A. J. Cartwright, the most library-minded man on the board. Public library standing in Hawaii today owes much to these men: Bishop, Cartwright, and Hyde.

THE SOCIAL SCIENCE ASSOCIATION

The Monday Evening Club of Haverhill[15] supplied a counterbalance to the tensions and demands of a daily routine, and an outlet for Dr. Hyde's social and intellectual yearnings. This was to be true in Honolulu although it took five years—a long time by his standards of impatience— to get such a group together. "I have tried since I came here, to get together the few who would be interested in such an organization and form a Monday Evg Club for social and literary improvement but could not succeed."[16]

It is little wonder that he "could not succeed." He had so many irons in the fire that adding one more would scarcely find enough heat to more than warm the project. But he persisted and before long the minutes of another organizing committee were a matter of record:

A number of gentlemen met by invitation at the house of C. M. Hyde, 122 Beretania Street, February 27, 1882, at 7:30 p.m. to consider the proposed plan for organizing a Honolulu Social Science Association . . . The Association was formally organized by the choice of L. McCully, President, W. O. Smith, Treasurer, and C. M. Hyde, Secretary . . . The evening was spent in informal conversation on various topics, chiefly special peculiarities noticed in the Hawaiian language. At 9:00 the Assn adjd for a collation, to meet again March 27th at the home of W. O. Smith, L. McCully to act as chairman and W. D. Alexander to furnish the essay.[17]

Here was Hyde at his typical best; he assembled the group, opened his home for the meeting, was elected Secretary, led the discussion on a favorite subject of his, and wrote and signed the minutes! The order of the program, frequency and circumstances of meeting, constitution, size of group, general purposes, and the collation were then and are even today closely similar to the Monday Evening Club. The annual reports are so nearly identical that, except for the names, they could be exchanged one for the other.

Dole assisted in working up the group. He and Walker some years earlier had started an informal club, a social center for a series of public meetings, at their bachelor home. Some of the members formed a part of the new group.

The roster of the Social Science Association included these men:

Dr. J. M. Whitney, dentist
C. J. Lyons, surveyor and geologist
A. Pratt, principal Punahou School
William Owen Smith, attorney
Lawrence McCully, judge
W. L. Jones, teacher Punahou School
Sanford Ballard Dole, attorney and judge
William R. Castle, attorney and business man
William D. Alexander, historian, president Punahou
W. N. Armstrong, attorney
C. T. Rodgers, physician
A. O. Forbes, clergyman
Thomas Rain Walker, British vice-consul
Charles McEwen Hyde, clergyman

These were top-drawer community men. All were friends and associates of the founder. This was, aside from his religious beat, largely the circle in which he moved in Honolulu. Here was stability, here a balance among men, here the source of strength to enter the forums of business and political life, here an opportunity to indulge in social action theory.

The members, according to the association's consititution, were expected to give an essay as their names appeared on the membership list. The first casualty was the speaker for the initial regular meeting. "C. M. Hyde was the essayist for the evening in place of W. D. Alexander. The topic was 'What ought to be the dominant idea in the policy of the Hawaiian government in regard to alcoholic beverages, licenses, free trade, or prohibition?' The Essay took strong ground in favor of prohibition. Much interest was manifested in the after talk on this subject, which continued all through the time spent around the host's well spread board."[18]

He not only had stepped into the breach in quickly filling in for Alexander but he was well prepared. Just at this time he was whacking away at temperance wrongs: speakers, correspondence, meetings.

A steady pride in the Social Science Association occasioned many letters to the American Board; one, a few days after that second meeting, gives a sense of that feeling and also points up one of Hyde's continuing concerns. " . . . I have recently started a Honolulu Social Science Association. Some fifteen gentlemen here, have united to discuss the many social problems of vital importance constantly pressing on public attention in the community, yet whatever question we may take up, the one great question in this department that underlies every other is the relation of this fading Hawaiian race to the other and more vigorous races that have come into the country and must ultimately control here . . ."[19]

Eight months later he wrote of an essay by A. O. Forbes on that subject, "Decline of the Hawaiian Population." This was the first essay to be published.[20] From time to time, certain of the essays were considered to be of public interest and were published—pamphlet form and in newspapers, magazines or journals. Some led to articles for the Historical Society, others were expanded into full length books.

In January 1883 A. Francis Judd "read a very sensible paper on the Hawaiian currency." This was a promising subject so Hyde invited Charles R. Bishop to the meeting. Attendance was not a lead-in to membership but he was elected three years later. With his election four of the Bishop Estate trustees were members: C. R. Bishop, C. M. Cooke, C. M. Hyde, and W. O. Smith. Only Samuel M. Damon was not a member.

As secretary he was not required to do an essay but he invariably took his turn, sometimes as a fill-in. He presented six papers during his time:

License or Prohibition	April 3, 1882
American Colleges	February 26, 1883
Representation in Civil Government	January 31, 1889
Notes of a Tour in Europe	November 20, 1893
A Graduated Income Tax	January 27, 1895
Tour in Japan	December 13, 1897

The list of all essays is printed in the "75th Anniversary Program" of the association.[21] Taken as a whole, it documents the thinking of community leaders in such fashion as to reveal the history of social thinking in Hawaii. This was so apparent by this anniversary that Dr. Stanley D. Porteus was commissioned to write a full-sized book, a review of the approximately 700 essays by members up to that time.[22]

He gives Dr. Hyde full credit for his role in creating the association but does not mince words in his comments on the secretary's essays. Says Dr. Porteus:

It is interesting to note the trends of policical thought seventy years ago among what could then be called the "best people." Those trends reveal to us a strange mixture of idealism and liberalism, strongly affected by prejudice, much of it religious or sectarian. Men wanted to be tolerant, but what they regarded as their wholesome prejudices would not allow them to be so. Such conflicting tendencies were illustrated in a paper by our first Secretary, C. M. Hyde, on "Principle and Method of Representation in Civil Government."

The essayist declared that voting under prescribed forms was what he called a natural, not a derivative right, but was limited by fitness to exercise that right. The demented, the dependent, the pauper, the alien and the criminal were among those unfit to vote. Prejudices appeared when the essayist objected to the admission of "ignorant and bigoted Portuguese." . . .

But the speaker reserved his most decided strictures against extending the franchise to Asiatic foreigners . . .

A more liberal view was apparent in the essayist's opposition to making property qualifications the criterion for the right to vote, "as securing for the capitalist class an advantage over the laboring class," . . .

. . . He was an excellent secretary, a little tart when someone missed his turn in providing a paper, but some of the members evidently wished he were not so radical in some of his ideas. There was, for example, the paper in which he proposed, of all things, "A Graduated Income Tax"!

Hyde admitted that no perfectly satisfactory system of taxation had ever been devised . . . paying taxes was a civic duty, governed by the ability to pay. But conditions change and hence taxation must be flexible . . . Contrary to arguments that income tax collection was impracticable and its methods inquisitorial it offered an excellent solution . . . Its progressive nature should be self-limited, so that it should never amount to confiscation . . . This almost socialistic view, as we well know, finally captured practical politics.

It is probably surprising that such discussions took place forty years before income taxes became such an important factor in all our lives. That coming event certainly cast a long shadow.[23]

Hyde wrote nothing on leprosy for his fellow Social Science members before the Robert Louis Stevenson-Father Damien imbroglio. Afterwards his feelings were such that he refrained from inflicting his personal inner conflict upon them. Five essayists did discuss leprosy:

William O. Smith, "Lepers," April 27, 1903.

Dr. Walter Brinckerhoff, "The Leprosy Nuisance in Hawaii and How It is To Be Abated," December 7, 1908.

Dr. W. C. Hobdy, "Some Aspects of the Leper Situation in Hawaii," March 3, 1919.

Harry Kluegel, "Leprosy in Hawaii," January 6, 1941.

Dr. Thomas K. Hitch, "Some Notes on Leprosy Today In Hawaii," June 2, 1969.

It will be noted that all of these essays were presented after Hyde's death. No one, apparently, including Hyde, considered a discussion of the Stevenson-Damien matter before then and no essayist touched upon the subject until more than half a century had passed and that was in a paper of my authorship. This effort constitutes part of the reason for this book.[24]

The Social Science Association as founded by Hyde had elements of longevity probably undreamed of at the time. Now 90 years old, it is still vigorous and meeting regularly—under a constitution virtually unamended since 1882.

THE HAWAIIAN HISTORICAL SOCIETY

Anyone could have predicted that Hawaii would eventually organize an historical society. The islands were rich in history, the pre-Cook story, the trade in sandalwood and whale oil, the missionaries, foreign nationals, governments, royal family, churches and schools. There were also history-minded Charles R. Bishop and Charles M. Hyde.

The idea of such a society slowly broadened in the thinking of Bishop as he indulged in the financing of writers, translators, and artists, and ultimately in setting up a museum. Hyde was merely standing by mentally. All his thinking needed was a spark. He of course was a history enthusiast. He had written histories, and maintained and added to an overflowing file of notes and correspondence which was a backup to innumerable pamphlet-size commentaries. Probably the reason additional

full-length histories did not issue from his facile pen was his unwillingness to give "full-length" time to such projects.

One early hint of Hyde's thinking is found in his starting to collect
Hawaiian printed materials soon after his arrival in the islands. Within
four years he had a sizable collection and he prepared a "Mss Catalogue"
arranged both "chronologically and alphabetically."[25] A member of
the American Oriental Society was also an ABCFM correspondent—
conveniently—for a Hyde inquiry. "I am interesting myself in some
special studies of Hawaiian Antiquities, and propose to organize a
society for the better prosecution of this work. I believe you are a member
of the Am. Oriental Society. Will you please send me a copy of the Constitution and any of the published proceedings you can get that you think
will be of service to me."[26] At this juncture, this interest might have led
to a museum or an historical society. As things developed it lead to both.

A year later Hyde wrote, "Dr. Clark has sent me a Constitution of
the Amer. Oriental Socy, which I wanted, to get some hints for the formation of a Hawaiian Antiquities Society. Archaeology Society might
be a better term, as I propose that we should investigate the origin of
the Race, as well as carefully preserve implements, dresses etc illustrating
old modes of life . . . "[27]

In November 1891, the USS *Pensacola* docked at a Honolulu wharf.
Aboard was the Rev. (Chaplain) Roswell Randall Hoes and his family.
Dr. Hyde met the chaplain and "found him a very pleasant Christian
gentleman." He also found the key to his aspiration to form some kind
of historical association, the idea he had been pursuing as the Hawaiian
Antiquarian Society. Hoes was a history major in college and knew
library guidelines.

As Hoes' stay in Honolulu was a tour duty of several months, a few
informal meetings were quickly arranged which led to an organization
session:

December 29, 1891
A few gentlemen interested in Hawaiian Antiquities and Comparative
Ethnology met at the rooms of the Hawaiian Board, 108 Beretania Street,
to consider the expediency of forming an organization for co-operation
in the study, preservation, and utilization of material relating to the
condition and progress of the Hawaiian people and cognate races.

There were present, W. D. Alexander, G. P. Andrews, C. R. Bishop,

S. B. Dole, J. S. Emerson, N. B. Emerson, O. P. Emerson, C. M. Hyde, L. McCully, of Honolulu, and Chaplain Hoes of the U.S.S. *Pensacola.*

On nomination of J. S. Emerson, who called the meeting to order, Prof. W. D. Alexander was chosen Chairman and Rev. C. M. Hyde Sec'y.

At the request of Mr. Emerson, Prof. Alexander read a letter which he had received from New Zealand, proposing the organization of a Polynesian Society with branches in the different groups.

The Secretary read a copy of the constitution of the American Oriental Society, sent to him with the view of organizing a similar Society in Honolulu.

After a general discussion of the project, Mr. Emerson presented a resolution which embodied what seemed to be the general opinion of the meeting, and it was accordingly

Resolved, that in view of the opportunity before us, the time has come in our opinion for the formation of a local Antiquarian and Historical Society, affiliated with the proposed Polynesian Society of New Zealand, but acting as an independent organization in its methods and administration.

After the adoption of this resolution the question of preliminary measures came up for discussion and it was

Voted, That a Committee of three be appointed to draft a Constitution and Bylaws

The Chairman appointed C. M. Hyde, S. B. Dole, J. S. Emerson.

Judge Dole declined in favor of the Chairman of the meeting Prof. W. D. Alexander, and putting the question to vote, it was so decided.

The Committee was by vote instructed to present their report as soon as possible, authorized to invite the attendance of any others who might be interested in the project, and requested also to invite some gentleman to read a paper or give an informal talk on some subject pertinent to the objects of the proposed organization.[28]

He must have known he was helping to make history that evening and that his secretarial remarks would be important to later researchers for he used his most careful penmanship. The constitution was ready two weeks later, January 11, 1892, for the organizational meeting, held in the parlor of the Honolulu Library Association. Hon. C. R. Bishop was elected president, C. M. Hyde recording secretary, and R. R. Hoes librarian. The newly elected secretary read the constitution which with appropriate amendments was adopted. The list of "Original Members" consisted of those in attendance. Fittingly the first four signatures in order were Bishop, Alexander, Hyde and Hoes. Queen Liliuokalani by prearrangement with the New Zealand group was elected Patron of both societies.[29]

Pleased, Hyde reported these rapidfire events to the American Board:

I have felt constrained to accept an additional work of some respon-sibility, the organization of a Hawaiian Historical Society, of which I have been chosen Recording Secretary. Hon. C. R. Bishop is President, J. S. Emerson is V.P. and will bear the chief burden in the administration of the Society's affairs. Prof. Alexander is the Cor. Secy. We start off with a membership of 125 and funds in the Treasury ($25 from initiation fees of $5). Prof. Alexander read the first paper Thursday Evng on "Traces of Spanish Influence in Early Hawaiian History." We shall publish this in pamphlet form and I will send you a copy when printed. I planned such a society some years ago, but postponed active measures as long as Kalakaua lived, who would have meddled with any such or-ganization and made us trouble.[30]

The Historical Society held its first annual meeting ten months after the organization meeting. Hyde's pride was obvious:

We held the Annual Meeting of our Hawaiian Historical Society in Queen Emma Hall Monday evening, as the YMCA Hall was engaged for that evening. I put up a few extra lights and cleaned up the assembly room (formerly Queen Emma's parlor) and it looked bright and pleasant. We had an audience of over 100, and Judge Dole gave us an interesting paper on "Evolution of Hawaiian Land Titles." We shall publish it as No. 3 of our series of specially prepared papers. Including the materials transferred to our shelves from the Honolulu Library Association, we have a collection of 2447 books relating to the Islands and Pacific gener-ally.[31]

Hyde's last meeting with the Board of Managers, as the trustees were then called, was November 29, 1898. He passed away before another one. In the minutes of the 1899 annual meeting Miss M. A. Burbanks, librarian, paid tribute to "the Rev. C. M. Hyde, D.D., its Recording Secretary who took a deep interest in the objects of the Society of which he was one of the founders, and who was an indefatigable worker in the rich field of Hawaiian ethnology."[32]

Substantial evidence of Miss Burbank's tribute is found in still another posthumous entry. "The Annual Meeting of the Hawaiian Historical Society was held at the YMCA Hall on the evening of December 10, 1900 . . . Miss Burbank also presented her report as Librarian, referring, among other things to the valuable gift from Mrs. Hyde of the complete set of books in the Hawaiian Language which had been collected by the late Dr. C. M. Hyde, whose wish it was that the collection should ultimately belong to the Society."[33]

In 1906 the collection was arranged and indexed with the assistance of Miss Carrie Green in the translation. In the 15th Annual Report this statement is excerpted from the President's address. ". . . I am happy to state that an exhaustive bibliography of works published in the Hawaiian language is being prepared by Hon. Geo. R. Carter, who has arranged and indexed the Hyde collection, containing 81 bound volumes and 129 pamphlets."[34]

Thus ends the story of this "sub-career" of Hyde's full life. He was a true student of history and his grasp of current happening was in the tradition of those who think in the broad sweep of the historian.

LITERARY EFFORTS

Some phase of writing accompanied each of the Hyde activities. Not only the book-length histories of Lee and Brimfield emerged from his pen in Massachusetts; he wrote the minutes of his churches, set forth painstakingly in a pattern of writing which also characterized his Honolulu years. As secretary or scribe he kept the minutes of the Hawaiian Historical Society, Social Science Association, Punahou School, Charles R. Bishop Trust, YMCA, and the like. Such writings can be classed as part of his literary effort and actually no small part of his total literary production, since he regularly recorded monthly meetings for over twenty years.

Another aspect of his literary work rests in his prolific correspondence. He had many major correspondents among the educators, scientists, and clergy. The letters constituting his most important single effort were those to the American Board of Commissioners for Foreign Missions in Boston.

Solid incursions into the writing field were made in the pulpit, the daily press, and in the *Friend, Maile Wreath, Hawaiian Gazette, Hawaiian Annual,* in a stylized reporter pattern often flecked with religious overtones. There were, of course, his own career supplements in writing and publishing the almost endless Hawaiian language tracts, lessons, sermons, letters.

He carried this zest for addressing himself to the public reader into the editorial rooms. He wrote of one such affiliation not long after arriving in the islands:

I was asked a year ago, if I would not join some five or six other gentlemen who wanted to maintain an independent newspaper on the right side in politics, morality and religion but the matter fell through. This year this matter was agitated anew, and I consented to do something in that way. Some five or six of us are therefore now engaged in writing for the *Hawaiian Gazette,* which was lately sold by the Government and bought in by the printer. It is not I presume generally known that I have any connection with it. I think it best to advise you of my connection with the enterprise. I have no pecuniary interest nor any editorial responsibility but meet the others of the corps of writers every Thursday aft'n for an hour to talk over our affairs, compare views and prepare leading articles and editorial paragraphs. I hope in this way without any great expenditure of time and effort to keep myself informed on the social and literary, scientific and religious questions of the day and exert some influence in forming and directing public opinion in our small community.[35]

The *Hawaiian Gazette* could be relied upon to be sympathetic to Hyde causes. Almost simultaneously another newspaper sale was effected. The government purchased the *Daily Pacific Commercial Advertiser* for $20,000 and Walter Murray Gibson, an ill-starred adviser to the king, was named manager. Originally a Mormon, he was excommunicated, professed Protestantism about the time Kalakaua became king and was soon made head of the cabinet as premier. The backroom editorial committee of the *Gazette* was to engage in a running feud with the government-managed paper for the next several years.

Thrum's Hawaiian Almanac and Annual. Started in 1875 and still published, was a useful compendium of advertisements, statistics, rosters of
officials, reviews and special articles. Hyde contributed many papers,
most of unusual interest, with special emphasis on Hawaiian ethnology.
Notes on his articles reveal the depth or in some instances the lack of
depth in his approach and research. These articles included:

Some Hawaiian Proverbs.[36] H. L. Sheldon submitted a page or so of proverbs, figurative phrases, and rhetorical epithets to which Hyde added
six pages of his own gleanings. This effort was connected with his study
of the Hawaiian language. He invited the native students in the North
Pacific Missionary Institute to collect expressions of proverbial wisdom
and his school thus became an ideal source of materials. His students
were of somewhat higher intellectual attainment than other natives.
All were pure Hawaiian or largely so and spoke Hawaiian as their first
tongue. Rivalry sprang up to recall and dress up Hawaiian expressions
for possible inclusion in the article.

The native sayings had a rich and colorful content and variety. Many
were rhetorical allusions, slang phrases, snatches of songs or *meles,* terms
of admiration, flattering titles of chiefs, attachments for local places,
racial characteristics, barbs at quarrelsome people, ridicule of pride,
phrases of encouragement, Hawaiian habits, landscape and nature appreciations and the like. Hyde added to his skill in the language through
this project.

*A Chronological Table of Noted Voyages, Travels, and Discoveries in the
Eastern, Northern, and Southern Pacific.*[37] This article, while incomplete,
has been generously utilized by subsequent compilers. It starts with
Vasco Nunez de Balboa from a mountain top in Panama in 1513 and
ends with *Wanderings, South and East,* by Walter Coote. In between are
eight listings for the 16th century, five for the 17th, 21 for the 18th, and
48 for the 19th—a total of 82.

Hawaiian Names of Relationships, of Consanguinity and Affinity.[38] Hyde
wrote of a book by the Hon. Louis H. Morgan,[39] in which he noted some
errors in orthography and "facts in regard to Hawaiian names of relationship as well as some incorrect inferences." He proceeded to correct
them and draw a striking conclusion: "These Hawaiian names of relationship express no relationship at all to the tribe or family; but only to
one or more generations. It is evident that lineal descent and individual
relationship to particular persons, with special ties of affection as we

express by father, mother, brother, sister within one family, are lost out of sight in the Hawaiian particularization of the relative date of intermediate birth, and succession of different generations." But the corrector found himself corrected! Abraham Fornander could not rush into print in picking up Hyde errors because the next *Annual* would not be out until a year later. But what Hyde took two pages to print, Fornander took eight pages to disprove. Actually his comment was courteous in tone and somewhat more in the nature of further explanation than correction.[40]

Helps to the Study of Hawaiian Botany.[41] This little article first lists botanical publications relating to Hawaii. Hyde looks forward to the forthcoming *Flora of the Hawaiian Islands* by Dr. W. Hillebrand, mentions Horace Mann's *Enumeration of Hawaiian Plants* and reminds his readers that Mann and William T. Brigham "investigated the botany of these islands, traveling over all of them from May 4, 1864 to May 18, 1865." Following this section appears a tight list of "Botanical Names of Hawaiian Plants" concluding with a section devoted to "Hawaiian Odoriferous Plants."

Some Hawaiian Conundrums.[42] In this paper, Dr. Hyde drew again on his native students for most of the riddles. These have been widely used in other publications as supplementary sections in tour and guide books, and even in school books. A few samples illustrate the objective figures of speech that emanated from the propensity of the native for imagery:

Nane (question): *Kuu punawai kau i ka lewa;* my spring of water high in the clouds? *Haina* (answer): *Niu;* coconut

Nane: Kuu imukalua loa a loike; my long underground oven? *Haina: he;* a grave.

Nane: Kuu wahe kuahiwi, lauliilii; my mountain with little trees? *Haina: poo;* the head with its hair.

Hawaiian Poetical Names for Places.[43] Poetical imagery used in place names is a voluminous subject. In four pages Hyde voices a hopeful urgency that someone research the subject exhaustively. Poetical objects include places, persons (genealogy), islands, channels and bays, surfing areas, mountains, and rivers. Winds and various rains make up most of such references; Maui has at Hana the "rain of the low lying heavens," at Waiehu the "rain that pricks the skin," the "fine mist of Waihee," Kaupo with its wind that "drives one to the rocks for shelter," and there is the "rainbow forming rain of Piiholo" while Makawao has its "driving chilling rain." These references apply to a part of Maui only and illustrate the widespread popularity of poetical imagery employed in names of places and things.

Hawaiian Words for Sounds.[44] His fondness for the Hawaiian language emerges interestingly in this article. Some of the peculiarities in its onomatopoetic words, its imitations or representations of sounds lead to words of many types of conversation: the talk of the multitude, gossip, news, fault-finding. Also treated are sounds of phrases of oratory, musical sounds, unmusical sounds, water and animal sounds.

"The Kamehameha Schools."[45] Hyde departs from the earlier categorizations and writes in this article as a trustee. He reviews the life of Bernice Pauahi Bishop, details of early days of her estate, school staff, program of study, campus layout and Mr. Bishop's continuing concern and support.

"The Educational Work of the American Mission for the Hawaiian People."[46] This is another of the more historical of his pieces. The American Board of Commissioners for Foreign Missions had a lengthened and profound influence on the islands starting in 1820. This paper, prepared in 1892, is perhaps the most succinct review ever written of the work of the Board in Hawaii. Hyde gives but a brief paragraph to his own eventful direction of the North Pacific Missionary Institute.

Fornander's Account of Hawaiian Legends Resembling Old Testament History.[47] Essentially a book review of a portion of Fornander's Volume One, *The Polynesian Race,*[48] it was put together first for the *Saturday Review.*[49] Fornander was writing of the parallels of the Hawaiian legends with Old Testament history: the Creation, Flood, Jonah and the Whale, the Tower of Babel and the like. The article was revised by Hyde and resubmitted for the 1900 Annual. It appeared posthumously. Subsequently Thrum included it in several successive editions of his *Hawaiian Folk Tales.*[50]

Hyde did not speculate on the Fornander position in regard to the parallels; he was merely summarizing the very involved, somewhat technical, and even tiresome versions as put in order and refined by the author.

Fornander's Volume Two elicited praise from him. "Have you seen Judge Fornander's Second Volume on the Polynesian Race published by Scribner & Co.? It is a marvel of industry and gives an account of the wars and doings of the petty chieftains of these islands for two or three hundred years, drawn from the Hawaiian *meles* and legends. It ends with the conquest by Kamehameha of the whole group."[51]

An interesting diversion, still in the legend file, appeared in a letter to an editor telling of the origin of the Legend of Kamapuaa with its locale in the fire pits of Kilauea on Hawaii island:

I have long wondered why a pig should have been supposed by the Hawaiians to be the mate of their goddess Pele. I can see resemblance of the word Pele to other words for fire, heat, flame, burning, etc. In other languages we have Baal, Belus, etc., the sun-god or fire-god. The Hawaiian Pele is the goddess of subterranean, volcanic fire. On a recent visit to the crater of Kilauea on approaching Dana Lake, the noise of the steam escaping from Halema'uma'u (house among the ferns), sounded exactly like the squealing of hogs, so that I involuntarily stopped to ascertain where was the pig-pen from which the noises proceeded. It occurred to me at once that the sounds I heard had given rise to the belief in Kamapuaa, the monstrous pig of the Hawaiian legends, the husband of Pele. The Hawaiians would naturally attribute to that animal the sounds heard in the crater of Kilauea, and hence originated the old Hawaiian legend of Kamapuaa.[52]

Hyde translated into Hawaiian a very popular sermon, "The Blood," preached by the famous evangelist Dwight L. Moody given in English on a visit to Honolulu.[53]

A catalogue of the bound books in the library of the Historical Society was another Hyde venture. The list included his own library which he had contributed. The titles were chiefly of voyages and the usual miscellany of dictionaries, histories, and biographies. These books and pamphlets were largely out of print then and have great value in today's market.[54]

Hyde had a consuming interest in the local political scene where the leading actors were, successively, King Kalakaua and Queen Liliuokalani. He could apply the reasonable constructiveness of Bryce to Hawaiian government and he deplored the contrast. The authors of democratic government in Hawaii had their model in the Constitution of the United States but had imposed it in a situation where emotion and personal ambition were not subordinated to the wisdom and discretion of the people.

An opportunity was offered him to write his ideas on religious conditions as they affected the islands, for inclusion in the Blount Report.[55] Simultaneously he prepared an article of similar length on *Hawaiian*

Annexation, Its Necessity and Its Urgency, from the Islands' standpoint. This in some respects is his most reasoned and forceful statement among his political utterances.

His pen was active and a good case can be made for assembling his Honolulu writings into a "works of Hyde" volume that would carry considerable merit for its comments on literary, religious, political and social matters.

NOTES

1 Library of Hawaii, *Trustee Records,* March 1, 1879.
2 Ibid., March 8.
3 Ibid., June 24.
4 Ibid., Sept. 6.
5 Ibid., Sept. 18.
6 Honolulu Y.M.C.A., *Minute Book,* Feb. 21.
7 Library of Hawaii, *Trustee Records,* Jan. 7, 1882.
8 Letter, Hyde to the Rev. N. G. Clark, ABCFM, May 6.
9 Honolulu Library Association, *Catalog of the Loan Exhibition, May 8–16, 1882,* Honolulu.
10 Library of Hawaii, *Trustee Records,* Feb. 7.
11 Letter, Hyde to Clark, May 14, 1884.
12 The *Friend,* May 1886.
13 Letter Hyde as Sec. of Punahou School to library trustees, Jan. 18, 1898.
14 Library of Hawaii, *Trustee Records,* Apr. 17, 1899.
15 Monday Evening Club, *25th Anniversary Booklet,* 1885, p. 48.
16 Letter Hyde to Clark, Jan. 30, 1880.
17 Social Science Association, Minutes, Feb. 27, 1882.
18 Ibid., April 3.
19 Letter Hyde to Clark, April 8.
20 *Hawaiian Gazette,* April.
21 Social Science Association of Honolulu, *75th Anniversary,* May 17, 1957.
22 Stanley D. Porteus, *A Century of Social Thinking in Hawaii* (Palo Alto, Calif., Pacific Books, 1962).
23 Ibid.
24 Harold W. Kent, *Charles McEwen Hyde* (Kamehameha Schools Press, 1954).
25 Letter Hyde to the Rev. H. H. Hagen, ABCFM, July 4, 1881.
26 Letter Hyde to Clark, Aug. 1, 1884.
27 Letter Hyde to the Rev. Judson Smith, ABCFM, June 15, 1885.
28 Hawaiian Historical Society, Board of Managers, p. 3.
29 Ibid., p. 37.
30 Letter Hyde to Smith, Feb. 2, 1892.
31 Ibid., Dec. 7.
32 Haw. Hist. Soc., 7th Annual Report, 1900, p. 8.
33 Ibid., 8th Annual Report, 1901. p. 6.
34 Ibid., 15th Annual Report, 1907, p. 7
35 Letter Hyde to Clark, Jan. 30, 1880.
36 *Hawaiian Annual,* 1883, pp. 52–58.

37 Ibid., 1884, pp. 53–58.
38 Ibid., 1884, pp. 42–44.
39 Louis H. Morgan, *Smithsonian Contributions to Knowledge*, No. 218, 1871.
40 *Hawaiian Annual*, 1885, pp. 46–53.
41 Ibid., 1886, pp. 39–42.
42 Ibid., 1886, pp. 68–69.
43 Ibid., 1887, pp. 79–82.
44 Ibid., 1888, pp. 55–59.
45 Ibid., 1890, pp. 62–65.
46 Ibid., 1892, pp. 117–127.
47 Ibid., 1900, pp. 138–148.
48 Abraham Fornander, *The Polynesian Race* (London, Trubner & Co., 1878), pp. 77–103.
49 *Saturday Press*, Honolulu, Sept. 24, Oct. 1, 1881.
50 Thomas G. Thrum, *Hawaiian Folk Tales* (Chicago, A. C. McClurg & Co., 1907).
51 Letter Hyde to Clark, June 4, 1881.
52 *Pacific Commercial Advertiser*, Sept. 13, 1888.
53 Dwight L. Moody, sermon, "The Blood," Honolulu, Hawaiian Gazette Press, 1890.
54 C. M. Hyde, *Catalogue of Bound Books in the Library*, Hawaiian Historical Society, 1897.
55 Hon. J. S. Blount, *Executive Documents*, House of Representatives, 1893–1894, No. 26.

Chapter 14

"TO REIGN AND NOT RULE"

POLITICS IN HAWAII had a direct bearing on Dr. Hyde's religious work but it was even more his interest in good government for its own sake that made the challenge forceful to him.

He had lived in Honolulu only a few months when he first met King Kalakaua and he immediately provided full details of the event for the American Board. U. S. Minister Hon. H. A. Peirce was recalled in 1877. When about to present his successor he asked Dr. Hyde to attend with him in his call upon the king at the original Iolani Palace:

Entering the palace, a one storied building, having the appearance of comfort rather than architectural elegance, we delayed a few moments in the hall which served as a waiting room, and then were ushered into the reception room. At one end on a platform stood the king and arranged in line on either side were the various legal and executive functionaries of the government, the former in citizen's dress, the latter in military attire. The room was simple in its furnishings the portraits on the walls attracting the attention more than the other appurtenances of the room. The ceremonies were simple and appropriate. The retiring minister presented his letter of recall, and read a farewell address to which the king had a written reply, as he did also to the written address of the new minister.

. . . I was presented to the king, who then stepped from the platform and entered into general conversation with the company present. I took occasion to express to the King my pleasure at being sent, and present— on the occasion of this official presentation; unofficially to represent the

people and the society who had done so much for the Hawaiian people
and still felt a warm and deep interest in their spiritual welfare and national prosperity. I bespoke his kindly interest in the work especially
assigned to me in connection with the Missionary Institute of the North
Pacific. In reply, he spoke of the need of thorough training on the part
of those as were set-for the defense of the gospel as well as sent-for the
spread of the gospel, especially in days of change and light attachment to
all merely traditional faiths. I assured him that one who believed the
gospel believed in the fullest, present inquiry into its foundations and
its tendencies; knowing well that liberty, and light, and love were its
marked characteristics as well as its beneficial effects . . .[1]

Hyde came away impressed with the warm personality of an individual
apparently cognizant of and sympathetic to his purposes. This first impression was to give way to a deep disenchantment and it was to involve
Walter Murray Gibson, a political adventurer who had ingratiated
himself with Kalakaua. An unsavory partnership developed between
the king and Gibson, one which would sorely try the patience of Hyde
both in his church work and in his concept of what good government
should really be. In writing about the overextended sugar situation he
worried about the population decline of the "perishing Hawaiian people"
and the effects of the tight money market and the plantation system
upon their social welfare. "To do the most good to the Hawaiians it has
seemed to me that I must secure the confidence of the leading element
in the affairs of the people as well as the Hawaiian people. Whatever I
could do to secure this has seemed to me a legitimate part of the work I
came to do . . ."[2]

Thus he justifies his interest in government in and of itself and as it
affected his mission. His correspondence with the American Board is
an invaluable contribution to this period of Hawaiian history. He could
scarcely know that his series of letters from early Kalakaua days to annexation would constitute a running explanation of the evolution of
Hawaiian government from kingdom, through provisional government
and republic, to annexation. He included himself in the gallery of political
minds as he wrote a kind of "kick-off" letter:

There are materials here as never before for a fearful strife if government
loses its head and people lose their temper. Half educated Hawaiians,

ignorant Chinese, savage Micronesians, vicious hoodlums,—but so far all has been moved without riotous violence.[3]

The latest news is that Kalakaua has had the effrontery to send to all foreign powers requesting them to recall their representatives and revoke their appointments! He is trying the experiment of absolute rule, appointing too, only natives and half whites, heretofore kept out of higher public offices not because of color but for lack of necessary specifications. He is repeating Kamehameha V's experiment who openly proclaimed his intention to upset missionary influence, but was obliged to retreat and retrieve his wasting strength by calling back to office persons whom he had dismissed . . .[4]

In another letter a few weeks later:

. . . The fact is, the whole moral tone of government is lowered by the notorious interference of the present King with the decent operations of every branch of the government: and there is no *one* here strong enough to influence or control him, or any combination that could do it. As I cannot interfere in political affairs it makes me still more anxious to see the religious condition of the people in a more satisfactory light. I have not the power to stir and sway and move them in public address. What I do must be through personal influence with individuals. I propose to take one of my students and set him to work as a City missionary, here in Honolulu. I shall go with him myself and visit from house to house trying to get the people to attend church, to send their children to S.S., to buy Bibles and Bible dictionaries, and to listen to words of friendly advice and Christian exhortation . . .[5]

Influence through such a neighborhood hike could be spotty and ineffective; nonetheless, Hyde did exactly as he indicated. But this knocking-on-doors backed by editorial comment in the *Gazette* had some value. His friends were sorted out, a few strung along with his crusades, more gave casual support. The end product of this enterprise drove him more and more into a human loneliness and closer comradeship with his loyal friends.

He saw the king at a going-away party. "At the state dinner given last Friday on the eve of his departure for the tour of the world, the King spoke to me again of his interest in the Chinese Church. I was gratified to hear him, for the first time, express any interest in such a thing. His leaving the Kingdom at this time for a pleasure excursion is not wise, but he is bent on having his own way and no one can stop him. He travels incog. as 'Alii Kalakaua,' goes to San Francisco, Japan, China, from Asia to Europe, thence home through the United States. W. N. Armstrong goes with him as companion friend under the nominal guise of Hawaiian Commissioner of Immigration . . . "[6]

An election for representatives to the legislature was held and the results while not in tune with Hyde's political humanism were considered important news:

Gibson has proved too cunning and active for our easy going good people. I wanted to have some organization begun three months ago to enlighten the people, and prepare for elections. I did not think it was my business to *do* the work. I brought the subject up in our Temperance Committee and had a Committee appointed: there the matter rested. They did not think it best either to make an open campaign of it, or to begin any public agitation till a week before the election. Then a few of our leading men met and agreed on the name of J. O. Carter as their candidate. The result is that the native element went solid for Gibson. He was on 15 tickets! The King took no active part in the elections. 1457 ballots, in all, for four representatives; over 21 candidates' names, Gibson had 1153 votes, J. O. Carter 350. The highest, next to Gibson had 603 votes. It is evident that Carter had hardly any but the foreign born voters to support him. The military was marched up in a body and voted in a body![7]

In May the king overturned his own ministry and "appointed a new set who began their career by a 'drunken carousal.' "[8] Gibson was the head of the new cabinet. By July, conditions in Hyde's opinion, were deteriorating:

. . . The King has got under his control all but 9 of the Legislature. There is little hope of any good while he is on the throne. The Legislature has voted him all the money he has asked for. The Appropriation Bill calls for an expenditure of money nearly twice the estimated income. How much longer the foreigners, who pay most of the taxes, will endure this foolish squandering of money, is a question of the greatest moment.[9]

But there were brighter moments. In the same letter he commented on the unusual success of the Fourth of July demonstration with the "numbers and influences of the American element. So heartily and fully did they enter into it that even the benediction, which was the only part assigned to me, was applauded."[10]

August 27: . . . Our political affairs are in a disturbed state again. The American Citizens are beginning to express themselves freely in regard to the reckless extravagance of Kalakaua and the set he has about him. A complimentary dinner was given to the retiring U. S. Minister. The new Minister R. M. Daggett was there and the speeches savored much of the war times, at home. We all feel that the purchase of the Gatling guns and arming the natives is a menace to the foreign residents. I was one of the invited guests and the first one called on to respond to a toast after the officials had spoken . . .[11]

September 25: The King had a $15,000 appropriation passed for the education of Hawaiian youth abroad and then sent 7 to England, to military and naval schools! Far more ridiculous this than the teaching of the missionaries in reading, writing, arithmetic, geography . . .[12]

November 18: His latest folly was sending a note to the Nobles and members of the Privy Council, saying that it was his desire they should appear in court in suitable attire. He had ascertained that a suit would cost $200 and they were requested to send him at once their checks for that amount, in order that the money might be remitted by this steamer's mail.[13]

March 10, 1883: . . . The decent and respectable portion of the community have been scandalized and incensed by the . . . performances that closed up the two weeks Coronation festivities . . . I would like to speak out, but it is very little use to make any demonstration unless others are willing to unite.

The King has been trying also to get the Hawaiian pastors to break away from our Evangelical Association and form churches and associations of their own to suit his ideas of Christian worship and work! So far he has not been able to make any breach.[14]

June 29, 1884: The Gibson administration still keeps on its shameful course. Last Saturday a vote was taken on Mr. Dole's Resolution of a want of confidence in the Ministry. The vote stood 19 to 24, all four of the ministers voting for themselves. Coming out of the Hall, Gibson taunted Mr. Henry Waterhouse with being defeated, and told him his bribery had not made him successful in his attempts to get rid of the Ministry. For this insulting falsehood Mr. Waterhouse promptly floored him . . . Gibson is acting entirely in Spreckel's interest and the community are determined that the sugar monopolist of California shall not control and ruin the business interests of the Islands. In this state of political affairs you can see there is little opportunity for religious growth and progress . . .[16]

October 15: Kalakaua has kept on his course of folly, extravagance, and vice: but however he may outrage common sense or common decency, in his proceedings, this community will quietly endure it all. Many are dependent upon the government for daily bread and do not dare to speak. Business men are interested in government contracts and do not want to do anything to interfere with any possible profits. Kalakaua has turned out of office Col. Allen for 20 years the Collector General of Customs, Marshal Parke, for 38 years in Government employ . . .[17]

December 30: . . . With the Wilder Cabinet, and with the Green Cabinet, who had charge of the Government for the first five years of my residence here, I always sustained most friendly and cordial relations. Of course I declined all official relations, excepting that once at Mr. Carter's request, because I had so repeatedly urged the Government to enter into the Universal Postal Union, I did serve on a Committee to inquire into the details of such an arrangement, report reasons in its favor, and a schedule of postal rates. Mr. Thrum did most of that work. Mr. Atkinson wrote the report. You will see in the letters I wrote, however, when Gibson came into office, that I opposed his taking or holding office as effectively as I could. Of course I also did this in no official way, only as a private individual interested in the welfare of the people. I made up my mind very soon that the proper role for me to take in regard to Gibson was to ignore the fellow and his set entirely, and to build up an influence outside by evident devotion to the public good, not by any denunciation or depreciation of them. I think it has proved to be a wise policy. When I started the idea of a Hospital for Leper Children, Gibson invited me to his office to talk over the project with me. I would not disclose any of my plans, and I had thought out the whole scheme; place, organization etc but finding that he was maneuvering for some such thing himself, I dropped the matter.[18]

January 26, 1886: . . . The King has just gone with some soldiers to Kailua, where he is determined to put down Pelipo, the opposition Candidate. He has such a personal spite against him as the Russian Emperor had against Alexander of Bulgaria. I hope he is destined to a similar disappointment.

Gibson and his set will stop at no lie or trickery to keep their offices. Flattery or intimidation, gin and fair promises, are their chief methods of work and reliance for success.

. . . If the elections go for his candidates, we may expect a determined effort to break the missionary influence entirely, break down our Chinese organization, upset the Hawaiian Board, and wreck things generally. The King hates us, for the same reason that bad men hate the Bible . . . If the elections go against the King's candidates, I do not know on what he would sooner pour out the vials of his wrath than on such an institution as the NPMI where there is plain talk about right and wrong, and an earnest spirit to make righteousness triumphant . . .[19]

February 15: The election of Feb. 3 has resulted in Gibson's nominees' election, 18 of them against 10 of the opposition party. There is not much possibility of this minority making any headway at all against the iniquitous legislation proposed, the licensed sale of opium, a ten million loan, abolition of the life tenure of the Supreme Court etc etc.[20]

This letter spoke also of the troubling exodus of many of the white ministers. Racial animosity was evident. The activists of the time clamored for the "Yankees to go home." Deterioration in government accelerated its pace in 1886. Gibson, an increasingly ambitious personality in the Kalakaua rule, was taking the government to a brink from which there was no stepping back. The sale of opium was licensed, public offices were bartered—even sold, customs revenue was subverted to royal causes, kingdom lands were illegally leased, lepers were excused from deportation to Kalaupapa, public roads were neglected—and the churches of the Hawaiian Board were being divided on racial lines.

At the end of this year the political Hawaiian League was secretly formed of what turned out to be two factions: one supporting continuation of the independence of the kingdom with a genuinely constitutional monarchy in which the powers of the king were limited and the other supporting an overthrow of the monarchy with ultimate annexation by the United States. Excerpts from the Hyde letters in the first half of 1887 describe the step-by-step measures culminating in drastic revision of the Kalakaua government and the hasty escape of Walter Murray Gibson in early July:

January 14, 1887: . . . I am glad to be able to say that our government affairs are in a better condition than ever. The deadlock between the Legislature and the King is at an end, and the King has submitted to the inevitable. He assented to the appointment of S. B. Dole as 4th Associate Judge of the Supreme Court and at the earliest opportunity the five judges declared the Act of the Legislature unconstitutional, reducing the number of judges to three with the intention of getting rid of Judge Bickerton . . . But the King was made to see there was no hope for him in any idea of personal rule, and appointed Col. Jonathan Austin (the nominee of the League for first President of their expected Hawaiian Republic).[21]

March 5: How much longer this community will endure this state of things I cannot tell. So many are interested in government contracts and government salaries, that they are unwilling to make radical changes that are necessary to secure good government and good order in church and state.[22]

March 5: I feel the need as much as anyone of some radical changes; but as the political situation must be endured until things are ripe, so let us endure this unhappy and wretched condition of things in our churches, till the changed conditions of things will warrant an aggressive movement. Let *first* things be *first*.

This is not *waiting* when God wants us to act; this is not meddling in *politics*, when it should be our purpose and endeavor to save souls; but as I look at missionary work, it is the building up of a Community on the basis of consistent, intelligent piety . . . Some time, perhaps soon, the political situation will go beyond the limits of human endurance. Then a change will be made, which will remove the dangerous and impracticable element out of the religious situation. Here is the patience as well as the faith of the saints. It is the old story of the sun and the wind as potent agencies in removing the traveller's cloak . . .[23]

April 11: . . . The trouble is in the fundamental idea of the Constitution—an irresponsible sovereign—and only by extraconstitutional methods can this be remedied . . .[24]

May 17: I am trying to organize a Bible study for the week succeeding our June meeting with the hope of turning it into revival work. I think the King has lost his grip on the Kaumakapili Church, and if so we may manage to bring the people back to spiritual life.[25]

June 1: . . . Political matters are in a ferment and a crisis, not a bloody one, I hope, is imminent. I send you some newspapers from which you may see for yourself how wicked, and just now, how irritating is the conduct, and the attitude of the King. You may be surprised to see an article over my name, and think I have no business to be dabbling in politics. Read it carefully and you will see that it is in the interest of the Hawaiians, and a plea for peaceful and Christian action. Then, consider this fact that I have been several times lately asked, and I have as often refused, to buy a rifle and join a secret association, that has distributed out the various important offices of the new government which they mean to establish and I think you will agree with me that it was high time some one should speak out calmly and clearly in favor of peace measures . . .

But the time has gone by for arbitrary rule. There was a time when I hoped this community would assert itself and put some checks on the King's follies, extravagances, and criminalities. But as things look now, the wish seems to be to oust him entirely.[26]

June 6: I want to see justice done to the Hawaiians. I want such a statement made of the situation that the statement itself will be half the battle, so plain and true that every one will acknowledge its force. Then I would like such a statement backed up by the signatures of men, whose names would be a guarantee for social influence and personal worth and property control. But I am very much afraid, that the people, who ought to take hold of such a movement, are involved in another style of effort, which 'men of honor' would hesitate about approving. Yet this may all flatten as so many undertakings in Honolulu have done. My experience is that one is not sure of his backers in Honolulu. When I spoke to Mr. Bishop Saturday, about presiding at such a meeting, I judged from his reply, that his experience had been similar to mine. Yet Mr. Bishop is not a man, who needs backers, but rather one who could command a following. But how things will turn, I cannot foresee. I hope whatever is done, the Hawaiians' interests will be duly regarded.[27]

June 15: I have just returned from Kaumakapili Church and the sermon on Home Missions by Rev. W. M. Kalawiaa. Five graduates of NPMI were on the platform, taking part in the services. The house was filled. But I was the only white person present. That tells the story of the utter separation now of the Hawaiians from the foreigners . . . The Hawaiians are to all intents and purposes a separate organization, only a few preachers meeting in the Hawaiian Board for some matters of common interest . . .[28]

June 29: The sure result of the King's course of wickedness and folly, as I long ago wrote to you, is swiftly coming upon us. A Public Meeting is called tomorrow at 2 p.m. to be held in the Armory of the Honolulu Rifles, only a block away from my house. But it is not such a meeting as I hoped to see called. This is simply a mass meeting calling all to assemble 'to take into consideration the present maladministering of Public Affairs, and to consider means of redress.' It is signed simply, *Per Order.*

. . . I am interrupted just here by a man who lives opposite to me, an English Jew, who has a Hawaiian wife. He has come to tell me, 10:30 p.m. that my house is to be burned tomorrow afternoon when the mass meeting is in session; that the King has natives distributed all around town for this purpose, other houses being marked for destruction as well as my own. Mr. Lazarus has a son, who is an Express driver, a great friend of Junius Kaai, the official who was the King's go-between in getting the $70,000 from the Chinaman. The palace is undermined and a tunnel leads under the street to the Parliament house on the other side. This is to be the King's exit in case the Palace gates are forced and an attempt made on his life. But I am not easily scared, and shall keep on writing to you now that my kind neighbor has gone . . . [29]

July 1: I wrote to Secy Smith yesterday and mailed it early, not knowing what might happen. The result, I have so long anticipated, of Gibson's chicanery and Kalakaua's folly, was too much for the patience of this community. For six months some of our people have been organizing, until when things were all ready, the movement was made. When the last stmr from the Coast came down, the customs officials refused to deliver the arms that had been imported. Hall & Co., Waterhouse, Castle & Cooke have dealt in fire arms & ammunition for years. There was no shadow of law for any impediment. Writs of replevin were sued out at once, and the arms were given to the importers. When the stmr. came in Tuesday, the goods were delivered as usual. It was a strange sight to see scores of men at noon carrying away their muskets from these stores. The Honolulu Rifles, our volunteer military company, has been increasing their numbers, till finally there were more than 500 men enrolled. They were ordered out yesterday by their officers to appear in uniform with full cartridge belts. After they had been under arms an hour or so, the order for them to appear was issued from the govt office, making a virtue of necessity. The mtg of which I wrote Secy Smith was held in the Skating Rink, a block away from my house. Mr. P. C. Jones presided, assisted by Hon. W. L. Green. At the very beginning of the meeting, a letter was read from the King, addressed to Hon. C. R. Bishop, promising to give whatever might be asked. He is thoroughly frightened and has no support whatsoever. He ordered his Hawaiian military to assemble at the palace Friday night, but only 20 assembled out of 200. When he asked them how many would fight for him, only 2 said they would! Tuesday, 2 a.m. he dismissed Gibson and the other ministers; and when the Committee of Thirteen went to him with the resolution from the Mass Meeting, without reading them, he said, he was ready to give his reply at once . . .

The city, and virtually the government, is now in the hands of the Citizens' committee. Gibson is kept under guard in a warehouse on the wharf. He sent a note to the meeting, yesterday, asking, that a company of the Rifles might be detailed to guard him against *Hawaiians,* whom he has professed all along to love and befriend! But it was thought he would try to slip out of the country, and that the safest place to guard him would be between stone walls. So this morning he was removed to the Warehouse. The Honolulu Rifles patrol the streets in the vicinity, and also Gibson's dwelling house. The city is perfectly quiet, and the change of administration has come without any disturbance . . .

The backbone of the whole movement is the money furnished by some of our capitalists, while the brains came largely from the 'missionary ring' and the muscle from the sturdy mechanics, carpenters, and masons and machinists who have no great regard for royalty but do believe in right and justice. I am thinking that our little Episode coming so soon after the reception given by Victoria to Kapiolani will do much towards making ridiculous the absurd pretensions of crowned heads to be above and beyond the laws that govern the intercourse of ordinary people.[30]

July 11: When the Committee called upon him [Kalakaua] he was ready to grant every demand. This put a new and unexpected phase on the situation. He was assured by the diplomatic representatives when he called them together to consult, that the demands were reasonable and ought to be granted. He offered to resign his sovereignty into their hands for safekeeping, but they declined to accept the trust. He asked them to nominate the new ministers for his Cabinet. This they declined to do. Nothing was left for him but to accept the situation and appoint the four ministers acceptable to the 'League,' committed to the proclamation of a new Constitution. Then there was long and earnest consultation in the Councils of the League as to the new constitution on a monarchical basis. Finally one was agreed upon but the Supreme Court Judges wanted the privilege of examining it first, and the foreign diplomats also. So there was additional delay.

. . . After this had been signed (Thursday July 7) came the work of translating it into Hawaiian, and then the printing of this Hawaiian version. So much work had been done by the others, who were tired out that I was asked to attend to the proofreading . . . at 5 p.m. the Marshall took printed copies and riding through the principal streets, proclaimed the new Constitution giving a copy to all who wished. And so the thing was *done*.[31]

July 25: The King tried his utmost to get the ministers of our Hawaiian Evangelical Churches to break away from all connection with foreigners and start an independent association but he could not succeed. There was an unusually large attendance [annual church conference], and I fully expected that the matter would be brought up, and there would be a contest over it. I wrote to you that we were 'ready for the fray;' but much to my gratification, we had no contest at all. The King's ideas were unpopular from the first, and he could get no support whatever except from a very few who saw that the undertaking was hopeless and dropped it entirely . . .[32]

July 29: The whole secret of it [change in government] is that it was managed by men who had the best interests of the community at heart, and especially the Hawaiians. There was never so complete an overturn of a government so quickly effected. But it had been carefully planned. The only disappointment is that Kalakaua was so ready to yield anything and everything. In this, however, God's providence mercifully interfered. So long as the person of the King was not molested, the Hawaiians did not care a straw who was in office or who was out, or how the government was changed.[33]

Mr. Oleson, who was preparing the Kamehameha School for Boys for opening, did not have his hands too full to prevent a political excursion. "Mr. Oleson," wrote Hyde, "has developed such level headedness and organizing ability in the League, as one of the Executive Committee of Thirteen, that he has been sent off to Hawaii [island] to compose some internal dissensions between the districts and widely separated communities of that large island, so as to ensure the success of the Reform Party at the coming election." Hyde continued with a description of the political changes:

August 26: You speak as if the King were led, i.e. persuaded to dismiss the Gibson ministry and promulgate a new Constitution. The truth is he was *compelled* to do it. The few men that managed the League could not have accomplished what they did, however, if they had not simply expressed the sentiment of the community. The king found himself on one side, alone, unsupported; on the other side, the community demanding rights and privileges, which he must either accord, or they would be taken and he put out of the way. The native Hawaiians were not consulted in the movement at all. They had nothing to do with it. They looked on in blank astonishment, but they accepted the situation . . .

The Minister of Finance, W. L. Green, the head of the Cabinet, is the only elderly man, the only one with any previous experience in government affairs. He is an English gentleman of high abilities and high spirit, nothing mean or tricky about him. Lorrin A. Thurston, Minister of the Interior, is a grandson of the veteran missionary, a young lion in the boldness of his attacks on the Gibson ministry in the recent legislature. The record of his electioneering tour on Maui and Molokai is as fascinating as a romance. He went to Gibson's own island of Lanai and the people voted enthusiastically for him in spite of all that Gibson could do.[34]

October 20: The elections as I wrote to you were overwhelmingly in favor of the new movement. The Hawaiians never before voted so freely, with the absence of all pressure to vote only for a certain set of candidates. But they voted against Gibson and Kalakaua. Everyone of the 48 members of the Legislature was elected on the Reform platform.

While the new government is on a better basis than the old one, and so far is an occasion for thankfulness, it is just as evident that Hawaiians, as such, have lost the position of prestige and influence given them by the older constitution. These islands are no longer to be managed in the interest of the Hawaiians, but of the cosmopolitan population now resident, exclusive of the Chinese.[35]

As the months rolled on he found dissatisfaction again. This time he leaned more to the side of Kalakaua, who after bowing his head to the reform changes, was not certain of his powers. In one of his longest letters to the American Board Hyde poured out his anguish:

March 13, 1888: . . . All political questions connect themselves with moral considerations . . . even after I had become interested in studying out the political situation, I could not take in or express even in my own thoughts, what at last I saw clearly was the actual condition of things . . . you will remember that the Reform movement was a secret affair. I was told of the existence and objects of the League, and invited to join it: but I refused, objecting to the secret, underhand plottings involved in such a style of procedure. It is this underhanded way of doing things that has given opportunity for the recent political maneuver . . . The present Constitution was drafted by a Committee of the League. It was presented to the Supreme Court Judges for amendment or approval.

It was also submitted to the European diplomatists here. (Art. 48). All these persons knew what the provisions were . . . giving a personal, independent veto power to the King. Three of the Judges of the Supreme Court wrote Article 78 to avoid frequent repetition of the phrase "by and with the advice and consent of the ministers." Article 78 is to the effect that what the King does is really to be done by his ministers: but had no reference to the King's veto power which was understood by all concerned to be a personal independent power. When the Constitution was presented to the King, he asked if it gave him such veto power. The Premier of the Cabinet told him that it did. Would you believe it credible that in the face of these facts, when the King sent in his veto messages of some important measures, the Cabinet and Legislature tried to get out of the unpleasant predicament in which they found themselves not by a two thirds vote constitutionally overriding his veto; but by trying to make out that the Constitution did not give *him* the veto power, but his *ministers*! Would you believe that honorable men would lend themselves to connive at any such proceedings? Yet of all who know the facts, not one opened his mouth to tell the truth. I did not know the facts till since the decision of the Supreme Court. What ought I to think of such proceedings? Am I showing a lovely Christian spirit by upholding any such actions? Or am I rancorous and rabid, because I believe and say that this style of doing things is iniquitous and dishonorable?

. . . In the isolation of life here, and the loneliness in which I find myself in my present attitude in reference to political maneuvers, I am impelled to notice how individualized after all the work of salvation is. God is dealing with me personally, as it were, singling me out in His providence for just such discipline, as I need, if I am but wise to see what He means to have me learn.[36]

Kalakaua was overcome with his failures and further depressed with the scolding he received from his sister for not fighting off the "foreign" reformers. Generally, however, he stayed with the new constitutional rule although he was ever seeking loopholes and attempting counter-measures. But the Cabinet solved these skirmishes in July, 1889 and Hyde so reported:

You will be glad to know that our political atmosphere is the clearer and brighter after the fire and smoke of last week, Tuesday, The Cabinet,

before taking any further steps insisted that the King should acknowledge
that this was a ministerial government, that he was to sign such papers
as his Cabinet presented for signature, and that the Minister of Foreign
Affairs according to Military Law was to have control of all the munitions
of war, the King no personal right to issue orders or make appointments . . .[37]

January 17, 1890: As regards the political situation, I think it probable
that the present government will be continued in office another biennial
term. The opposition is not well organized, has taken Wilcox (the rioter)
and Bush (one of Gibson's associates) as its candidates. So accustomed
are they to stealing, that they have actually stolen the Platform of the
Reform Party and the name, calling themselves by way of distinction the
National Reform Party . . .the Reform Party has a queer mixture
on their ticket. How any can think it, or call it, 'Missionary concern' is
utterly without reason.[38]

This letter contained the last Hyde reference to the politics of Kalakaua. He had written fully on the situation in Hawaii; decrease in Hawaiian population, the heterogeneity of the people, social extremes, new
plantations, well-digging, and all and sundry problems, but no more
on Kalakaua in politics. There would be more on the king in death.
In November 1890 Kalakaua announced a trip to San Francisco where
he would go for medical advice. He was indeed a very sick man. The
real reason for the trip was initiation into Islam Temple of the AAONMS
(Ancient and Accepted Order of the Nobles of the Mystic Shrine, a
masonic-related agency). There was no Shrine Temple in Honolulu so
he applied to Islam Temple. He attended a brief portion of the ceremonial
on Wednesday evening, January 14, 1891. He was returned to the Palace
Hotel to his bed which he did not leave again. He died there January 20.
Dr. Hyde wrote in considerate terms of the monarch:

The news of the King's death was not unexpected. He was very weak
when he went away, and the fatal character of his ailment (Bright's disease of the kidneys) was well known. I do not see how the circumstances
of his death could have been more kindly ordered. The feeling of anger
against him for his wanton abuse of his position that culminated in the
Revolution of '87 had died away. Any grudges; not a particle of mali-

cious ugliness apparently in his disposition. He died away from the islands, so there can be no possible foundation for any accusation of poisoning, or of praying him to death. His visit was under such circumstances that he was received with all the pomp and show in which he delighted as if it were a form of divine worship. He thought himself a bigger *kahuna* [native priest] than any living Hawaiian and claimed to know more about God than any of the missionary set. The people of California & the federal officials most certainly treated him with the highest possible distinction. The *Charleston* brought back the body with all possible honor, and the display from the men-of-war in port added greatly to the impressiveness of the funeral ceremony in removing the body to the palace. The *Charleston* was telephoned [a lookout on Diamond Head] soon after 8, and the news was spread through the city. The schools were dismissed and the stores closed, and mourning emblems displayed . . . In common with other organizations, the students of the NPMI drew up and presented in person at the palace written testimonials of condolence and sympathy. One of the most impressive incidents connected with the ceremonies was the sight of the widowed Queen— all alone by herself—on the second story verandah—in the palace front —as the body was brought into the palace yard. Arches had been prepared for a joyous welcome. These were hastily draped in black, and about 5 p.m. the body was borne through the streets. Just over the palace was a most lovely rainbow, and as the sun was low, the arch was apparently all within the palace grounds. In fact if Kalakaua had had the arrangement of all the circumstances I do not think that anything could have been more appropriately arranged.[39]

He added a paragraph of his impressions of the amenities and proprieties observed in the funeral:

We have entered a new page of Hawaiian history. Kalakaua's death on Jan. 20 is now followed by his funeral Feb. 15. All the ceremonies connected with it have been decorous and appropriate. Mrs. Dominis, now Queen Liliuokalani, has insisted upon perfect orderliness and decency about the palace. There has been no drinking, no hula, no heathenism. The funeral procession last Sunday was as well ordered as any that was ever seen in this city, and there was no hitch about it in carrying out the programme . . . I did not want to walk in the procession as a mark of honor to Kalakaua; but in this world it is sometimes best to do what we do not want to do: So I headed the Protestant Clergy.[40]

Queen Liliuokalani was sworn in as Hawaii's ruler on the day of the *Charleston's* arrival in port. She had been named successor by Kalakaua April 10, 1877, immediately upon the death of William Pitt Leleiohoku, his younger brother, whom he had named heir apparent upon becoming monarch.

There was to ensue the same cycle of early hope and later disenchantment with Liliuokalani as there had been with Kalakaua. Dr. Hyde wrote to the American Board even as he was writing about Kalakaua's death:

The change of sovereigns was effected with even less commotion than the arrival of a mail steamer. Everything seems favorable for a prosperous future. Mrs. Dominis is too old (54) to care for the frivolities of life and has recently appeared to be strongly in favor of whatever is right and good and distinctively *Christian*. She said not long ago to Rev. H. H. Parker, that she was a changed woman. We have every reason to hope only good things from her.[41]

This inspiriting optimism was short-lived. It lasted a week. Troubles began at the Palace at the outset:

The Queen Regnant and the Dowager Queen had different opinions about the proper disposal of the coffin in which the King's body was brought from the States, the Dowager Queen saying that it was an indignity to the States not to use the coffin sent from it. The Queen Regnant wanted a coffin made of Hawaiian woods. I do not know how the matter was settled.

Yesterday was to have been the day for proclaiming the Heir apparent to the throne; but the Queen was not ready. Now it appears she wants to get rid of the present Ministers; but that involves a special interpretation of the Constitution or rather a single phrase of it "the Sovereign shall appoint" in opposition to the whole tenure. The complication is an unfortunate one, just at this juncture, this opposition to the controlling sentiments of the community, for the Queen's avowed purpose is to appoint Hawaiians.[42]

To friend General Armstrong he reworded the problem, "The Queen has made a *faux pas* at the outset, but no one is disposed to make trouble about her foolishness (not wickedness). She wants the present ministry to resign and appoint her nominees, Iaukea, Charlie Wilson, Sam Parker, Antone Rose—Hawaii for the Hawaiians. It can't be done, and I hope she will be taught distinctly the lesson that she is *to reign and not rule.*"[43]

Economics mixed with politics in his next letter. The Queen had her hands full with the McKinley tariff, the swarming in of native workers from Japan (1000) and China (1500), the cable scheme, a steamship line subsidy, Pearl Harbor activity in Congress, the continuing decrease in the native Hawaiian population—and all this in addition to her determined attempts to readjust the elements of her rule. It is likely, too, that matters of government were affected by Liliuokalani's matters of family. Her husband, Consort John Owen Dominis, died August 27, 1891.

An election was held in January 1892, a year after her assumption of the throne. The "hoodlum" element placed 13 in office as opposed to 35 conservatives. "The men elected to the Legislature," he said, "are mostly pledged against a Constitutional Convention. Whatever amendments may be made, there will not be very soon any radical changes."

Simultaneously one item of good news cropped up:

The Queen is making provision for the Education of Hawaiian girls in our Seminaries. Out of the estate of her late husband, a fund of $20,000 will yield an income for the support of 25 or 30 girls in the various boarding schools. There always comes some gleam of light when things seem particularly dark and discouraging.[44]

By the middle of 1892 he was slashing away at her political moves in successive letters to the American Board. The Queen was moved in her political strategy by an unquenchable devotion to the principle of native supremacy in the executive branch of the government. She would misrule if need be but she would rule.

Hyde was in a most difficult dilemma. His own devotion to the very same natives was countered in principle with the realities of misrule by the sovereign. This was his quandary and he had only one path to follow and it was narrow. The paragraphs of commentary on politics in his American Board letters far exceeded, in length and number, those on

Micronesia, the Hawaiian Board, or his North Pacific Missionary Institute. His emotions regarding truth and justice in this field transcended any other major discussion in his lifetime, even that of the recently endured Robert Louis Stevenson attack.* And the queen gave him the material for his paragraphs as indeed earlier had the king:

July 27, 1892: We are in the midst of another political crisis. The Queen appointed Paul Neumann Attorney General. He was supposed to be connected with a bill just introduced into the Legislature to incorporate a Lottery Company. The Legislature demanded resignation of the Cabinet by a vote of want of confidence, 31 to 10 . . . as soon as the bill was introduced . . . decent people talked and acted against it. I prepared a set of resolutions & a petition against the establishment of any such law, which were adopted at a large meeting of our best ladies. I preached against the Lottery in Kaumakapili Church & published the sermon in the native newspaper; I have prepared resolutions, petitions, leaflets in Hawaiian, and we are trying to arouse the native population against the fraud.[46]

August 8, 1892: The race between the "Lottery" Cabinet and the Reform Party is really not so much that as a contest as to whether the "personal" government of the regent is to come back again or not. There is much talk that Hawaii should become a British Protectorate. Stand by in the meantime.[47]

October 20: The mail that will bring news of the Presidential Election will be anxiously awaited. One point of special anxiety will be the probable attitude of the incoming adminstration towards the Hawaiian Islands, and the continued aggressiveness of England in the struggle for the commerce of the Pacific. America's policy (foreign) has been one of neutrality hitherto, but the Harrison adminstration has taken a more active part in the transactions of other nations than has hitherto been deemed advisable. I hope that this is not attributable to growing "bumptiousness" as the country keeps on growing. Intelligent and watchful interest (and interposition if need be) is surely not out of place in what concerns the commercial and political development of the Pacific. That England should have taken possession of the Gilbert Islands is a matter

*See chapters 15–19.

of gratulation only as such seizure prevents such action by Germany or France. Yet the spirit of this occupation and annexation of uncivilized peoples and lands is not the ideal development of these islands in their relation to the spread of the Gospel and the upbuilding of Christ's Kingdom.[48]

A small morsel of comfort was found in the request of the queen to George Wilcox that he form a cabinet. "The new ministers are such men as to command the respect and confidence of every intelligent citizen."[49]
This hopeful reflection soon faded:

. . . political complications come in to add to our troubles. The Queen persists in claiming her right to choose and appoint her ministers. The leaders of our political movements insist upon appointment by the Legislature to whom & through whom the Ministry is responsible. Another complication as I wrote you has entered into the quarrel to embitter and prolong it. Our British residents support the Queen in her desire to assert and maintain her royal prerogatives. They are bitter against the U. S. Govt. for its assertion of sovereignty in the Behring's Straits and the seal rookeries. So they kindle a backfire here, and talk about the Reform Party as disloyal annexationists. They try to block attempts of the U. S. to get a foothold in Pearl River Harbor. They want an English loan with its pickings and stealings. They want closer relations with Canada, a telegraph cable, and a steamer line from the terminus of the Canadian Pacific Railway . . . What will rouse the Yankee nation to give over praising John Bull and playing second fiddle to his self asserting snobbery snubbing the Yankee whenever he can get the chance to do it.[50]

January 11, 1893: I very much fear the Queen will sign the [Lottery] bill. In fact I think she is maneuvering to oust the present Cabinet. She wants ministers of a different stripe. It was a surprise to me that she would appoint such good men. I shall be happily disappointed if she will uphold them now, all against the Lottery Bill.[51]

He sensed a change but how and where he could not divine. Three days after this letter was dated, the queen prorogued the legislature and announced that she was promulgating a new constitution! On January 17, the "Committee of Safety" proclaimed the abrogation of the monarchy and establishment of the Provisional Government "to exist until terms of union with the United States of America have been agreed upon." Two days later a five man commission left for Washington to discuss annexation.

February 1, 1893: So far as I have talked with the Hawaiians they think that the Queen deserved to be dethroned, for letting loose upon the country such unmitigated evils as liquor, opium and the lottery. But when they think that this means loss of all political control, the taking away of the elective franchise from them, they naturally feel sore. I hope that no such piece of injustice is contemplated as utterly to ignore the Hawaiians.

The Provisional Government has complete and firm control . . . as I do not know all the facts I am not in a position to speak positively of the unwisdom of any of their measures. But the law against seditious utterances, verbal or printed, seems to be a curtailment of the liberty of speech that is of questionable expediency.[52]

February 9: I did not know at the time I took to the P.O. my last letter, that the U.S. Flag had been raised at 9:00 on the government building, this country placed under an American Protectorate. It is one step forward to the inevitable. We cannot afford to let the English gobble up these islands. We hope to hear that Congress has agreed upon terms of annexation, and political standing secured. The Provisional Government have pushed matters with a firm hand, steadily and wisely. I have written letters to many of the Hawaiian pastors. The answers I have received have been most satisfactory, showing a strong conviction of the folly and wickedness of the Queen, and unfaltering confidence in the outcome of the overturn as on the whole for the best. Captain Wiltse of the *Boston*, deserves great credit for his coolness, prudence, sagacity, decision in the management of his part in the events that have transpired. While the presence ashore of the U.S. troops may have had its due part as a factor in the changes that have taken place, the suddenness and completeness of the collapse of the Hawaiian sovereignty was only the outward visible proof of *its* inward corruption and utter weakness. It existed only by sufferance. The Queen did a most foolish thing when she dismissed the Wilcox Cabinet, men of integrity and ability, who would have stood by her and supported her through thick and thin, if she had taken a stand for the right. She appointed as weak and brainless a set of men as she could have found, thinking only that they would be her subservient tools. She found them failures in every *point*. When the Committee were leaving W. O. Smith's office to go to the Govt. Building & declare a Provisional Government two of her ministers were having a champagne lunch at the hotel and the other two were in the Police Station so frightened that they did not know what to do . . . But the cool, steady audacity of the leaders in the revolution carried everything without the use of force. Captain Wiltse never did the first overt act to implicate the U. S. government. He told President Dole, he must establish himself in actual command before he could be recognized, must have in actual possession the barracks and the police station as well as the Government Building. It is simply marvelous how it all came about, one point after the other.[53]

February 28: Mere pity should not control our actions, neither as guide nor limit. But we cannot help feeling pity for the changes that have come over the lives and hopes of the Hawaiians, while our sympathies are with the party of progress.

We have heard by the *Australia* that Pres. Harrison has signed the treaty of Annexation and that it was to be sent to the Senate at 3:30 p.m.

Feb. 15. We shall have no news for an interval of 16 days . . . It would seem that annexation was a foregone conclusion as soon as the project was broached. I had never supposed that it would be possible for years to come, anymore than people could have imagined that American slavery would be done away with the stroke of a pen . . . It is the only possible, practical thing for the Hawaiian people . . .

The English Commissioner here, Major Wodehouse, and the Japanese Consul, seem to be working in sympathy, not antagonism perhaps to annexation . . .

This whole matter has its bearings for good or for evil on the work of the Board among the other nationalities. Hawaii is the first country in which the American missionaries have labored, whose political relations to the United States have been changed as the result of missionary labors.[54]

There was not enough time for the Senate to adopt the annexation treaty before March 4. Grover Cleveland returned then as president of the United States for his second term; Harrison's term of four years had come in between. Cleveland was an avowed foe of foreign conquest and upon the advice of Walter Q. Gresham immediately withdrew the treaty for the time being and dispatched U. S. Commissioner James H. Blount to Hawaii to make a study.

Blount met with Hawaii's leaders and gathered statistics and opinions. His voluminous report recorded the view of community leaders of all faiths, races, and careers; among them the views of the Rev. Dr. Hyde.[55] The latter summed up the capabilities of the native for managing church and government affairs in a 3500-word analysis.[56]

The Blounts and Hydes struck up a warm friendship which was soon to cool. The Commissioner and his lady attended services, including Easter, at the recently built Central Union Church on Beretania and Richards Streets. Mrs. Hyde took Mrs. Blount to the Woman's Board meetings.

Dr. Hyde was more restrained at first than his fellow Honolulans, who, including Bishop, were downright suspicious of Blount, even caustic in criticism:

I wish people in the United States could be convinced that it is simply the necessary setting aside of an obsolete decrepit, effete social and political system. What is desired here is a radical change and the only way to secure it is by annexation. Mr. Spreckels [arrived the Tuesday before— *Australia*] talks about Republic but we have not the material here out of which a stable republican form of government could be assured. Annexation, to my mind, involves a temporary government by Commission, or in some such way, till the social elements here are so changed, that we can have a territorial government, or some transitional form till Statehood can be reached . . . I had no idea that annexation was so near at hand. No one could have anticipated that the Queen would commit such an act of folly, when every feature of the situation looked hopeful & good for the Hawaiian people and Kingdom, while the Queen seemed so desirous of doing what was respectable and right.

I have written out my views of the situation and passed the document over to Mr. Blount. He apparently thinks that he has gathered about all the material facts necessary for the formation of an opinion, and after visiting the other islands will be ready to return to Washington. The situation is such, that I do not see why we can expect any change till

Congress meets. We hear of a plan to have Congress meet in September, but there, other matters will be brought to the front and the Hawaiian question will be relegated to some season that will suit the convenience of the leaders.

I have seen Hon. C. R. Bishop since his return, and find that he is very pronounced on the necessity and urgency of annexation. He has taken up the idea of annexation as the only way out, just as other thinking men among us have done, following the logic of events dating back to the closing days of the Legislature.[57]

Having submitted his statement for the Blount Report and having brought his Institute to the close of another year he and Mrs. Hyde left Honolulu, May 20, on the *Australia*, for an extended tour of the United States and Europe, climaxing this with a look-in at the annual meeting of the American Board at Worcester, Massachusetts.[58]

He was thus somewhat out of touch with annexation news, particularly Honolulu reaction. But he was sufficiently in touch to be disappointed in Blount when the full results of that investigation came to light. He began to sense Cleveland's backing away from annexation and the grow-ing possibility of failure of the Provisional Government. However he thought Dame Fortune might be smiling on him when upon boarding the *Australia* for the return trip, San Francisco-Honolulu, he found that Albert S. Willis, the new U. S. Resident Minister to Hawaii, and Mrs. Willis were fellow passengers. Perhaps he should have been more wary of a first acquaintance; he had had dream castles tumble about him in the too quick, too close placing of trust in prominent personalities. But from the first shipboard meeting the Hydes and Willises seemed to have much in common and the opportunity for explaining the annexation mind-set of Honolulu leaders was not lost.

By the time of disembarkation at Honolulu Willis was not so certain of the intent of the instructions he was carrying from Cleveland who had sent him out to Hawaii with "power to act." About a week after his return, Hyde mailed his first letter in several months to Boston, a long letter of many pages of updating material:

I have just returned in time to take my part in the affairs of these last two weeks. It would seem like a special providence that brought Mrs. Hyde and myself to the islands in the same vessel with the new U. S.

Minister Resident (Willis) and his wife. We were very much pleased with them as intelligent, kindly, courteous Christian people. We had the opportunity of telling them some facts which otherwise they might not have known. It would seem, at any rate, as if we had dissipated their prejudices, and prepared their minds to a comprehension of the situation, as they found it when arrived at their destination.

It seems to be utterly at variance with the ideas they had formed of the affairs and people here from Mr. Blount's report, perhaps, or from other misrepresentations. It seems (and I have to use that word constantly in speaking of the position in which Cleveland's pig-in-a-poke policy has placed us), as though Mr. Willis has not done what he was instructed to do. He has said in a published letter, that a *contingency* has arisen, not contemplated when he left Washington. It seems, as if he meant "a *condition* of affairs, which he did not comprehend." At any rate, he has not put Liliuokalani on the throne, nor does there seem to be the least likelihood of his doing so. It seems as if he would prefer being recalled rather than carry out Cleveland's program.

Cleveland has played his game in a very underhand way. I don't wonder that the Senators at Washington feel sore over the bamboogle-ment in which it seems Cleveland has succeeded in keeping *them*. A dastardly part of the Cleveland policy is that while nothing has been said to Americans about it, information has been given somehow to Hawaiians, English, and Japanese. They knew the day fixed for the restoration of the Queen. Perhaps Admiral Irwin knew it too, for on the night of Nov. 9, the *Philadelphia*'s boats with gatling guns were kept in the water alongside the vessel till 4 a.m.

Then, too, we have seen in the harbor an English man-of-war, kept here in violation of tacit understanding with the English govt. and the U. S. to bolster up a fallen dynasty. Strange to say also, a Japanese man-of-war came into the harbor yesterday morning, as if to be on hand to aid the Queen's party, who promised if they be re-instated in power to give the Japanese the right of suffrage as compensation for the support this war vessel might render.

As yet all these schemes seem to have been defeated because Cleveland sent as U. S. Minister a Christian gentleman of prudence and the fear of God, instead of the boorish Georgia "Cracker" that Blount proved himself to be. He tried to make it appear that he was securing information about the resources of the Country, the experiences of the past, and the probabilities of the future with reference to annexation. But his real object seems to have been to manufacture or manipulate testimony so as to make out a plausible case against the Harrison administration. But on that he seems to me to have signally failed. Aside from the direct falsehoods in his report, his perversions and prevarications only bring out in stronger light, his disregard of truth and righteousness in his dealings with the main question.

He has apparently no word to say of the villainy, duplicity, and perniciousness of the Queen's policy, which made it no longer endurable. I think Mr. Willis got the idea from Mr. Blount's report that the officers of the Provisional Government were a band of atrocious and diabolical thieves. He was utterly taken aback when he found they were high toned, high principled men, men of standing, men of affairs, who were pursuing a policy that simply sought in perfectly proper and legitimate ways, to secure and promote good order, good government, the common welfare, while opposed to them were pimps and prostitutes, gamblers and drunkards, with a few sore headed, sour minded, disappointed office seekers to give a fictitious glamour of respectability to a very disreputable crowd. He avowed himself, in his letter published here, an American, thoroughly so, and it seems as if [he] had very little in sympathy with the royalist party. In fact, they at once declared him "too-missionary."

The strangely favoring Providence that has so often been manifested in Hawaiian history, seems again to have most graciously interposed for our deliverance: and while the people and the press of the U. S. have been denouncing Cleveland's "restoration of a rotten royalty," nothing has been done here by Cleveland's appointee to carry out any such policy. The announcement of it in Gresham's letter simply unified and vivified the sentiment of those opposed to the Queen.

We could not have anticipated any such program from any President of the U. S. But now that we know the worst, we have prepared ourselves for it. The Provisional Government can only be put out of the way by the armed intervention of a foreign power. Will Cleveland order any such steps in the face of the overwhelming tide of indignation that has asserted itself all over the land against his Hawaiian policy?

We feel sorry for Mr. & Mrs. Willis, who mingle very little in society, though they come to church regularly.

Eschewing politics, Dr. Beckwith gave us a fine Thanksgiving sermon on the "New England Home." There was a large congregation, U. S.

Minister Willis was present and though a Southerner must have enjoyed such a presentation of the blessedness and blessings of Yankee home life.[59]

A few days later he could give no higher praise of Willis than to say, "I see no reason to change my opinion in regard to U. S. Minister Willis. He is 'too missionary' to suit the royalists, i.e., is a true American Christian gentleman, sensible and judicious. A kind Providence seems to have sent him here."[60]

But once again the unblindfolding process affected the Willis image and this time, it took another long letter for Hyde to express his disaffection for Willis and analyze the purposes of President Cleveland:

I must confess I am personally disappointed in Mr. Willis' course. I gave him credit for being a fairminded man, for I did not discover in him any unwillingness to be informed of the facts that might appear in opposition to prejudices and prepossessions. But he has shown himself in his public actions so incapable of looking at a question in all its phases, or so unwilling to do so, that information is thrown away upon him and warning is trampled underfoot.

Cleveland's dastardly and underhanded policy of infamy has had a fitting foil in this incompetent diplomat, who has made such a mess of the President's unthinkable schemes of restoration. The royalists and Britishers here have been kept well informed of Cleveland's policy and plans, but not a word for all these months of weary waiting and anxious expectancy has been vouchsafed to the Provisional Government.

Gresham's letter, announcing Cleveland's policy, when it was received here, gave a fitting opportunity to press Mr. Willis to make some official communication to the Government to whose friendship he had been accredited in terms of approval and hopefulness. But Mr. Willis' unofficial talks had awakened forebodings of possible perils that no one had imagined would be brought upon us by any action of the administration at Washington. He said to one of the Cabinet, "Who are you anyway? I have come here to carry out Cleveland's policy, which he had determined upon before he entered the White House: and no power on earth can change it. I have three war vessels in this harbor, and could crush you in a moment," doubling up his fist before the eyes of his astounded interviewer. What was there left for us but to prepare for the worst? So thorough organization was made against any hostile attack. Squads of men were armed, and received orders as to their special post of duty. Native policemen not in sympathy with the Government were summarily dismissed. Everything around the Executive and Judiciary buildings was put in readiness for resistance. Sand bags piled up, machine guns placed at points of advantage. The 300 men that might have landed from the U. S. vessels would have found no easy task before them. They were under orders to land at a moment's notice, fully armed, and with Gatling guns.

A conflict seemed imminent. Mr. Willis, pressed for some specific declaration of intentions, said he would be ready in 48 hours. You can imagine how intense the excitement was. You can imagine also the intense rebound of relief that came when the substance of his weak and silly talk was made public, a statement of Cleveland's determination and a request to them to step down and out. There was no need of any speedy reply. There could be only one, a most decided refusal to do anything of the kind . . .

The point of danger is passed for the present. The question has passed out of Cleveland's control. The press and the public generally seem to be united in condemning Cleveland.

I marvel that our *Congregationalist* should be so prejudiced against the claims and rights of good government and Christian civilization, and be willing to hand us over to misrule and degradation, as far as any influence it might exert to the contrary is concerned. Here are English and Japanese war vessels lying in our harbor, watching for the first mistake or misadventure that would give them a pretext for interference and disposing of us to suit themselves.[61]

Many more pages of this sort illustrate the week-to-week vicissitudes of personal worry of Hyde, citizen and patriot; they also serve as one man's version of the history of a confused interplay among nations and races and personalities. These excerpts from successive Hyde letters to Boston depict with a free-flowing clarity the smokeless fire of government news as viewed through his eyes.

January 5, 1894: It is evident that we cannot expect annexation under Cleveland with territorial government. Steps are being taken to organize speedily a lower house with suitable limitations on suffrage qualifications, leaving the present Executive and Advisory Council to constitute the upper house.[62]

January 11: The center of the political contest is now transferred to Washington. It seems from all newspapers received that Pres. Cleveland's policy has received and will receive almost universal condemnation. I have seen nothing of Mr. and Mrs. Willis. He seems to associate chiefly with the English Minister, Mr. Wodehouse. Mr. T. H. Davies has been writing some bitter articles in the *Evening Bulletin,* against the Missionaries' sons, who have "stolen a kingdom." As he is interested in Kaiulani's[63] future, he seems unable to look at the situation apart from the possibility of her occupying the throne in which he would be the big man at court.[64]

February 3: The publication of Mr. Willis' report of his interview with her [the Queen] and his futile endeavor to persuade her to abandon her wish to decapitate all the revolutionists, confiscate their property, and banish their families, ought to convince everyone how unfit she is to be trusted with sovereign authority. The last mail with its disclosure of the Queen's vindictive malice led to a good many jokes about necks and heads. It was the pluck of the people here that made the revolution successful. They showed the same pluck in getting ready to defend themselves against the U.S. forces, if the attempt should have been made to restore the Queen by force.[65]

March 3: Now that annexation seems far off, if not impossible, our politicians are preparing for some more permanent form of government. The Annexation Club has appointed a Committee of Thirteen to prepare a platform, and perfect a party organization. Pres. Dole is at work on a new Constitution.[66]

With annexation almost hopelessly mired down in Washington, the Provisional Government organizers made plans to establish a permanent government of republican nature:

Our Constitutional Convention has done good work. The draft submitted by the Executive Council had been carefully prepared with the aid of various jurists in the United States. The Convention, a truly representative body, modified it in some respects. It is hoped to have it ready

so as to promulgate the new Republic July 4. The Queen is still obstinate
& ugly tempered, threatens to cut off the head of any Hawaiian that
votes for the new Constitution which gives the Hawaiians larger political
advantages than they ever had. But that is her love (?) for her dear
people (?).[67]

Two weeks later he could report happily to Boston:

We celebrated the Fourth of July with double eclat with all the usual
fervor remembering the Natal Day of the American Nation, and proclaiming in simple and appropriate style the Republic of Hawaii. There
is every indication that Pres. Dole and his associates will administer the
Republic as acceptably and successfully as they have its predecessor,
the P. G. [Provisional Government].[68]

Storm clouds were constantly hovering over the men of reform in
government. One individual on the local scene was in some respects
a continuous link in fomenting trouble—Robert W. Wilcox. It was he
who staged the summer rebellion of 1889. He participated in another
attempt in 1892 but his most dramatic effort was the insurrection con-
trived in late 1894 and launched in January 1895. The will and resiliency
of the new republic were tested and proved equal to the challenge. Hyde
was not a part of this action, yet was exposed to it in a minor way:

January 10, 1895: . . . My son Charles came running home soon after
the hour for church service saying the long threatened attempt to overthrow the government had been begun in good earnest, and that while
the police were searching a house out beyond Waikiki for arms, Charles
Carter (son of Hon. H. A. P. Carter, now a prominent lawyer here, and
one of the Commissioners who went to Washington two years ago) had
been [fatally] shot, that the church was being deserted, Citizen's Guards
rallying at their different rendezvous.
He was out all night acting as messenger, and late on towards morning
relieving one of the Guards. I went out myself several times in the night
and could now learn much more. The morning brought definite intelligence & the whole city was aroused. Business was suspended & the
work of suppressing the uprising was begun in earnest. Not until Tuesday
morning was martial law declared, and the fifth night finds the leaders

of the movement still armed and untaken, though the attempt has proven a failure in everything except as an indication of the strength of the government, the wise and abundant provision made for such an emergency & the universal determination to put a stop for once for all to this fatal & fatuous foolhardiness of some scatterbrained unprincipled adventurers who have been treated all too leniently in the past. The poor natives, ready to do anything asked of them by those whom they regard as leaders, are coming in, starved and cold, but I am afraid no wiser by any such experience. There seems to be nothing left but summary and severe measures, & this seems to be the universal sentiment.

Personally I can but grieve over such a state of affairs. It seems likely only to separate and segregate the Hawaiians still more from any participation in public affairs. They are utterly unfit as well as unfitted for the complicated political machinery of the 19th century. They have been out of the current of civilization so long that they cannot catch on as the locomotive of modern progress rushes along their way.

We have kept up our program for the Week of Prayer. There have been 40 on an average at the various district meetings morning and evening. But no allusion is made to the present situation by anyone but myself. I do not think that the "pious" natives are engaged in this affair at all. It is the hoodlum element, the harum scarum ragamuffin element of boys who never work for their living, but wander around "bumming" on their acquaintances, knowing little of any principles involved in the affair & caring for nothing except some new excitement and a chance to get a free drink of gin.

That such a set should be able to throw this community, every once in a while, into this feverish unrest & disquiet, shows how little severity there is in the exercise of governmental authority in managing an indolent tropical race. But this community with $20,000,000 of American capital involved in business here, cannot afford the damage & loss to the pecuniary interests of this large proportion of our wealth. The fiat has gone forth & the leaders will be shown no mercy.

Other interests are imperiled as well as the commercial. One of the boys of Kamehameha [school] was brought in as a prisoner today. It is reported that John Wise, whom the American Board educated at Oberlin, is one of Wilcox's followers. One of the clerks in Lewers & Cooke's employ where my son Charles is, is a Lieutenant in one of the Wilcox companies. The other Lieutenant is the youngest son of Judge

Widemann, who went on to Washington & Europe in the entourage of the Queen. But there are few educated men concerned. It is as foolish and fatal an undertaking as any fatuous foolhardiness could have conceived. None the less it is criminal and outrageous & deserving of punishment.

Friday, Jan. 11 . . . The military and the sharpshooters have been on the mountains hunting the fugitives, but without any success. Patience and perseverance must win the day. But the difficulties are great in these precipitous mountains with their tangled undergrowth, many sharp ridges running out from the central backbone of the island. I hope that this is the last of such abortive attempts at insurrection.[69]

Robert Wilcox was a chameleon. Educated at Kalakaua's expense, he turned against him. A royalist in Liliuokalani's cause he joined the Annexation Club when President Harrison seemed likely to succeed with the annexation treaty. He returned to royalism and thereupon engineered the January insurrection after Cleveland withdrew the treaty.

President Sanford B. Dole and his associates in their judicious adherence to the principles of the democratic process made a deep impression on Dr. Hyde:

President Dole's proclamation of Monday last declared the work of the Military Commission at an end, and martial law no longer in force. The men who are in control, have the courage of their convictions, and yet as the Attorney General tells me, feel that *behind* the law is an undefined power of public sentiment sustaining and enforcing it. As a small island community with a heterogeneous population of widely differing degrees and methods of civilization, the conditions are so peculiar as to call for peculiar measures of legislation and administration. But it seems to me that the shrewd, farseeing wisdom of the government is well attested by the acknowledged absence of any serious mistakes in the various steps they have taken for the establishment, maintenance, and advancement of social order and good government.[70]

He felt constrained to comment on missionary positioning in regard to reform movements, especially that of 1893:

Of course the missionaries came in for more than a fair share of the odium that attaches to such a radical change; but if ever there was a movement, free from all questionable motives in its origin, and from all dishonorable measure in its methods, it was the Hawaiian Revolution of '93. But it is one of the disciplinary experiences in the school of Divine Providence, that the followers of Christ, like their Master, should be misinterpreted by those who have their own ulterior purposes to serve by slander and detraction. I have taken no active part in political measures, though everyone knows with which party in this matter my affiliations and sympathies must be. It is a matter of regret to me personally, that the Hawaiians, whose welfare is my first consideration, should have had such rulers. But no amount of warning or pleading would avail with such persons as Kalakaua or Liliuokalani.[71]

Some insight into the Kalakaua mind is gained from a Hyde letter on the subject of the use of the *kahuna,* the pagan priest, in a supportive role in engaging the natives for political purposes. "One of the Hawaiian ministers, whose uncle has recently died, brought to me the Kahuna's outfit which he found in his uncle's room. I took it up to the Museum and Prof. Brigham displays it with the title 'Modern Heathenism, articles used in praying for the restoration of the Queen.' The man was a member of the secret order of the priesthood, established by Kalakaua, as head of the Hale Naua . . . [He] mixed up the rites and shibboleths of Free Masonry (he was a 33⁰ Free Mason) with the mummeries and orgies of heathenism. The ritual of the Hale Naua is a literary curiosity as well as a sociological puzzle."[72] No amount of praying by a *kahuna* was strong enough to restore the Queen.

The Republic could now stand erect and confident until the annexation question would be resolved. It finally took a foreign war of the United States—the war with Spain—to rouse Congress to take up the dormant resolution on annexation. The sovereignty of the Republic of Hawaii was transferred to the United States, August 12, 1898.

The war brought more than annexation to Hawaii. Shiploads of servicemen were given a respite in the long journey from California to Manila, which placed the need for immediate hospitality measures in the willing hands of the local people:

June 4, 1898: The 2500 troops from California for Manila arrived

Wednesday. They have had the freedom of the city for two days, and left this morning at 9:30. You can imagine what excitement and confusion there has been, and we are expecting the second detachment to arrive next week.[73]

July 26: We have been very busy looking after the comfort of the Boys in Blue enroute to Manila, and I need not assure you Honolulu hospitality has been generous and unrestricted. As the Red Cross Society has its hospital in the Kindergarten close by our house we have abundant opportunity to learn of the soldiers' needs and provide for them in various helpful ways. Mrs. Hyde is chairman of the Executive Committee and has her hands full of work for which fortunately she has the leisure now that there is so little to do for the Woman's Board or the Kindergarten.[74]

There was a real concern about the welfare of the mission stations in Micronesia. Involved also was the safety of the *Morning Star*. The Spanish, in administering their captured island groups, had acted arbitrarily in uprooting the local governments and church leaders. If the natives there, along with their missionary advisers were drawn into this war, and if the *Morning Star* were molested there would be worry enough. As events turned out the quick termination of the war eased the minds of all.

One final word on annexation in typical Hyde language provides a suitable conclusion to this chapter. "Thanks for your congratulations and your welcome to the sisterhood of states. Little Hawaii will give a good account of herself in every way, socially, commercially, ecclesiastically. But we need your sympathy and interest as much as ever and now that we are 'one of the family,' don't suppose that fact relieves you from further care and oversight."[75]

NOTES

1 Letter, Hyde to the Rev. N. G. Clark, ABCFM, Oct. 9, 1877.
2 Ibid., Apr. 24, 1879.
3 Ibid., Sept. 27, 1880.
4 Ibid.
5 Ibid., Dec. 18, 1880.
6 Ibid., Jan. 17, 1881.
7 Ibid., Feb. 11, 1882.
8 Ibid., June 3.
9 Ibid., July 31.
10 Ibid.

11 Ibid., Aug. 27.
12 Ibid., Sept. 25.
13 Ibid., Nov. 18.
14 Ibid., March 10, 1883.
15 Letter Hyde to the Rev. Means, ABCFM, April 9.
16 Letter Hyde to Clark, June 29, 1884.
17 Letter Hyde to the Rev. Judson Smith, ABCFM, Oct. 15.
18 Ibid., Dec. 30.
19 Ibid., Jan. 26, 1886.
20 Ibid., Feb. 15.
21 Ibid., Jan. 14, 1887.
22 Ibid., March 5.
23 Letter Hyde to the Rev. E. K. Alden, ABCFM, March 5.
24 Letter Hyde to Smith, April 11.
25 Letter Hyde to Alden, May 17.
26 Letter Hyde to Smith, June 1.
27 Letter Hyde to Rudolph W. Meyer, Molokai, June 6.
28 Letter Hyde to Alden, June 15.
29 Letter Hyde to Smith, June 29.
30 Letter Hyde to Alden, July 1.
31 Letter Hyde to Smith, July 11.
32 Ibid., July 25.
33 Ibid., July 29.
34 Ibid., Aug. 26.
35 Ibid., Oct. 20.
36 Ibid., March 13, 1888.
37 Ibid., August 7.
38 Ibid., Jan. 17, 1890.
39 Ibid., Feb. 7, 1891.
40 Ibid., Feb. 18.
41 Ibid., Feb. 7.
42 Ibid., Feb. 18.
43 Letter Hyde to Gen. S. C. Armstrong, Feb. 24.
44 Letter Hyde to Smith, Feb. 11, 1892.
45 Ibid.
46 Ibid., July 27.
47 Ibid., Aug. 8.
48 Ibid., Oct. 20
49 Ibid., Nov. 8.
50 Ibid., Nov. 18.
51 Ibid., Jan. 11, 1893.
52 Ibid., Feb. 1.
53 Ibid., Feb. 9.
54 Ibid., Feb. 28.
55 Executive Documents, Blount Report, House of Representatives, Second Session, 1893–1894.
56 Ibid., No. 26, Statement of C. M. Hyde, Apr. 3, 1893.
57 Letter Hyde to Smith, Apr. 26.
58 ABCFM, 83rd Annual Meeting, Worcester, Mass., Oct. 10–13.
59 Letter Hyde to Smith, Dec. 4.

60 Ibid., Dec. 9.
61 Ibid., Jan. 1, 1894.
62 Ibid., Jan. 5.
63 Princess Victoria Kaiulani, frequently mentioned in connection with the Hawaiian throne—Mr. Davies acted as her guardian.
64 Letter Hyde to Smith, Jan. 11, 1894.
65 Ibid., Feb. 3.
66 Ibid., Mar. 3.
67 Ibid., June 23.
68 Ibid., July 10.
69 Ibid., Jan. 10, 1895.
70 Ibid., Mar. 20.
71 Ibid., Apr. 29.
72 Ibid., June 17.
73 Ibid., June 4, 1898.
74 Ibid., July 26.
75 Ibid., Aug. 17.

Chapter 15

THREE MEN, EARLY 1889

CLEARLY THE PICTURE of Dr. Hyde to this point is that of zealot, wise man and humble, avid scholar, "doer of the word," and overall a truly good example of that New England-bred community-minded leader which throughout the course of several generations has formulated the pattern we speak of as the American way.

But removing an obscuration which has clouded his entitlement to a position of precedence and remembrance more befitting his work is a strange task, and the telling of it is not simple.

Dr. Hyde's first contact with Father Damien was made in September 1885. He had planned a leper-settlement visit three summers earlier but when Hollenbeck, the famed temperance speaker, unexpectedly became available for a crusade, he cancelled the trip, for his presence was required in town. But now (1885) he gathered up all the "old clothes and clothing he could get and anything else that would be of benefit" to the patients and sailed off to Molokai.

A convention of native branches of the YMCA was scheduled at Pukoo, Molokai. Down at Kalawao-Kalaupapa, the leper settlement, on an isolated peninsula of the island were two Hawaiian (Congregational) churches, one new and the other restored, both ready for dedication. His training school would not resume classes until October and the YMCA and church celebrations could be conveniently arranged for one trip.

At the settlement, having participated in the church dedications, he turned to visiting. He went from patient to patient in the hospital and talked with his own people among whom were patients, *kokuas*,[1] and settlement employees. He also spent considerable time with Father Damien and discussed leprosy with him, its ravages and reported cures. His regular visits to the Honolulu receiving station had acquainted him with the physical and social effects of the disease and he had corresponded widely, seeking to gather the best opinions as to its cause and cure. He was closely identified with some Board of Health officials and staff in Honolulu and others resident in the settlement. But here was the heart of the country's effort to care for the lepers. He made notes which he expanded into a 5000-word article in two parts for the *Hawaiian Gazette*.[2] Dr. A. A. Mouritz, resident physician at the settlement, gave a description of Hyde's visit:

It was his first visit to the leper settlement, his business was to look after "church matters" and also consecrate the newly erected church at Kalaupapa. He accepted such hospitality as I could extend him and remained in the Settlement some weeks.

During the following days Dr. Hyde was busy with church affairs; later he made a careful examination . . . the homes and schools . . . emphasized the benefits that would accrue in having more commodious and up-to-date buildings in every respect, for girls and single women, for boys and single men; nursing was also debated and the conclusion reached that paid foreign nurses were out of the question, Sisters and Brothers of Catholic organizations being alone available and promising success. Father Damien only too eagerly acquiesced and hoped ultimately to see those changes carried out.

Dr. Hyde's visit was directly and indirectly of untold benefit to the lepers. The doctor had the ear and confidence of wealthy men connected with the then Fort Street Church, now Central Union; both Mr. Charles R. Bishop, and Mr. Henry P. Baldwin of Maui were connected with this church . . .[3]

Another visitor went to the settlement on the heels of Dr. Hyde. Charles Warren Stoddard, artist and writer, was on a sentimental Journey and he sentimentalized at a great rate. In a small booklet, he, like Hyde, covered the entire trip from the island's chief port, Kaunakakai, describing the dusty horseback ride to cliff-edge overlooking the settlement and the winding, steep zig-zag trail to the bottom.

He was impressed with the friendliness and comparative cleanliness of the patients and he felt the Board of Health had, years before, chosen an ideal spot for this segregation. He also spent much time with Father Damien and drew from him the story of his life, his decision to volunteer at the settlement, his problems with the Board of Health, and in general the conditions of Kalawao-Kalaupapa. He also met government officials.[4]

Four years later in the waning weeks of 1888, Robert Louis Stevenson and his family party were impatiently waiting out the remasting of their charter ship *Casco* at Papeete, Tahiti.

Stevenson was not only a sick man physically, but he had not recovered from the effects of a break with one of his closest friends, William Ernest Henley. Biographer Steuart commented on the proposed Pacific islands trip on the *Casco* that it was not with "bounding exhilaration of spirits" that he set forth . . . "to give any such impression is utterly untrue to fact."[5]

The vessel left on Christmas Day, experiencing even more delay because of a "deplorable passage" of punishing storms and frustrating calms between Papeete and Honolulu. So long overdue was the *Casco* that Mrs. Strong, Stevenson's stepdaughter, then a Honolulu resident, had given the voyagers up for lost. But the ship sailed into Honolulu harbor and was moored in the stream off the Oceanic Steamship Company wharf January 24, 1889.

Stevenson had achieved great literary fame; *A Child's Garden of Verses, Treasure Island, Kidnapped, Dr. Jekyll and Mr. Hyde,* and a long list of others, had brought the author high esteem. He was a welcome addition to Honolulu's literati and its social circles. His arrival was anticipated because Mrs. Strong had alerted the local press.

Meanwhile Stevenson was under obligation to the McClure Syndicate for a series of letters on his Pacific sailings. He was also completing the *Master of Ballantrae* which had already started appearing as a magazine serial.

As he took up residence in Waikiki he had not the slightest hint of what the next fifteen months would bring of interplay among Father Damien, Charles M. Hyde, and himself. Damien was little more than a name; of Hyde he knew nothing. In the hospitable warmth of Honolulu he began a round of social calls, ultimately becoming very friendly with King Kalakaua. He also was able to concentrate on writing.

By coincidence, Hyde mentioned both Father Damien and Stevenson in a letter to the American Board. The Damien reference was one of several that he had been sending of late to the Board, and which revealed a shift from the somewhat restrained praise accorded the leper priest following the 1885 visit to Molokai. The observation regarding Stevenson was routine: "Robert Louis Stevenson (author of *Dr. Jekyll and Mr. Hyde*) is visiting the islands. He is voyaging in a yacht and comes here from Tahiti where he spent two months. He visited the Marquesas on his way up and speaks very highly of the Hawaiian Missionary Kauwealoha."[6]

This passage bespeaks an early meeting of Stevenson and Hyde. There were several meetings, one of which was purely business. Stevenson, with his chronic illness, was an impatient man. His health and spirits seemed more buoyant at sea. So no sooner was he settled than he looked around for a sailing charter or passage anywhere in the Pacific; the *Casco* charter had been terminated at Honolulu. One day the *Morning Star,* the missionary packet, arrived from Micronesia for its turnaround and he saw this ship as it moved towards Honolulu harbor.

The little ship occasioned the next meeting between the two:

. . . He would like to go to Micronesia on the next voyage of the *Morning Star* as a passenger with his wife, paying whatever may be judged a fair compensation.

He would write his impressions but would submit his Mss. to you [American Board] as well as to us here with the privilege of erasing any statements we might deem erroneous, or injurious to the missionary work. He is not a religious man, himself, nor is his wife a pious woman. Very far from it: but his mother is a godly woman, now with him here, the daughter of a Scotch minister. So he knows how religious people view things, yet considers himself a gentleman bound to regard with respect the opinions and wishes of his hosts, would not broach his own opinions, differ though they may from ours in regard to the need of salvation, the observance of the Sabbath, and so on.

He says, "Even if I saw reason to differ in a hundred points with the policy of the missionaries, I should remember, first, that I agreed and hoped with them in a thousand others; second, that they were men of devoted lives, and I that very poor person, a man of the world; third, that I was their guest and (I hope) a gentleman; and fourth that I was in a position (through their kindness) where I might hope to help a little, but where if I ever in the least abused it, I must infallibly and perhaps fatally hinder.

"I hope and believe, if your Board should see fit to accept my proposal, the Mission will be in all ways a gainer! Even upon points of difference, should any arise, the eye of the outsider is sometimes clearer than that of the master, and there might prove to be some truth in what I might find to call in question." He says also "From my childhood I have been thrown much in contact with mission workers, and count among them several of my friends. Though, perhaps from the accident of special knowledge I had not previously been very much interested in any mission but the Zerana Mission in India, I have conceived a very high impression of the necessity and the excellence of the work in the South Seas. Had it been otherwise, oxen and wainropes could not have taken me on board the *Morning Star*."

I copy the above from Mr. Stevenson's note to Mr. Damon [F. W.] with whom he sought an interview first in making his request to be permitted to go out as a passenger on the *Star*. I told Mr. Damon that I thought the Board here might hesitate about granting the request without consultation with you at Boston and offered to write to you by a sailing vessel advertised to leave at noon today. I have written this very hurriedly in order to catch this mail. I have had no time to interview members of the Hawaiian Board. What would be your thoughts in regard to this request? I wish you could come to some decision as soon as possible and telegraph it to Mr. Flint in S. F. He may have the opportunity to forward it by some chance opportunity previous to the regular steamer mail.[7]

There was not much inclination on the part either of Hyde or the

American Board to honor Stevenson's request—as is obvious from this excerpt: "I have to acknowledge the receipt by SS. *Umatilla,* this ev'g, your letters of May 1 & 17. One object in writing to you about Mr. Stevenson was not to give any abrupt refusal, but take such time for consideration as in all probability would result (as proved to be the case) in a change of plan. Capt. Garland [of the Star] has no reason to fear any unwelcome passengers."[8]

But all to no purpose. The intervening hand of disaster provided commercial passage. On April 6 the Oceanic steamer *Alameda* docked in Honolulu with tragic news of the worst hurricane ever known in Western Samoa. Another Oceanic ship, the *Equator,* would be following with injured sailors from the wrecked ships in Apia roadstead. The news included word that after proceeding to a turnaround in San Francisco, the *Equator* would touch at Honolulu on a return trip to Apia.

Stevenson turned from the *Morning Star*[9] with an eager sigh of relief which was likely matched by Hyde and his associates. He chartered the *Equator* for four months, not for Micronesia but Apia, Western Samoa. Stevenson hedged his *Equator* future, suggesting to Hyde that if there were any change of plans he might like to complete the balance of the south Pacific voyage by possibly returning to Honolulu on the *Star* and chartering another vessel to Fiji. This plan did not materialize.

The Samoan tragedy which resulted in a change of ships for Stevenson involved Hyde in another way. The news of the devastating hurricane with stories of heroism and severe loss of life and property roused the sympathies of Honolulu citizens to fever pitch. Kinship of the Polynesian Samoans and Hawaiians, combined with the currency of international rivalry of the Americans, British, Germans, and Spanish for power in the Pacific, projected the story for days on end in the Honolulu press. Churches took it up:

The Samoan disaster, of which the up steamer brought us the news, has aroused profound interest here. The Catholics had a requiem mass Tuesday evg. The Anglicans followed suit with memorial services Wednesday afternoon. The Central Union people had a crowded church at the evening service held there yesterday (Thursday) evg. Much to my surprise I found myself the orator of the occasion. I had no thought of occupying any such position, but managed to read a few sentences I had hurriedly thrown together yesterday after.[10]

Left: Bishop Hall, lava stone classroom building of the Kamehameha School for Boys. Erected 1887. *Above:* Punahou Preparatory School in the remodeled Armstrong home on Beretania Street, now the site of the Anglican Cathedral. *Below:* Kawaiahao Seminary's first building, formerly the Mission Printing House, later site of Hawaiian Board of Missions's headquarters, presently part of the City of Honolulu facilities.

Above: Bernice Pauahi Bishop Museum, Palama, Honolulu, founded by Charles Reed Bishop as a memorial to his wife. First construction in 1889. *Right:* First building of the Honolulu YMCA at the *makai-ewa* corner of Hotel and Alakea Streets. Dedicated in 1883. *Below:* Honolulu Library and Reading Room Association. Erected on the *mauka-ewa* corner of Alakea and Hotel Streets in 1884.

Top left: The Rev. Mr. Elias Bond of Kohala, Hawaii Island. Great friend and benefactor of Charles M. Hyde. *Top right:* Judge Laurence McCully, Hyde's closest Honolulu friend. *Bottom right:* Mr. and Mrs. Charles Reed Bishop, 1866. He was the banker of Hawaii, she the great-granddaughter of Kamehameha I.

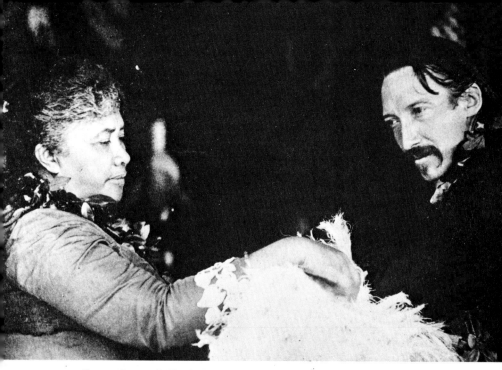

Above: Queen Liliuokalani of Hawaii and Robert Louis Stevenson, 1893.
Below: Author Robert Louis Stevenson visiting with King Kalakaua of Hawaii, 1889.

Three days after Hyde dispatched this letter to the American Board, Father Damien passed away at Kalawao, Molokai. He had been busy at Kalawao, but sick as he was and getting sicker, Father Damien had stayed with his routine of visits, interviews, daily chores, and the Mass. He could hardly have known much of Stevenson or been aware of the *Casco,* plunging and ploughing and halting northward to Honolulu in January—nor were he and Stevenson to meet.

He did know Hyde from the visit a few years earlier and from the stream of contributions supplied for the patients' welfare by the women of Central Union Church, by the students' families of the North Pacific Missionary Institute and several agencies of the Hawaiian Evangelical Association.

Despite his grave illness, Father Damien enjoyed satisfactions. The Bishop Home for Girls, provided by the efforts of Dr. Hyde with Charles R. Bishop, and staffed by the Sisters of St. Francis, had been opened in late 1888. The young girls would be well cared for by the nurses of that order. Father Moellers followed Mother Marianne and her nurses into Kalaupapa as the sick Damien was failing; so help, both in people and facilities, was coming and his mission would be continued.

On the minus side might be mentioned his continuing conflict with his superior, Father Lenor, a relationship in which the latter was the stalking critic and Father Damien unreplying and somewhat self-effacing. But this kind of trouble was nothing in the face of the physical torture he was suffering. He tried every new ointment and oil in search of a relief that would never come. Each passing day brought sharper cuts into his life until finally on April 15, 1889 he passed away, at the too-young age of forty-nine. "He made his will," wrote John Farrow, "leaving what few belongings he had to be disposed of at the Bishop's discretion . . . to Belgium went the last letter: Kindly remember me to all the Fathers in Louvain . . . I am still able, but not without some difficulty to stand every day at the altar, where I do not forget any of you. Do you, in return, pray and get prayers for me, who are being gently drawn toward the grave."[11]

Shortly after Father Damien's demise, Stevenson, in need of background material for more letters for his McClure contract,[12] took ship for Hawaii island. There he looked at erupting Kilauea, examined a ranch for possible purchase, visited native villages and attended a court in session. The notes of this early May tour were drawn on later not only for the letters but also in his writing the *Bottle Imp* and *Isle of Voices*.

He was personally averse to visiting the leper settlement and he kept putting off a decision but the need for more notes for more letters led him to call upon Dr. N. B. Emerson, President of the Board of Health. There was some urgency, for the sailing of his *Equator* charter was imminent.

Dr. Emerson proved uncooperative and illuminated his personal journal with his reactions:

May 15, 1889: . . . Mr. Stevenson, the author in at the office today requesting of all things, the permission of the Board to visit Kalawao! Naturally I refused, but with that pleading look he is so well known about town for I almost gave in. Told him to fill out an official request by letter and I would see what I could do about the matter.

May 16, 1889: . . . Called to the Palace by H. M. [King Kalakaua] today to discuss the matter of Stevenson . . . puzzled by H. M. being in the act, it seems Belle Strong put pressure on the King. He was very nice about it all, saying he did not wish to interfere with the work of the Board, but would appreciate it as a personal favor. I stated my feelings in the matter, that once we make exception to him others will want to also go over and play tourist. H. M. feels he can do Hawaii a great service by allowing RLS to go as he is in a position to do Hawaii much good in that he can tell the world how good our strides have been in isolating and curing the disease. It will let people everywhere know how safe it is to live in the islands. My opinions were to a deaf ear. I left feeling brainwashed—H.M. sounds like an Oceanic S. S. travel poster— much good for Hawaii can come from this—! ! ! Bah . . .

May 18, 1889: . . . Stevenson to have his letter. Came to the office today with Joe Strong, who was as usual—DRUNK . . .[13]

Stevenson had gone over Emerson's head in dispatching Isobel Strong to Kalakaua and counting on intervention by the king wrote a letter to Emerson fromally requesting permission to visit. Although he dated the letter May 15 he did not deliver it until the 18th:

I beg to apply for permission to visit the Leper Settlement on Molokai.

My object is in the first place to write some account of the settlement, as to be in a position to do so, not probably by itself, but in the body of my proposed account of the Polynesian Islands. I am aware how much you must be inclined, in these days of newspaper correspondents, to look askance on such a proposition; but I trust you will consider that I scarcely belong to the same class, and that I visit the settlement with no design to make capital. My second object is to see with my own eyes how the sufferers are disposed; as I have already had occasion to see something of the horrors and dangers of the disease in other islands less considerately managed.[14]

In this letter he gave careful wording to his deportment and purposes if he were permitted to go. There was no reference to Father Damien. Shortly thereafter he obtained approval in a courteous letter of reply[15] and went over immediately from Honolulu. Several days were spent in talking with the nursing sisters at the Bishop Home, the brothers at the Baldwin Home, Brother Dutton, patients and government workers. From these experiences he gathered enough material, including a brief appraisal of Father Damien, for several letters for McClure. Upon his return to Honolulu the Stevenson party packed and prepared to board the *Equator* for a June 24 departure for more Pacific action.

Up to this point, Dr. Hyde had corresponded rather fully with the American Board regarding Father Damien and Stevenson, but as the next period opens up an almost complete hiatus is noted; and yet, with the record filled in from other sources, his role in the approaching confrontation with Stevenson is well documented.

NOTES

1 *Kokua*, a helper. In the case of the leper settlement, a friend, usually a relative, who chose to live with or near a patient.
2 Charles M. Hyde, "A Visit to Molokai," *Hawaiian Gazette*, Sept. 14, 23, 1885. Description of Molokai island with special attention to the leper settlement.
3 Dr. A. A. Mouritz, *Path of the Destroyer* (Honolulu, 1916), p. 289.
4 Charles Warren Stoddard, *The Lepers of Molokai* (Notre Dame, Ind., Ave Maria Press, 1885).
5 John Alexander Steuart, *Robert Louis Stevenson, Man and Writer* (London, Sampson Low, Marston and Co., Ltd., 1924), Vol. II, p. 116.
6 Letter Hyde to the Rev. Judson Smith, ABCFM, Feb. 8, 1889.
7 Ibid., Mar. 25.
8 Ibid., May 31.

9 J. C. Furnas, *Voyage to Windward* (New York, William Sloane Associates, 1951), p. 341. Furnas stated that when the mission denied the Stevensons passage they "repined the less" because an alternative appeared. The denying was Stevenson's.

10 Letter Hyde to Smith, Apr. 12, 1889.

11 John Farrow, *Damien the Leper* (New York, Sheed and Ward, 1937) pp. 196–197.

12 Stevenson, *Letters Upolu Samoa* (New York *Sun*), Feb. to Dec. 1891.

13 [Private] Journal of Dr. N. B. Emerson, President Board of Health, Hawaii. Extracts used with permission of Robert C. Van Dyke.

14 Letter Stevenson to Dr. Nathaniel B. Emerson, Board of Health, May 15. This letter is used with permission of Robert E. Van Dyke.

15 Letter Board of Health (N. B. Emerson) to Stevenson, May 20.

Chapter 16

A LETTER IS PUBLISHED

THE REV. HENRY BARTLETT GAGE is an important factor in the Damien-Hyde-Stevenson story. Indeed the plot could list four instead of three characters and the fourth would be Gage.

After spending one year as a divinity student at Princeton Theological Seminary, a Presbyterian school, Gage left for Colorado where he became known as a missionary pioneer. He started several new churches and conducted revival and temperance meetings. He was appointed trustee of a college, served on committees on Presbyterian records, and edited a modest church journal.[1]

In 1886 he moved to Riverside, California, as pastor of suburban Arlington Presbyterian Church. He also served a pastorate at Long Beach and as a director and trustee of the San Francisco Theological Seminary at San Anselmo.

It is scarcely known that Gage visited Hawaii. He started a three-week holiday there on June 12, 1888 and became acquainted with Dr. Hyde.

The services of a visiting minister were always welcome and Gage was a willing guest. He "assisted at the Lord's Supper in Central Union Church, and preached in the evening with great acceptance [July 1]. Mr. Gage is an active champion of total abstinence."[2] Like Hyde he was a proud wearer of the temperance Blue Ribbon badge.

Gage arranged a week's trip via the S.S. *Kinau* to the volcano pots of Kilauea on Hawaii island as a part of his Hawaiian holiday before departing Honolulu, S.S. *Australia*, July 3. There is no record of his having visited Kalaupapa and at the moment there was no great pressure on him to do so.

He wrote two travel-type stories for the *Riverside Daily Press* in which he made no mention of Father Damien or the leper settlement.[3] He also favored the highly respected *Herald Presbyter* of Cincinnati with an article (August 29, 1888), on religious work in the islands. In this resumé he referred to the work of Dr. Hyde.

However, the laudations which were enhancing the image of Father Damien as the settlement's pioneer processor of law, human welfare, and religious zeal among the lepers stoked controversy. Fires were fueled by such ministers as Gage. He, in protest, sent another article to the *Herald Presbyter*.[4] This was a diatribe about such unfounded praise—his first. It was a generalized popular type of criticism of the "Romish" church and the priests of Molokai. This initial attack carries but a brief mention of Father Damien and spells the name Damion. The concluding paragraph speaks of Hyde as the one who "gave me substantially the same facts as gathered during twelve years in Hawaii, and knowing the native pastors who became lepers, and were sent to Molokai, and in visiting the leper settlements and preaching among the lepers."[5]

Gage's contribution in the *Herald and Presbyter* caused little comment in either Catholic or Protestant news organs and practically none in the lay press. Argument over pre-Damien conditions, Father Damien himself, and the leper settlement, in the weeks immediately surrounding the leper priest's death was mild. Gage was quiet, Stevenson made his visit to Kalaupapa but said little and in Honolulu the *Friend* and *Hawaiian Gazette* talked of other matters.

Then, suddenly, two months after Father Damien's death. The Rev. Sereno E. Bishop authored a lengthy article, "Father Damien's Work." His was a vigorous protest against the downgrading of leper life and welfare before 1873. He quoted extracts which he termed "the grossest

slanders" from *Longman's*, the *N. Y. Tribune*, and the *Christian Union*. He
pointed out that these slanders "upon the Hawaiian Government, which
represents our Christian civilization, are. . . inextricably intermixed
with the laudations of Father Damien. . ."

His purpose was to answer those "slanders" and to set forth the facts
as he saw them, not to discuss Father Damien as such. He called him an
"unquestionably benevolent and devoted priest. . . heroic. . . in undertaking and performing his duties in the face of the liability of becoming
a leper himself," but, ". . . we think it an unworthy exaggeration to
erect this good priest into a rare and wonderful martyr." He dismissed the
gossip which Honolulu heard of Father Damien. "We purposely abstain
from setting forth several acknowledged facts which would put this matter
in a stronger light, and which many here will feel disappointed not to see
published herewith. Enough has been said for our purpose in vindicating
our Hawaiian civilization from the disgraceful inhumanity imputed to
it."[6]

The Bishop article was reprinted in the *Paradise of the Pacific*,[7] quoted in
an editorial in the *Hawaiian Gazette*,[8] and widely used elsewhere. Use of
it, made simultaneously in a letter in the Presbyterian *Occident* of San
Francisco[9] and an editorial in the *Pacific*,[10] directly caused Gage to write
a letter of inquiry to Dr. Hyde July 25 or 26, 1889.[11]

Hyde made immediate reply in a letter dated August 2. It was this
letter that became the *cause celebre*, the target of Robert Louis Stevenson
seven months later. It was brief and devoted merely to refuting what
Hyde considered over-praise and inaccuracy:

In answer to your inquiries about Father Damien, I can only reply that
we who knew the man are surprised at the extravagant newspaper
laudations, as if he was a most saintly philanthropist. The simple truth
is, he was a coarse, dirty man, headstrong and bigoted. He was not sent
to Molokai, but went there without orders; did not stay at the leper
settlement (before he became one himself), but circulated freely over the
whole island (less than half the island is devoted to the lepers) and he
came often to Honolulu. He had no hand in the reforms and improvements inaugurated, which were the work of our Board of Health, as
occasion required and means were provided. He was not a pure man in
his relations with women, and the leprosy of which he died should be
attributed to his vices and carelessness. Others have done much for the

lepers, our own ministers, the government physicians, and so forth, but never with the Catholic idea of meriting eternal life.[12]

The Rev. Mr. Gage did not wait (nor did he ask) for permission to use the letter. He carefully rewrote his February 20 *Herald Presbyter* article, added the Hyde letter at the end and read the paper at a meeting of his church members. There was immediate insistence that he submit it to a religious journal. Forsaking his Cincinnati standby he sent it up the California coast to the *Occident* for its August 28th issue. Damien's name was still spelled Damion.[13]

Hyde had followed his personal reply to Gage's inquiry with an almost identical letter to the American Board. He used a few days to ponder such a move but finally wrote it out and dispatched it, almost a carbon of the other. This version has never been published.[14]

Neither the Gage letter of inquiry nor the original of the Hyde reply have ever been located. If Hyde made specific admonitions as to its not being published, such are not known. There is ample proof, however, in his own words as well as in circumstantial evidence, that he never intended it to be anything but a personal opinion expressed hurriedly to a request from a chance ministerial acquaintance. He is, for example, on record to this effect in a letter to the American Board. "I see that the *Congregationalist* has published a letter I wrote to Mr. Gage in answer to his inquiry about Father Damien. It is clear and conclusive but curt rather than courteous in tone, and I did not expect that he would publish it. . . ."[15] This letter was written five months before Stevenson published his "Open Letter" and was not a defensive statement related to that. Hyde wrote countless papers for public consumption but there is no single instance of his having published a slanderous statement. Fundamentally, the private nature of his reply to Gage does not break that record.

He was a skillful writer, a scholar, and one in whom discretion was all-pervading. He wrote dictionaries, translated hymns, preached sermons, prepared critiques, eulogies, scientific and religious articles—and letters. He was a prodigious letter writer.

In none of these public literary efforts did he express himself in the tone and manner of the letter to the Rev. Mr. Gage.

The letter is not written in the style or careful phrasing that he employed in writing public papers. Even his closing salutation is not in formal style— "yours etc." This would have been a most unusual, not to say careless or hasty, sign off for an open public letter.

It could have been expected that his fellow trustees in the several Bishop trusts would either have been consulted as to the propriety of making such a reply for publication or would have brought up the subject in discussion in the meetings after its publication, particularly after the Stevenson letter was published in Honolulu.[16] The minute books of the trusts are silent. More, there is no reference to be found in any of the minute books of the Woman's Board of Missions, Honolulu YMCA, Hawaiian Mission Children's Society or any other of the Hyde-related agencies.

This was a private letter, and, accepting it as such, Dr. Hyde cannot be condemned for expressing a personal opinion to a friend. Whether it be a thought reserved to silence in the mind or given to the privacy of perusal in a private letter does not matter. One's private life is secured to one's self. Where this tenet of personal privacy is broken, by publication, as it was by the Rev. H. B. Gage, the blame for the tragedy of broken faith is to be laid at his door. This man escaped with never a shred of criticism, even from the one whose life and career were terribly belittled and insulted in the process.

Hyde could never bring himself to utter a word of protest to Gage before or after the appearance of the "Open Letter." Furthermore there is no record of explanation or apology for his action from Gage himself. Perhaps none was needed but the result placed the entire burden of the published letter upon Hyde. There was not the slightest hint of an offer to share the odium of the publication.

I am reminded at this point of a sentence in a letter that Julien D. Hayne, editor and publisher of a short-lived periodical in 1896, *The Hawaiian,* wrote to Alatau T. Atkinson editor of the *Commercial Advertiser.* "Now, I think you will agree with me, Mr. Atkinson, that, morally and legally, the unpublished writings of an author are quite as sacred as his sealed letters." Hayne was a bitter outspoken foe of Hyde and devoted pages of unlimited abuse to him—but not a word about Gage's position in hastening into publication of Hyde's private letter. He had not remembered his concern with Atkinson's having published private materials without notice.

But now the die was cast for a second level of stepped-up debate which

Above: Bishop Home for Girls, Kalaupapa, Molokai, constructed by Charles R. Bishop for girls and young women leper patients, in 1888. This building is one of several comprising the compound. *Below:* Steep zigzag trail used by horses, mules, and humans, extending from the cliff on topside Molokai to the leper settlement at Kalawao-Kalaupapa.

Left: The small building is the Catholic Chapel built at Kalawao prior to Father Damien's arrival. The larger structure is the church built by him. The entire structure, later superseded by a larger one, is St. Philomena's Church. *Center:* Kanaana Hou Hawaiian (Protestant) Church in Kalaupapa. This is the second church of that faith in the settlement. *Bottom:* Siloama Hawaiian Church in Kalawao. This was the first church in the settlement. Founded in 1866, the picture shows it remodeled in 1885, when C. M. Hyde visited the settlement to lead in its dedication.

Right: Father Damien in an early year of his work at Kalawao, Molokai. *Lower left:* This statue of Father Damien by Marisol Escobar stands in the Capitol, Honolulu, Hawaii. An identical statue stands in the Capitol, Washington, D.C. *Lower right:* Brother Joseph Dutton standing at the grave of Father Damien, Kalawao, Molokai. The remains were transferred to Louvain, Belgium in 1936.

Stone marker over the grave of Charles McEwen Hyde, Oahu Cemetery,
Honolulu, Hawaii.

echoed and reverberated largely in religious journals. Copies of the *Occident* of August 28 carrying the Gage article tag-ended by the Hyde letter, made their way through the customary exchange paths to Presbyterian journals and others in the United States and around the world. Feuds between religiously oriented journalistic rivals erupted in Honolulu, Sydney, London, Boston, and other places.

This was the religious press level of the war over Father Damien as set off by the Rev. Mr. Gage. True, the commercial press was drawn into it but usually on a minor news basis except where a commercial paper had an editor supportive of religious interests. The subject was more emotional and editorial than factual and newsworthy. The religious press went at it with a fervor that widened the cleavage between Catholicism and Protestantism. There were notable exceptions; earlier, the Prince of Wales and adherents of the Anglican Church had organized to erect a monument to Father Damien and this was warmly supported by the commercial editors. Then there was fund raising for the work of Father Damien, some prior to his death and some as late as January 1890 by Protestant leaders in London.

But in London, the *English Churchman,* the *London Times,* and the *British Weekly* were hard at the matter of taking sides. In Boston, it was the *Congregationalist, Pilot,* and *Evening Transcript.* In New York, *Longman's Magazine, New York Independent, Catholic Review,* and *Christian Union.* San Francisco had its *Occident, Pacific, Call, Chronicle,* and *Examiner.* Sydney was alive with controversy in its *Presbyterian, Herald,* and *Star.* Skirmishing actually broke out everywhere that the religious press was represented. The in-fighting spread among church groups in the various cities, all before the Stevenson letter.

The seemingly eternal flame of conflict was searing the normally peaceful and calm temperament of Dr. Hyde. Rudolph W. Meyer came to his mind and he turned to him in a letter. Meyer was the kingdom's Board of Health superintendent and representative for the settlement from its inception in 1866 to his death in 1897. He lived on the heights overlooking the settlement from which he could manage Charles R. Bishop's Molokai Ranch and oversee the affairs of the leper colony. Despite his somewhat removed oversight Meyer was knowledgeable and highly regarded. Father Damien had maintained a flow of letters to him locally mentioning such things as shopping lists for Meyer visits to Honolulu: plumbing supplies for the Board of Health bathroom in his quarters, cloth and thread, beer, the newest medicines and his oft-repeated plea for nursing sisters.

Hyde had conferred regularly with Meyer in the latter's Honolulu visits, one of which resulted in a successful Damien-to-Meyer-to-Hyde request of Charles R. Bishop that he build a home for girls and young women in the settlement. So to this strong man of Molokai, Dr. Hyde now turned:

I think it only courteous to tell you that I should let you know something of the controversy into which I have been drawn in regards to Father Damien. I enclose the newspaper clippings which will speak for themselves. Please return them to me.

If there is anything I despise it is the spirit that pick flaws in other's reputation and sneers at any supposed goodness in others. Please notice that I made no attack on anybody. I simply answered a letter of inquiry. Without my permission or knowledge my answer was published, and the publication has led to other inquiries.

I do not ask you to take any part in the matter, for or against me personally. I have learned since I came to the Islands, to take my own stand and not look to others for support. But I am not so independent as to be neglectful of the position others occupy, and accord them the same freedom I wish to maintain for myself, with due recognition of their place and worth.

I have an esteem for you, which I regret to say I did not have for Father Damien, but in what I have said in private or in public about him, I expressed only a belief, which was as clear as daylight to me in view of the facts that had come to my knowledge. It is solely in the interests of truth and justice, that I have spoken and written as I have done, and as I trust also in the spirit of Christian charity with malice toward none.[17]

Hyde's attempt to write off his critics in this message to Meyer is not altogether acceptable but he does make clear his one point of privacy in personal correspondence. Meyer made immediate reply:

. . . I regret that you have been drawn into this extraordinary controversy relating to the late Father Damien.

I was intimately acquainted with Father Damien from the day he landed at the Leper settlement in 1873 or 1874 to within two weeks of his death, and during all this time of 15 or 16 years I came in very frequent contact with him in business, private and other matters, and was always on friendly terms with him.

These extraordinary laudations, bestowed upon Father Damien, were not made by anybody living on these islands; they were made by a few stranger visitors, and I fear from interested motives, to serve their own ends.

During a conversation, which I had with the Rev. S. E. Bishop, relating to this matter, some time during August or September last, I advised to say or write nothing more about it than what had already been said in the *Friend*.

Father Damien was dead, and anything which might perchance be said against him now, as he cannot defend himself, would not be favorably received by most people—and Mr. Bishop came to the same conclusion, adding "if people want to set up an Idol, let them do so," to which I replied that I thought it the most correct way of looking at it, and we parted. . .

As I have been connected with the Leper settlement ever since its establishment in 1866, I must here state that all such aspersions, that the Lepers were neglected until the arrival of Father Damien, *are utterly false*.

Every Administration of the Hawaiian Government from the very commencement, has ever done what they could for these unfortunate sufferers, and every succeeding administration improved upon the one immediately preceding—independently of any particular exertions or influence on the part of Father Damien.

But in justice to Father Damien, let me acknowledge that in my management of the affairs of the Leper settlement, his advice and assistance, especially in the promotion of peace and order, have been very valuable to me.[18]

Hyde warmly appreciated Meyer's reasonableness and started a letter back to him the same day:

Thanks for your letter. It was just what I expected of you, kind, candid, considerate.

I wished you to understand that I did not attack Father Damien. I answered a friend's letter of inquiry, which he indiscreetly published, and without any authority to do so from me.

Then I was attacked for altering [uttering?] falsehoods: but in defending myself, I made no attack on Father Damien, and was careful to understate rather than give publicity to all, that I have good reason to believe from what has been said to me, which might have been truthfully said about him.

I did not wish you to suppose, as has been charged against me, that I attacked Father Damien...[19]

If Dr. Hyde was indiscreet in including a comment on Father Damien's immorality in his reply to Gage, he was still standing on solid ground in subsequently emphasizing the principle that secures privacy to the writer in personal correspondence. But the one critic who violated the "mutual tolerations of man" in a torrent of misbestowed public denunciation was Robert Louis Stevenson.

NOTES

1 Andrew Evans Murray, "A History of Presbyterianism in Colorado," Princeton, N. J., thesis.
2 The *Friend*, July, 1888.
3 *Riverside Daily Press*, July 11, 18.
4 *Herald and Presbyter*, Cincinnati, Feb. 20, 1889.
5 Ibid.
6 The Rev. Sereno E. Bishop, "Father Damien's Work," The *Friend*, July. See Chap. 18.
7 *Paradise of the Pacific*, Honolulu, Aug. 1889.
8 *Hawaiian Gazette*, July 16.
9 *Occident*, San Francisco, July 24.
10 *Pacific*, San Francisco, July 24.
11 Letter the Rev. H. B. Gage to Hyde, July 25 or 26.
12 Letter Hyde to Gage, Aug. 2.
13 *Occident*, Aug. 28.
14 Letter Hyde to the Rev. Judson Smith, ABCFM, Aug. 7.
15 Ibid., Oct. 25.
16 R. L. Stevenson; *Father Damien, open letter to the Reverend Dr. Hyde of Honolulu* (Sydney, Ben Franklin Printers, Feb. 25, 1890) published Mar. 27.
17 Letter Hyde to Rudolph W. Meyer, Molokai, Jan. 7, 1890.
18 Letter Meyer to Hyde, Jan. 15.
19 Letter Hyde to Meyer, Jan. 15.

Chapter 17

A LETTER IN REPLY

AND SO MATTERS STOOD around the turn of the year 1889–1890. The defenses, rationalizations, accusations, viturperations rolled on, largely still in the narrower world served by the religious press, especially bitter in Boston and Honolulu; perhaps because Dr. Hyde's directives for his missionary work emanated from the first place and his operations centered in the second.

This was the time when, in a moving letter, Elizabeth Stuart Phelps wrote an "open letter" regarding an unknown woman who wanted to go to the leper settlement to take upon herself the mantle laid down by Father Damien. [1]

This was also the time when Anglican poet, the Rev. H. B. Chapman, wrote his support of Father Damien in the *London Times*.[2] There was also another Hyde letter. He answered an inquiry, this for publication, from the Rev. W. T. McCormick, a correspondent for the *English Churchman*. This letter was in the same vein, without the charges as contained in his letter to Gage.[3]

But it was also the time when a San Francisco correspondent of the Sydney, Australia, *Presbyterian*, the Rev. T. J. Curtis, appeared as a member of the cast. This journal printed his column, "Our American Letter," regularly. In his October 26, 1889 column he quoted the Hyde letter leaving out the Gage lead-in.[4] It was buried in the column's items of religious views and news. It initiated an interchurch argument in Sydney. But why did the Sydney commercial press not comment editorially or receive letters from "disturbed readers" re-

271

garding Hyde's letter? It had been in print in 1889 since August 28 in the United States and since October 26 in Australia. The fact is, there was no general public outrage, no motivation. There was really no place for the debate to go except as it swirled about the clergy. Under usual circumstances it would have rested dormant in the emotions of the antagonists. But destiny was as ever unpredictable. An eruption was in the making!

Robert Louis Stevenson had purchased some land in Samoa, started work on clearing and building, for here he decided he would settle down—after whatever journeys might be ahead. In early February, foregoing sail for steam, the Stevenson party boarded the SS *Lubeck* for Sydney as a port of call on a trip that was possibly to wind up in a visit to London. Stevenson was excited about the prospect of seeing London but was overwhelmed with the warmest welcome and reception he had ever experienced as he established himself first at the Oxford Hotel and then the Union Club in Sydney.

It was about a year to the day of his visit to Dr. Hyde in Honolulu asking passage on the *Morning Star,* when someone, who had saved the October 26, 1889 issue of the *Presbyterian,* showed the Curtis column to him. His immediate reaction was his natural inclination to defend the weak, the poor, and in this case, the criticized. He could have been incensed at any time beginning with Gage, February 20, 1889, two months before Father Damien's death, could he have chanced upon some Presbyterian journal or other somewhere along the road.

He, nowhere, makes reference to the original Gage article printed in the *Herald Presbyter* and reprinted elsewhere, as he entered upon the writing of his "Open Letter." He certainly was unaware of the Gage piece when he visited the leper settlement and made his notes, although it had appeared three months earlier. And since the Presbyterian columnist dispatched the Hyde letter, unsupported by the Gage article, all that Stevenson had to go on was the Hyde letter. Indeed, enough to go on, but there was no immediate way he could bring Gage into it, even had he desired, without checking. So there was no research, no homework, despite the real need for such; and his emotional state allowed none of this. So it was clearly Robert Louis Stevenson and Charles McEwen Hyde alone.

Stevenson took to a writing table in the Union Club and, in a mood of furious exaltation, hastily constructed a literary guillotine to knife down the life story of Dr. Hyde. He was an inaccurate and careless executioner but he had a world-wide audience.

He did not cool off for some time. His biographers wrote of the incident as if he were in a frenzy during the penning of the "Open Letter" and immediately thereafter. "Do I dare publish it? Will I be sued for libel?"

Seldom did Stevenson rush off into print as he did with his letter. What was his motivation? He had not known Father Damien. His contacts with Dr. Hyde in Honolulu, while casual, were friendly. He had written little for six months. Perhaps a latent urge to do something was given quick release. He was in ill health and impatient but always the writer. His quick reach for the Hyde letter was almost an involuntary reaction to his mood and physical state. An on-the-scene printer read it and ". . . thought it read like the work of a writer straining for effect, and was somewhat theatrical. . ."[5]

What was his motive in paying any attention at all to an old letter, largely inconspicuous within a larger letter, set in very small type, written August 2, 1889 by Hyde and printed in the Sydney journal, October 26? The letter was six months old and the clipping three months old—a long time for a newspaper clipping to stay alive. But we just don't know. As Doris N. Dalglish said in her book on Stevenson, "But although forever talking of himself, he never enlightened his readers much, and we can only guess, vaguely guided by a leniency displayed here or a vehemence shown there (form your own conclusion, for example, on *Father Damien*), what blackness remained behind."[6]

Never, in any of his previous mss., had he dispatched copy to a printer[7] with an order to print directly, without galley or page proof, a miniscule run (25 copies). Because there were no page proofs, someone in his household made corrections in pen and ink on each of the copies and this person did not make uniform corrections among the copies. This hasty handling bespeaks a greater hysteria in Stevenson's writing of the "Open Letter" than has been appreciated hitherto.

Distribution was effected to a few leading citizens and journals around the world. Except those to a few favored friends, each was mailed without a covering letter. One copy, of course, was sent to Dr. Hyde. This is now on file in the library of the Hawaiian Historical Society. This booklet of 8000 words, *Father Damien: An Open Letter to the Reverend Dr. Hyde of Honolulu,*[8] was reprinted by the *Scots Observer,*[9] the *English Churchman,*[10] *Elele,*[11] and issued in small book form by Messrs. Chatto and Windus,[12]

Thomas B. Mosher,[13] and the *Ave Maria Press*.[14] It has appeared freely and usually unabridged in Catholic and Protestant journals, in the commercial press, and in countless biographies of Father Damien and Stevenson. With the passing years new editions appear, one as recently as 1968.[15] The "Open Letter" is reproduced also in the appendix of this ms.

Reference has been made to circulation levels as related to the reading public. The pre-Gage discussion involving Father Damien was rather limited within the religious community. Important visitors to Molokai, except for medical men, were few. Chapman and Stoddard were probably the most persuasive foreigners who went to the settlement. Visiting by Hawaii residents was not encouraged.

The Gage-to-Hyde period, short as it was—February to August, 1889—contained largely religious journal dialog; the Hyde-to-Stevenson period, August 1889 to March 1890, was marked by increased debate with some overtones in the public press. The Stevenson letter changed the temper of the discussion to a bitterness that surfaced wherever newspapers and magazines as well as books, were published.

Stevenson was indeed like "a bull rushing at the gate." His emotional fog, all-encompassing, and the swift raking of his jeremiad rushed over readers, including the hapless Hyde, like a mental bulldozer. Normal perceptiveness was overwhelmed; the bulldozed were pulverized, and some, willy-nilly, became disciples of the machine.

The "Open Letter," while hailed as a classic among the great letters of literature, never achieved the solid acceptance of the general run of Stevenson productions. For the purpose of this ms. it merits a temperate and careful analysis. If any evidence of Stevenson error exists in respect to Dr. Hyde, it lies within the "Open Letter" or in association with it.

Hyde's adjectives and adjectival phrases employed in describing Father Damien, with a single exception, bear an astonishing parallel to the words and phrases expended by Stevenson in a letter he wrote after his Kalawao-Kalaupapa visit.[16] Dr. Hyde's list included *coarse, dirty, headstrong,* and *bigoted*. Stevenson used *peasant, dirty, bigoted, untruthful, unwise, tricky*.[17] He altered his notes of that visit to fit his "Open Letter" by adding *ignorant, shrewd, lack of control, slovenly ways, false ideas of hygiene.* Unlike Dr. Hyde, however, he compensated for his listings by affirmative stress on the "overvailing virtues" of Father Damien.

No matter! Stevenson was conferring no favor upon Damien by

his characterization; the favor came in the attack upon Hyde. But both men had obviously listened to other men's tales of Damien. No person can ever compare the informants of either Hyde or Stevenson. The only real difference in the situation was that Hyde knew Damien personally.

Stevenson did not know Damien except through local informants and actually at the time of his last minute visit to Molokai had no special object regarding Damien. He did not mention him in his letter of application to go to the leper settlement, merely that he wished to gather notes.

Richard Aldington, in his *Portrait of a Rebel*, lists several of Stevenson's literary martyrdom-like interventions wherein "all he knew. . . he got in the newspapers."[18] One of these, for example, the incident of the Irish farm, he blew up into an impossible distortion that caused biographer J. A. Steuart to write in a footnote, "I lived five years in Ireland, and from actual observation knew something of the matters which agitated Stevenson. His presence in Kerry in the character of martyr would have provoked nothing deadlier than derision."[19]

Aldington goes on to say that the fury over Dr. Hyde's letter seemed the more curious since many of its phrases and those in Stevenson's might be interchanged. "It is said," he continued "that Stevenson feared that Dr. Hyde's letter would prevent the setting up of a public memorial to Damien. The fact is that for some reason Don Luis Roberto de la Mancha was ready for another attack on windmills, and thirsting martyrdom. He knew his sizzling pamphlet was libellous, and once again, as over the Irish farm, Fanny and Lloyd [Osbourne] professed their willingness to die—at least pay heavy damages—with him. . . The fact is that Dr. Hyde's letter, however unjust and bigoted, was a private one and never intended by him for publication. In this event Stevenson upset himself more than his antagonist, since he passed several agitated months awaiting a suit for libel which he certainly would have lost. . . but once again the romance of destiny rescued Stevenson from a situation which might have been both unpleasant and crippling—a verdict in Hyde's favour would have turned against Stevenson the power of the whole venal and gutter presses."

Arthur Johnstone in his *Recollections of Robert Louis Stevenson in the Pacific* devotes a chapter to the Hyde-Stevenson letters and makes a reasonable, careful analysis of their anti-Damien comments.[20]

So, unless the scorn, with which Stevenson unfolds the phrases, or the reference to sainthood, ". . . on the day when Damien of Molokai shall be named Saint. . . " are the reasons that the writers called "foul" on Dr. Hyde, there remains only one charge of his which is not compatible with his notes. This is the charge referring to Father Damien's alleged relations with women. It is this charge in which we find Dr. Hyde standing on softest ground. Catholic fathers and others wrote vehemently, submitting sworn statements of Father Damien's purity, of mistaken identity in the morals charge, but none of this was even helpful because Dr. Hyde, when challenged to produce evidence, declined. They were jousting with subjectivity.

If he could say it in the first place, he should have supported it but he either skirted the adducing facts or stated a firm disinclination to be specific. This was illustrated most clearly in the one major self-justification article which he was to write after the appearance of the Stevenson letter.[21]

In my research, I have watched carefully for any scrap of evidence about Father Damien's morality. I have discovered none. I therefore must aver that Dr. Hyde's position in this aspect of the Damien story must be considered unsupportable.

Again it should be noted that we are treating and in a sense trying the wrong man for the unjustified and improper publication of a private letter.

Stevenson's right to fly off any literary handle is not in question. But let a query be posed: What did he aspire to in his unilateral semantic battle as he grossly overwrote his compulsive emotions into an incredible production of 8000 words? He was actually replying to a 26-word single sentence in Hyde's letter to Gage. Where in the history of English literature has a score of 8000 words to 26 been recorded? This container-sized Pandora's box of literary enthusiasms of Stevenson provided the space for packing in the innuendoes and nuances, the irrelevancies and repetitions, the distortions and errors of a nervous and worried Stevenson. The document taken as a whole underwrites doubt, not to say disbelief.

Another query: Why did Stevenson not ask personally of Hyde that he state his sources of authority to back up the single 26-word sentence or ask him to review and comment editorially or in any manner upon the "Open Letter" before publication? These queries become rhetorical for there will never be answers.

Francis Watt offers a comment: "The student of R.L.S. would do well to con it carefully [the open letter], and this same student will find it a curious revelation of R.L.S. character. It is not logical, and it is no proper defense of Damien at all. Much is made of the comfortable house of Dr. Hyde, his leisured and cultured life, and the fact that he never went to Molokai. This is the most obvious fallacy. The point under discussion was not the character and work of Dr. Hyde but the character and work of Damien. In defending Damien R.L.S. is still more peculiar. What, he asks, in effect, if the charges were true?"[22]

Emma Lyons Doyle, granddaughter of revered Lorenzo Lyons (Liana), wrote of her memories of the day that the Stevenson letter was printed in the *Elele*:[23]

One day the town was like a raging inferno with talk about a sensational letter that had just appeared in the *Elele*, a newspaper on Kauai. In fact everytime one would pick up the phone for days "central" had something new to add to the matter which was dividing the community into a very broad faction of Catholics against Protestants. The story of the famed letter of Dr. Hyde and his private opinions of Father Damien is too well known to go into in my reminiscences, but I should record a few brief facts.

The day of the news hitting Honolulu like a fierce slap from the back of a hand, papa had me stop the carriage at Dr. C. M. Hyde's residence on Beretania St. as we made our way home. Of the missionary fathers still living in the city, C. M. Hyde was among the youngest, having come out in 1877.

Dr. Hyde was devoted to Grandpa Lyons, whom he had met shortly after coming to the islands. Grandpa had aided him in the study of the language and it was because of his help that Dr. Hyde became so proficient in it in such a short time.

The whole family loved him and we children called him "Daddy Hyde". After Grandpa Lyons death, there were thousands of books in the old homestead at Waimea, for naturally everything that had ever come into the place had been saved. Dr. Hyde was one of the founders of the Hawaiian Historical Society and had encouraged Grandma Lyons to give many of the historical books and particularly the early imprints in Hawaiian to the society when it was founded. There were many duplicates which he kept for his own collection, which later Mrs. Hyde gave to

Rev. Westervelt and he in turn gave them to the University of Hawaii. I tho am leaving my train of thought on that afternoon. I turned into the drive and Papa and I went to the door where we were met by Mrs. Hyde, a lovely and vivacious woman of many talents and interests. She threw her arms around papa and wept bitterly. The phone had rung all day long, people were dropping in to pay their respects, and now "Daddy" Hyde was in his study in a state of sheer exhaustion, Dr. Robert McKibbin had just left and had ordered rest and quiet.

I always knew Daddy Hyde to be a kindly man with a twinkle of delight and fun in his face and his eyes were alive with enthusiasm in everything. That afternoon, he seemed to be an extinguished candle with the last remnants of life ebbing out of the light that had been. He was crushed, distracted and himself on the verge of tears.

Rising from his lounge as we entered the room, the venerable gentleman clasped both of papa's hands and said "Oh Curtis, what have I done?" His voice trembled in random thought and for some length they talked about the matter. He turned to me, and said "My dear never, never in life write a privacy or express an opinion in writing for you never know what will become of it. I have just suffered the greatest undoing of my entire life. I have always tried to be a good Christian, and heaven only knows I am perhaps too opinionated but I am honest."

This was perhaps the only flaw in his character, he was outspoken but of everything that could be said of him he was a man of great integrity.

He went on. . . "I am now being crucified by the most widely read author of our day and on the charges of telling the truth about that sanctimonious bigot on Molokai."

A curious fact struck me later that not once in the conversation was Robert Louis Stevenson mentioned by name. The whole town was to talk for many months about the matter and for years those echoes were to be heard everytime the subject of Stevenson or Damien was to be aired. It seems now so odd that Dr. Hyde is all but forgotten here in the community, and yet he by that curious quirk of fate was to gain immortality on a universal plane because he had so chosen to take upon himself the writing of a private letter.[24]

Long before the appearance of the Stevenson letter, the Hydes had planned a New England holiday in the summer of 1890. But with the appearance of the letter, both could use the trip to refresh their mental well-being. He of course was carrying a double burden: the opprobrium of the attacks by his critics and the silent suffering endured over his own unwillingness to condemn the Rev. Mr. Gage.

On the dock at San Francisco, a reporter interviewed Dr. Hyde:

"Stevenson's letter answers itself," said Dr. Hyde. "He admits the truth of my statements in the letter to Dr. Gage concerning Father Damien, and goes on to excuse the priest's acts. That they are true cannot be gainsaid, as everybody in Honolulu knows. I would not now recall my letter if I could, although I do not think Dr. Bragg [sic][25] was discreet in making public the contents of a private missive. Personal animosity was not the sentiment that impelled Stevenson to write about me. He visited me often, and I found him a very pleasant man, between whom and myself the most friendly feelings have hitherto existed. He is somewhat of a crank, however, and his defense of Damien originated in a desire to take up the Catholic side of the cause, not because he was interested in the matter, but simply because he was a crank and wanted to have something to say."[26]

By mid-July he could say, ". . . Have been able to possess my soul in patience thus far and trust that I shall not lose my equanimity now."[27]

NOTES

1 Letter Elizabeth Stuart Phelps, *New York Independent*, Dec. 10, 1889.
2 Letter the Rev. H. B. Chapman, Vicar of St. Luke's, Camperwell, England, *London Times*, Jan. 1890.
3 Letter Hyde to the Rev. W. T. McCormick, *English Churchman*, Mar. 8.
4 The Rev. T. J. Curtis, *Presbyterian*, Sydney, Australia, Oct. 26, 1889.
5 Letter, James Grant to the *Australian*, July 29, 1922.
6 Doris M. Dalglish, *Presbyterian Pirate* (Oxford Univ. Press, London, 1937), p. 200.
7 Ben Franklin Printing Co., Sydney.
8 The complete wording on the title page of the pamphlet reads, "With Mr. R. L. Stevenson's Compliments, *Father Damien: An Open Letter to the Reverend Dr. Hyde of Honolulu* from Robert Louis Stevenson, Sydney, 1890 [Mar. 27]. The letter carries the self date. Feb. 25.
9 Ibid., *Scots Observer* (Edinburgh), May 3, pp. 659–662; May 10, pp. 687–690.
10 Ibid., *English Churchman* (London, May 1890).
11 Ibid., *Elele*, Supplement (Honolulu, May 10).
12 Ibid., Messrs. Chatto and Windus, (London, 1890).
13 Ibid., Thomas B. Mosher (Portland, Maine, Apr. 1905).
14 Ibid., *Ave Maria Press* (Notre Dame, Ind. 1911).

15 Ibid., *Cobble Hill Press*, (New York, 1968).
16 Letter Stevenson to Sydney Colvin.
17 Hyde, Letter to the Rev. H. B. Gage, Aug. 2, 1889.
18 Richard Aldington, *Portrait of a Rebel* (London, Evans Brothers Ltd., 1957).
19 J. A. Steuart, *Robert Louis Stevenson, Man and Letter Writer* (London, Sampson Low, Marston & Co., Ltd., 1924). Vol. II, p. 84.
20 Arthur Johnston, *Recollections of Robert Louis Stevenson in the Pacific* (London, Chatto & Windus, 1905). This is a useful analysis and interpretation of the respective roles of Hyde and Stevenson.
21 "Hyde, Father Damien and his Work," article (*Congregationalist*, Boston, Aug. 7, 1890). Reprinted (Boston, *Thomas Doll*, Septimo, 1890). The article was written after he arrived in Ware, Mass., in early summer 1890. He checked it with the American Board before submitting it to the *Congregationalist*.
22 Francis Watt, *R.L.S.* (Lond, Methuen & Co., Ltd. 1913).
23 *Elele* (supplement), May 10, 1890.
24 Emma Lyons Doyle, *Reminiscences of My Life* (typewritten, 1958–1963), presented by the author to Robert E. Van Dyke and used with his permission.
25 Obviously Gage.
26 Hyde interview, *San Francisco Examiner*, May 17, 1890, also quoted in the *Daily Pacific Com'l-Advertiser*, Honolulu, May 30.
27 Letter Hyde to the Rev. O. B. Emerson, Honolulu, July 12.

Chapter 18

MOLOKAI, 1866–1873

THE MOST COMMON distortion reported in connection with Molokai is the assumption that the improved leper life began with Father Damien. Sympathetic writers have written horrendous tales of conditions reflecting the lack of religious influences and law controls in the seven years during which the settlement existed prior to his arrival in 1873. Most of the writers, and they are legion, made no allowance for the slow, steady, and constructive improvement that marked the little colony from the start.

Quotations abound decrying conditions as writers pictured them before the arrival of Father Damien:

The sense of delicacy which made us throw a veil over the faces of the sufferers obliges us also to throw a veil over their morals.[1]

. . . estranged from God and abandoned by men, in want of food and clothes, reduced to the lowest depths of misery: heretics, mormons or pagans, creatures given to every vice, living in lawless disorder, without faith, without hope.[2]

. . . without decent homes, half clad or naked, living in promiscuous intercourse and drunkenness, without nurses, schools or church, they were a scandal to the government and to the Christian charity of these islands.[3]

. . . the dying were cast out of the huts and laid behind a stone wall and left to die there in the ditch.[4]

281

Philibert Tauvel, in a French book later translated into English, not only described the settlement in lurid prose in one of the above quotations, but turned his pen on the Protestant missionaries as well. He did not try to know that there is no single instance of missionaries "abandoning their ministry. . . to devote themselves. . . to more lucrative positions."[5]

Tauvel checks off Board of Health actions in the pre-1873 years but ends with the strange conclusion that "what was absent. . . was life." He also said that the Catholic Church would have to step in. . . "she alone being able to fill this crying want. . . these unfortunate sheep were not, however, forgotten by their pastors. A missionary visited them occasionally, in so far as necessity demanded. . . " The pre-Damien "necessity" was taken care of by the visits of Fathers Raymond and Aubert immediately prior to Father Damien's arrival. Tauvel's "necessity" seemingly blossomed into a first class bestiality just as the priest arrived.

The Rev. Sereno E. Bishop of the Hawaiian Board was concerned about the flood of misstatements that characterized the spring months of 1889:

A chief source of these misstatements seems to have been an article in *Longman's Magazine*, signed Archibald Ballantyne.[6] The character of this article is indicated by the exaggerated strain of its opening sentence; "Perhaps no spot on the face of the earth can equal for concentrated misery and hopeless horror, a little village-settlement in the Pacific island of Molokai." What of cancer hospitals, penitentiaries, insane asylums? To such Kalawao is a Paradise . . . The malady is mostly painless . . . They are commonly better housed and fed than in their former homes. In a lovely spot, once the favorite abode of a large population, and with abundant society, the closing years of these poor people are generally not devoid of much happiness . . .

Mr. Ballantyne represents the settlement as abandoned to disorder and neglect until Father Damien's arrival in 1873 secured amelioration. The *New York Tribune* enlarging upon this, says: "The brutal indifference of the Hawaiian Government had thrust these poor creatures away upon a barren peninsula . . . Damien found them a colony of men and women forgetting God and hating man, utterly wretched in body and mind, and abandoned in their desperation to every form of wickedness . . . His labors in time transformed this nest of disease-stricken savages into a Christian community."

Even our valued *Christian Union* joins the calumnious crowd and says: "Thirteen years ago these villages were the homes of indescribable misery . . . The miserable huts huddled together, filled with wretchedness and debauchery which greeted him as he landed in 1873, have now been supplanted (through his efforts) by groups of neat cottages . . ."

In . . . the grossest slanders upon the Hawaiian Government, which represents our Christian civilization . . . the truth is . . . that no such abominable disorder among the lepers or neglect on the part of the government existed, either at Damien's arrival in 1873 or at any previous time . . . The Government always took care to have faithful and capable agents, and gave zealous attention to the wants of the settlement without waiting for Damien to importune them.

. . . Mr. Ballantyne says: "Though the other Hawaiian Islands had abolished idolatry and adopted Christianity, in Molokai—where there was no missionary, no priest—the old paganism, with all its horrible consequences, reigned supreme."

. . . Why Bishop Maigret left his Catholic people at Kalawao for so many years destitute of spiritual care, we do not know . . . Father Damien did a worthy and noble thing to volunteer in 1873 to serve them . . .[7]

Elizabeth Hough Sechrist and Janet Woolsey, in *It's Time for Brotherhood*, say this:

Unfortunately for the people who were sent there, the Hawaiian government had set aside no money for dwelling places and very little for food, clothing and supplies . . . This was the almost hopeless situation among some eight hundred lepers on the island when Father Damien landed there in 1870 [1873].[8]

These authors also refer to the "Great Gray Island" [Molokai], a description erroneously inferred from the popular Hawaiian song, *Molokai Nui Ahina*. In stressing the "great gray walls of rock . . . prison walls for those who had been exiled there" they charge the Government with neglect in care and handling the lepers, The word *hina* in

Hawaiian does mean gray, but when used as in the title of the song, Hina refers to a pagan goddess identified since legendary times with Molokai island. But these writers did not personally research this point; the entire reference is copied from Stevenson's "Open Letter," and as has and will be seen, his research was not only faulty, but he also substituted emotional fictions to serve his purposes.

Herman Hagedorn in one of his selected biographies treated the life of Father Damien but again with the common errors. "He . . . was going where no priest or missionary, Catholic or Protestant, had been before. He was bound for that most miserable gathering-place of rejected men—the island which the king of the Sandwich Islands had set aside for lepers." He also quoted the oft-repeated words of Bishop Maigret, "My children you have been left too long alone and uncared for."[9] This is more repetition of the charges of abdication of the Hawaii authorities of responsibilities in the leper settlement. It should be noted that the creation of the settlement was not an act of the king but was enacted by the legislature.

Before the leper settlement was opened in 1866 the villages of Kalawao and Kalaupapa were no different than other villages scattered over beach and shore areas on all the islands. All were well populated. The companies of missionaries divided up after reaching the islands and fanned out to all these living places, initiating a teaching ministry that was providential; and they reached into Kalawao-Kalaupapa.

After the Rev. Harvey R. Hitchcock and his wife were stationed at Kaluaaha, on the lee side of Molokai, in 1832 some of more than 1000 residents of Kalawao-Kalaupapa began to climb the high cliff dividing the island or paddle around to occasional meetings. In 1838 Kanakaokai, a young Lahainaluna graduate, was stationed at Kalaupapa and directed the building of a large meeting house of stone as well as a thatched house for a missionary. A more substantial meeting house replaced that first building during the next decade.[10]

The story of this missionary effort in Kalawao and Kalaupapa, before the purchase by the government for segregation of the lepers, appears in a book by Miss Ethel M. Damon.[11] She lists the first churches, the ministers-in-residence and the missionaries who included the peninsula on a circuit of regular visits.

Kanakaokai's church continued to serve the villages for nearly 30 years, until in 1866 the legislature authorized the purchase of the area for the housing of lepers. The original residents were moved away, mostly to Waialua on the south-eastern coast of Molokai. Shiploads of leprous patients were delivered regularly with a special upsurge in 1873 when King Lunalilo campaigned to flush all lepers out of hiding and into the settlement.

Among the first arrivals, practically all natives, were 35 members of the Hawaiian (Congregational) Churches from the various islands, including some lay ministers and licentiates. The Aha Paeaina, or annual meeting of the Hawaiian Evangelical Association, released these 35 to form a church by themselves at Kalawao. The Rev. A. O. Forbes, then stationed at Wailuku, Maui island, was named pastor by the elders in the Maui and Molokai Presbytery in October 1866. Forbes and his associate resident minister-to-be, the Rev. S. W. Neuku, in December made the journey over the Kalaupapa switchback trail to organize the church named Siloama (Church of the Healing Spring).[12]

The Rev. S. W. Neuku (1866–1874), the Rev. S. P. Heulu (1870–1873), the Rev. S. Holokahiki (1874–1876) and their successors as resident ministers of Kalawao-Kalaupapa had their part in the record of Protestant ministry, unbroken from the village church in 1839 to the Kanaana Hou Church of today—more than 130 years!

There was some Catholic activity as early as 1871. Fathers Raymond and Aubert each gave several weeks of ministry to the lepers. Miss Damon speaks of other Catholic activity in Kalawao prior to the coming of Father Damien. "Priests . . . came when they could; one, Brother Bertant built in 1872 at Honolulu a wooden chapel which he managed somehow to convey to Kalawao and to set up on the hillside not far from the Church of the Healing Spring . . . a small clapboarded chapel, added by Father Damien west of and adjoining the larger one brought by Brother Bertant in 1872, still remains as a partial transcept of the stone church which replaced . . . the original chapel. This stone church was erected and almost completed by Father Damien, and close beside it he was buried."[13]

The spirit, so warmly exemplified in the Siloama Church, tempered the evil minded and non-conformist alike. But there was a degree of lawlessness, Miss Damon reports, and likewise a "resentment against white men for having enforced the cruelties of segregation on Hawaiians who themselves has no fear of the disease.

"This attitude of resentment seems to have been reflected in the report that at first some of the patients shunned Father Damien when he first came among them, a stranger, in 1873. Pastor Heulu and his deacons of Siloama Church, however, realizing how much the new priest's help would mean to the stricken multitudes went up and down through the scattered villages, urging the people to accept the care of the newcomer, assuring them that he had come to live with them and to help them, even though he was a white man . . ."[14]

The practically unanimous projection of wretched, unsolved, uncared for conditions pictured by many writers affronted two Honolulu agencies in particular, the Hawaiian Board of Missions and the Board of Health of the kingdom.

Disregard for the work of the Protestants contributed to the feeling of the Hawaiian Board of Missions and a large segment of Honolulu opinion that their efforts were being given no consideration in the spreading laudation of Father Damien.

One voice spoke up for the Hawaiian church as the criticisms mounted. The Rev. W. D. Westervelt placed squarely on the record in 1889 a clear and reasonable explanation of the Damien publicity. He wanted to do two things; first, to relate a history of a virtually unknown hero he considered commensurate with Father Damien, and second, to correct the common error that the Rev. Mr. Hanaloa was a leper:

There are now two Congregational church buildings for the accommodation of the widely scattered sufferers. There is however, only the one organization, which bears the significant name Siloama.

Over this church there has been a noble native pastor. His wife was afflicted with the leprosy. Instead of separating from her, he said, "This leper church needs me." He would go better than the other pastors. Let us remember that it took real self-sacrifice and consecration for the dark-skinned minister to take this leper church. White missionaries who had left pleasant scenes in America preached to the natives the necessity of self denying missionary work. Some of the native missionaries went to the cannibal islands, further west to preach the gospel. Rev. J. Hanaloa went to the leper settlement. The published accounts of his work are necessarily meager. It has all been done in the native language and among natives. The visitors who have written about the settlement, sometimes have stated that a "leper" minister was preaching for the natives. They could not understand Hawaiian and Hanaloa could not speak English, so they naturally consulted the Catholics and reported the work of Father Damien, while the earnest toil of the humble Hawaiian preacher was passed over. Yet it is worthwhile to recognize his self-sacrifice. He too gave up his opportunity of preferment. He went to a church that gave the scantiest support. He labored almost "at his own charges." He faithfully and patiently, for almost twenty years, has preached the Word, and carried the gospel message to the large number of the sick and dying among his own church members as well as those who were not members. His consecration has not been blazoned around the world. He has not had the stimulus of outside praise, save as some of the excellent white ministers have visited Kalawao, preached for the natives, and given him a few words of encouragement.

Now this man *was not a leper.* He has carried on his faithful work these many years *and is not yet a leper.* He is well spoken of by both Catholics and Protestants. He is an old man now—an assistant has been given him, Rev. S. Waiwaiole, late pastor of one of the native churches near Honolulu.

The widely known Father Damien went to the settlement in May, 1873 and has done a good work worthy of the fame that has been accorded to him. The pastor with the dark face and strange tongue, and his work, are, however, worthy of a place side by side with the white priest in the record of consecration and self-denial.[15]

The other aspect of Kalawao-Kalaupapa welfare that was ignored as if it in itself were a plague was the work of the government from 1866 to 1873. The impression was given that Father Damien prodded officials and suddenly order was brought out of chaos. No quarrel can be had with his prodigious labor in spreading the gospel, ministering to the sick, and working on physical improvements; but to overlook the labors of the Board of Health or accuse it of ineptness or neglect or general failure to provide was to affront the government officials, faithful and competent Rudolph Meyer, the doctors, a substantial segment of public opinion in Honolulu, as well as the Hawaiian Church. In this area of public opinion again we find Dr. Hyde. The concerted invective of the writers had its changing effect upon his reaction to Father Damien.

In a statement prepared in February 1890 for Bishop Herman of Honolulu, Brother Joseph Dutton, who spent many years at the settlement, discussed the role of the government:

. . . There has been much misapprehension upon this point, principally, it seems to me, growing out of the fact that more has been published about Father Damien than about the Government—leaving the impression that he was in charge of the settlement and had made all the improvements—an impression quite incorrect.

The history of the leper settlement shows that it has always been operated by the Hawaiian Government through its Board of Health, the regular and general expenses being all paid by the Government—including a fair ration and clothing allowance for each leper. At first a good many families and groups of people built their own cabins, but more recently the Government has constructed a considerable number of comfortable cottages . . .

There has always—as is well known here—also been a superintendent of the place, under the official title of "Agent of the Board of Health," often called "superintendent." He has always had charge of the business affairs of the settlement and of its general management . . . The same person has always held this place—a worthy gentleman . . .

He assisted in establishing the leper settlement here, and has, I am informed, never been out of office as its practical manager . . .

If in the earlier years of its existence, the conditions at the settlement were in any degree unsatisfactory, I do not believe, from all I heard and know, that the charges against the Hawaiian Government for this state of affairs have good grounds. The place is isolated, and various drawbacks tended to prevent a very rapid improvement; but, considering the nature and characteristics of the people to be dealt with, it would appear, from the history of the settlement, that the Hawaiian Government has always given it fair support, and made reasonable progress in the necessary construction.

. . . even in July, 1886, some of the conditions were still imperfect; some remain so yet; some are beyond remedy—but all along there has been tendency towards improvement and I believe all parties having to do with the management of the place have honestly tried to deal justly with it.

Certainly there have been some delays, some oversights, occasionally an apparent neglect, but I will say that the real grounds for complaint have been very few.[16]

An official accounting is to be found in the biennial reports of the Board of Health. Here, as if climbing a ladder with a step upwards every two years, is found the progress story of the settlement. The first report spoke of the settlement site acquisition, included a budget for the initial operation, and gave the impression that the whole operation was a great guessing game. There were no rules for guidance in planning available. It was obvious that mistakes would be made. Fault was found with the first plan for raising garden foods by patients able to work. Administrators and staff members could scarcely be found who would go to the settlement. Carpenters, upon learning that the Bishop Home they were to construct was in Kalaupapa, declined to go.

At the very start the Board of Health recognized the extraordinary problems of initiating the segregation ordered by law. There was conflict involving health officials, police, legislators, kings and perhaps, chiefly, the natives whose families were broken up. The perspective gained in each two-year look-back gave the officers of the Board of Health the chance to apply modified solutions; not in sufficient depth and not quickly enough, yet by some providence a going concern was created amidst the welter of trying complications and public impatience.

Conditions were not instantaneously changed for the better following Father Damien's arrival. On the contrary, things worsened at that very time because King Lunalilo abruptly decided to search out and transport to the settlement every diseased person in the islands. It was this deluge of sick humanity that probably overwhelmed Father Damien and caused, through "the tarnish of his missionary spectacles," descriptions of conditions of defeat contrasting with those he had just left in the outside world.

Uninformed, he could make no allowance for the plodding work of a dedicated Board of Health; he could not, in his first impression, realize that a leper settlement at its very best would be a sorry sight in terms of his past environments. He was honest with himself in his evaluation but he was unknowingly lending support to the legend that settlement life began with him.

During his time, progress continued and he had much to do with it. The pattern of progress in bettering conditions held beyond his decease according to Dr. A. A. Mouritz, settlement physician in the middle

1880's: "Owing to the rapidly failing health of Father Damien . . . his relief . . . Father Wendelin . . . labored nobly.

"Under his [Wendelin's] splendid administrative ability, the churches, the schools, the Baldwin and Bishop Homes reached a high degree of spiritual efficiency . . .

"Marked changes and improvements took place. The lepers had better housing, and their material comfort was vastly improved . . ."[17]

Another voice spoke out for the Board of Health. Isabella Bird, a respected author of a many-editioned book wrote: "It is not surprising that officials called upon to meet this sad emergency [1866 settlement opening] are assailed in all quarters of the globe by sentimental criticisms and misstatements regarding the provision made for the lepers on Molokai. Most of these are unfounded, and the members of the Board of Health deserve great credit both for their humanity and for their prompt and careful attention to the complaints made by the sufferers."[18]

Stevenson in his "Open Letter" wrote that "all of the reforms of the Lazaretto . . . are properly the work of Damien . . . Many were before him in the field . . . even you will confess they had effected little . . ."[19] Father Damien would be the first to disagree with such an assumption and he would be the first to correct it. Enhanced living conditions, improvements generally, a higher moral tone in the lives of the patients, were to be expected but could not be achieved overnight. The history of the settlement from the beginning has been that of an agonizing crawl up a mountain, of slow progress—almost Sisyphaen in nature.

The many agencies involved in Kalawao-Kalaupapa, however, tried and began their trying in 1866; and Father Damien tried when he arrived in 1873; and every person and group who ever went there tried.

NOTES

1 *Damien Institute Monthly Magazine*, Feb. 1895.
2 Ibid., Mar., p. 21.
3 *Catholic Review*, New York, May, 1890.
4 John Henaghan, *Father Damien* (Dublin, Clonmore & Reynolds, 1954).
5 Philibert Tauvel, *Father Damien* (London, Art and Book Co., 1904) trans. from the French.
6 Archibald Ballantyne, "Father Damien and the Lepers," *Longman's Magazine*, Vol. IV, May, 1889.
7 The Rev. Sereno E. Bishop, "Father Damien's Work," the *Friend*, July.
8 Sechrist and Woolsey, *It's Time For Brotherhood* (Philadelphia, Macrae Smith Company, 1962), pp. 78–79.

9 Herman Hagedorn, *Eleven Who Dared* (New York, Four Winds Press, 1967), pp. 80, 84. Abridged and revised by Dorothea Hagedorn Parfit.
10 Ethel M. Damon, *Siloama, Church of the Healing Spring* (Honolulu, Hawaiian Board of Missions, 1948), p. 50.
11 Ibid.
12 Ibid., p. 10.
13 Ibid., pp. 17–18.
14 Ibid., p. 5.
15 Letter the Rev. W. D. Westervelt, *Congregationalist,* June 28, 1889. p. 246.
16 Brother Joseph Dutton, *Statement,* signed Feb. 12, 1890. Typewritten, corrected, and initialed, May 7, 1908. The excerpts appearing here were omitted by Father Yzerdo-orn, *History of the Catholic Mission in Hawaii* (Honolulu Star-Bulletin, 1927). See appendix.
17 Dr. A. A. Mouritz, *Pathway of the Destroyer* (Honolulu, 1916) p. 256.
18 Isabella L. Bird, *Six Months in the Sandwich Islands* (New York, Putnam, 1876), p. 294.
19 Stevenson, op. cit., p. 27.

Chapter 19

ERRORS TOLD AND RETOLD

A PERMISSIVE SOCIETY may carefreely discount the emotional distortions of Robert Louis Stevenson's sharply worded philippic, the "Open Letter,"[1] but a multitude of his avid protagonists adopted it as gospel. There is probably no parallel in literary history where the distortions and errors of a basic document have been so continued, repeated, and compounded as by the willing hands of the post-Stevenson era.

"It may offend others; scarcely you, who have been so busy to collect, so bold to publish, gossip on your rivals."[2] This is Stevenson's first error in his "Open Letter" and it is egregious. Hyde made no effort to *collect* gossip nor to *publish* it. The letter was personal, published and re-published without his permission or knowledge. And why does Stevenson mention *rivals?* Were there others? The answer is negative, but the assumptions in the sentence provide the basis for Stevenson's leap into the unknown.

"It will at least be news to you, that when I returned your civil visit, the driver

of my cab commented on the size, the taste, and the comfort of your home.'' Here aside from the questionable propriety of snidely alluding to the "mansion" status of the home of a host, is something which Stevenson pumps up to major emphasis. These allusions troubled Hyde for honest reasons. He wrote to the American Board: "He [Stevenson] attacks me for living so comfortably & elegantly. That is a matter of taste, as one gentleman said, 'Give Dr. Hyde any salary however small, his home would seem a palace. Give Stevenson three times the amount & he would live in a pigsty.' It is a radical opinion about the sanctity of dirtiness."[3]

Stevenson's emphasis on the quality of the home gives purpose to his attack. He speaks of the *pleasant room* twice, mentions once the *pleasant parlor on Beretania Street, the fine house,* and *charming mansion.* Other uses include, "But the clean Dr. Hyde was at his food in a *fine house* . . . from the *house on Beretania Street* . . . *the house on Beretania Street* that the cabman envied . . . to the retirement of your *clerical parlor* . . . the *Honolulu manse.''* He pointedly built up a picture of luxury as a marked contrast to Father Damien's conditions of home life. His repeated use of the street name, Beretania,[4] reflected a touch of nostalgia for his homeland. But the fact remains that he exaggerated the tasteful ordinariness of the Hyde house into a pretension for his own purposes.[5] His artificial contrivance of the contrast of Damien living and Hyde living stares out of the Open Letter pages as a form of literary venom. He deliberately makes Damien dirtier in his squalor and Hyde more confortable in his grand living style; but in so doing creates aura of boredom out of the effort.

"You belong to a sect—I believe my sect . . ." This reference is made again, *"Your sect (and remember, as any sect avows me, it is mine) . . ."* Repeating himself in the close quarters of his letter is evidence of a quick one-time rush at writing but the error rests in the denomination. Hyde was Congregational, Stevenson Presbyterian.

"In the course of their evangelical calling, they [missionaries to Hawaii] *or too many of them—grew rich . . ."* Again the endless repeating, " . . . *Your sect . . . has not done ill in a worldly sense in the Hawaiian Kingdom."* This is a popular distortion. The facts are well documented. The missionaries as missionaries did not profit from business activity or land speculation. Many of them died in the mission field virtually penniless; others returned to the United States, too ill to continue. Three did transfer to the service of the kingdom, invited by Kamehameha III to assist him in

placing finances, public education and government on a more settled road. The American Board carefully studied the requests for transfer and approved each one, in turn, on the basis that enlightenment resulting from education and good government was a handmaiden to the missionary effort.

Still others, such as Samuel N. Castle and Amos Starr Cooke, were authorized by the American Board to enter business when the mission work which they had undertaken was no longer needed. Neither was an ordained minister. Castle had been sent from Boston to manage the mission depository which supplied members of the mission with household, building and teaching materials, and many articles not otherwise available in Hawaii. Cooke, with his wife, opened and managed the Chiefs' Children's School for royal children. This valuable little institution, which educated several of Hawaii's monarchs, ran out of royal pupils about the time the mission depository, an expensive operation because of its small turnover, had to be closed out. The Prudential Committee of the American Board initiated the project whereby the firm of Castle & Cooke was permitted organization as a mercantile business, but still acting as the distributing agents of the Board.

It is true that missionary descendants entered into business, and to their credit it can be said they gave the country a strong economic foundation, highly favorable, albeit paternalistic. But they were not missionaries when they did this and their fortunes were modest compared to leading business men in most parts of the United States.

". . . it 'should be attributed' to you that you have never visited the scenes of Damien's life and death . . .," "Kalawao which you have never visited . . ." ". . . that place which oxen and wainropes could not drag you to behold . . ." Here is error in triplicate. Hyde's visits to the settlement are a matter of record.

"You, who do not even know its location on the map . . ." Stevenson fails, as he starts an extraneous full page of talk about Hyde's ignorance of geography, to recognize hyperbole when he sees it. This also tries credulity. It was possibly deliberate; nonetheless, the entire passage was both inconsequential and irrelevant.

"You were thinking of the lost chance, the past day; of that which should have been conceived and was not; of the service due and not rendered . . . when we have failed, and another has succeeded; when we have stood by, and another has stepped in; when we sit and grow bulky in our charming mansions . . ." Pure literary license, putting thoughts in another's mind and ascribing motives purely from opinion! Motives of envy!

"*. . . I marvel it should not have occurred to you that you were doomed to silence; that when you had been outstripped in high rivalry, and sat inglorious in the midst of your well-being in your pleasant room—and Damien, crowned with glories and horrors, toiled in the pigsty . . .*" Stevenson, now, after ascribing envy as the Hyde motivation builds it into rivalry.

"*. . . there followed a brief term of office* [settlement assistant supt.] *by Father Damien which served only to publish the weakness of that noble man. He was rough in his ways, and he had no control. Authority was relaxed; Damien's life was threatened and he was eager to resign.*" There is no Damien resignation in the file. He was not reappointed by the administrative committee of the Board of Health.

"*It is possible, for instance, that you . . . had heard of the affair of Chapman's money and were singly struck by Damien's intended wrongdoing.*" The Rev. H. B. Chapman, pastor of St. Luke's Anglican Church, Camberwell, England transferred a substantial fund raised for settlement work to Father Damien for distribution. Hyde had not included any mention of this incident in his Gage letter.

"*I have now come far enough to meet you on a common ground of fact; and I tell you, to a mind not prejudiced by jealousy, all the reforms of the Lazaretto, and even those he most vigorously opposed, are properly the work of Damien.*" His use of the word *opposed* is not clear but the preceding chapter of this book contains comment pertinent to this error that settlement life began with Father Damien.

"*At a blow, and with the price of his life, he made the place illustrious and public. And that, if you will consider largely, was the one reform needful . . . it brought (best addition of them all) the sisters . . .*" The nursing order was brought to staff the Bishop Home, construction of which was actually recommended by Hyde to C. R. Bishop who thereupon provided it.

"*There is not a clean cup or towel in the Bishop's-Home, but dirty Damien washed it.*" Father Damien never washed a cup or a towel in the Bishop Home. He was not a visitor at the Sisters' kitchen.

Moreover Stevenson mispunctuates the name Bishop Home into a hyphenated possessive Bishop's-Home on page 17 and an also incorrect hyphenated Bishop-Home on pages 26 and 28 of his original non-galley proofed version of his "Open Letter." All this under the careless assumption that the word Bishop in the name had reference to some official of the church. It is of interest that in a very recent reproduction of the "Open Letter" (1968), the Cobble Hill Press, among other editings, changes the three references in the original Stevenson version to Bishop Home.

"... *In him, his bigotry, his intense and narrow faith, wrought potently for good, and strengthened him to be one of the world's heroes and exemplars.*" Since Dr. Hyde's story has been largely told is it not fitting and appropriate that he be accorded like analysis and definition of his bigotry?

Stevenson's dexterous command of word and phrase was more than once characterized as a "scalpel" deftly applied to cut Hyde "down to size." But he did not cut him down to size and he had a purpose in not so doing. Twice, Stevenson addresses him as "portly." There is a disingenuous quality in this adjective. Dr. Hyde was actually wiry and of slight build and only average height.

There is an amazing contrapuntal tone in Stevenson's *Letters From Upolu, Samoan Islands.*[6] These were letters written for a fee from the McClure Syndicate—bread and butter letters. He would accept no royalties from any re-publication of his "Open Letter" but was pleased when his London publisher sent such proceeds to the settlement.

In these Upolu Letters, written after the "Open Letter," Stevenson did an about-face. He was writing from his notes—the notes used in supporting his letter—and here he scarcely mentioned Father Damien and Dr. Hyde not at all. No reference was made to the controversy. He used a travelogue technique and covered the geography, poked at the Board of Health, spoke of the Franciscan Sisters at the Bishop Home, described his rounds with Brother Dutton, detailed a few anecdotes. He even managed a few errors. But why the skimpy reference to Father Damien, none to Dr. Hyde or his "Open Letter"? Was he tired of his subject? Had he already said enough? Did he want to forget a letter he was already regretting? Was he writing for a different audience? The answer is not clear.

What status has the Gage-Hyde-Damien-Stevenson happening in history? While the Stevenson letter is described as a philippic, a classic and a satire, as English literature it is not taught at all in the public schools and is hardly used in the parochial schools. Taken alone it would be difficult to teach without adequate research on the causes and effects intermingled in the text. It is quite fair to say that practically no one of the writers building a biography of Father Damien around the "Open

Letter," or those making liberal use of it in a Stevenson biography, really did thorough research among the basic references. It simply is not an authentic piece of writing.

Ralph S. Kuykendall, the late eminent Hawaii historian, lists inferential items only regarding Stevenson's brief visits in Waikiki in his definitive history, *Hawaiian Kingdom*.[7] There is but a single entry about Dr. Hyde. There is no listing of Father Damien in the index. What does this suggest? Simply that the Stevenson-Hyde confrontation does not carry much weight in the secular history of peoples, although it does loom large in a certain context of religious thought.

There is practically unanimous agreement among the writers who followed publication of the Stevenson "Open Letter," even to the present, that Father Damien's public image was thereby greatly enhanced. Such remarks were usually accompanied by defamatory thrusts at Dr. Hyde:

Stevenson picked up his pen, and unexpectedly, most undeservedly the Rev. Dr. Hyde became immortal. . . that was when and where Dr. Hyde was chopped into inch pieces.[8]

The world in general does not know the greatness of our Father Damien, and its main source of information has been the magnificent letter of Robert Louis Stevenson.[9]

. . . And the words that sprang from the angry writer comprise a far greater monument to the leper priest than any structure of stone could have. . .[10]

Misquotation is common. John Farrow used a sentence from Dr. Hyde's article on Molokai, ". . . that noble hearted Catholic priest who went to Molokai in 1873 to care for the spiritual welfare of his faith *and whose work has been so successful.*" In place of the italicized portion Hyde actually said, *"But Father Damien. . . may yet consummate his self-sacrifice by becoming himself a leper."* Elsewhere, Farrow said Hyde was at work answering a colleague [Gage]. "On receipt of this amazing letter, the Rev. Mr. Gage displayed the bad judgment of sending it to the Sydney *Presbyterian.*" Aside from the usual errors it should be noted that Farrow here acknowledges the bad judgment of Gage.

In the *Heart of Father Damien*, Vital Jourdain wrote, "Then suddenly the Sacred Hearts Fathers stopped defending their confrere. An absolutely independent witness spoke up. The great English writer Robert Louis Stevenson answered Hyde. At the time Stevenson was living in Tahiti. He spent long months at Honolulu, stayed eight days at Molokai, made a searching inquiry, then wrote an open letter for the world to read."[12]

Jourdain's carelessness is regrettable. His only research could have been in secondary sources and in his use of them he was in error. Stevenson was not in Tahiti when he wrote the letter—he hadn't been there for more than a year. He was in Sydney, Australia. His "long months" in Honolulu came to about five months. Jourdain's listing of the sequence of residences, inquiry, and writing sounds as if Stevenson had made the "searching inquiry" in order to write the "Open Letter." Stevenson did not have the slightest idea that a Hyde-Gage letter or its subsequent publication would ever be in the making when he visited Molokai. Jourdain calls Gage a Methodist minister and refers to his letter to Hyde as if he were quoting.

The writers make Hyde a man of many denominations. Not only was he called a Methodist, but also the name Presbyterian was applied to him, likewise Anglican. Few spoke of him correctly as a Congregationalist. The Presbyterian label might have stemmed from his first seminary training which was Presbyterian or the Broome Street Presbyterian Church in New York where he was a member in his youth. But it is not likely that these early associations were the source of the Presbyterian nameplate of the post-Stevenson writers. It came from Stevenson who did not know. Of course the Rev. Mr. Gage was a Presbyterian and he published in Presbyterian journals. Dr. Hyde was ordained in the Brimfield, Massachusetts Congregational Church and remained a devoted adherent to Congregationalism all of his days.

Sister Mary Martha McGaw relights the Stevenson flame. "Not pausing to disprove the accusations that Dr. Hyde had made, which he felt were beneath his consideration, he leveled his adversary with a piercing irony and sarcasm seldom surpassed. . . In his reply [to Gage] Dr. Hyde cruelly maligned the priest, denied him all possible right to respect and honor as a man and as a priest, refused to recognize that he had any part in bettering the conditions at the leprosarium, and ended by giving credit to his own sect and the Board of Health for all the improvements. . . "[13] Sister Mary Martha should read Stevenson's letter again. He does attempt to disprove Hyde's accusations, and as for being Stevenson's adversary we remember that Hyde addressed himself privately to a man named Gage.

Ironically, the writers who pour on the condemnations do it as if in acknowledgment of Dr. Hyde's power as a great public figure. His voice must have been feared to have Stevenson and his followers so loudly denounce his bigotry, gleefully announce his obscurity and rejoice in what they termed his downfall.

Furnas supports this: ". . . Beyond that, the model of deliberate insult as personal as a love letter, this dismantling of a fellow-creature not with ax or scalpel but with a razor-sharp butcher knife that flays as handily as it disembowels, most magnificently arraigns Hyde as a type of whited sepulchre, of gimlet-eyed Pharisee, of the general scandal of diametrically un-Christian behavior among men holding posts in Christian cults. . . "[14] Dr. Hyde must have been an awesome personality to merit this kind of a reception among the post-"Open Letter" writers!

Irene Cauldwell in her *Damien of Molokai* repeats the errors and adds a few of her own in utterly misrepresenting Hyde's character, declaring he had never been on Molokai, placing Gage in Sydney. ". . . With a pen dipped in gall, he wrote his infamous letter to his brother minister in Australia. . . "[15]

Perhaps the pen that was "dipped in gall" was that of Irene Cauldwell. Forty years after, to have compounded the Stevenson errors, none of which had to do with Father Damien, bespeaks a lack of care in checking facts. Stevenson's material is colored enough with innuendo and distortion but hers is a careless broadsiding that lacks any useful service.

Thomas B. Mosher published an edition of the "Open Letter" with a preface of his own. ". . . Somehow, at the time, one fancies a sort of critical indifference; at best as who should say, why vex yourself over a Dr. Hyde? Have you not given us an imaginary *Mr. Hyde*? The lost souls of the imagination interest us vastly more than this obscure traducer and a far off leper colony."[16] "Traducer" indeed! The word is commonly employed in the barrage of condemnation.

The *Damien Institute Monthly Magazine* commented that Stevenson was a fair minded man and "when a bigoted minister, the Rev. C. M. Hyde, vilely slandered the martyr, Mr. Stevenson was the heroic priest's defender."[17]

Omer Englebert in his *Hero of Molokai* told of a slander against Father

Damien by a former employee and of the "foulness that dropped from this poisoned tongue [which] was later *communicated to the press by Dr. C. M. Hyde.*" The inference in the italicized clause is pure license.

". . . He took to the pen only after Damien's death when the news arrived, that under the patronage of the Prince of Wales, a committee had been organized in London to perpetuate the name of the leper priest.

"*Thereupon*, Dr. Hyde wrote to his colleague, Rev. H. B. Gage, the following *open* letter. . . " The italics are mine. Englebert makes it sound as if Hyde had been reading the newspapers and decided to write a letter. He was actually writing a private letter in reply to Gage's inquiry. And why the use of the adjective *open?* It is reasonable that he borrowed it from Stevenson. Employing such parallel use of the word, he assigns to Hyde a motive of seeking to appear in public print.

Continuing the defamation, Englebert quotes Father Albert to the effect that "the Doctor [Hyde] in terms of St. Paul, was a worldly man 'incapable of understanding any of the things which are of the spirit of God.' He appealed to Mrs. Hyde for corroboration." What the "corroboration" was intended to entail is not at all clear. There is an unbecoming rationale in the thinking that would ever prompt such a request.

According to another Albert quotation there had been only one minister, not of the Catholic Church, in the lazaretto [Stevenson's word for Kalawao-Kalaupapa], a kanaka [native] leper who had no alternative but life in the leper settlement.

Father Albert's conclusion is clearly in error; the reference to the native minister suggests a re-reading of the preceding chapter and Bishop Sereno's article in the appendix of this book.

". . . Then all of a sudden, the Picpus Fathers[18] ceased firing," said Engelbert. "Defense of their confrere by their arms was no longer necessary. Robert Louis Stevenson had waded into the thick of the fight with his letter in reply to Dr. Hyde. After the trumpet blast of the distinguished author had gone echoing around the world, there was nothing left of Dr. Hyde's charges and precious little of the doctor himself."[19]

Englebert was another who noted that Father Damien was called a bigot and explained the epithet as applied to him. Does he use the same explanation when the word is applied to Dr. Hyde? Father Damien and Dr. Hyde were both bigoted. They were products of their time and upbringing and then, moreover, the Hawaiian islands were provincial and isolated—a place to nurture obsession and pedantism.

Joseph W. Ellison had this to say: "One evening at a dinner, someone asked Stevenson whether he had read in a religious newspaper a letter written by Dr. Hyde, a Presbyterian missionary, severely condemning Father Damien. In this letter Dr. Hyde accused Father Damien of having died of illicit relations with the female lepers on the island of Molokai, in Hawaii. This is a degrading enhancement of what Hyde actually said, and Ellison lifted it from Stevenson with an alteration of his own—neither was quoting Hyde. The exaggeration is as unfortunate as the endless contrasts of Damien filth and squalor with the Hyde home. Somehow, to the writers, the route to immortal fame for Damien rests in making him look his worst as they proceed to vilify Hyde.

Archibald Ballantyne is quoted in the *Bibelot* as saying ". . . But to ignorant tolerance, which presumes to revile such a life as Damien's because he is not this and he is not that, may be very decisively applied the crushing rebuke which the brother of the dead Ophelia addressed to the 'churlish' priest in Hamlet."[20] The rebuke is scarcely a true Christian tenet.

Ballantyne also wrote the long *Longman's* article of tantalizing intellectual license, "Father Damien and the Lepers."[21]

Henri Daniel Rops thought the "island authorities were not too happy to see a single man do more for Molokai in a few years than they had accomplished in fifty."[22] His exaggeration blows up the actual seven years more than sevenfold! And on what does he base the jealousy of the "island authorities?"

Amleto Giovarnini Cicognani describes the Hyde-Stevenson correspondence. "An important Anglican minister, Rev. Dr. Hyde did not hesitate to send a scurrilous letter to his colleague, Rev. H. B. Gage, in which he besmirched the memory of the heroic apostle of Molokai. . . The reaction following the author's shameful letter was very strong. . . But it was above all, the famous English author, Robert Louis Stevenson, himself an Anglican like Rev. Dr. Hyde who took up the defense of Father Damien in a crushing reply in which he expressed his disgust and indignation. . . This masterful refutation was reprinted in the world-press and silenced the culminators once and for all."[23] Errors abound, not only in the above quotation but throughout the text which largely follows the Stevenson letter.

Debroey writes in a recent booklet, "The arbitrary accusations of a petty Congregational minister, a certain Charles McEwen Hyde who[?] living in Honolulu, were evidently dictated by mean and unworthy sentiments. They were embodied in a letter of August 2, 1889, to a colleague in Australia, Reverend H. B. Gage." Debroey quoted Bishop Maigret in a talk to the lepers assembled when he and Father Damien stepped ashore at Kalaupapa, "So far, my children, you have been left alone and uncared for, but you shall be no longer. . . " Father Maigret was another who fell into this error. Debroey also said, ". . . it was known that Europeans had brought that life-destroying disease to the Hawaiian Islands."[24] The evidence is overwhelming that the disease was introduced from the Orient and the tropics.

One of the most confused writers is Howard E. Crouch. He not only places the Rev. Mr. Gage in England and condemns pre-Damien conditions at the settlement but he gives this amazingly fictitious version of the writing of the "Open Letter:"

. . . Another man [Stevenson] read the letter written by Reverend Mr. Hyde. It disturbed him to the point of arranging a visit to Molokai to see for himself. From his home in Tahiti, he traveled to Honolulu and then to Molokai.

"Well," Stevenson exploded, "that's good enough for me! I've been wanting to answer Hyde but I had to be sure. . . It's merely a case of jealousy, and I aim to put Hyde in his place. . . . you'll be hearing from me. . ."

Indeed, Brother Joseph [Dutton] did hear from Stevenson. And the Reverend Hyde heard. . . All the world heard. . . The letter of reply to the Reverend Hyde was an immortal masterpiece. Today it is read by every student of literature. . .[25]

In 1917 Eleanor Rivenburgh penned a three-installment article for the *Bookman* entitled "Stevenson in Hawaii." She has a Honolulu Privy Counsellor, F. H. Hayselden, in telling a story, say this: ". . . He [Stevenson] was returning to Honolulu after a visit to the leper settlement *where for three weeks he lived with Father Damien*. . . " Hayselden also mentioned the " . . . sanitation and purity of the lives redeemed by the priest from squalor, filth and degradation,—it was the memory of all this that surged up in Stevenson a *few years later.* . . the most brilliant invective the world has ever read."[26] Hayselden was quite a story teller!

May Quinlan, author of *Damien of Molokai*, in extravagant and sentimental language, contributes her bit. "Stevenson, whose pen never faltered in speaking truth. . . Of these eight hundred survivors, perhaps two hundred in all were Catholics, the rest being Lutherans." The writer speaks of the problems before 1873: the rebellion of the lepers, deplorable housing, shortage of rations, poor water, inadequate clothing, no law, no religion.

"Hitherto the authorities at Honolulu had seemingly taken but little active interest in the welfare of the leper colony, but this inertness arose not from want of goodwill, but rather from lack of public funds, and from the absence of any leader in Molokai who could press the claims of the lepers, and see to the proper distribution of funds had any been forthcoming.

"But when Damien came, and after he had shown himself worthy of trust, the Hawaiian Government proved their willingness to cooperate by furnishing means to carry out those reforms which he so ably championed."[27]

There were no Lutherans among the lepers. The first Lutheran Church in Hawaii was not established until 1881. As for ascribing the administration of public funds to a minister or priest she shows no understanding of public finance. But her complete condemnation of all conditions before 1873 is not acceptable in any sense.

An incongruous little aside appears in *To You From Hawaii* by Sister Adele Marie: "Speaking of Father Damien reminds me that a few weeks ago we passed the site on Beretania Street where Robert Louis Stevenson's literary target, the despicable Rev. Mr. Hyde, used to live. . . "[28] This is the only sour note in a friendly diary-arranged book on Hawaii.

An esteemed Honolulu writer, the late Kathleen Dickenson Mellen attempted an incursion into the Hyde-Stevenson battleground and employed a considerable license in so doing. "In San Francisco," she wrote, "they [the Stevenson party] boarded the trading schooner *Equator* and travelled extensively throughout Micronesia. Arriving in Samoa six months later, they learned of a letter written by the Rev. C. M.

Hyde of Honolulu to a friend in Australia, in which he called Father
Damien, 'a stupid, dirty person who slept with female lepers,' . . . its
publication halting a world-wide subscription for a monument to Father
Damien."[29]

The errors tumble out in profusion: the party boarded the *Equator* in
Honolulu; Stevenson did not see the Hyde to Gage letter until he was
settled in Sydney; Hyde wrote the letter to acquaintance Gage in California; the Hyde reference to Damien in that letter is grossly misquoted
and there was no halt to a subscription campaign for a Damien monument. Anyone of these errors is an insignificant item but as a package
they confirm the unfortunate reliance on secondary research sources, and
the subsequent need to call into question the factual correctness and
effect of the entire reference.

Inaccuracy also invades the encyclopedia! In the *Americana* the writer
states that the colony was ". . . uncared for except for shipments of food
and clothing. . . Father Damien died April 15, 1888 [1889]. . . When
a Presbyterian minister. . . " etc.

In the *Britannica* sketch: "Struck with the sad condition of the lepers,
whom the Hawaiian Government deported to Molokai Island in 1873,
he volunteered to take spiritual charge of the settlement. . . Some ill-
considered imputations upon Father Damien by a Presbyterian minister
produced a memorable tract by Robert Louis Stevenson. . . "

Why the need to build up the Damien character and conduct con-
tinually with an assortment of negative references? Father Damien does
not require the razing and rebuilding of his human edifice as developed
in the rather questionable employment of a private letter in the penning
of an error-laden "Open Letter," and the excited condemnatory and
negative clamor of the writers.

Stevenson did not know his facts, and the post-Stevenson writers, in
their thinly veiled plagiarism, knew what they were talking about no more
than did he. The motive among the followers may have been an assumption that they were helping the Damien sainthood concept along.
It is strongly evident that the one element in the "Open Letter" that
stood out as its greatest favor to that cause was the passage: "For if that
world remember you, on that day when Damien of Molokai shall be
named Saint, it will be in virtue of one work: Your letter to the Reverend
H. B. Gage."

Ignorance can harm. If so many errors had not been made, before and after Stevenson's letter and in the letter itself, if there had not been general ignorance of settlement conditions, the storm would not have swirled around Dr. Hyde and Father Damien. Both were victims of circumstance. Hyde would not have been severely criticized were the facts known. Father Damien would not have been assailed for personal faults if he had been given his just dues rather than fulsome credit for what was accomplished even more completely by the Protestant Church and the Board of Health.

NOTES

1 The italics used in this chapter are mine.
2 Stevenson, *An Open Letter to the Reverend Dr. Hyde,* op. cit.; the italicized references in this chapter are all contained in the "Open Letter."
3 Letter Hyde to the Rev. Judson Smith, ABCFM, May 16, 1890.
4 *Beretania,* Hawaiian for Britannia.
5 Letter Hyde to Smith, Feb. 2, 1892.
6 Stevenson, *The South Seas* (New York, P. F. Collier & Sons Co 1912), reprinted from the *New York Sun,* Feb. to Dec. 1891.
7 Ralph S. Kuykendall, *The Hawaiian Kingdom III* (Honolulu, Univ. of Hawaii Press, 1967).
8 J. C. Furnas, *Voyage to Windward* (New York, Sloane, 1951) pp. 337, 364.
9 Hugh Walpole, preface to *Damien the Leper,* John Farrow.
10 John Farrow, *Damien the Leper* (New York, Sheed and Ward, 1937), pp. 202–206.
12 Vital Jourdain, *The Heart of Father Damien* (Milwaukee, Bruce Pblg. Co., 1955). Trans. from the French by the Rev. Francis Larkin and Charles Davenport, p. 347.
13 Sister Mary Martha McGaw, *Stevenson in Hawaii* (Honolulu, Univ. of Hawaii Press, 1950).
14 Furnas, op. cit., p. 338.
15 Irene Cauldwell, *Damien of Molokai* (New York, Macmillan, 1932).
16 Thomas B. Mosher, *"Open Letter"* (Portland, Maine, 1910).
17 *The Damien Institute Monthly Magazine* (Droitwick, England, Hadzor).
18 Picpus Fathers, the order of which Father Damien was a member.
19 Omer Englebert, *Hero of Molokai* (St. Paul Editions, 1962), trans. by Benj. T. Crawford.
20 T. B. Mosher, *The Bibelot, Damien* (New York, Wm. B. Wise, 1897.) The quotation from Hamlet Act V; Laertes: "I tell thee, churlish priest, a ministering angel shall my sister be, When thou liest howling."
21 Archibald Ballantyne, *Longmans* (Vol IV, May 1889) pp. 66–67.
22 Henri Daniel Rops, *The Heroes of God* (New York, Hawthorne Books, 1959).Trans. from the French by Laurence G. Blackman.
23 Amleto Giovanni Cicognani, *Father Damien Apostle of the Lepers,* 1944.
24 Steven Debroey, *Father Damien, the Priest of the Lepers* (Dublin, Clonmore & Reynolds, 1966).
25 Howard E. Crouch, *Brother Dutton of Molokai* (Milwaukee, Bruce Pblg. Co., 1958).
26 Eleanor Rivenburgh, "Stevenson in Hawaii," *The Bookman,* periodical (Dodd, Mead and Co., N. Y.), Vol. XLVI, 1917, pp. 306–307.

27 Mary Quinlan, *Damien of Molokai* (London, MacDonald & Evans, 1909) pp. 80–87, 102–103, 154–155.
28 Sister Adele Marie, *To You From Hawaii* (Albany, Fort Orange Press, 1950), pp. 53.
29 Kathleen Dickenson Mellen, *An Island Kingdom Passes* (New York, Hastings House, 1958).

Chapter 20

FEARS AND SECOND THOUGHTS

STEVENSON'S IMMEDIATE expressed worry as he finished his draft of the "Open Letter" was that Dr. Hyde might sue for libel. He need not have worried; it was not in the Hyde character to seek redress from personal injury—physical or mental.

But strangely, Stevenson was also worried about how the letter would be received by his mother, Mrs. Thomas Stevenson and his friends, Francis W. Damon, Mrs. Charles Fairchild, Charles Baxter, Sydney Colvin, and Andrew Chatto. There is incongruity in his writing such a letter and worrying about friends' reception of it—evidence that he realized he was too wrought-up to write with literary restraint or that there might be some question of his having used another's personal letter for public purposes.

Elsie Noble Caldwell sums up the psychological violence that was exciting Stevenson's mental processes:
There it is—cruelly vindictive and mean, boringly repetitious, shamelessly [sic] titled "An Open Letter [etc]." The pendulum of Celtic temperament swung the full arc of cold and calculated ruthlessness to reveal a Stevenson hitherto unknown. Exaggeration and reiteration of detail, with one misstatement of fact, betray the turbulence of his thoughts as he belabored

a man with unfair accusations to vent his spleen upon a community and a situation he found intolerable.

This is not the Stevenson we know and love. That he regretted his act did not soften the blow that crushed the career of Dr. Hyde, who, to his death, maintained a dignified and absolute silence. The misstatement is that Dr. Hyde "rushed into print" with his remarks regarding Father Damien, where as a matter of strictest fact, the letter was never intended for print.[1]

As Stevenson was readying the mailing of his "Open Letter," he wrote a letter to Charles Baxter[2] and marked it "private and confidential":

Enclosed please find a libel: you perceive I am quite frank with my legal adviser; and I will also add it is *conceivable* an action may be brought, and in that event *probable* I should be ruined. If you had been through my experience, you would understand how little I care, for upon this topic my zeal is complete and, probably enough without discretion.

I put myself in your hands, for Henley's[3] sake, not for mine. My case is beyond help. This leaves tomorrow the 13th; two weeks later, day by day, it will be followed by presentation copies, which for all purposes of action, is publication quite enough, is it not? Thus you will have no power to save me, and can, with a light conscience, follow my desires. That is to say: 1st. If you think Henley should try the gamble, you will let him have it. 2nd. If you think Henley shouldn't, you will kindly see whether the *Times*, *Scotsman* or other leading paper will touch it. 3rd. If none of them will, see if Chatto will issue it as a pamphlet. N.B. *Of Course in no case will I receive any emolument. . .*

What's more to the purpose, his [Hyde's] colleagues in Honolulu, whom I know, would probably—I think certainly—dissuade him with eagerness. But then there is the Boston Board of Missions—they may be a low lot. I don't know them from Adam—and the trouble may come from there. I own I cannot see what they would gain, unless revenge. . . It seems to me a rather spirited piece; but of course I am the last to know, and all of us here, knowing Dr. Hyde personally as we do, are apt to consider it more pungent than it can appear to an outsider. . .[4]

In a letter to his friend E. L. Burlingame, editor of Scribner's, Stevenson wrote his rhetorical fear of libel action. ". . . I speak much at my ease; yet I do not know, I may now be an outlaw, a bankrupt, the abhorred of all good men. I do not know, you probably do. Has Hyde turned upon me? Have I fallen. . . ?"[5]

He had written his mother a letter earlier. "Have you seen Hyde's (Dr. not Mr.) letter about Damien? That has been one of my concerns; I have an answer in the press; and have just written a difficult letter to Damon[6] trying to prepare him for what (I fear) must be to him extremely painful. The answer is to come out as a pamphlet; of which I make of course a present to the publisher. I am not a cannibal, I would not eat the flesh of Dr. Hyde,—and it is conceivable it will make a noise in Honolulu. . . "[7]

In September he wrote Mrs. Charles Fairchild. "It is always harshness that one regrets. . . I regret also my letter to Dr. Hyde. Yes, I do; I think it was barbarously harsh; if I did it now, I would defend Damien no less well, and give less pain to those who are alive. . . On the whole, it was virtuous to defend Damien; but it was harsh to strike so hard at Dr. Hyde. When I wrote the letter, I believed he would bring an action, in which case I knew I would be beggared. And as yet there has come no action; the injured doctor has contented himself up to now with the (truly innocuous) vengeance of calling me a 'Bohemian crank,' and I have deeply wounded one of his colleagues whom I esteemed and liked. Well, such is life."[8] The colleague was Francis W. Damon.

Robert Catton of Honolulu was troubled by the letter. In a talk to the Thistle Club he said; "But I have always thought that Dr. Hyde was harshly dealt with and that Rev. H. B. Gage, who took the liberty of publishing what I cannot imagine was intended for publication, was more deserving of censure.

"I was therefore, the more gratified to hear from Sir Sydney Colvin, some eighteen months ago, that 'R.L.S. regretted certain points in his letter about Father Damien; came to think he could have defended Damien better without making his attack on Hyde so savage. He says this distinctly in letters of '92/93 which I have not printed and am hesitating whether I ought to print in a new and much larger edition of the correspondence which I am even now busy seeing through the press. . . '

"I urged him to bring this out in the new edition of *The Letters of Robert Louis Stevenson* which he was then having printed."[9]

The editor of *Ave Maria* asked Mrs. Robert Louis Stevenson about any regrets her husband may have entertained. "As to the 'Open Letter to Dr. Hyde,'" she replied, "nothing can make me believe that Louis ever regretted the subject matter of that piece of writing. . . "[10] In a sense this has nothing to do with his genuine regrets about treating Dr. Hyde so harshly.

Katherine D. Osbourne of Palo Alto, California, makes a comment: ". . . Mr. Stevenson did regret that his article on Father Damien went so far as it did and he said so in a letter Mrs. Stevenson deleted from the collected letters. You see I saw all the letters handed in from the collections and know which ones were not allowed to be published. About the Church and Missionary situation when Stevenson was there [Honolulu]—his opinions were colored by Belle's [Mrs. Isobel Strong] views of antagonism to these societies and workers. In the long run Stevenson got true conceptions but he was too credulous and trusting in what one said to him for the time being and his indignation against any real or seeming injustice or hypocrisy was easily aroused."[11]

Stevenson in one letter expressed a soft regret, "You see I have queried the name of *Father Damien*. I quite agree that is is one of my best works, but I am kind of *wae*[12] for Hyde.[13]

But why the contest over regrets? What is wrong that he had regrets and expressed them? It is reasonable that he was a little sorry. Dr. Hyde and he were quite well acquainted and he therefore worried about the reactions of friends in Honolulu who moved in Hyde circles. Stevenson should be permitted his moments of regret. More, his feeling of regret bespeaks respect for Hyde.

Minor fires of argument broke out here and there. In 1895 Thomas G. Shearman used the columns of the *New York Evening Post* to reopen the case and attack Dr. Hyde. Titus Munson Coan, descendant of a Hawaii missionary, collaborated with Shearman in this, which quickly brought rebuttals from the Rev. Dr. Lyman Abbott in the *Outlook*,[14] and Gorham D. Gilman in the *Daily Pacific Commercial Advertiser*.[15] Dr. Hyde took notice of these attacks in a letter to the American Board. "The Shearman scandal has not ruffled me in the least," he wrote, "for people here know that I am no such man as he and T. M. Coan would fain represent to be. . . Mr. Shearman does not believe that one minister can tell the truth about another, and so prefers that Damien was all right, rather than that I told the truth. . . "[16]

Another fire erupted in Honolulu in 1905. This was correspondence in the *Sunday Advertiser*. Here Father James C. Beissel, E. C. Bond, and an anonymous "Byestander" dug up a confusion of names, Damien and Fabien [Fabian?] to discuss further the question of Father Damien's morality. Unpredictable volcano-like outbreaks like this continued and still do. I had a minor connection with one. My essay on Hyde for the Social Science Association in 1954[17] was reprinted in a Honolulu paper in 1964 and read by a local citizen, Mr. Emmett Cahill, who offered a reply:

"The Other Side of the Damien Letter" as told by Harold W. Kent in the full page Star-Bulletin article on January 1 was interesting, timely, and I am sure, accurate. Considering the opposition previously presented by Robert Louis Stevenson (who had risen in Damien's defense, after Mr. Hyde's unfortunate and uncharitable published slander of Father Damien) Mr. Kent's defense of Mr. Hyde is creditable.

However, Mr. Kent's article cannot be considered complete without a quotation from one more, and perhaps the most important letter of the period. It was written on June 16, 1905 to the Editor of the *Advertiser* by E. C. Bond of Kohala, the son of another missionary. In this letter he made it clear that he had unwittingly given Mr. Hyde the wrong information about Damien.

"It was," wrote Mr. Bond belatedly but honestly, "merely a case of mistaken identity."

Thus 16 years later, thanks to Mr. Bond, Father Damien's honor was finally vindicated.[18]

There are two areas of discussion in this letter which surface the controversy again. First, is the assumption implied in the use of the word *published* in the context, that Dr. Hyde did *publish* his letter to the Rev. Mr. Gage. Had Mr. Cahill written, ". . . unfortunate publication of Dr. Hyde's private letter by Gage etc etc. . . " it would have fitted the circumstances.

The other area is not at issue either in the essay or this book: the point of Damien morality, the one constituting the basic difference between the Hyde and Stevenson productions. It is in no wise considered, especially in this book, except as hearsay. Father Damien does not need defending.

Mabel Wing Castle, member of a *kamaaina*[19] family, contributed a calm and studied commentary on the Stevenson letter:

. . . A few months before this [publication of the "Open Letter"] a personal letter of his [Stevenson] had been published without his knowledge and he complained. "How disagreeable it is to have your private affairs and your private unguarded expression getting into print! It would soon sicken one of writing letters."

If Stevenson could have known that Hyde's letter was private! If he could have remembered his own discomfort under similar circumstances!

. . . In all these points—knowledge, fairness, logic, and adherence to facts, I am forced to admit that Stevenson's letter is somewhat lacking. There is also a literary charge to prefer against him. . . the letter is lacking in proportion and the quality of restraint—the finest of literary virtues.

. . . I must ask you to remember that Stevenson. . . did not recognize Dr. Hyde's letter to be a private one, never intended for print, published without Dr. Hyde's knowledge, therefore not open to public criticism. . .

I cannot discover that he made any apology to Hyde, but I give the substance of two letters he wrote to a friend in Honolulu. The first is from Sydney: "I am doing something that will give you great pain. . . I feel that you will sympathize with Dr. Hyde and I am sorry that this will cut our friendship." The second was to the same gentleman, after Stevenson had come to Honolulu for a second time, and lay ill at Sans Souci. He hoped sufficient time had elapsed to blunt the edge of any resentment against him, and begged that their former cordial relations might be renewed. If that could not be, why, he would understand. His letter, I am glad to say, did not plead in vain.

When, furthermore, Stevenson alluded to the matter with another candid and sincere admirer of his, this friend said: "Let me say to you frankly. . . that you played a little to the gallery. Some of your expressions were unworthy of you, I think." And Stevenson accepted the judgment in silence, and so may we also, with the knowledge of the facts.[20]

Stanley Porteus, honorary member of the Social Science Association, summarizes:

If Sanford Dole was the Association's most noted member, there is little doubt that C. M. Hyde, our Secretary for its first years, was the center of the greatest controversy. And that fact is in itself a paradox, for Hyde, according to all accounts, was not a very controversial type of man. . .

Whatever effects Stevenson's famous letter of castigation had on outside opinion, it had little upon those who knew Hyde best. . . [Their description of him] is certainly not a picture easily reconcilable with Stevenson's outburst.[21]

And whither now? Father Damien is treading a fairly well lighted path to the pantheon of angels, and the articulation of his life and works at Kalawao-Kalaupapa, now in process, may be considered likely to result in beatification. This is in the eminent hands of his church and while a tedium of years and decades must pass and mountainous obstacles of extrusion must be mastered, the index of the dial of progress in that direction will not be stilled or turned back.

Robert Louis Stevenson has gone his way. His literary genius has mounted a massive tome of poetry, prose, and letters. But when he surrendered to arraignment of a clergyman, hitherto comparatively unknown, a man of humble yet lofty purposes, he waved emotional disaster over a true and kind Christian person.

As for Charles McEwen Hyde, one can but marvel at the restraint exhibited in the turmoil of a broken common understanding among men. But his was a disaster in the night. His day has come and the real Hyde emerges as a Son of God, a fellow with Christ, and a zealous master of his educational craft—a teacher of people—as diligent a worker in the vineyard, perhaps, as any mortal who ever lived with the exception of the Man from Galilee, down from Gethsemane.

Let Charles Hyde's life and contributions ring out a clarion call to create a better fellowship among men, a better world.

NOTES

1 Elsie Nobel Caldwell, *Last Witness for Robert Louis Stevenson* (Norman, Oklahoma, U. of O. Press, 1960) p. 142.
2 Charles Baxter was an intimate friend and acted as R. L. S.' literary agent.
3 W. E. Henley, intimate friend, publisher of *Scots Observer*, in which he published the "Open Letter," May 3, 10, 1890.
4 Letter Stevenson to Charles Baxter, Mar. 12.

312   DR. HYDE AND MR. STEVENSON

5 Letter Stevenson to E. L. Burlingame, July 13.
6 Francis (Frank) W. Damon, Honolulu friend of R.L.S.
7 Letter Stevenson to Mrs. Thomas Stevenson, Mar. 5.
8 Letter Stevenson to Mr. Charles Fairchild, Sept.
9 Robert Catton, *A Little Bit of R.L.S.* (Edinburgh, Andrew Elliot, 1916), Thistle Club, June 28, 1912.
10 Vital Jourdain, op. cit., p. 362.
11 Letter Katherine D. Osbourne to Robert Catton, Dec. 21, 1921.
12 *Wae,* Scottish word, sad, grief-stricken.
13 Margaret Mackay, *The Violent Friend* (Garden City, N. Y., Doubleday, 1968).
14 *Outlook,* June 15, 1895.
15 *Daily Pacific Com'l Advertiser,* Apr. 10.
16 Letter Hyde to the Rev. Judson Smith, ABCFM, June 17.
17 Essay Harold W. Kent, *Charles M. Hyde* (Honolulu, Kamehameha Schools Press, 1954); reprinted Honolulu *Star-Bulletin,* Jan. 1, 1964.
18 Emmett Cahill letter to Star-Bulletin, Jan. 7, 1964.
19 *Kamaaina,* born of the soil, one whose love is deeply rooted in Hawaii.
20 Mabel Wing Castle, "Robert Louis Stevenson," *Honolulu Advertiser,* Apr. 14, 1902.
21 Stanley D. Porteus, *A Century of Social Thinking in Hawaii* (Palo Alto, Pacific Books, 1962).

Chapter 21

GOLDEN DECADE

WITH THE STEVENSON LETTER preoccupation it might appear that return to normalcy in any onward thrust of Dr. Hyde would be slow and difficult. There was a common reporting among the post-Stevenson writers that he was sent into "oblivion" or suffered an ignominious end. His consignment to any such ultimate riddance did not accord with the story. Horace wrote aptly in another time but appropriately, "*Mens Aequa in Arduis.*" Longfellow put it, "Sorrow and silence are strong, and patient endurance is godlike." Equanimity was his strength, and contrary to the saturnine consignments of the writers, he was to enjoy almost exactly ten years of mounting achievement between the inexpedient publication of his personal letter to Gage and his death.

It can scarcely be appreciated that the Stevenson episode was a superimposition and not an interruption of a continuous program and vigorous schedule of action. But such was the case. His intensity of purpose never wavered, even to the end.

Politically, the Hawaiian government was in jeopardy of malfeasance. Dr. Hyde followed the current events of royalty with a sharp eye on the welfare of his native flock. He watched carefully the impact of the rule of Kalakaua and Liliuokalani, the feeble, almost ineffective gropings of the Provisional Government, and the stronger headway of the Republic of Hawaii. And as his physical frame was deteriorating—soon to lay him low—he gloried in the constructive climax of annexation by the United States of America.

313

His church work was continuing with steady success. The North Pacific Missionary Institute acquired an associate leader and developed its finest curriculum. Work with the immigrant labor arrivals, Japanese and Chinese and Portuguese, was taken in stride, with no slackening in the work with the natives.

In the community he found time to help develop the public library, assist the free kindergarten movement, and give impetus to a historical society. He maintained a watchful eye over Punahou School, the Kamehameha Schools, and the Bishop Museum. He continued his secretarial work with the YMCA, Hawaiian Board of Missions, and the Social Science Association.

He became Charles R. Bishop's right-hand man in carrying out the banker's philanthropies: new facilities, grants-in-aid, scholarships and capital gifts. He and Mrs. Hyde traveled to the United States in 1890, 1893, and 1899. In 1897 a three months' trip to Japan was a fruitful source of newspaper articles on Japanese history, life, and religion.

Not to be overlooked in this roundup of the elements that constitute his story are such things as his consistent correspondence-treatment of the Kalakaua-Liliuokalani saga from elections to demise or dethronement; the Kawaiahao Seminary from land acquisition, building, and staffing to the climax of a mature program of studies; the museum concept from an early mini-collection of shells to trusteeship; the headway made in the Hawaiian language from the first encounter with the top-of-the-throat glottals to linguistic mastery in speech and writing—to mention a few. His career was marked with a passion for doing and improving.

The role of the crusader, zealot, reformer, seldom develops a warmly regarded public image. Crusading invokes resistance from the vested restraints of ease, apathy, status quo and institutionalism. Dr. Hyde was a crusader of rare discernment, intelligence, energy, vision and deep religious scruple.

It was this crusading spirit which primarily distinguished him from the missionaries who had sailed to the shores of Hawaii since 1820. He was a missionary too, but he rode his white charger into the lists of economics and politics, museums and libraries, churches and schools, periodicals and books. He thus entered sanctums, stepped on toes, affronted sacred cows and often found himself a "loner" whether engaged in the vineyard or the community domain. This singlehandedness could frequently be a liability. He received some of the credit when he succeeded but garnered most of the blame when he stumbled.

The golden decade was eventful. The Hydes made a trip to the United States in the late spring of 1890 to look up men for various phases of island church work and to attend the wedding of their son Henry who was cashier of the Ware, Massachusetts, bank.

The Stevenson "Open Letter" appeared just before his departure May 9, and although he left with a dissonant ringing in his ears, he bore up. In a letter to O. P. Emerson in Honolulu, written after the Hydes were settled in Ware, he wrote of his sorrow that Stevenson's letter should have given occasion to "yet other outpouring of abusive language. Discriminating minds, in reading the letter think it carries its own refutation. Have been able to possess my soul in patience thus far and trust that I shall not have lost my equanimity now."[2]

A deep loss was sustained by Hyde in the passing of his most intimate friend and supporter, Lawrence McCully, April 1892. To Judson Smith of the ABCFM he wrote worthy praise of his friend: "He was one of the few intimate friends whose companionship I have enjoyed ever since my arrival in 1877 . . . I have written an obituary notice to be published in the *Congregationalist*."[3]

Charles R. Bishop, another key associate, sailed away to San Francisco, March 2, 1894, never to return. This departure settled a heavier burden than ever upon Hyde through the demands of his trusteeships of the Kamehameha Schools and the Bishop Museum.[4]

In the middle of this golden decade he paid a last visit to Kalawao-Kalaupapa. For the *Friend* he reviewed the work at the settlement from its beginning in 1866 to 1895. He attributed the changes to the reorganization of the Kalakaua government in 1887. He spoke highly of the work of Brother Dutton, of the improved Bishop Home for Girls and the Baldwin Home for Boys, the nature of the rations, the matter of supply by land and sea, communications[5]—but nowhere a mention of Father Damien. This visit was five years and more after the publication of the Stevenson letter. His omission of such mention, if indeed it was an omission, can only be accounted for in his having placed the matter squarely behind him. Actually, he made no allusion to Father Damien after the fall of 1890 to the time of his death. He was, for example, invited by Dr. B. B. Warfield, an eminent editor and contributor of the *Presbyterian Review*, to do an article on the Damien-Stevenson proceedings and he mentioned this request to the American Board. He considered it, but in the late months of 1890 decided against it and in fact against any future statement.

The cholera epidemic of 1895 was a community disaster with its epicenter in downtown Honolulu. Dr. Hyde offered his services as an inspector, made visits each day to all homes in his assigned district, one of the worst of the imperiled sections, and reported sanitary conditions as well as newly stricken victims. In a sense this was routine with him for he never turned away from the leprous, the epidemic victims, or other afflicted persons.

The cholera epidemic had scarcely abated when he took to bed with a bout of disease which confined him for the first half of 1896. He wrote of his pains and plans to the Rev. O. P. Emerson:

. . . Doubtless before this reaches you, you will find how sick I have been. The trouble dates back some months, so that when the Assn met at Honolulu, I was too weak to attend the meetings. I managed however to be present at such times as to carry through some measures I had in mind . . . Grippe left me with a congested liver, next the lungs were sympathetically affected, then the kidneys and finally the heart weakened under the accumulated strain. For three nights I have had to struggle for breath: then the doctor bethought himself of a remedy he had not tried, put a little powder on my tongue, and I have had no trouble with my breathing since that time. I was very weak, however and only gradually have I regained my strength.

I have got out from under the doctor's care, but find that I cannot do work as I used to do. I shall have to take care of myself, and my diet, not overwork, nor worry, nor hurry. The sickness has upset all my plans. I wanted to devote June and July, to raising an Emergency Fund of $6000 for Hawaiian work. I wished to put every Hawaiian Church into good working condition, and make sure of a suitable support for every Hawaiian pastor. Something of this kind must be done. I have been talking with Mr. Gulick about my plans for work, and we expect to discuss the project next week.

The Portuguese Church is progressing nicely. The first time that I rode out, I went around Punchbowl Street to see the building. It will be very neat, commodious and attractive.

We are putting the floor timbers on the new Memorial Chapel at the

Kamehameha School, and will be at work next week building up the walls. School opens soon, and we hope for a successful year. Mr. Townsend's summer school has been a great success. The teachers are all visiting the Museum today. Prof. Brigham returns next week. Mrs. Hyde joins me in regards to you and Mrs. E.[6]

Dr. Hyde seldom went to the photographic gallery for a sitting and as a result there are few photographs of him in existence. Once, he sat for a portrait, this for William Yates, the English artist, who was in Hawaii, 1896-1897. Yates painted a large number of Honolulu's leaders most acceptably, among whom was Judge Hartwell. So pleased was the Judge that he arranged an exhibit in the artist's honor. Yates described his Hyde portrait in a newspaper story on the show: "Dr. Hyde is my most recent canvas, a portrait completed under 12 hours, which, from all comments I have heard, is admired by all the Doctor's friends." The disposition of this portrait is not known.

There remained one final accomplishment. The Hawaiian Board of Missions had been operating as an autonomous agency since 1863. Hyde had performed in full cooperation with the Mission, subject to the advice and consent of the American Board. As his terminal illness was hastening his end, he initiated an important intra-church affiliation. The Hawaii churches had their own association and they reported their statistics and progress generally to the American Board. But they did not belong to the National Council of Congregational Churches of the United States.

Dr. Hyde wrote to the Rev. Henry A. Hazen, D. D., Secretary of the National Council suggesting affiliation. To this he received the following reply:

What you say about the transfer is well said. It needs to be done, if done, with care and wisely.

Of course overtures are to come from you, if such is your desire and pleasure. You sent your delegate to London in 1891, which implied that you were Congregationalists; and if that is the fact, it will be for your welfare as well as ours, to recognize the fact, and join hands in proper fellowship.

At the same time, it is easily conceivable, that you may have sensibilities to deal with, which should not be too roughly handled, and the final result may be all the healthier for their due consideration.

If it is your pleasure to report your churches to me, for due record in the Year Book for 1899, I will send you a supply of blanks, such as I furnish to our States . . .

If you do come in . . . I shall have 3 new names to put [on] our roll; Alaska and Delaware, which have just organized their first churches, and Hawaii. That will put every State and Territorial name on our list not counting Jamaica and Manila!

You will want to look after the appointment of a delegate to the International Council, in Boston, in 1899. Why should you not come on to that? I hope your health will not be a bar to your coming.[7]

The affiliation was effected in 1899 at the National Council meeting, and the transition was made after eighty years of American Board direction and association to the growing national Congregational body. Dr. Hyde wanted to be on hand—he was in the East—but he was scarcely able to do more than feebly race with death in a return to Honolulu.

His last twelve months had been difficult. He could foresee the results of his physical deterioration. As the correspondence on the transfer of the church was being completed he took another final personal step that must have been heartrending. He presented his resignation as Secretary of the Hawaiian Board:

I find that since my last attack of illness, I lack the physical vigor of former days, and it seems advisable in order to more speedy and complete restoration to health, that I should be released from some of the work and the responsibilities that I can no longer efficiently discharge. I beg leave herewith to tender my resignation as Secretary of the Board, and to assure my associates and friends that though asking to be released from duties which I have found it a pleasure and privilege to perform for the past 21 years that I have been connected with them, I hope to be able to continue in touch with the Board and its work as one of the membership though no longer in an official capacity.[8]

His activity with the Social Science Association, one of his highest loyalties, also began drawing to a close for him. October 17, 1898 he was elected secretary again for what was destined to be his last time.[9] He died a year later, almost to the day. In an item in the local press, he was "reported as absent from the February 6, 1899 meeting. It was his first miss in 18 years. He is not ill—only slightly indisposed and fearful of damp weather." He must have been heavily indisposed to suffer this absence. Weather ordinarily never kept him from any duty. He attended the March meeting; the minutes are in his hand. He was at the May meeting; the minutes are unsigned and not in his writing.

A few days after this meeting he left for a mainland trip on his doctor's advice, accompanied by Mrs. Hyde and Irene Ii (Mrs. Charles A.) Brown. The latter was the young part Hawaiian girl who lived her childhood years as a member of the Hyde household, was married in a "bower of flowers, ferns, and vines" in the Hyde home, and then returned with her husband after a honeymoon on the mainland to live with the Hydes for many months. The husband was in the insurance department of Bishop & Co. Irene continued in her devotion to the Hydes and gave warm support to their charitable and religious projects. She accompanied them on two mainland trips; one in 1893 as a traveling companion, and this last one when she and Mrs. Hyde acted essentially as nursing companions to Dr. Hyde. Irene was also in Ware, Massachusetts, in 1917 when Mrs. Hyde died and she brought her ashes back for burial in Honolulu.

The object of the trip, aside from the hope of physical relief, was to visit their son in Massachusetts. Hyde passed a fairly restful summer. He could rally with any sign of change for the better in his health. He described one trip by horse and buggy. "We drove," he wrote, "to Dana (Mass.), 12 miles to eat our Fourth of July dinner at an old fashioned N. E. (New England) diner; we drove back, reaching home at 7:30 and I was not at all fatigued. This is an ideal place for an outing. The village is at the head of the Ware River Valley. Wooded ridges run parallel to this all through this section into which roads cut at all angles. Every afternoon we take a ride on wooded roads. I am drinking Saratoga water from Lincoln Springs, said to be a specific for kidney troubles, and think it is doing me good . . ."[10]

Later, he wrote, in weakening hand, another letter to Uldrick Thompson, principal of the Kamehameha School for Boys, "I have just returned from a three days visit at Brimfield. I had previously arranged with Mr. Beadle . . . to teach at Kamehameha. I send you also a copy of the Boston Course of study for the Mechanic Arts High School . . . I am improving all the time."[11]

It was from Ware that he wrote his last letter to anybody. It was to the

Rev. Judson Smith, ABCFM, his most frequent correspondent, in answer to an invitation to attend the annual meeting of the American Board. He regretted the absolute necessity, due to waning strength, of turning homeward to Hawaii, thirty days and a third of the way around the world from death.

This last letter is a noble expression of never-ending hope, of plans, of recognition of physical limitation, and ample evidence of a mind clear and sound to the last. It is mute testimony, in gentle terms, of a courage and purpose that shall forever hallow his name. It was posted at Ware:

Yrs recd inviting us to stay over to the Annual Meeting of the Board. We should be glad to do it, and receive some of the inspiration that always comes with these Annual Meetings, especially desirable now as we enter upon new phases of the work. But the truth is though all my preparations are made to return, I am utterly unable to take up any public work. I can take part in Trustees' meetings and the deliberations of the Hawaiian Board, and I hope to do some good in that way, but to teach in the NPMI is beyond my ability, and I shall have to be excused from undertaking it. I do not know what arrangements have been made by the Hawaiian Board but I will try to secure something definite as soon as possible & will let you know.

I go back not to lie idly by, but to do whatever I can do for the good of the cause. We are well equipped now with Mr. Richards in the Hawaiian work, Mr. Gulick in the Japanese, and "young ministers" anxious to be utilized and do most effective work.[12]

His persistence in the face of his declining health evoked a sympathetic comment from the *Friend:* ". . . For years he had charge of this little sheet [Hoahana], and the last lessons printed are a pathetic reminder of the heroic persistence of a faithful man in the face of mortal weakness. When not able to more than sit up, he patiently translated these lessons; and almost the last work of his hands were the sheets now in print. There are few instances of greater pluck and self-forgetfulness than are shown in the last days of C. M. Hyde."[13]

His son reported, "The journey home seemed much longer and it required all the devotion of his wife, as well as his own fortitude, to enable him to reach the home he loved so well. Once there he sank rapidly. His younger son on Hawaii was sent for and after he had seen him and passed his wedding anniversary he seemed to have accomplished all that he desired and fell peacefully asleep on October 13th 1899 in the sixty-eighth year of his life."[14]

The funeral sermon was preached by the Rev. William Kincaid at Central Union Church to a grieving assemblage that overflowed the new edifice. Even in death, Charles McEwen Hyde was true to Hawaii. As he returned from his early homeland to Hawaii to die, so he wanted burial of his mortal remains in his adopted land. He was laid to rest in the Hyde family plot in Oahu Cemetery in cool and beautiful Nuuanu Valley, beside Mrs. Hyde's mother, Thirza W. Knight, and her sister, Eunice B. Knight. Eighteen years later, his wife and in 1920 his son Charles K. Hyde were buried there too. The latter had spent most of his adult life in plantation work on Hawaii island.

No Social Science Association activity stirred in October 1899 when the eighteenth season should have been getting underway. The members, in sadness, awaited the inevitable outcome of the mortal struggle in the home on Beretania Street. About a month after his passing, the widow invited the association to meet at her home. Son Charles was there; as was also the Rev. John Leadingham, director of the North Pacific Missionary Institute. President Hosmer of Punahou was appointed secretary *pro tem* in Dr. Hyde's place, and the association proceeded to elect William R. Castle to fill the position.

The program consisted largely of individual eulogies. President Dole described Hyde as "the life of the society, its head and front," and Prof. Scott called to mind his interest in all things pertaining to the good of the community as a whole, not alone to individuals, but to the schools, the kindergarten, the museum, the public library and other institutions. Dr. Whitney characterized him as "a broadminded, great-souled man, very modest withal, of a very lovely character, always cheerful and optimistic." Prof. Alexander spoke of his fidelity to duty, even to the end of his life. Mr. Hosmer "called to mind his excellent epitomes of the essays, his well turned phrases, his happy allusions," and called him "an excellent example of the American gentleman of our century with scholarly attainments, keen judgment, sense of humor, and sound common sense." The society passed a resolution lauding his inspiration and his faithfulness as a secretary: "Many times his resume of the paper of the evening presented the points made even more clearly than they were written. As executive officer he never failed to produce harmonious action."[15]

These were not the only tributes paid the memory of Dr. Hyde. His passing brought a flood of obituaries, resolutions, and tributes from publications, organizations, and friends. Many of the personal letters were printed by Henry K. Hyde in his biography of his father.

Honolulu newspapers spoke in deep respect of him as a great community leader. The *Semi-Weekly Star* called him a "leading spirit in religious and charitable work of all kinds. . . a notable and influential mind."[16]

The *Pacific Commercial Advertiser* printed the substance of the Rev. Mr. Kincaid's sermon preached at the funeral.[17] The *Friend* devoted a page to his life review.[18] Other comments appeared in the *Hawaiian Gazette*, the Hawaiian language papers, bulletins of the Japanese, Portuguese, and Chinese churches. Far away, Williams College published a long review in its *Williams College Bulletin*. The Hawaiian Board of Missions observed his passing.[19] One review, typical of most, appeared in Austin's *Hawaiian Weekly*. In part, it said, "Dr. Hyde's influence upon the moral life of the Islands is far-reaching in time and distance. His time was constantly occupied to its briefest minute in the toil he loved. Inaugurator, teacher, trustee, and member, he was indefatigable in doing the thing he laid his hands to, promptly and well. Heralded by heredity, gifted by grace, enlarged by education, the doctor's mind was a store-house of thought and knowledge freely open, freely expressed to all. In his death the community at large suffers an irreparable loss sustained by the thought that in a wider sphere he attains the only reward he would wish a larger capacity and opportunity for doing good."[20]

The Hawaiian Mission Children's Society carried a notice, in which it said, "Rev. C. M. Hyde so intimately associated for the last twenty-two years in all the *modern* missionary work of Hawaii, and who literally wore himself out, in 'labors more abundant,' returned in the Fall from his visit to Ware, Mass., and eight days after, October 13, 1899, breathed his last in his own Hawaiian home."[21]

The Missionary Herald printed a lengthy review of Dr. Hyde's life story, including the Massachusetts pastorates, his call to Honolulu, and subsequent work there: "None can understand so fully the value of this service as do the people of Hawaii. . . "[22] It quotes the *Pacific Commercial Advertiser*: 'From this institution [NPMI] have gone forth, under the training of Dr. Hyde, the whole circle of younger men who today fill the pastorates of the Hawaiian churches. . . These men are the best witnesses to the faithful and painstaking service of this most indefatigable of teachers.'[23]

Bishop Estate trustees said in part, ". . . the work of Dr. Hyde since the establishment of the Trust has been marked by intelligence and fidelity and a rare consecration."[24] From the trustees of the Bishop Museum came this message: ". . . by his death the continuing trustees have lost a colleague always eager for the duties of the office and prompt to efficiently discharge them, and the Museum has been deprived of the services of one who found much pleasure in its work.[25]

The Honolulu Library Association issued a resolution: ". . . We remember his long services as Trustee and Vice President, the careful thoughtfulness and untiring energy which added so much to the success of the Association."[26]

Oahu College (Punahou School) trustees said in their resolution, "In his death all good causes have lost an effective, efficient helper. His talents and rare executive capacity were ever and freely at the service of educational, religious and social progress. His kindly voice and helping hand never failed when others needed a calm faith in God, a clear and discriminating judgment to untangle the intricate web which often made living a weariness.

"Oahu College has lost one of its most faithful and willing servants. His aid and advice will be painfully missed in the important developments of the near future. But his example and the memory of his long and kindly service will not be lost."[27]

A touching resolution was adopted by the teachers of the Kamehameha Schools—a little unusual in that this was a spontaneous offering by an informal action.

His enabling agency, the American Board of Commissioners for Foreign Missions adopted this tribute:

The most marked event of the year in the Hawaiian Islands is the lamented death of Dr. Hyde, which occurred October 13, 1899. Going to Honolulu early in 1877 as a missionary of the American Board, he has for more than twenty years been closely identified with the religious and educational work of the country. As Principal of the Institute he has had in his hands the training of all the Hawaiian pastors and missionaries of this generation: he kept in close touch with them till the end of his life and they greatly miss his friendship. With great industry, executive ability, and power of leadership, he made himself felt as an influence for good in many departments of Christian work. As a teacher, a writer and counselor, his presence was invaluable; his power and willingness were constantly felt, and burdens were laid upon him which no one else was found ready to bear."[28]

A few years after Hyde's decease a Honolulu subdivision was developed in lower Manoa Valley and one of the streets was given his name. No obituary this, but a practical marker of the beloved missionary's memory. What is the Rev. Dr. Hyde's legacy? His life is a magnificent sermon— magnificent in that it is personal conversation with his congregation, the native Hawaiians, the men in the market place, the leaders in politics and among the churchly and the children. It is the detailing of large measures and minute infinitesmals as he walked among his fellow humans —it is this book which is his sermon. No saint or sinner he; just a toiler in the vineyard, a servant of God.

The legend on the marker in Oahu Cemetery carries the terse caption: "Charles M. Hyde 1832—1899."

NOTES

1 Letter Hyde to the Rev. Judson Smith, ABCFM, Mar. 7, 1890.
2 Letter Hyde to the Rev. O. P. Emerson, July 12.
3 Letter Hyde to Smith, Apr. 26, 1892. *Congregationalist,* May 19, pp. 159–161.
4 Letter C. R. Bishop to Hyde, Feb. 11, 1897.
5 The *Friend,* Sept. 1895.
6 Letter Hyde to Emerson, Aug. 22, 1896.
7 Letter the Rev. H. A. Hazen to Hyde, Sept. 13, 1898.
8 Letter Hyde to the Hawaiian Board, Oct. 4.
9 Social Science Association, Minutes, Oct. 17, 1898.
10 Letter Hyde to Uldrick Thompson, Kamehameha Schools, July 6, 1899.
11 Ibid., Aug. 3.
12 Letter Hyde to Smith, Sept. 15.
13 The *Friend,* Nov. 1899, p. 91.
14 Henry K. Hyde, op. cit., pp. 90–91.
15 Social Science Association, Minutes, Oct.
16 *Semi-Weekly Star,* Honolulu, Oct. 17.
17 *Pacific Commercial Advertiser,* Honolulu, Oct. 16.
18 The *Friend,* Nov.
19 Hawaiian Evangelical Association, *Thirty Seventh Annual Report,* June 1900.
20 *Austin's Hawaiian Weekly,* Honolulu, Oct. 21, 1899.
21 Hawaiian Mission Children's Society, *Forty-eighth Annual Report,* June 4, 1900.
22 The *Missionary Herald,* Boston, Beacon Press, Dec. 1899, pp. 527–529.

23 *Pacific Commercial Advertiser*, Oct. 14.
24 B. P. Bishop Estate, *Minute Book*, Oct. 17, p. 234.
25 Bernice Pauahi Bishop Museum, *Minute Book*, Oct. 20.
26 Honolulu Library Association, Minutes, Dec. 15, pp. 24–25.
27 Punahou School, *Secretary's Record*, Oct. 16.
28 ABCFM, *Annual Report*, Oct. 10, 1900, pp. 126–127.

Appendix A

TRIBUTES

Quoted from *Charles McEwen Hyde*
by Henry Knight Hyde

PROF. W. D. ALEXANDER
Honolulu

I count it a rare privilege to have enjoyed the friendship of such a man, and to have been associated with him in a few of the many lines of Christian work which he carried on with such untiring zeal and devotion. He was many-sided in his talents and also in his labors for the welfare of his fellow-men in all departments of the life that now is, as well as in that which is to come.

It was in the line of educational work that I came into touch with him most frequently. He was especially gifted as an instructor, and as a leader and organizer of educational work. Like an able general, he constantly kept in view the whole field, and laid comprehensive and far-reaching plans for future progress. In all the different boards with which he was connected, his mature judgment and experience had great weight. He not only founded and conducted for a quarter of a century the North Pacific Mission Institute in which nearly all the present Hawaiian pastors have

DR. HYDE AND MR. STEVENSON

been trained, but continued to guide and assist his former pupils through their after-life.

For twenty-two years he bore a leading part in the councils of the board of trustees of Oahu College, which lay very near his heart, and it was there I first came to know and appreciate him. Enjoying, as he did, the entire confidence of Hon. C. R. Bishop, it fell to his lot, to do a great work in assisting to organize and carry on the Kamehameha Schools and the Bishop Museum. In all our institutions of learning his influence will long be felt, and "his works do follow him."

It was in 1883 I think, that he started the "Social Science Association," of which he continued to be the inspiring spirit, and which has served to draw out the best thoughts of some of our leading minds on social questions.

Of his relations to the Public Library Association, I have less personal knowledge, but I do know that he did much towards building it up and widening its sphere of usefulness.

He also took an active part in founding the Hawaiian Historical Society, and was a valued co-worker in the field of Hawaiian language and folk-lore.

I have mentioned only a part of his manifold activities, but into them all he carried a spirit of devout consecration to his Divine Master.

If ever a man seemed to be indispensable to this country, it was he, and when he was called to go up higher, we felt like saying with Elisha, "My father, my father, the chariots of Israel, and the horsemen thereof."

HON. TARO ANDO
Tokyo, Japan

It was in 1886 when I went to Hawaii as Japanese Consul-General. There were then about three thousand Japanese laborers mostly engaged in different sugar plantations, but their moral condition was in such a state that unless they were properly guided, the consequences would surely prove fatal to the development of Hawaiian resources, as the islands entirely depended upon immigrant laborers, among whom the Japanese were then regarded as the most important element.

Under these circumstances Dr. Hyde, who was then the president of the Hawaiian Mission Board, offered his services for the training of the

Japanese residents in Honolulu, as well as in various other places. He then opened regular religious meetings in the buildings of the Hawaiian Y.M.C.A. and other commodious places, where he devoted his exertions to instruct the Japanese morally and spiritually, as far as his time could permit him to do so. His work was ably assisted by his cheerful and talented lady in singing and musical and other various social gatherings, which always gave needed comfort and pleasure to those who were far away from their homes. Such devotional services rendered by these virtuous and experienced workers naturally brought about an excellent success; the Gospel and temperance found their way among the Japanese immigrants who have almost entirely changed their moral and social condition to such an extent that the Japanese that had been once defamed, gradually restored their good name and in consequence their number has since come up to nearly thirty thousand souls at present in those islands.

In fact, in the latter part of 1887, the evangelical work by the M. E. Church in San Francisco commenced in the island, and they secured a pretty good success among the Japanese as well, but I can positively declare that this they have greatly owed to the indefatigable efforts of Dr. Hyde.

In this remarkable movement, I am happy to say that, I was so situated as to be able to cooperate with this worthy doctor, for I was with him all the time from the beginning, say 1886 till 1889, that is, for the space of nearly four years. I am equally proud to assert that no one but myself could tell more correctly and accurately the account of this wonderful achievement in holy work among the Japanese in the Pacific paradise.

HON. CHAS. R. BISHOP
Founder of the Bernice Pauahi Bishop Museum

I trust that you will permit me, one of his friends, to offer a few lines in testimony of my respect for him and my high appreciation of his work and influence in the Hawaiian Islands. He was a whole-souled missionary, a faithful friend to the Hawaiian people, and during all the years of his residence in Honolulu, he took a deep and active interest in all that concerned their moral, social and physical welfare. Much of his time, thought and strength were given to general education and uplifting of the various races represented in the islands, and he was especially devoted to Oahu College, the Kamehameha Schools and the North Pacific Institute.

It was my good fortune to be associated with him as trustee of Oahu College; of the Estate of Mrs. Bernice Pauahi Bishop; the Bernice Pauahi Bishop Museum and other trusts, and I am indebted to him for many wise suggestions and efficient aid. In the management of the schools and museum his experience, culture and broad intelligence were of great advantage and value. He was systematic and rapid in his work, and hence, by constant application, accomplished great results. But few had so wide an acquaintance in the islands as he had, or will be so missed now that his work is done. His name and influence are deservedly held in honor by all who knew him well and will not soon be forgotten.

REV. SERENO E. BISHOP, D. D.
Editor of the *Friend,* Honolulu

It was my great privilege to be brought into somewhat close relations with him soon after his arrival here. I became at once greatly impressed with his ripe maturity as a scholar, a Christian, and as, for a preacher, a man of affairs. He very early took a strong grasp upon his special work as a trainer of preachers and pastors, and upon that of a counsellor in ecclesiastical business, in both departments speedily developing a remarkable efficiency, and establishing himself in the confidence of the Hawaiian churches, as well as of his missionary brethren, several of whom were then still in somewhat active work. 'Kauka Hai' became a name of authority and ascendancy.

Dr. Hyde soon gained by scholarly industry a good working command of the native language. He acquired a copious and exact vocabulary, and became a ready and fluent speaker in Hawaiian, although at the age of forty-five he was incapable of idiomatic nicety of accent or expression. His written Hawaiian was excellent, both in diction and grammar. He possessed a rare expertness in clerical work, and has left behind him long and accurate records made with peculiar facility, as Recording Secretary of the Hawaiian Board. An especially serviceable aptitude was shown in the discussions of the Board, but more particularly in our Church Association meetings, in discerning the points in which conflicting or confused ideas could be brought to harmonize. It was a usual thing that some resolution or measure formulated by Dr. Hyde would meet with general acceptance and close a long and perhaps trying debate. Although not lacking in tenacity in his own propositions, he was not impracticable or averse to reasonable compromises of opinion. In controversy, he was courteous and calm, and somewhat diplomatic in no bad sense. His influence was habitually for harmony and Christian compliance. His impressive personality and quiet, steadfast, yet reasonable demeanor became thus a strong and most happy educative force upon the native membership of our Island Associations, as well as in the annual meetings of our general "Hawaiian Evangelical Association." I think it may be said that no other individual did so much to shape their action.

During Dr. Hyde's twenty-one years of active labor in the North Pacific Missionary Institute, the great majority of the present pastors of the Hawaiian churches gained their training at his hands. It is a marked and obvious fact that during that period the character of the native pastors has greatly advanced in intelligence and dignity, and I think also in depth of piety and faith, and in firmness of Christian integrity. While a part of this progress coincides with a general advance of the native people in education and character, it must largely be attributed to the wisdom and piety of the chief instructor of these pastors, as well as to his excellent assistants, Mrs. Hyde especially included.

No one who well knew Dr. Hyde could fail to be impressed with the devout spirituality of his piety, the strength and sincerity of his Christian faith, or the chastened ripeness of his moral excellence. No one is faultless, but I have rarely known a man with so few or slight blemishes upon his moral brightness as Dr. Hyde. His life has been a noble and beautiful one. To a rare capacity for efficient and excellent work, and for influencing and controlling men, he added a deep and unselfish consecration to the service of our Lord in saving and uplifting the lowly.

PROF. WILLIAM T. BRIGHAM,
Director of the Museum, Honolulu

What Dr. Hyde was to the Bishop Museum few beside the museum staff could appreciate, for his good work was not done "to be seen of men." Long before the birth of this museum he had seen the insufficiency of the Government museum, and the great need of some more efficient means of preserving the fast disappearing remains of Hawaiian primitive industry. His interest in the Hawaiian people and their works led him to study with his usual painstaking care the native names of implements, of animals and plants, and his notes are to-day in possession of the museum. When at last it became possible to realize his hopes in the memorial museum which Charles Reed Bishop founded to contain the collections of his wife, Dr. Hyde as one of the trustees entered most heartily into the plans of the newly appointed Curator to make this more than a mere cabinet of curiosities.

As the plans were developed and the museum grew into a scientific living institution, ranking with the more important museums of its kind in the world, Dr. Hyde was the foster-father, cheering the only laborer in that museum for years with his sympathy and counsel. In a community where the greed of gain might easily turn earnest men from higher pursuits, it was especially helpful to have the sympathy of an intelligent and good man. More than physical, more than pecuniary aid, was the appreciative word given often when the museum and its interests seemed to have passed from the notice of all other men.

When a new and important collection was added to the museum, it was always a pleasure to drive to his house the next morning to tell him of it, for he was always pleased and could understand the value of each addition. With prophetic insight he could see in the struggling time of small beginnings the great possibilities concealed in the germ. While others thought it unwise to exchange so much good money for books and specimens,—books in some foreign language they could not read— specimens that were obsolete or out of fashion, relics of a decaying race, he well understood that these things rightly used were not mere curiosities, but educational material: not to amuse an idle tourist, but to be read as a chapter in the great history of man's development: to show, so far as inanimate things can show, how far these people of the Pacific islands had traveled on the road from primitive barbarism to civilization, and to preserve the record for all to read when the last of the islanders shall have passed away or been absorbed into other races.

Personally my first meeting with Dr. Hyde was in 1880. I had come to Hawaii to study an expected eruption of Mauna Loa, and soon after my arrival Dr. Hyde called to offer any assistance in his power. An interval of eight years passed, and on my return to Hawaii he was among the first to greet me, and from that day I was assured of his help in any attempt to improve the local opportunities for study and advancement. Although not a scientist he understood fully the importance of scientific methods, and from the first was ready to work with all his power to prevent the new museum from becoming a mere passing entertainment. Hence his constant advocacy of the purchase of books for the needed library of scientific reference, his approval of all acquisitions of scientific material even if not attractive to the ephemeral tourist.

With all this it never seemed to me that the museum was in any sense a hobby. He was quite as much interested in his school for native ministers, in the Kamehameha schools, in the Historical Society, in the Public Library. It was simply his earnest interest in anything he believed was likely to do good service to his fellow men, and we of the museum felt grateful to him for the large share he gave us.

MR. GOO KIM FUI
Chinese Vice-Consul, Honolulu

Dr. Hyde came to the Hawaiian Islands to preach the Gospel. From the time I believed in Jesus I ever found him a real helper of the Chinese. In 1879 Dr. Hyde with J. T. Waterhouse and others helped in building the Chinese Church. I was one of the first elders and whenever I went to Dr. Hyde for help or advice I always found a ready response.

After the Chinese Church was opened for preaching services in 1881, Dr. Hyde directed the affairs of the Chinese Christians in their new chapel. He aided them in forming the church rules, administered the Lord's Supper, baptized the new members and helped in the other services of the Church. Dr. Hyde assisted me in starting the Sunday School and helped to make the Gospel truths more clear to the Christians. The early workers ever found Dr. Hyde ready to help them in their work and to give good counsel and advice in all their efforts.

I wished to start a Christian school for studying English and found a true supporter in Dr. Hyde. Miss Payson became the teacher of this school.

In all these efforts for upbuilding, educating and advancing the Chinese of the Islands, for more than twenty years, Dr. Hyde gave his hearty support, and his memory will long be cherished in the hearts of those who knew and loved him.

REV. CHAS. J. HILL, D. D.
Stonington, Conn.

When I went to Williams College in 1849 I became acquainted with a young man who was familiarly called "Charlie Hyde." He was one of the six "Charlies" of our class—all good fellows.

He was physically one of the finest looking men in the class. He was about medium height, with a good figure, thick black hair, a smooth face, a clear blue eye and a manly bearing. He was not much of an athlete, and I do not remember that he cared very much about the gymnasium, but he was fond of walking, and I recall with pleasure the walks we took together up West mountain and over the hills which surround Williamstown.

He always dressed well and coming from New York brought its style with him. He was a genial, kind, courteous gentleman. We all loved him and acknowledged that he was the most popular man in our class.

As a scholar he was easily pre-eminent, always accurate, ever ready to respond to his name, never careless in his preparation and always equal to any demand put upon him. It was no surprise to any of us when he took the valedictory.

Socially he was very popular. Though he did not connect himself with any of the secret societies he would have been welcomed by all of them. He was kind and courteous in his intercourse with every member of the class, and while of course he had his particular friends, he made every one feel that he was a true friend. He won the esteem and love of each one by his manly and gentlemanly bearing.

His Christian character was so sincere that we all felt his refined, gentlemanly influence. He could easily talk with any one, and many found him their wise and sympathizing counsellor in times of sorrow or hours of doubt. He never obtruded his religion or made any one feel that he esteemed himself any better than the rest of us (though we all thought that he was.) I think that with one other exception he was the only one who did not smoke at the class supper when our course was finished.

After a year of teaching we became classmates in Union Theological Seminary of New York. There he showed the same scholarly and religious character, and won the esteem and affection of those with whom he daily associated. But it was not college. The careless, happy days in Williams were over and we were beginning the serious preparation for our life-work. It was then, and I presume still is, the practice of students to engage in city missionary work. I asked to be sent to the worst district in the city and was appointed to work at the Five Points (where by the way, I acquired a better preparation for the ministry than I did by studying the "Five Points of Calvinism").

At the Five Points House of Industry there was need of some one to keep the books. Knowing that Mr. Hyde was a good accountant, I asked him to take the work, and he kindly agreed to give two half days a week to settling the money affairs of the Institution. It was just as much missionary work as visiting the poor and sinful in their wretched rooms. He did that work for a year.

When the time came for me to marry the daughter of Rev. Dr. Todd of Pittsfield, there was no one that I wanted for my best man, but my old college friend. Though my wife has left me there is still upon our side-board the beautiful gift he gave her, and my children will know that "Charlie Hyde" was my most beloved college classmate.

REV. J. D. KINGSBURY, D. D.
Bradford, Mass.

I knew him intimately as he served as pastor of the Center Church in Haverhill during the years 1870-75.

He was a rare man. In breadth and accuracy of scholarship he stood easily among the first, having critical knowledge of language and a wide acquaintance with literature and a somewhat profound conversance with the schools of philosophy and of theology. But his knowledge, which was often superior to the apprehension of his associates, always wore the veil of modesty. He never appeared as one having mastered all things, but rather as a disciple seeking and striving to know.

He was a loving pastor, devoted to his flock, and greatly beloved in the houses of those whose hearts were pressed by want, or anguished in grief.

His preaching was the simple, forceful gospel, giving hope and faith and joy to those who believe in the divine revealing to men.

His genial spirit and artless manner made him a valued companion in any circle. He was a true gentleman, noble and commanding in favor, appreciative always of the opinion and wishes of others, amiable, courteous, strong and tender in sympathy, ever ready with kindly words or ministries, and keenly alive to the demands of every duty and occasion of life, where God had given him a part.

He was a man of great wisdom in the affairs of more public nature in the city or in the Commonwealth. His views of duty were positive and he never shrank from the utterance of them, whether they were favored or opposed by men.

In theology he was conservative but sufficiently progressive to keep him abreast of present day thinking. He was never rusty or old-fashioned, but in his forms of thought, his views of truth, his methods of investigation, he kept pace with the advance of scholars, and those who knew him intimately recognized the freshness, originality, and sincerity of his intellect, his heart and soul.

It is a great pleasure to bear testimony to the life and character of my friend whose years were all too few among us, here in the valley of the Merrimac.

REV. H. H. PARKER
Pastor, Kawaiahao Church, Honolulu

Dr. Charles M. Hyde came to Hawaii in the summer of 1877 and entered forthwith upon his work in the training school for Hawaiian pastors in this city. The design of the school was to prepare young Hawaiians by a three or four years' course of study and religious training for pastorate work in the native churches, and also to fit other Hawaiians, as Providence should open the way for them, to carry Christian civilization to the islands beyond. And with this intent "Father Alexander's" old "school of the prophets" which had been located many years previous at Wailuku, Maui, was moved to Honolulu, where it eventually became the North Pacific Institute with Dr. Hyde at its head. In this school Dr. Hyde began a work which continued without interruption, through a period of twenty years of faithful, conscientious service in behalf of the people of Hawaii, his main object being to build up and equip a native ministry for the Hawaiian churches. The interest he manifested in this field of effort to which he was called was warm and ardent, bordering on enthusiasm, and it was an interest not to be cooled by difficulties which he frequently encountered. His faith at that time in the future growth and usefulness of the native ministry was large.

Dr. Hyde was always true to the best interests of his students as he understood them, and he was honored and respected by the students as well as by the native people generally. I well remember his first attempt to address an audience of native Hawaiians in their mother tongue. It was one of those occasions that is always sure to draw a large crowd, and not very long after his arrival on the islands. At the close of the service not a few persons came forward to greet the stranger, for of course he was really a stranger to the greater portion of the crowd; but from that day on the Doctor was no stranger to the natives of Honolulu, who then and there gave him his native name of "Kauka Hai" by which he was universally known among the Hawaiians.

"The Doctor was an untiring worker for the young peoples' societies and Sunday schools. He accomplished a great deal in the way of preparing reading matter for the native youth, editing up to almost the last month of his life a Sunday school magazine for use in the native Sunday schools. He wrote and translated much in the way of providing useful reading for the native pastors.

Dr. Hyde had a very marked personality which always impressed itself upon those who chanced to come within the sphere of his activity. Where his life touched the life of others it was sure to leave its impression which was uniformly a healthful and happy impression. His life was fruitful. He was a man of many parts, easily at home in any field of Christian philanthropy, and always ready to do good to all men. His demise has created a vacancy not easy to fill. And yet

"When you have lived your life,
When you have fought your last fight and won,
And the day's work is finished and the sun
Sets in the darkened world, in all its strife,
When you have lived your life,
'Twere good to die."

MISS IDA M. POPE
Principal of the Kamehameha School for Girls at Honolulu

Dr. Hyde was closely identified with the educational interests of Hawaiians for many years and it is fitting that the Kamehameha School for Girls pay tribute to his memory.

From the inception of the school until his labors on earth ceased, Dr. Hyde was faithful to his obligations, as trustee, as member of the educational committee, as wise counsellor and trusted friend.

Dr. Hyde was pre-eminently a leader, a man who had a keen grasp of affairs religious, political, educational and social; a rare executive ability that entered into the carrying out of details; he was an example of an indefatigable worker, who spared not himself and asked the best of others.

Scarely a week passed by but found Dr. Hyde a welcome visitor at Kamehameha, interested and conversant with the routine work, helpful with advice and suggestion. Not alone in class-room work but in every department of the school was his concern manifest; in sewing-room, kitchen and laundry; favoring shop work for girls as well as boys; advocating a training class for nurses and the giving of instruction in various branches of horticulture.

On Public days, Founder's Day, at musicales, entertainments, commencements, alumni reunions his presence cheered and encouraged. He was punctilious in the performance of every duty.

Dr. Hyde was ever ready to consider what was for the benefit of the school in the future and it is good for us to know that one of the last letters he wrote was in favor of the erection of a hospital, where the pupils could receive professional training and become self-respecting, self-supporting women.

Dr. Hyde hath wrought Hawaii and Hawaiians lasting good. No more will he go in and out among us a familiar presence, but the good that he hath done will abide forever and ever, and along with Bernice Pauahi Bishop will be another "Blessed Memory."

PROF. M. M. SCOTT
Principal of the High School, Honolulu

The people of Honolulu will remember, not without gratitude, the late Dr. Hyde's many-sided activities for the public good. For more than twenty years his name has been connected with the various institutions most pronounced in their beneficent effects on the public welfare.

He was connected with the Library and Reading Room Association from its incipiency, and as one of the trustees and as one of the committee of three for choosing of books, his advice and literary taste were always at the service of the institution. He never failed to be present at all of its meetings, however pressed he might be in other directions.

As an intimate friend of the wealthy banker, Mr. Charles R. Bishop, he was largely instrumental in securing from that gentleman endowments amounting altogether to more than forty thousand dollars to put the Library upon a permanent financial basis. His broad views and excellent business qualities were of great assistance in the plans and construction of the present building.

His educated literary tastes were shown to great advantage as a member of the Literary Committee. While having decided views of his own in regard to its management and the selection of books, with a view to the education and direction of the reading and literary tastes of the community, he was always conciliatory, in his mental and moral make-up, to those differing from his views. During his entire connection with the Library, he never missed a meeting excepting when absent from town, or when necessarily kept away by indisposition.

At his death, the trustees recognized the fact that they had lost one of their most intelligent, courteous, and conscientious members and a testimonial engrossed to that effect was sent to his family.

He was the originator and the main support of the Social Science Club, an organization whose functions are similar to those of a like nature in other places, and containing the scholarship, scientific tastes and business enterprise of Honolulu. From the beginning until his death, he was its secretary, in which capacity he looked after and directed, to a large extent, the character of its contributions, places of meeting and all other matters pertaining to its welfare and efficiency.

Each year, it held its first meeting at his house. As secretary of the club, his summing up of the main points of the papers was a marvel of definite and incisive reporting of the chief excellence of the essay, which when read at the meetings was in some respects superior to the original.

All the members knew that at his death no one could fill his place. At the final meeting, after his decease, a resolution was carried, embodying his unequalled excellency as secretary, and his general usefulness in keeping the club to its high standard of efficiency.

In every community, especially in a developing commercial and industrial one, there are needed some men of the highest culture and the most devoted public spirit to take the lead in calling the attention of men of wealth, but absorbed entirely in their own affairs, to the public needs.

Dr. Hyde pre-eminently filled that place for the last twenty years in Honolulu. It was largely through his initiation and through his energy and high public spirit that many of the noblest monuments of public utility exist in Honolulu.

REV. CHARLES AUGUSTUS STODDARD, D. D.
Editor of the "Observer," New York City

Mr. Hyde was with me two years in Williams College. He was one of the purest and best young men in the college. His life was blameless, but it was influential. He had the respect of all the students because he was a fine scholar, a friendly and companionable man, and a consistent Christian. His character was well rounded, and his life in college had the poise and finish which is rare at so early a period. His influence upon others, which was always considerable, seemed to come from the man himself rather than from any efforts or actions; it was like sunshine or pure air, every person in his company felt and enjoyed it.

I was very sorry that he went to live in Honolulu, though I am not unmindful of the good work which he did there, for I hoped and believed that even more important and honorable work might have claimed him in the United States. I have met him but twice since his graduation from college, but on both occasions found him the same man, grown larger in all that makes true manhood.

REV. A. V. SOARES
Pastor, Portuguese Church, Honolulu

I count it an honor to have the privilege of adding my loving tribute to the memory of the dear man whom I learned to love and reverence, not only because I am indebted to him for many kindnesses and favors and help given me, but also for his unselfish devotion to the Master's cause.

It was in 1890 that I first met Dr. Hyde, in my own home in Springfield, Illinois, whither he had come to try and obtain workers to engage in religious work among the Portuguese people in the Hawaiian Islands. It had already been proposed to me that I should take up this work, but my acceptance seemed doubtful, until Dr. Hyde came and in a kind and placid manner, which was so characteristic of him, presented the subject in such a light that my wife and I after a time of prayerful consideration decided to go.

Dr. Hyde was a firm, kind, interested, helpful friend of the Portuguese Mission in Honolulu as long as he lived.

I shall never forget how often he visited our little congregation and the encouraging, helpful words he gave us from the pulpit. Although a man of numerous duties, for he was interested in every educational, moral and uplifting enterprise for the good of his fellow-men, he was never too busy to receive me when I went to him for advice; he was a man of sound judgment and foresight, one upon whose judgment it would be safe to rely. He was very unselfish with his valuable library, and not only gave me the privilege of using it, but he himself would choose those books he deemed most helpful to me and would even himself bring them to my house. On one occasion I said to him, 'Doctor, you spend a great deal of your time on me.' In his usual kind tone he replied, 'Mr. Soares, that is what I am here for.' Helpfulness to all who needed his help was always found in him as in the Christ whom he loved.

I remember one time he carried an armful of books from his carriage to my door. With his permission I kept some of his books for a year or more. After his death, I carried a number of his books, which I still had in my possession, to Mrs. Hyde who, after looking them over and finding they were helpful to me, kindly offered them to me. By the death of Dr. Hyde, the religious, moral and educational cause in Honolulu lost a faithful friend, but outside of his bereaved family, none, perhaps, lost as much as I did. Of him it can truly be said, "His works do follow him."

Appendix B

KAMEHAMEHA SCHOOLS PROSPECTUS

by Charles M. Hyde

BERNICE P. BISHOP ESTATE
Minutes of Meeting held December 23rd., 1885

A Special Meeting of the Board of Trustees of the Kamehameha Schools was called at Three O'clock P. M.

Present:—Hon. C. R. Bishop, Rev. C. M. Hyde, S. M. Damon and C. M. Cooke.

Mr. Bishop stated that the object of the meeting was to consider the report by Dr. Hyde of the Prospectus of the Kamehameha Schools, which is as follows:

KAMEHAMEHA SCHOOLS
An Official Prospectus[1]

In accepting the Trust created by the last Will and Testament of the late Hon. Bernice Pauahi Bishop, the Trustees therein named have deemed it best to prepare and publish this prospectus of the Kamehameha Schools. This action has been considered advisable both for their own guidance in administering the trust, and for the purpose of making such public announcement of their plans as shall meet the constant inquiries of those interested in the right disposition of this great educational gift to the youth of these islands.

In accordance with the terms of the will, the Boys' School will be established first. The will does not make any provision for branch schools on the different islands, and the Trustees see no good reason now for desiring or attempting any such institutions. The two schools will be located in Honolulu; but in opposite quarters of the city. The Girls' School will be near the Lunalilo Home in Makiki, the Boys' School beyond the Reformatory on the Western limits of Palama. The will expresses a wish that land belonging to the estate should be chosen for the location of the two schools rather than that money should be spent in purchasing a site. The Trustees have decided that these locations are not only admirably adapted for school purposes, but better than that could be bought outside. The present assessed value of the estate is $474,000. Its estimated annual income will be so large that the Trustees hope by judicious expenditure of the income for the first two years, together with the cash balance on hand at the time of the settlement of the estate, to put up the building for Boys' School without entrenching very largely upon the invested funds, though they are authorized by the will to expend one-half of the estate in the erection of buildings.

The tract of land at Palama belonging to the estate extends from the sea-shore to the ridge of the mountain, affording every variety of soil and situation for the various purposes of the school. It is purposed to put into suitable shape for suburban residences the land on the *makai* side on the road to Ewa, the lots to be disposed of in such a way as to furnish additional income as well as a safe and desirable investment. The Boys' School will be located some distance from the road, on the *mauka* side on a ridge of land, commanding a fine prospect of the city and its environs. The distance from the centre of the city is just far enough to give both easy access and desirable retirement. Water will be supplied from an artesian well, the contract for which will be made as soon as the plans for building are somewhat further matured. The utmost possible regard will be had to the observance of all needful sanitary requirements in location and construction of buildings, as well as in the provision to be made for all matters of detail which the best sanitary engineering may consider requisite. It is intended that the school shall have as much as possible the character of a home rather than that of an institution of public charity. To this end as well as with a view to special adaptations to climatic as well as other conditions, a group of cottage-like buildings has been determined upon, rather than an immense structure of imposing architecture. There will be a central school hall with its large assembly room, and adjoining class rooms, and other facilities for the course of literary and scientific instruction which has been deemed best adapted to the wants of the boys who will enjoy the privileges afforded by the school. There will be a building specially devoted to the industrial department, which is both specially mentioned by the will and specially desired by the trustees. Instruction will be given in the use of tools and materials, and some trades may be taught. So far as practicable, the boys will have the privacy, the wholesome freedom, and the loving watch and care, which are considered such essential requirements of Christian home life.

It is intended that the course of study shall be specially adapted to the circumstances and needs of our island community, present and pro-spective, with no rigid requirements designed to turn out finished products of one particular pattern; but under regulations, sufficiently flexible not to exclude on the one hand any boy whom it may be deemed advisable to welcome, nor on the other hand to keep on any boy in a profitless round of perfunctory tasks. It is desired that the Kamehameha Schools shall be a help and a stimulus in their relations to the Kingdom, and in no sense or shape to interfere or compete with the governmental provisions made for the general good. Such qualifications will be required for admission as it will make an honor and a prize for any public school scholar to secure the highest privileges of these advanced schools. While they will be conducted with special reference to advantages to be afforded to Hawaiians by preference, as the will requires, they will not be exclusive-ly Hawaiian. Hilo and Lahainaluna, Makawao and Kawaiahao may well be devoted to such special work; but the noble minded Hawaiian Chiefess who endowed the Kamehameha schools, put no limitations of race or condition on her general bequest. Instruction will be given only in the English language, but the schools will be open to all nationalities. Hawaiians must compete with other nationalities in the struggle for national existence. It is wise to recognize this beneficent but inexorable law of competition in human society, a fundamental law of all physical life. It is hoped to help the young Hawaiian to hold his own from the first in this honorable rivalry, so that he shall work out his own future under the conditions most favorable for his success. To this end some industrial training is for the great majority more essential than any high degree of literary qualifications. The course of study will require several hours of manual labor—every day, the controlling purpose of the school being to fit the boys to take hold intelligently and hopefully of the work of life. The best methods in vogue in other countries will be adopted, so far as they are adapted to our social conditions and needs.

To how large a proportion of the scholars these advantages will be furnished free of cost the trustees are now not prepared to say; but they do deem it advisable that specific though moderate charges should be made for the advantages offered by the school, any exception to the rule to be considered on its own merits, the testator's designs being evidently not to establish an orphan asylum or a charity school but to furnish advantages for education of Hawaiian youth, to supplement the ordinary means and methods, not to supplant them.

The Principal and his associates will be chosen with reference to their special fitness for the work thus marked out, knowledge of Hawaiian character being considered in the appointment, as well as the social and personal attainments of the appointment. The wise provisions of the will in regard to moral and religious training are in full accord with the sentiments of the trustees, who hope to carry out such measures and methods as will tend to make good and industrious citizens, interested in maintaining and developing the principles, usages, and institutions of the highest Christian civilization.

The Course of Study, the Rules and Regulations adopted in regard to admission, and expenses in the Kamehameha Boys' School will be prepared and published in due season—some time before the opening of the school, which the trustees now hope will be at the beginning of the school year in September, 1887. Mr. Damon made a motion that the report be accepted and placed on file. Carried.

Mr. Damon presented a proposition in regard to enclosing the land at Palama, proposed for the Boys' School, two sides with stone-wall, and the Kalihi road and East side with rail fence. Voted that Mr. Damon proceed to make arrangements to enclose the lot as proposed.

Adjourned.

(Signed)   CHAS M. COOKE,
                                                        Secretary.

FATHER DAMIEN,
AN OPEN LETTER

from Robert Louis Stevenson
to the Reverend Dr. Hyde of Honolulu

Sydney, February 25, 1890.

Sir,

It may probably occur to you that we have met, and visited, and conversed; on my side, with interest. You may remember that you have done me several courtesies for which I was prepared to be grateful. But there are duties which come before gratitude, and offences which justly divide friends, far more acquaintances. Your letter to the Reverend H. B. Gage is a document which, in my sight, if you filled me with bread when I was starving, if you had sat up to nurse my father when he lay a dying, would yet absolve me from the bonds of gratitude. You know enough, doubtless, of the process of canonisation [sic], to be aware that, a hundred years after the death of Damien, there will appear a man charged with the painful office of the *devil's advocate*. After that noble brother of mine, and of all frail clay, shall have lain a century at rest, one shall accuse, one defend him. The circumstance is unusual that the devil's advocate should be a volunteer, should be a member of a sect immediately rival, and should make haste to take upon himself his ugly office ere the bones are cold; unusual, and of a taste which I shall leave my readers free to qualify; unusual, and to me inspiring. If I have at all learned the trade of using words to convey truth and to arouse emotion, you have at last furnished me with a subject. For it is in the interest of all mankind and the cause of public decency in every quarter of the world, not only

344

that Damien should be righted, but that you and your letter should be displayed at length, in their true colours, to the public eye.

To do this properly I must begin by quoting you at large: I shall then proceed to criticise your utterance from several points of view, divine and human, in the course of which I shall attempt to draw again and with more specification the character of the dead saint whom it has pleased you to vilify: so much being done, I shall say farewell to you forever.

Honolulu, August 2, 1889.

"Rev. H. B. GAGE.

"Dear Brother:

"In answer to your inquiries about Father Damien, I can only reply that we who knew the man are surprised at the extravagant newspaper laudations, as if he was a most saintly philanthropist. The simple truth is, he was a coarse, dirty man, headstrong and bigoted. He was not sent to Molokai, but went there without orders; did not stay at the leper settlement (before he became one himself), but circulated freely over the whole island (less than half the island is devoted to the lepers) and he came often to Honolulu. He had no hand in the reforms and improvements inaugurated, which were the work of our Board of Health, as occasion required and means were provided. He was not a pure man in his relations with women, and the leprosy of which he died should be attributed to his vices and carelessness. Others have done much for the lepers, our own ministers, the government physicians, and so forth, but never with the catholic idea of meriting eternal life.

"Yours, etc.,

"C. M. HYDE."[2]

To deal fitly with a letter so extraordinary, I must draw at the outset on my private knowledge of the signatory and his sect. It may offend others; scarcely you, who have been so busy to collect, so bold to publish, gossip on your rivals. And this is perhaps the moment when I may best explain to you the character of what you are to read: I conceive you as a man quite beyond and below the reticences of civility: with what measure you mete, with that shall it be measured you again; with you at last, I rejoice to feel the button off the foil and to plunge home. And if in aught that I shall say, I should offend others, your colleagues, whom I respect and remember with affection, I can but offer them my regret; I am not free, I am inspired by the consideration of interests far more large; and such pain as can be inflicted by anything from me must be indeed trifling when compared with the pain with which they read your letter. It is not the hangman, but the criminal, that brings dishonor on the house.

You belong, sir, to a sect—I believe my sect, and that in which my ancestors laboured—which has enjoyed, and partly failed to utilise, an exceptional advantage in the islands of Hawaii. The first missionaries came; they found the land already self-purged of its old and bloody faith; they were embraced, almost on their arrival, with enthusiasm; what troubles they supported came far more from whites than from Hawaiians; and to these last they stood (in a rough figure) in the shoes of God. This is not the place to enter into the degree or causes of their failure, such as it is. One element alone is pertinent, and must here be plainly dealt with. In the course of their evangelical calling, they—or too many of them—grew rich. It may be news to you that the houses of missionaries are a cause of mocking on the streets of Honolulu. It will at least be news to you, that when I returned your civil visit, the driver of my cab commented on the size, the taste, and the comfort of your home. It would have been news certainly to myself, had anyone told me that afternoon that I should live to drag such matter into print. But you see, sir, how you degrade better men to your own level; and it is needful that those who are to judge betwixt you and me, betwixt Damien and the devil's advocate, should understand your letter to have been penned in a house which could raise, and that very justly, the envy and the comments of the passers-by. I think (to employ a phrase of yours, which I admire) it "should be attributed" to you that you have never visited the scene of Damien's life and death. If you had, and had recalled it, and looked about your pleasant rooms, even your pen perhaps would have been stayed.

Your sect (and remember, as far as any sect avows me, it is mine) has not done ill in a worldly sense in the Hawaiian Kingdom. When calamity befell their innocent parishioners, when leprosy descended and took root in the Eight Islands, a *quid pro quo* was to be looked for. To that prosperous mission, and to you, as one of its adornments, God had sent at last an opportunity. I know I am touching here upon a nerve acutely sensitive. I know that others of your colleagues look back on the inertia of your church, and the intrusive and decisive heroism of Damien, with something almost to be called remorse. I am sure it is so with yourself;

I am persuaded your letter was inspired by a certain envy, not essentially ignoble, and the one human trait to be espied in that performance. You were thinking of the lost chance, the past day; of that which should have been conceived and was not; of the service due and not rendered. *Time was*, said the voice in your ear, in your pleasant room, as you sat raging and writing; and if the words written were base beyond parallel, the rage, I am happy to repeat—it is the only compliment I shall pay you— the rage was almost virtuous. But, sir, when we have failed, and another has succeeded; when we have stood by, and another has stepped in; when we sit and grow bulky in our charming mansions, and a plain, uncouth peasant steps into the battle, under the eyes of God, and succours the afflicted, and consoles the dying, and is himself afflicted in his turn, and dies upon the field of honour—the battle cannot be retrieved as your unhappy irritation has suggested. It is a lost battle, and lost forever. One thing remained to you in your defeat—some rags of common honour; and these you have made haste to cast away.

Common honour; not the honour of having done anything right, but the honour of not having done aught conspicuously foul; the honour of the inert: that was what remained to you. We are not all expected to be Damiens; a man may conceive his duty more narrowly, he may love his comforts better; and none will cast a stone at him for that. But will a gentleman of your reverend profession allow me an example from the fields of gallantry? When two gentlemen compete for the favour of a lady, and the one succeeds and the other is rejected, and (as will sometimes happen) matter damaging to the successful rival's credit reaches the ear of the defeated, it is held by plain men of no pretensions that his mouth is, in the circumstance, almost necessarily closed. Your church and Damien's were in Hawaii upon a rivalry to do well: to help, to edify, to set divine examples. You having (in one huge instance) failed, and Damien succeeded, I marvel it should not have occurred to you that you were doomed to silence; that when you had been outstripped in that high rivalry, and sat inglorious in the midst of your well being, in your pleasant room—and Damien, crowned with glories and horrors, toiled and rotted in that pigstye of his under the cliffs at Kalawao—you, the elect who would not, were the last man on earth to collect and propagate gossip on the volunteer who would and did.

I think I see you—for I try to see you in the flesh as I write these sentences—I think I see you leap at the word pigstye, a hyperbolical expression at the best. "He had no hand in the reforms," he was "a coarse, dirty man;" these were your own words; and you may think it possible that I am come to support you with fresh evidence. In a sense, it is even so. Damien has been too much depicted with a conventional halo and conventional features; so drawn by men who perhaps had not the eye to remark or the pen to express the individual; or who perhaps were only blinded and silenced by generous admiration, such as I partly envy for myself—such as you, if your soul were enlightened, would envy on your bended knees. It is the least defect of such a method of portraiture that it makes the path easy for the devil's advocate, and leaves for the misuse of the slanderer a considerable field of truth. For the truth that is suppressed by friends is the readiest weapon of the enemy. The world, in your despite, may perhaps owe you something, if your letter be the means of substituting once for all a credible likeness for a wax abstraction. For, if that world at all remember you, on the day when Damien of Molokai shall be named Saint, it will be in virtue of one work: your letter to the Reverend H. B. Gage.

You may ask on what authority I speak. It was my inclement destiny to become acquainted, not with Damien, but with Dr. Hyde. When I visited the lazaretto, Damien was already in his resting grave. But such information as I have, I gathered on the spot in conversation with those who knew him well and long: some indeed who revered his memory; but others who had sparred and wrangled with him, who beheld him with no halo, who perhaps regarded him with small respect, and through whose unprepared and scarcely partial communications, the plain, human features of the man shone on me convincingly. These gave me what knowledge I possess; and I learnt it in that scene where it could be most completely and sensitively understood—Kalawao, which you have never visited, about which you have never so much as endeavoured to inform yourself: for, brief as your letter is, you have found the means to stumble into that confession. *"Less than one-half* of the island," you say, "is devoted to the lepers." Molokai—*"Molokai ahina,"* the "gray," lofty and most desolate island—along all its northern side plunges a front of precipice into a sea of unusual profundity. This range of cliff is, from east to west, the true end and frontier of the island. Only in one spot there prcjects into the ocean a certain triangular and rugged down, grassy, stony, windy, and rising in the midst into a hill with a dead crater: the whole bearing to the cliff that overhangs it, somewhat the same relation as a bracket to a wall. With this hint, you will now be able to pick out the leper station on a map; you will be able to judge how much of Molokai is thus cut off between the surf and precipice, whether less than a half, or less than a quarter, or a fifth, or a tenth—or say, a twentieth; and the next time you burst into print, you will be in a position to share with us the issue of your calculations.

I imagine you to be one of those persons who talk with cheerfulness of that place which oxen and wainropes[3] could not drag you to behold. You, who do not even know its situation on the map, probably denounce sensational descriptions, stretching your limbs the while in your pleasant parlour on Beretania Street. When I was pulled ashore there one early morning, there sat with me in the boat two sisters, bidding farewell (in humble imitation of Damien) to the lights and joys of human life. One of these wept silently; I could not withhold myself from joining her. Had you been there, it is my belief that nature would have triumphed even in you; and as the boat drew but a little nearer, and you beheld the stairs crowded with abominable deformations of our common manhood, and saw yourself landing in the midst of such a population as only now and then surrounds us in the horror of a nightmare—what a haggard eye would you have rolled over your reluctant shoulder towards the house on Beretania Street! Had you gone on; had you found every fourth face a blot upon the landscape; had you visited the hospital and seen the butt-ends of human beings lying there almost unrecognisable, but still breathing, still thinking, still remembering; you would have understood that life in the lazaretto is an ordeal from which the nerves of a man's spirit shrink, even as his eye quails under the brightness of the sun; you would have felt it was (even to-day) a pitiful place to visit and a hell to dwell in. It is not the fear of possible infection. That seems a little thing when compared with the pain, the pity and the disgust of the visitor's surroundings, and the atmosphere of affliction, disease and physical disgrace in which he breathes. I do not think I am a man more than usually timid; but I never recall the days and nights I spent upon that island promontory (eight days and seven nights), without heartfelt thankfulness that I am somewhere else. I find in my diary that I speak of my stay as "a grinding experience": I have once jotted in the margin "*Harrowing* is the word"; and when the *Mokolii* bore me at last towards the outer world, I kept repeating to myself, with a new conception of their pregnancy, those simple words of the song:

" 'Tis the most distressful country
That ever yet was seen."

And observe: that which I saw and suffered from, was a settlement, purged, bettered, beautified; the new village built, the hospital and the Bishop's-Home excellently arranged; the sisters, the doctor, and the missionaries all indefatigable in their noble tasks. It was a different place when Damien came there, and made his great renunciation, and slept that first night under a tree amidst his rotting brethren: alone with pestilence; and looking forward (with what courage, with what pitiful sinkings of dread, God only knows) to a lifetime of dressing sores and stumps.

You will say perhaps, I am too sensitive, that sights as painful abound in cancer hospitals and are confronted daily by doctors and nurses. I have long learned to admire and envy the doctors and the nurses. But there is no cancer hospital so large and populous as Kalawao and Kalaupapa; and in such a matter every fresh case, like every inch of length in the pipe of an organ, deepens the note of the impression; for what daunts the onlooker, is that monstrous sum of human suffering by which he stands surrounded. Lastly, no doctor or nurse is called upon to enter once for all the doors of of that gehenna; they do not say farewell, they need not abandon hope, on its sad threshold; they but go for a time to their high calling; and can look forward, as they go, to relief, to recreation, and to rest. But Damien shut to with his own hand the doors of his own sepulchre.

I shall now extract three passages from my diary at Kalawao.

A.   "Damien is dead and already somewhat ungratefully remembered in the field of his labours and sufferings. 'He was a good man, but very officious,' says one. Another tells me he had fallen (as other priests so easily do) into something of the ways and habits of thought of a Kanaka; but he had the wit to recognise the fact, and the good sense to laugh at" [over] "it. [sic] A plain man it seems he was; I cannot find he was a popular."

B.   "After Ragsdale's death [Ragsdale was a famous Luna, or overseer, of the unruly settlement] "there followed a brief term of office by Father Damien which served only to publish the weakness of that noble man. He was rough in his ways, and he had no control. Authority was relaxed; Damien's life was threatened, and he was soon eager to resign."

C.   "Of Damien I begin to have an idea. He seems to have been a man of the peasant class, certainly of the peasant type: shrewd; ignorant and bigotted, yet with an open mind and capable of receiving and digesting a reproof, if it were bluntly administered; superbly generous in the least thing as well as in the greatest, and as ready to give his last shirt (although not without human grumbling) as he had been to sacrifice his life; essentially indiscreet and officious, which made him a troublesome colleague; domineering in all his ways, which made him incurably unpopular with the Kanakas, but yet destitute of real authority, so that his boys laughed at him and he must carry out his wishes by the means of bribes. He learned to have a mania for doctoring; and set up the Kanakas against the remedies of his regular rivals: perhaps (if anything matter at all in the treatment of such a disease) the worst thing that he did, and certainly the easiest. The best and worst of the man appear very plainly in his dealings with Mr. Chapman's money; he had orginally laid it out "[intended to lay it out]" entirely for the benefit of catholics, and even so not wisely; but after a long, plain talk, he admitted his error fully and revised the list. The sad state of the boy's home is in part the result of his lack of control; in part, of his own slovenly ways and false ideas of hygiene. Brother officials used to call it 'Damien's Chinatown.' 'Well,' they would say, 'your Chinatown keeps growing.' And he would laugh with perfect good nature, and adhere to his errors with perfect obstinancy. So much I have gathered of truth about this plain, noble human brother as [sic] father of ours; his imperfections are the traits of his face, by which we know him for our fellow; his martyrdom and his example nothing can lessen or annul; and only a person here on the spot can properly appreciate their greatness."

I have set down these private passages, as you perceive, without correction; thanks to you, the public has them in their bluntness. They are almost a list of the man's faults, for it is rather these that I was seeking; with his virtues, with the heroic profile of his life, I and the world were already sufficiently acquainted. I was besides a little suspicious of Catholic testimony; in no ill sense, but merely because Damien's admirers and disciples were the least likely to be critical. I know you will be more suspicious still; and the facts set down above were one and all collected from the lips of Protestants who had opposed the father in his life. Yet I am strangely deceived, or they build up the image of a man, with all his weaknesses, essentially heroic, and alive with rugged honesty, generosity, and mirth.

Take it for what it is, rough private jottings of the worst sides of Damien's character, collected from the lips of those who had laboured with and (in your own phrase) "knew the man";—though I question whether Damien would have said that he knew you. Take it, and observe with wonder how well you were served by your gossips, how ill by your intelligence and sympathy; in how many points of fact we are at one, and how widely our appreciations vary. There is something wrong here; either with you or me. It is possible for instance, that you, who seem to have so many ears in Kalawao, had heard of the affair of Mr. Chapman's money, and were singly struck by Damien's intended wrongdoing. I was struck by that also, and set it fairly down; but I was struck much more by the fact that he had the honesty of mind to be convinced. I may here tell you that it was a long business; that one of his colleagues sat with him late into the night, multiplying arguments and accusations; that the father listened as usual with "perfect good nature and perfect obstinacy"; but at the last, when he was persuaded—"Yes," said he, "I am very much obliged to you, you have done me a service; it would have been a theft." There are many (not catholics merely) who require their heroes and saints to be infallible; to these, the story will be painful; not to the true lovers, patrons and servants of mankind.

And I take it, this is a type of our division; that you are one of those who have an eye for faults and failures; that you take a pleasure to find and publish them; and that having found them, you make haste to forget the overvailing virtues and the real success, which had alone introduced them to your knowledge. It is a dangerous frame of mind. That you may understand how dangerous, and into what a situation it has already brought you, we will (if you please) go hand in hand through the different phrases of your letter, and candidly examine each from the point of view of its truth, its appositeness, and its charity.

Damien was *coarse.*

It is very possible. You make us sorry for the lepers, who had only a coarse old peasant for their friend and father. But you, who were so refined, why were you not there, to cheer them with the lights of culture? Or may I remind you that we have some reason to doubt if John the Baptist were genteel; and in the case of Peter, on whose career you doubtless dwell approvingly in the pulpit, no doubt at all that he was a "coarse, headstrong" fisherman! Yet even in our Protestant Bibles, Peter is called Saint.

Damien was *dirty*.

He was. Think of the poor lepers annoyed with this dirty comrade! But the clean Dr. Hyde was at his food in a fine house.

Damien was *headstrong*.

I believe you are right again; and I thank God for his strong head and heart.

Damien was *bigoted*.

I am not fond of bigots myself, because they are not fond of me. But what is meant by bigotry, that we should regard it as a blemish in a priest? Damien believed his own religion with the simplicity of a peasant or a child; as I would I could suppose that you do. For this, I wonder at him some way off; and had that been his only character, should have avoided him in life. But the point of interest in Damien, which has caused him to be so much talked about and made him at last the subject of your pen and mine, was that, in him, his bigotry, his intense and narrow faith, wrought potently for good, and strengthened him to be one of the world's heroes and exemplars.

Damien *was not sent to Molokai but went there without orders*.

Is this a misreading? or do you really mean the words for blame? I have heard Christ, in the pulpits of our church, held up for imitation on the ground that his sacrifice was voluntary. Does Dr. Hyde think otherwise?

Damien *did not stay at the settlement, etc.*

It is true he was allowed many indulgences. Am I to understand that you blame the father for profiting by these, or the officers for granting them? In either case, it is a mighty Spartan standard to issue from the house on Beretania Street; and I am convinced you will find yourself with few supportors.

Damien *had no hand in the reforms, etc.*

I think even you will admit that I have already been frank in my description of the man I am defending; but before I take you up upon this head, I will be franker still, and tell you that perhaps nowhere in the world can a man taste a more pleasurable sense of contrast, than when he passes from Damien's "China Town" at Kalawao to the beautiful Bishop-Home at Kalaupapa. At this point in my desire to make all fair for you, I will break my rule, and adduce catholic testimony. Here is a passage from my diary, about my visit to the Chinatown, from which you will see how it is (even now) regarded by its own officials: "We went round all the dormitories, refectories, etc., dark and dingy enough, with a superficial cleanliness, which he" [Mr. Dutton, the lay brother] "did not seek to defend. 'It is almost decent,' said he, 'the sisters will make that all right when we get them here.' " And yet I gathered it was already better since Damien was dead, and far better than when he was there alone and had his own (not always excellent) way. I have now come far enough to meet you on a common ground of fact; and I tell you that, to a mind not prejudiced by jealousy, all the reforms of the Lazaretto, and even those which he most vigorously opposed, are properly the work of Damien. They are the evidence of his success; they are what his heroism provoked from the reluctant and the careless. Many were before him in the field; Mr. Meyer, for instance, of whose faithful work we hear too little; there have been many since; and some had more worldly wisdom, though none had more devotion than our saint. Before his day, even you will confess they had effected little. It was his part, by one striking act of martyrdom, to direct all men's eyes on that distressful country. At a blow, and with the price of his life, he made the place illustrious and public. And that, if you will consider largely, was the one reform needful; pregnant of all that should succeed. It brought money; it brought (best individual addition of them all) the sisters; it brought supervision, for public opinion and public interest landed with the man at Kalawao. If ever any man brought reforms, and died to bring them, it was he. There is not a clean cup or towel in the Bishop-Home, but dirty Damien washed it.

Damien *was not a pure man in his relations with women, etc.*

How do you know that? Is this the nature of the conversation in that house on Beretania Street, which the cabman envied, driving past?—racy details of the misconduct of the poor, peasant priest, toiling under the cliffs of Molokai?

Many have visited the station before me; they seem not to have heard the rumour. When I was there I heard many shocking tales, for my informants were men speaking with the plainness of the laity; and I heard plenty of complaints of Damien. Why was this never mentioned? and how came it to you in the retirement of your clerical parlour?

But I must not even seem to deceive you. This scandal, when I read it in your letter, was not new to me. I had heard it once before; and I must tell you how. There came to Samoa a man from Honolulu; he, in a public-house on the beach, volunteered the statement that Damien had "contracted the disease from having connection with the female lepers;" and I find a joy in telling you how the report was welcomed in a public-house. A man sprang to his feet; I am not at liberty to give his name, but from what I heard, I doubt if you would care to have him to dinner in Beretania Street. "You miserable little——," (here is a word I dare not print, it would so shock your ears) "You miserable little—," he cried, "if the story were a thousand times true, can't you see you are a million times a lower—for daring to repeat it?" I wish it could be told of you that when the report reached you in your house, perhaps after family worship, you had found in your soul enough holy anger to receive it with the same expressions; ay, even with that one which I dare not print; it would not need to have been blotted away, like Uncle Toby's oath, by the tears of the recording angel; it would have been counted to you for your brightest righteousness. But you have deliberately chosen the part of the man from Honolulu, and you have played it with improvements of your own. The man from Honolulu—miserable, leering creature—communicated the tale to a rude knot of beach-combing drinkers in a public house, where (I will so far agree with your temperance opinions) man is not always at his noblest; and the man from Honolulu had himself been drinking—drinking, we may charitably fancy, to excess. It was to your "Dear Brother, the Reverend H. B. Gage," that you chose to communicate the sickening story; and the blue ribbon which adorns your portly bosom forbids me to allow you the extenuating plea that you were drunk when it was done. Your "dear brother"—a brother indeed—made haste to deliver up your letter (as a means of grace, perhaps) to the religious papers; where, after many months, I found and read and wondered at it; and whence I have now reproduced it for the wonder of others. And you and your dear brother have, by this cycle of operations, built up a contrast very edifying to examine in detail. The man whom you would not care to have to dinner, on the one side; on the other, the Reverend Dr. Hyde and the Reverend H. B. Gage; the Apia bar-room, the Honolulu manse.

But I fear you scarce appreciate how you appear to your fellow men; and to bring it home to you, I will suppose your story to be true. I will suppose—and God forgive me for supposing it—that Damien faltered and stumbled in his narrow path of duty; I will suppose that, in the horror of his isolation, perhaps in the fever of incipient disease, he, who was doing so much more than he had sworn, failed in the letter of his priestly oath—he, who was so much a better man than either you or me, who did what we have never dreamed of daring—he too tasted of our common frailty. "O, Iago, the pity of it!" The least tender should be moved to tears; the most incredulous to prayer. And all that you could do, was to pen your letter to the Reverend H. B. Gage!

Is it growing at all clear to you, what a picture you have drawn of your own heart? I will try yet once again to make it clearer. You had a father: suppose this tale were about him, and some informant brought it to you, proof in hand: I am not making too high an estimate of your emotional nature, when I suppose you would regret the circumstance? that you would feel the tale of frailty the more keenly, since it shamed the author of your days? and that the last thing you would do, would be to publish it in the religious press? Well, the man who tried to do what Damien did, is my father, and the father of the man in the Apia bar, and the father of all who love goodness; and he was your father too, if God had given you grace to see it.

ROBERT LOUIS STEVENSON

Appendix D

FATHER DAMIEN, STATEMENT

by Brother Joseph Dutton

Catholic Mission, Leper Settlement,
Kalawao, Molokai, H. I.
Feb. 12th, 1890

To His Lordship,
Bishop Hermann, Honolulu, H. I.,
Right Rev. and Dear Sir:—

The Rev. Fathers Mathias and Wendelin have recently informed me that they were directed by you to make an examination here regarding the life of the late *Rev.*[4] Father Damien Deveuster; his virtues and characteristics; his relations with the work at this leper settlement, and with the officials of the Hawaiian Government, etc.—making report of the examination and embodying therein my statement in these matters.

After we had all made the same a subject of prayer for three days, Fathers Mathias and Wendelin met with me, and took some notes of what I had to say in regard to the things in view, but afterwards they concluded to hold their report to enable me to make my statement in writing, giving it somewhat more scope than at first intended.

Since the return to Honolulu of the Rev. Father Mathias, the Rev. Father Wendelin has suggested that I address the statement to you: making it complete—not only speaking of things undoubtedly favorable in *Rev.* Father Damien's character and relations here, but also embracing points in which [any] disparaging statements have been made, so far as I know; and particularly to point out the part taken by the Hawaiian Government in the management of the affairs of the leper settlement.

All this I will strive faithfully to do, but giving the statement rather in outline form than making attempt to relate many particulars.

As directed by the Fathers, I first state regarding myself, that I came here from the United States to work with *Rev.* Father Damien, arriving at Kalawao the evening of July 29th, 1886, and from that evening until his death—on April 15th 1889—I was intimately associated with him in his work among the people, particularly with his orphan boys, and in having the care of his two churches (of only one church, though, in the latter part), in serving his Masses, and in assisting about his various ministrations, as far as a layman could; though, in this last, I was some-what restricted after the summer of 1887, being from that time principally occupied in dressing sores, and in the care of the sick orphans, but my place for work was close by his house and for about half the time I ate with him at his table.

Several priests had been with him at different times before I came, but there was no one with him at that time; nor was there any other white person belonging to the Mission until May, 1888, *when Father Conrardy came.*

Regarding *Rev.* Father Damien, will speak first of his zeal and earnest-ness—for these were the traits that first impressed me and [which] seemed with him always prominent. He had a great natural vitality and strength. These powers coupled with his zeal seemed to enable him to be ever ready to pursue with vigor whatever seemed to him ought to be done. In everything that concerned the welfare of the place here and of the people, he was always alive and pushing. In fact often taking an active interest in affairs of which others—Government officials, etc., had charge.

There were but few things done here of which he did not have some knowledge. His advice was frequently asked in matters outside of his own duties—asked by Government officials and others.

He was not restricted, as the priests are now, to ordinary parish duties, but actually took a hand in various affairs going on for the improvement of the place; doing with his own hands more or less of nearly every sort of work in both parishes—more especially doing carpenter work, but able to turn his hand to almost anything. When there was—or when there was not—a Government physician here, he kept a supply of drugs and prescribed for many of the sick. Quite a number of the natives would call for him in preference to the regular physician.

This treatment of the sick he continued, in [quite] a general way, until the summer of 1887, when he turned the drugs over to me and I kept them for use at the Mission house, under direction of the physician. Father Damien got the most of his drugs from the physician; some were purchased by the Mission. In replenishing, I [obtained] got them from the Government, [either from the physician or directly from Honolulu].

As to Father Damien's relations with these physicians, it somewhat depended upon who the physician was; some were satisfied for him to practice as he did; others—one in particular—opposed it, and he discontinued partly because of this opposition.

Up to the summer of 1887, Father Damien also dressed lepers' sores from time to time and gained considerable knowledge in this and also in the use of medicines, in a general way. All of these *special* occupations, however, were very much broken into by other duties and therefore not followed with any particular regularity.

His method was to drive ahead at what he deemed the most important until something else seemed more so, when he would jump over into that; so that he left a track of unfinished jobs, though a certain share would be completed. It seemed sometimes that he tried to do more than one person could expect to finish.

He was very hospitable and made a practice of meeting the weekly steamer at Kalaupapa, for the purpose of greeting any newly arrived lepers or visitors there might be. For a long time the steamer arrived very early in the morning, and, in order to reach the landing in time, he used to say his Mass, on those mornings, at about four o'clock; so that he was among the foremost in meeting any passengers that were being landed.

If there were any lepers who could not, at the moment, be provided with quarters, he was sure to bring them to the Mission here—if any would come—and have them cared for until they were regularly located. The assistant superintendent, who had charge of all these matters, permitted this. Young boys so arriving, were generally placed at the Mission, in the institution *or refuge for care of boys,* that Father Damien was trying to build up.

About the beginning of 1888, this "institution" having become somewhat systematized, the placing there of all young boys, who were not with their parents or some near relative, was regularly authorized by the Government. Larger boys—and men also, who desired or could be induced, were placed in the same way—under Father Damien's care.

Having thus referred to this "institution" for boys and men on the Mission grounds here, (grounds used by the Mission, but the property of the Government) it may be well to state in connection, what the Hawaiian Government had to do with it, and at the same time will explain the general relations of the Government with the leper settlement as a whole.

There has been much misapprehension upon this point, principally, it seems to me, growing out of the fact that more has been published about Father Damien than about the Government—leaving the impression that he was in charge of the settlement and had made all the improvements—an impression quite incorrect.

The history of the leper settlement shows that it has always been operated by the Hawaiian Government through its Board of Health, the regular and general expenses being all paid by the Government—including a fair ration and clothing allowance for each leper. At first a good many families and groups of people built their own cabins, but more recently the Government has constructed a considerable number of comfortable cottages—also built the residence of one of the priests; otherwise, the Mission here and at Kalaupapa—located on Government grounds, portions of the settlement here—has paid its own expenses.

The expense for construction of the "Home" for girls at Kalaupapa, on like public or Government grounds and under the charge of the Franciscan Sisters, was principally borne by a charitable Protestant gentleman in Honolulu—but the Government operates it in like manner as it operates the "Boys Home" at Kalawao and the rest of the settlement, giving the Sisters a support.

Father Damien's efforts towards founding the "institution" heretofore referred to, resulted in the regular establishment of the "Boys' Home" close to the church here. Two of the Sisters drive over from Kalaupapa on pleasant days to visit the "Home" and it is hoped that three of them will eventually be located here.[5]

In the first part of the construction of the "Boys' Home," Father Damien did a good deal of the work with his own hands; but later the Government put up larger and better buildings including a very neat one for the Sisters. The Government paid the main expense of all— Father Damien adding some on the Mission account in the earlier part.

In the latter portion of the period in which Father Damien cared for the institution—then merging into the "Boys' Home" proper—he was paid by the Government a monthly salary for this care; and Father Damien once told me that he was employed by the Government as assistant superintendent of the settlement for a while, before I came here, there having been, generally some one—a member of the settlement—so employed. Since I came here there has always been one, and until just recently a half white, a leper, has held the place. Now a gentleman from one of the islands—a white non-leper—has been engaged and sent here for that purpose.

There has always—as is well known here—also been a superintendent of the place, under the official title of "Agent of the Board of Health," often called "superintendent." He has always had charge of the business affairs of the settlement and of its general management and is represented here by the assistant superintendent, for the agent has never lived here but makes occasional visits. The same person has always held this place—a worthy gentleman and large land-owner on this island. He lives on the "pali" above us, or rather about a mile back from the cliff—some five miles from here and about three from Kalaupapa.

He assisted in establishing the leper settlement here; and has, I am informed, never been out of office as its practical manager. This gentleman and Father Damien were friends, for, though they occasionally "agreed to disagree," their real friendship never ceased. Father Damien was never, properly, in charge of any of the Government affairs of the settlement—only as stated above. He supplied some "extras" to the inmates of the institution at the Mission; also to many lepers outside, but of this I will speak further on, *so as to finish here what is to be said about the Hawaiian Government.*

If in the earlier years of its existence, the conditions at the leper settlement were in any degree unsatisfactory, I do not believe, from all I have heard and know, that the charges against the Hawaiian Government for this state of affairs have good grounds. The place is isolated, and various drawbacks tended to prevent a very rapid improvement; but, considering the nature and characteristics of the people to be dealt with, it would appear, from the history of the settlement, that the Hawaiian Government has always given it fair support, and made reasonable progress in the necessary construction.

I believe it is an acknowledged fact that the official reports of expenditure show as generous outlay on account of this leper settlement as that made for any similar refuge in any country at this time—and with possibly one or two exceptions, more generous than any other. Any way, since July, 1886, I have been conversant with the fact that the Hawaiian Government has made provision, reasonable, suitable and sufficient, for the support of the lepers who have been segregated here.

Many very useful improvements have been made since that date; for even in July, 1886, some of the conditions were still imperfect; some remain so yet; some are beyond remedy—but all along there has been a tendency towards improvement and I believe that all parties having to do with the management of the place have honestly tried to deal justly with it.

Certainly there have been some delays, some oversights; occasionally an apparent neglect, but I will say that the real grounds for complaint have been very few—and as well as I am able to judge, many of the members of the settlement, probably I might say a large proportion of them are now in better circumstances as to shelter, food, clothing and medical attendance than they ever were before; and if given permission to leave here, many of them would not go so long as the present provision would last.

Of the Government buildings other than those heretofore referred to, there is a storehouse at the steamer landing, besides several other buildings elsewhere for storage of supplies; a butcher shop and other shop buildings, a store where a general stock is kept, at fair prices; a hospital outfit of some ten buildings new and old, under the charge of an active and well paid Government physician who is furnished with a comfortable residence.[6]

The necessary employees are provided for attending to these various things; some are white lepers, some native lepers and some native kokuas or helpers.

The assistance that Father Damien gave to inmates of his "institution" and to others—those outside—to the people generally was referred to above. By this is meant such help as went towards their provision or support, *but it was not any part of the regular support.* It consisted in giving help, generally, in special needs where a family had in it some *kokuas* not drawing rations, the family thus being short of supplies, of family thus short through waste or neglect—or some of the few whites or others needing some special kind of food, etc. etc.

The expense of what he thus gave was paid by the Catholic Mission, so it was quite the practice among the people to come to Father Damien for any special aid required. Yet some would not come to him at all—some Protestants, and at times some Catholics, those persons with whom he had difficulties.

Though these people easily forget what they may deem, at the time, harsh treatment, and in most cases would return to Father Damien in their next distress to again ask his aid, there were some who would not do so. There were some, too, who often came for aid, but who, when not in Father Damien's presence, would abuse him most shamefully. No matter what may have occurred in the past, if Father Damien could give the help asked for, he was pretty sure to give it. He was at times very vehement and excitable in regard to matters that did not seem to him right, or if opposed by any one when he was satisfied that his judgement was correct—sometimes doing and saying things he would afterwards regret, but he had the faculty, in a remarkable degree, of putting resentment aside. Very soon after a heated altercation he would be towards the opponent as if no such thing had happened, seeming to have forgotten the matter; only, if there was anything to be done *that he felt assured should be done* in a certain way, he was not likely to rest until it was carried out in that way.

Probably I am safe in saying that in all these differences he had a true desire to do right. To bring about what he thought would be for the best, no doubt he erred sometimes in judgement, as we all do. These things stated, his relations with the Government officials will be more readily understood. With some they were better than with others; with all, better at some times than at other times.

In certain periods he got along smoothly with every one, and at all times he was urgent for improvements or what he thought would be such. The carrying out of some things done by the Government was facilitated by his action; in other cases it made confusion, as the different authorities would not always agree with him. Will add that I believe his efforts for the people here—for material improvement—to have been, on the whole, beneficial for the place. In spiritual matters there is no doubt that he did great good.

The question of his purity has been brought up in the public prints. In this I can merely state my first belief that he was wholly devoid of sensuality during the time I knew him.

Will introduce here something repugnant but apropos; leprosy, in its course, shows some curious freaks in this regard. I have taken some pains to investigate the same for the information of a well known medical gentleman in New York. The effects upon sensual passions appear differently in different forms of the disease, and again differently in different stages. Without going into the various particulars, I will state that what Father Damien told me about himself in that regard, seems to hold good in many cases of his type, and what he said was this; that for several years of the latter part of his life he felt no tendency towards sensual excitement. He volunteered this and his conversation led me to infer that in the earlier years here on the islands he had to resist such movements. In going over the country it was sometimes necessary to stop over night with some native family. He told me that one night, when in one of these huts, a young native woman being about to sleep near him, he left the house and stayed out doors.

It never occurred to me to question his life-long adherence to virtue—in this regard at least. He seemed while I knew him to have no thought for such things—no thoughts tending towards sensuality; and this condition, in my opinion, was the cause of there being certain idle reports or gossip indulged in by some people.

The charges on this point, published since his death, are not new ones; I heard the same things—at least some of them—here while he was living; that is, I was informed of them but the parties so informing—intelligent men—always asserted their belief that Father Damien was innocent of the charge except in so far as he gave (apparently unwittingly) grounds for suspicion by his want of caution, in allowing women to be about his house, etc., being apparently blind to what might appear evil in the eyes of others.

These things I myself could not help seeing, yet I never saw what would cause me to suspect that there was anything wrong, unless in appearance.

Coupled with the above charge as published, was one to the effect that he was unclean in his personal habits. Of this I can not say so much in denial. When visitors were here he used to keep in presentable appearance, but ordinarily he paid very little attention to the cleanliness of his person or to his dress; did not pretend to neatness in his personal belongings. He told me that he considered this a defect. He was very simple in his bodily wants and was quite able also to subsist upon the coarsest fare.

As to his obedience, it is of course a subject for his superiors. Father Damien had in his heart—when tranquil, when not moved by excitement or by some absorbing purpose—a most tender feeling, as I have been often made to know; yet you will bear me out in stating the fact that no one found it pleasant, at all times, to be with him for a very long period.

If my association with him was longer continued than that of others, it was partly because I admitted my own fault in that regard, and partly because I ever saw him place in me the most entire confidence and have in his heart a deep love, no matter what his exterior might be; and also, I used to be quite free with him in speaking of all these things, and he likewise to me; and this seemed to give confidence in each other.

He would wish the whole truth to be told, and if he had the selection of the one to speak of his last few years here, he would I think, certainly select me. I do not speak thus in boast, but rather to show the depth of our love for each other.

In truth, Father Damien was in many ways a good priest, a good man; and I am glad to have, by your direction, the opportunity of describing him precisely as I knew him—perhaps not precisely as he has been pictured by some pious souls, but by a description in which you will recognize Father Damien as he was; you who knew him so much better than I, though not so intimately during the years of which I speak. Father Damien was very devout and in his tranquil moments, seemed to take a supernatural view of things—I may say of almost everything. His meditation in the morning was generally of an hour's duration and he had a regular practice of making a visit to the Blessed Sacrament at night before going to bed.

He offered the Holy Sacrifice long after he seemed to have become unable to do so, and recited his offices nearly to the last—for some time after being dispensed and while his one eye was hardly able to see. The sight of one eye was ruined, he told me, in childhood. He had to use many devices, toward the end, to be able to see at all with the other. For nearly a year it often gave him great pain. It seems to me that the recitation of his offices under the circumstances showed marked heroism.

His devotion had many ways of showing itself in his last days—reciting the Rosary every evening—asking for spiritual reading, etc. His love for the people of the leper settlement—all of them—was very great. He gave himself for them freely; a sudden call of charity; one in distress, would cause him to drop at once what he might be engaged upon (except when at the altar) and to quickly give his aid. In his ministrations with the natives he was untiring; especially in his attendance upon the dying was he earnest and helpful. So frequently being with him in this office, I was particularly impressed with it and often thought that he must have been a great comfort to many souls in these moments.

He thought that I had a faculty for knowing the death signs, and charged me to always give him warning. When he felt that his end was approaching, and having quite a number of pieces of unfinished work on hand—about the new church, etc.—he strained every nerve and muscle to get them completed. I am sure that those engaged upon the work and all who noted his efforts in those last weeks will join me in asserting the belief that by these extra exertions he considerably hastened his end.

I do not know of any miracles. In my private correspondence, three incidents have recently been related to me wherein cure of, or relief from, severe illness has been ascribed by relatives to the use of little pieces of Father Damien's old habit that I had sent by concurrence of Father Wendelin. My god-mother describes two instances in the case of her husband, Mr. B. J. Semmes, Memphis, Tennessee, and the third instance is related by Rev. Father F. X. Dutton,[7] Cincinnati, Ohio—the case of a child in his parish.

Fathers Wendelin and Mathias informed me that I might be called upon to qualify by oath in this matter and I am ready to declare that the things stated as facts, are in fact true, to the best of my knowledge and belief; that the things given as hearsay, were so understood by me and in matters of opinion I have shown my reasons for the opinion—at least aimed to do so.

You are of course at liberty to make what use you think best of this statement, but I believe it to be my right to hold that if any part of it is used for any purpose, it all ought to be—without mutilation. Good Father Damien—may he rest in peace, and may all of our acts in this and in every other matter be done solely for the glory of God.

Very truly and respectfully,

Your obedient servant,[8]

/s/ Joseph Dutton

FATHER DAMIEN AND HIS WORK

by Charles M. Hyde

The *Congregationalist*, August 7, 1890

So many and various have been the demands on my time that I have had no leisure till now to prepare a reply to the many long articles sent me from the office of the *Congregationalist* which were published some time ago in the Boston papers, the *Pilot* and the *Transcript*. Under the circumstances of the case I trust I shall be pardoned for trespassing on the patience of your readers if my reply should seem prolix and personal.

The attempt made to glorify Father Damien, the leper priest, who died at Molokai, April 10, 1889, and to magnify the work he did among the Hawaiian lepers segregated at the settlement on that island, is not merely an exaggeration or perversion of the facts, but many statements made in his behalf are in direct contravention of the truth. *I was not aware, when I wrote my letter to Rev. H. B. Gage, Aug. 2, 1889, in answer to certain inquiries from him, that he had himself published statements of a similar tenor derived from other sources.*[9] But it appears that in the *"Herald and Presbyter"* of Cincinnati Mr. Gage had published an article, dated Feb. 20, 1889, giving facts which during his visit to the islands he had learned from the resident government physician and others in reference to "the work of the Romish priest among the lepers of Hawaii." That article was read before the Ministerial Association of Riverside, Cal., Mr. Gage being the pastor of the Presbyterian church in that town. It was reprinted in the *Occident* of San Francisco, with the addition, as a postscript, of my letter to Mr. Gage. That letter took its form from his specific inquiries, and being clear, positive, brief, has, for these reasons, been widely published. Many other private letters, of the same general tenor, have been written from the islands by others, in answer to similar inquiries. Many more replies, evasive and non-committal, have also been written by those who fear lest they also may be deluged by such a torrent of abusive language as has been let loose upon me for presuming to make the statements given to the public over my name.

In view of this outburst of scurrility and denunciation from those who have no personal knowledge of the facts and are ignorant of the evidence that can be cited in corroboration of the testimony I have given, it is plain that I cannot ask my friends even to attest my competency and veracity, unless I am willing to see them in the same predicament in which I find myself—exposed to all the malodorous and scarifying missiles any blackguard may use who has access to the public press. I have no desire to push this matter further into public notoriety, any more than I have to withdraw or modify any statement formerly made, based on facts which had gradually come to my knowledge in the course of thirteen years' residence at the islands.

Very few people, even in Honolulu, have visited Molokai as I have, or had any personal knowledge of Father Damien, his character and his work. In answering the courteous inquiries of a friend as to my estimate of Father Damien and his work, I fail to see that I have transgressed the limits of personal duty in any measure. I believe that the God of holiness and justice requires a merciful spirit in those who would trust in His mercy; but I do not believe that the God of truth and love has ever commanded us to give admiration and approval to one whose principles and actions are in violation of the morality He enjoins.

I am indebted to Mr. R. L. Stevenson for sending me the pamphlet which he published in Sydney in relation to Father Damien, with special reference to the statements I had made on Damien's character and work. But I am sorry that he should have written his own condemnation as one indifferent to truth and justice, not to say Christian charity, in such a philippic against me, without making any inquiry as to my personal knowledge of Hawaiian leprosy, or the concurrent testimony I could cite for my statements in regard to Father Damien. His invective may be brilliant, but it is like a glass coin, not golden, shivered into fragments of worthless glitter when brought to the test of truthfulness. He had been in hot haste to condemn me for keeping aloof from Hawaiian lepers, for knowing nothing of Father Damien, and for being ignorant of the geography of Molokai. I beg your indulgence for a brief statement of facts, personal to myself, yet pertinent to the question at issue.

When I began, in 1877, my assigned work for the A.B.C.F.M., the charge of the North Pacific Institute, for the training of Hawaiian pastors and missionaries, this matter of leprosy confronted me as a most direct and personal question. Accustomed as I was to the purity of a New England home, there yawned before me, in Hawaiian social and family life, an abysmal depth of heathen degradation, unutterable in its loathsomeness. Obscenity takes the place, among Hawaiians and other heathen nations, of the profaneness that pollutes our Christian civilization. Hawaiian home life, apart from Christian life, is abominably filthy. Of the five students in the first class I taught, one has been for years a confirmed leper, one has a daughter in the leper home, one had a leper brother, and the other two were sons of a leper father. Could I safely hold intercourse with such a set? I investigated the question for myself. I found that in many cases of supposed leprosy one physician would declare it to be that disease (not the leprosy of the Bible, but in medical parlance called *Elephantiasis Graecorum*); another would say it is only an aggravated form of syphilis. I wrote to various countries where leprosy prevailed and received varying replies as to its origin and contagiousness. I consulted all accessible medical authorities, finding the preponderance of medical opinion against its contagiousness (as that word is popularly understood), but admitting its hereditary character. Day after day I sat in the Honolulu dispensary and saw the cases of leprosy treated, and the improvement manifest. I visited the lepers at their homes, and cared for them in their sickness. I went regularly to the Receiving Hospital, paying friendly visits to those with whom I had become acquainted, acting as executor and guardian in the care of their property and their relatives, holding religious services with them Sunday afternoons. I went to Molokai more than once, visited the homes, the hospital, the schools, stores, and other buildings. I was introduced to Father Damien, rode with him through the settlement, visited at his house, and talked with him about his work. I have kept up a constant correspondence all these years with individuals at the Leper Settlement. In regard to Mr. Stevenson's brilliant invective, I have only to say that, so far as I am concerned, it lacks the essential elements of truthfulness.

By all that I saw and heard and read, I was soon convinced of this one fact, that leprosy is one of the results of licentiousness. It is a disease, symptomatic of nervous exhaustion, like the blowing out of the tubes, or the accumulation of mud in the boiler when one is running a steam engine.[10] Since the law enforcing segregation was passed by the Hawaiian Legislature, Jan. 3, 1865, the total number of lepers segregated has been, up to date, 4,218, of whom 2,893 have died. There are now resident at the settlement 1,159. Of this total perhaps thirty have been Chinese; fifteen have been white men, all of notoriously immoral lives. The disproportion between the number of white men segregated and the number of Hawaiians is surely an indication that leprosy is not so eminently contagious as has been alleged; while the fact stated in regard to the character of the white men who have contracted the disease is a marked testimony as to its probable origin and nature. I find no record, in all the publications I have examined, of any nurses, or physicians, having contracted the disease from their personal care of lepers. The Moravians have had many missionaries at work among lepers in various parts of the world, but not one has ever had the leprosy. There have been several government physicians, with their wives, resident at the Leper Settlement. In no instance has there been any development of the disease. One feature of its slow morbific tendency is the extremely low vitality and sluggish development of the characteristic *bacillus*. For the first seven years of my connection with the institute it was my painful duty to drop a student each year, because of developed leprosy. I can never forget the last instance. The boy was one whom I had learned to love and admire. Never had a foul word been heard to pass his lips, a remarkable testimony in regard to any Hawaiian. I believed it to be my duty to say to him that he must be dropped from the school, and could not expect to be a minister of the gospel. When, after a night of sleepless sorrow, I told him so, he smiled in my face, and said, "All right. There is work yet, other work, that I can do for Jesus." If my belief in the origin and nature of this disease is an erroneous one, I may yet be myself a victim to its alleged contagiousness, for I have never shrunk from ordinary social intercourse with Hawaiian lepers, though I have not been negligent of such pre- cautions as every prudent man would be careful to take.

Interested, as I have been, from the very first, in this question of Hawaiian leprosy, and what was to be done for its extirpation or al- leviation, I was specially interested in the children; for the saddest cases, among the numberless sufferers whom I have seen, were the children, in whom leprosy begins to show itself at dentition, with a second outburst at the age of puberty. If neglected, as these children too often are by the careless, ignorant Hawaiian parents, the sores and distortions are frightfully hideous. I published, in the Honolulu newspaper, an appeal for contributions for a Children's Home, and secured about $2,500, with good prospect of more. Mr. Gibson, who was at that time the head of the Cabinet, invited me into his office one day, and told me that he would like to have part also in such a commendable work of charity. My reply was, "If you take hold of it, I shall drop it." I wished to keep aloof from all entangling alliance with one whose motives and methods I had abundant reason to distrust. He was making of this national calamity a lever to hoist himself into place and power, as well as what politicans call "a pull," to force men into acquiescence with the schemes he wished to push forward. He was afterwards ignominiously sent out of the country for his insidious treachery to the best interests of the community.

Under the manipulations of such a man the result was what might have been expected. Mr. Gibson, who was a Roman Catholic, having built at Honolulu the Kapiolani Home for Leper Girls, largely through gifts solicited from members of Evangelical sympathies, put it in charge of Franciscan sisters whom he invited from New York. Their sweet patience, loving care and skillful fidelity no one can honor more than I do. The Bishop Home, built afterwards at the Leper Settlement with funds contributed by Hon. C. R. Bishop, one of the trustees of the Central Union Church, is also under their care. The Boys' Home, for which Hon. H. P. Baldwin, son of one of the A. B. C. F. M. missionaries, has recently given $5,000, is under the charge of the Catholic priests. The Catholic bishop has just demanded the proportionate distribution to Catholic schools of the $120,000 appropriated by the Legislature for the educational department of the government. In the development of the Catholic Church at the islands, the priests have simply done what they have done elsewhere, appropriated to themselves institutions founded at public expense, or even by the generosity of Protestant Christians. Suffice it to say that every boy in the Leper Home, some of them children of our Hawaiian Evangelical pastors, has been baptized by the priests, and much to the grief of their Hawaiian parents, is claimed by them as belonging, body and soul, to the Roman Catholic Church. The girls of Protestant parentage were for a time forbidden to read their Bibles, or to attend Protestant worship. Under Father Damien's administration many gifts, contributed by the community and by liberal Protestants from other countries, were withheld from Protestant lepers, and lavished, injudiciously, too, on Catholics, or those who might be bribed to become so. Remonstrances and warnings, if not threats also, were necessary to make Father Damien comprehend that such exclusive and supercilious treatment, however proper it might seem to a Catholic priest, was not considered by other people as the policy of common honesty.

In order to enchance Father Damien's work for Hawaiian lepers, Catholic writers have falsely represented their conditions as "purely bestial; without nurses, schools or church; a scandal to the community, and to the Christian charity of those islands; a living grave, a leper hell." But the fact is that at no time have the lepers on Molokai been any worse off than the average Hawaiian, and during these recent years they have been far better housed, clothed and fed than the people outside of the settlement. The Catholic lepers told the bishop when he took Damien to them: "We are very well off here. The government takes good care of us. The one thing that has failed us is the residence of a priest." There was only a little chapel, dedicated to Saint Philomena. That was eight years after the work of segregation had begun. At the Leper Settlement at that time was a regularly organized Hawaiian Evangelical church, under its Hawaiian pastor, and regularly visited by the A. B. C. F. M. missionary, who had for some years resided on the other side of the island. In those early years there was great difficulty in even ordinary communication with Molokai, and the government was hampered in its management by want of men as well as means. It is to the government, especially since its emancipation from the Gibson misrule, that credit is due, not to the Catholic priesthood, for the generous and systematic provision for the care of the lepers. That government was established through the influence of the American missionaries, but of late years has been more or less under the control of those inimical to their principles and their methods. In the adoption and administration of the various measures of the government for the improvement of the lepers' condition, Father Damien has been a hindrance rather than a help. According to the last biennial report, the Board of Health spent $201,176 for the Leper Settlement, and $65,000 additional expenditure may properly be put to the account of expenses for leprosy. The whole expenditure, as nearly as it can be computed for the entire period of governmental segregation is $937,507. It is because so much has been done by this little community of 80,000 people for these 4,000 sufferers that public attention has been called to it. Great Britain, with its millions of untold wealth, had done almost nothing for its 135,000 lepers. At the settlement on Molokai the lepers have built and own 235 houses—that does not look like incurable poverty; 196 buildings are owned by the government, including schools, jail, hospital; ample weekly rations are served out to an average of 1,035 resident lepers (who own 786 horses), besides an allowance of ten dollars to each leper annually for clothing.

Not all has been done that could be desired or suggested; but there has been no reluctance nor unwillingness on the part of our Evangelical community to do whatever was possible. Money, time, thought, systematic and sympathetic efforts have been freely rendered. In the annual conference of the Evangelical churches, as in every biennial session of the Legislature, much time for earnest discussion has been given to the question, "What more can we do for the sufferers at Molokai?" Just before the first Sunday in April last, one of the leper girls wrote to me asking me to get for her to wear at the approaching Sunday school concert "a dress of white nun's veiling (which she wished Mrs. Hyde would make for her), eight yards of pink ribbon, one and one-half inches wide, and a white straw hat trimmed to match." Through the kindness of friends the articles requested were furnished, and several other dresses sent for other girls. In fact, every Christmas season, and at frequent intervals, year after year, boxes of toys, clothing, books, papers and other acceptable gifts are sent to the lepers by our benevolent people. Constantly special favors are done for individuals among the lepers by friends interested in their welfare. There are two churches for the lepers of Evangelical faith, with a pastor supported by the Hawaiian Evangelical Association. Two new church buildings have been built, largely through funds contributed by members of our churches. It must be remembered that since 1863 the American Board has withdrawn from the islands as no longer one of its mission fields. I was sent out in 1877 for a definite work at Honolulu, almost the only representative of our Congregational churches for forty years. The Catholic Church has never ordained a single Hawaiian to the priesthood, but has maintained and increased its large staff of priests, teachers and nurses by constant additions from abroad. Our Hawaiian churches, with one exception, have all been under the care of Hawaiian pastors. The lepers at Molokai have been treated, as every other Hawaiian community has been treated, as an independent church organization under its own Hawaiian pastor.

I have not the slightest desire to enter into any sort of rivalry with the Roman Catholic priesthood in the objects they seek to accomplish, the political and religious supremacy of the Papal Church, nor the methods they pursue, based on unquestioning obedience to its priesthood. I believe the true object of foreign missionary work is to lift up a people out of their superstitious practices and heathen degradation. In carrying out this object, the Christian home life of the missionary is an important factor. Mr. Stevenson is pleased to criticise the modest house which the generosity of friends in Honolulu has furnished for my occupancy. He holds up to ridicule the good judgment and unpretentious taste of the missionary's wife which has made the home so attractive and restful. He puts this in comparison with 'the pig-sty' in which he says he found Father Damien, whom he thereupon lauds, as if there were superior sanctity in dirt. The same spirit of detraction I have heard recently venting itself in a similar way over the new buildings which the further generosity of friends at the islands has enabled me to build for our students. "That big building? Oh, that is Hyde's palace for his Kanaka boys."

The statements I have made, however true, are distasteful also, I am aware, to those in sympathy with the prevailing humanitarian sentiment that would send any villain, or ruffian, straight to heavenly glory, if only he has been kind to others in suffering, or rescued those in peril, at the cost of his own life or great personal loss, like Bret Harte's Jim Bludsoe. There is an enthusiasm of humanity which bases salvation on some supposed meritorious acts. It has small regard for historical verities, but says that, "no *matter whether true or not,* the story of Father Damien is calculated to draw us up into a purer and nobler atmosphere, and such hero-worship is beneficial to the human race." To give a correct estimate of this alleged saint and martyr is ruthlessly to shatter such an ideal.

If any one will take the pains to read carefully the statements published, contradictory of the estimate I have given, t will be noticed that such apparent contradictions are either official generalities, or evasive replies, or the utterances of a partisan sympathy, or written by those who have no personal knowledge of the facts. But no proof is given that Damien was other than I have represented him to be. Mr. Edward Clifford made no inquiries of those persons, whose testimony would have confirmed all that I have said. With the credulity, not the charity, that believes all things, he asked no questions that would disturb his preconceived ideal. His imaginary portrait, profanely adored by some female writer as "the Hawaiian Christ," is no more like the Father Damien that figures as the frontispiece of the Catholic biography, than the picture of Hawaiian volcanoes in that book is like anything to be seen on the islands. Vice-Consul Hastings would have been more guarded in his language, and less effusive in his praises, if he had known who it was in the circle of his own acquaintances at Honolulu, holding the same opinions that I do, who made the statement published in the *Congregationalist* of Sept. 12, 1889, but not over my signature. Captain Palmer denies the name of Christianity to the faith which his fathers held, and says that the Christian religion was first introduced to the Sandwich Islands, August, 1819, when the chaplain of the French frigate *Uranie* baptized Boki, the Hawaiian chief, then acting as Governor of Oahu. Mr. Stevenson, educated like myself in the tenets of Calvinistic Orthodoxy, has departed so widely from the faith of his parents that he has come to regard Evangelical doctrines and methods as an outrage on human nature, and an insult to the God whose honor he is proud to defend against the misrepresentations of the Calvinistic faith. Mr. Stevenson himself says, what yet he contends that I have no right to say, of Father Damien, that Damien was—to use Mr. Stevenson's own language, "a man of the peasant class, certainly of the peasant type, shrewd, ignorant, bigoted, rough in his ways, indiscreet, officious, domineering, unpopular with the Kanakas, with a mania for doctoring, with slovenly ways and false ideas of hygiene, adhering to his errors with perfect obstinacy."

I submit that such testimony from such a source, confirming what I have said of Father Damien, is presumptive proof that I had equally good reason for saying what else I said in regard to him. That testimony came to me, not as gossip that I heard in some bar-room, but in the course of many years' correspondence and conversation with residents, white and native, on Hawaii and on Molokai, government physicians, agents, and other officials. Father Damien was a loyal Catholic, a zealous, hard-working priest. He was not close, sour, secretive; but headstrong, bluff, impulsive in his temperament. He had no thorough education, could not even write his own mother tongue correctly. He was ordained at Whitsuntide, 1864, at Honolulu, *in partibus infidelium,* as a member of the Society of the Sacred Hearts of Jesus and Mary, better known as the Picpus Fathers, from the name of the house where their headquarters were first established in the Faubourg St. Antoine. To this society the Sandwich Islands were specially assigned by Pope Leo XII in 1825. When Joseph de Veuster became "religious," he took the name of Damien, after the second of two brothers, Cosmos and Damien, both physicians, martyrs, saints in the Roman Catholic category. Before going to Molokai he had charge of two other parishes, where it is believed he contracted the disease, and left behind him an unsavory reputation. There is no doubt about his zeal and activity in his work, but the mere circumstance of his being a leper, or taking up his residence at the settlement, gives him no claim to the position assigned him as pre-eminent among those who have done good to their fellowmen. Other Catholic priests have had the leprosy and gone to Molokai, but they could not live with Damien. They quarreled, threw stones and cursed each other in the public road. Damien did not die from some fatal development of leprosy. The immediate cause of his death was an attack of pneumonia, for which he refused to take the remedies prescribed by the physician.

It has been anything but pleasant to write, as I have done, in regard to one who has passed beyond the reach of our praise or blame. I have not rushed into print in the statements which I have made. But to refuse personal testimony, when asked as I have been, to tell the truth in regard to him, would have been despicable poltroonery, not kindly forbearance. The exposure of fraudulent pretense is sometimes the unpleasant duty of a servant of the truth. No one in this world can know with what stress of pain I have taken the stand I have maintained as a witness for the truth, assailed on the one hand by the arrogant pretentiousness of the Roman hierarchy, and betrayed on the other by the fanciful falsities of a sentimental humanitarianism. I have written what I have at the suggestion and desire of friends, whom I thank most heartily for defending me when my competency and veracity have been assailed. I have written this reply in deference to these friends' opinion that the silence, which I myself had no desire to break, would only be construed as a concession to the truth of the invective with which I have been assailed. I leave it to any candid mind to judge on which side lies the calumny and the slander. There let it lie.

NOTES

1. B. P. Bishop Estate *Minute Book*, Vol. I. Dec. 23, 1885, pp. 3–5.
2. From the Sydney *Presbyterian*, October 26, 1889. This footnote appeared this way in the original pamphlet.
3. Favored Stevenson expression. See page 249. Line 24.
4. The italicized words, phrases and sentences are mine. Father Reginald Yzendoorn SS. CC. in his *"History of the Catholic Mission of the Hawaiian Islands,"* Honolulu Star Bulletin, 1927 *omits all* which I have italicized, many of which are significant. The brackets [ ] indicate where he has added his own phraseology.
5. This was before the Baldwin Home. J.D. This note is an entry in Dutton's handwriting.
6. The earlier buildings etc at Kalawao. By J.D. This note is in Dutton's handwriting.
7. Fr. Dutton was later chancellor of the Archdiocese—Died 1907. Entry in Joseph Dutton's handwriting.
8. This copy read over and signed May 7, 1907, "Joseph Dutton.
9. Italics mine.
10. It takes on two forms—either suppurating sores, or anaesthetic patches. Like every other epidemic, it decreases both in its virulence and in its spread. Domestication, as does also Pasteur's cultivation, diminishes the intensity, of the virus. Hawaiian leprosy, as an epidemic, has passed the extreme point, and the new cases are both less numerous and less virulent. Any one who knows the Hawaiian habit of promiscuous intercourse will acknowledge that segregation is necessary and must be enforced.

INDEX